Environmental Conservation

Environmental Conservation
fourth edition

raymond f. dasmann

Senior Ecologist
International Union for the Conservation of Nature
and Natural Resources, Morges, Switzerland

John Wiley & Sons, Inc.
New York   London   Sydney   Toronto

Books by R. F. Dasmann

Environmental Conservation
Wildlife Biology
The Last Horizon
The Destruction of California
African Game Ranching
The Pacific Coastal Wildlife Region
A Different Kind of Country
No Further Retreat
The Conservation Alternative
Ecological Principles for Economic Development

This book was set in Optima by
Ruttle, Shaw & Wetherill, Inc., and
printed and bound by Kingsport Press, Inc.
The text and cover were designed by Jules Perlmutter,
A Good Thing, Inc.; the drawings were designed and
executed by John Balbalis with the assistance of the
Wiley Illustration Department; Stella Kupferberg was the
picture researcher; the editor was Susan Giniger;
Reiko Okamura supervised production.

Library of Congress Cataloging in Publication Data

Dasmann, Raymond Frederick, 1919–
  Environmental conservation.
  Includes bibliographies.
    1. Conservation of natural resources. 2. Ecology.
3. Human ecology. I. Title.
S938.D37 1976   333.7'2   75–37657
ISBN 0–471–19602–9

Printed in the United States of America

10 9 8

acknowledgments

The original inspiration for this book came from the lectures and publications of the late Carl O. Sauer of the Department of Geography, University of California. Both Professor Sauer and A. Starker Leopold, of the School of Forestry and Conservation, University of California, influenced the philosophy and approach to the teaching of conservation, which I later applied to my courses at the University of Minnesota in Duluth and Humboldt State College, California, and to the first edition of this book.

Many people have commented helpfully on ways for improving this textbook. It is not possible to list all of their names, but their help has been greatly appreciated. I have been most fortunate in being able to work with and exchange ideas with many of the leaders in the fields of ecology and conservation. All of them have influenced my thinking, but most particularly I thank Sir Frank Fraser Darling, with whom I worked for some years.

This new edition reflects new ideas, and I have been assisted in developing these by such friends as Gary Snyder and Peter Berg in California, Robert Allen and Jimoh Omo Fadaka of the United Kingdom, as well as my colleagues in the International Union for the Conservation of Natural Resources. Particular thanks go to Elizabeth Dasmann who should, by virtue of her effort, be a coauthor. It has been her continual exploration of new fields of inquiry, and development of new concepts that has permitted this book to change with the times.

For comments and suggestions to improve the fourth edition manuscript, I an indebted to Professor Hugo A. Ferchau, of Western State College, Professor Robert E. Roth, of the Ohio State University, and Professors Stephen L. Smith and Pat D. Taylor, of Michigan State University.

R.F.D.

preface

Seventeen years have passed since the preface to the first edition of *Environmental Conservation* was written. During that period a tidal wave of humanity has flooded the earth—more than a thousand million additional people. Each of these wants a fair share of the earth's resources, and together they exert stresses on the life-support systems of the planet without precedent in human history. The trend toward growth of population and expansion of human demands on the earth's resources continues—but the planet is finite and infinite growth cannot be supported. The problems resulting from this dilemma are discussed in this edition.

The fourth edition of *Environmental Conservation* has been changed significantly from the earlier editions. This change reflects the growing urgency of the human situation and a recognition that the approaches used in the past to meet human needs and still protect the life of the planet are not good enough. New approaches are explored in this edition. Most importantly the need for decentralization of political and economic power and decision-making authority is stressed. If the goals of environmental conservation and the well-being of humanity are to be attained, a change must take place in the attitudes of people toward nature and toward themselves. There must be a willingness to seek life-styles that can be sustained, that reduce the stress upon the planet's resources, and that permit the survival of humanity into the foreseeable future. This change must take place in the individual and the local community—it cannot be decreed by national governments.

This book is written for the beginning university student and for the interested public. It provides a text for a one-semester course concerned with problems of the environment and conservation of natural resources.

The emphasis of the text is on North America, since it is on this continent that the changes in attitude and ways of living must take place if a dynamic balance between people and their environment is to be restored. However, the issues discussed are planetary in scope, and the book reflects my experience with international agencies and with global problems. Many global problems, it is pointed out, become nonproblems when responsibility for their solution is passed back to people willing to live in harmony with the land.

Morges, Switzerland and
San Juan Ridge, California
August, 1975

Raymond F. Dasmann

general references

GENERAL REFERENCES USED THROUGHOUT BOOK

Bresler, Jack, ed., 1966. *Human ecology.* Addison-Wesley, Reading, Mass.

Bronwell, Arthur B. ed., 1970. *Science and technology in the world of the future.* John Wiley, New York.

Bureau of the Census, 1964. *Statistical abstract of the United States, 1964.* 85th annual edition. Dept. of Commerce, Washington.

Bureau of Land Management, 1965. *Public land statistics,* Department of Interior, Washington, D.C.

Burton, Ian, and R. W. Kates, 1965. *Readings in resource management and conservation.* University of Chicago, Chicago.

Darlington, C. D., 1969. *The evolution of man and society.* Simon and Schuster, New York.

Espenshade, Edward B., Jr., 1960. *Goode's world atlas.* Twelfth edition. Rand McNally, Chicago.

Fraser Darling, F., and John Milton, 1966. *The future environments of North America.* Natural History Press, New York.

Fraser Darling, F. 1970. *Wilderness and plenty.* Houghton Mifflin, Boston.

Haden-Guest, S., J. K. Wright, and E. M. Teclaff, eds., 1956. *World geography of forest resources.* Ronald Press, New York.

Helfrich, Harold W., Jr., 1970. *The environmental crisis.* Yale University Press, New Haven.

Milton, John, and M. Taghi Farver, eds., 1971. *The careless technology.* Natural History Press, New York.

Nash, Roderick, ed., 1968. *The American environment: readings in the history of conservation.* Addison-Wesley, Reading, Mass.

Rand McNally, 1962. *Cosmopolitan world atlas.* Rand McNally, Chicago.

Stamp, L. Dudley, ed., 1961. *A history of land use in arid regions.* Unesco, Paris.

Thomas, William L. Jr., ed., 1956. *Man's role in changing the face of the earth.* University of Chicago Press, Chicago.

UNESCO, 1970. *Use and conservation of the biosphere.* Natural Resources Research, X. UNESCO, Paris.

LITERATURE CITED 1. Ehrlich, Paul R., 1967. The food-from-the-sea myth. *Commonwealth,* 61:115–117.

contents

conservation—
the alternative
for survival

Conservation is a way of looking at the world, and a way of action based on that point of view. Those who see the world this way seek to provide for the existence of the greatest possible diversity and variety of life on earth. Through this they hope to achieve for humanity not only a better chance for continued survival but also the opportunity for living in a world of richness and abundance in which the full range of human hopes and dreams can be pursued. We live in an uncertain universe where comets can go astray or suns explode. The future can never be guaranteed. We can, however, cease to be our own greatest danger and enhance the means for continuing life on earth. We can keep from destroying our own environment and, with it, ourselves. It is surely worth our time to see how we can accomplish this. That is what this book is all about.

Never before has the future of life on earth rested so completely in human hands. At no previous time in the last hundred thousand years has the survival of the human race seemed so doubtful. We have reached this state by taking control of enormous resources of energy. These resources can now be used for the destruction of life. They could equally be used for its improvement. Unfortunately, our control over these new sources of energy has not been accompanied by the development of the wisdom necessary to prevent their misuse. We lack understanding of ourselves, of others, and of the environment on which we depend. Most particularly we lack appreciation of the total interdependence that exists among all living things and the physical world that they inhabit.

During the past several centuries, and most notably in the past 50 years, there has been a severely unbalanced development of human knowledge. In the physical sciences, and the technology derived from them, a sophistication has been gained which permits us to shatter atoms and send rockets to Saturn. But there has been no similar growth of knowledge of how living creatures interact. There has been even less gain in understanding of the factors influencing our social interactions, or of the forces influencing the behavior of individuals. Consequently the human race today is like an ape with a hand grenade. Nobody can say when he will pull the pin. We are able to act with great skill and power without knowing why we act nor what the full results of that action will be. It is obvious it is perilous to continue in this way.

Environmental conservation is one approach toward achieving a better balance. At the very least it is an approach that will minimize the risks associated with our willingness to play with our newfound physical power. At best it will lead to an understanding of the interactions between nature and humanity that will allow us to develop ways of life that can be sustained. It is most likely these ways will provide greater satisfaction and fulfillment for the people who pursue them.

We are at a dramatic turning point in human history. Astrologers point out that, like it or not, we are entering the Age of Aquarius. More prosaic folk note only that we are reaching the end of a millennium — the second since the Christian calendar began. We have 25 years left before the twenty-first century begins. During that quarter century most of the human race is going to have a rough time. For reasons that will be examined in this book, civilization must change its course and it will not be easy to do so. For those who relax in the hope that things can go on as they have over the past few decades, it must be pointed out there is no basis for such hope. Life will not go on as it has been. There are various options to choose from, but there is no option that allows present trends to continue.

During the history of humanity, people have made many mistakes in their relationships to the world they lived in and to one another. Our ancestors, however, were able to postpone the day of reckoning. They were able to seek present profit without too much concern for its future effects. There were many who said, "Let posterity worry about it." You are the posterity they were talking about. During your lifetime you must find answers to this question: How can human beings continue to live on planet Earth without destroying the environment on which their lives depend? Sustainable ways of life must be discovered. Destructive ways of life must be abandoned. Without these there will be no posterity.

THE BACKGROUND OF CONSERVATION

Conservation, as a popular movement, began in the United States. It has had its greatest support and following in those continents most fully exposed to the impact of European immigrants — people who could draw on the power and resources of a civilization that was building a sophisticated industrial technology. These immigrants were capable of doing great environmental damage and of changing the landscapes and life they encountered. At the same time, they had memories of an older, long-settled continent where changes had not come so suddenly or had such dramatic consequences. They also saw the difference between what had been and what they had done in the "new" lands they were occupying. Thus a concern arose.

It is difficult to say when or where conservation started. A concern for wildlife conservation was expressed in the early British colonies as wildlife began to disappear before the onslaught of the colonists. Worry about the future of the forests may have been next, and then about the erosion of soils and the destruction of rangelands. Protest against pollution and poisoning, or concern with the urban condition was much later in arriving. In the 1830's, George Catlin, an artist and naturalist, expressed his feelings about the future of the buffalo and the Plains Indians that depended on it. He proposed a vast national park extending throughout the

Great Plains, in which Indians and wildlife would be left alone.[3] Nobody paid much attention, and when national parks were created there was no place in them for Indians. In the 1850's, Henry David Thoreau, writing in *Walden* and other journals, expressed his concern for the future of all wild nature and saw in wildness the hope for the preservation of the world. He had the foresight to realize that people are first inhabitants of the natural world "part and parcel of Nature," and only second members of society. He demanded attention first to the "more sacred laws" of nature when these come into conflict with the regulations of human society. But few were listening.[5]

George Perkins Marsh in the 1860's tried to put together what he had seen in the Old World and the New, and, in his *Man and Nature; or, Physical Geography as Modified by Human Action*, he provided the first textbook of conservation.[2] In the same decade John Muir and others pleaded for the protection of nature and were successful in the establishment of the Yosemite National Park. In 1872 Congress created the first official national park in Yellowstone. However, it was not until 1908 that Theodore Roosevelt provided the name of "conservation" to describe all of these activities. It is likely, however, that he acquired the concept from his chief forester Gifford Pinchot.[3]

As a popular movement conservation has grown by fits and starts. It was during the 1960's, touched off by the student revolt and by the increasing awareness of the dangers involved in pollution, population growth, and destruction of nature, that conservation became a mass movement with the capacity to elect or depose congressmen and governors and to influence presidents who, unlike Roosevelt, had little inherent interest in the subject. By then, however, the conservation movement was known by other names—it had become the "ecology movement" or the "environmental movement"—and those who followed it were known as "environmentalists."

The full recognition of man as a part of nature, inseparable from his environment, that Thoreau had foreseen, was to follow the development of the science of ecology. The pursuit of ecological knowledge was to reveal the existence of those "yet more sacred laws" which must take precedence over mere human regulations. Yet ecologists, as scientists, are often remote from any direct concern with the conservation of the life processes they study. Theodore Roszak questioned this:

Ecology already hovers on the threshold of heresy. Will it be brave enough to step across and, in so doing, revolutionize the sciences as a whole? If that step is to be taken, it will not be a matter of further research, but of transformed consciousness. . . . For many of our cultural drop-outs . . . ecology represents a last tenuous connection with the scientific mainstream. It is the one science that seems capable of assimilating moral principle and visionary experience, and so of becoming a science of the whole person. But there is no guarantee ecology will reach out to embrace these other dimensions of the mind.

It could finish—at least in its professionally respectable version—as no more than a sophisticated systems approach to the conservation of natural resources. The question remains open: which will ecology be, the last of the old sciences or the first of the new?[4]

Regardless of the penchant of individual ecologists, ecology forces one recognition on those who study it: the individual is coexistent with his environment, cannot be separated from it, and is continually changing and being changed by it. Thus ecology, albeit unwillingly, has come to a certain coincidence with the old nature religions of "primitive" people, and with the transcendental philosophies of the religions of Asia. Writing from the viewpoint of Zen, Alan Watts has stated, "The hostile attitude of conquering Nature ignores the basic interdependence of all things and events—that the world beyond the skin is actually an extension of our own bodies—and will end in destroying the very environment from which we emerge and upon which our whole life depends."[7]

To anyone who accepts the importance and necessity of environmental conservation it is apparent that conservationists must call into question the activities of governments, groups, and individuals. They must ask questions about the behavior and motives of people, and about ways of life and institutions. Since many who are in positions of power prefer no such questions to be asked, conservationists will encounter the strongest opposition. A conservation viewpoint, however, must challenge the right of nations, human institutions, and individuals to engage in activities which impair the long-term well-being of other humans, other species, or the environments on which they all depend.

The words of conservationists, no matter how well spoken, have shaken no empires thus far. They have caused no great worry among those who attempt to control the economic and political destiny of nations. Unlike the words of Marx or Lenin, they have inspired no violent revolutions. Yet, in their full implications, they are far more revolutionary to those who espouse a belief in the sacredness of continued economic growth and expansion. This will be apparent by the end of this book.

THE MEANING OF TERMS Before going further it is worthwhile to consider some basic definitions. The term *environmental conservation* is defined as the rational use of the environment to provide the highest sustainable quality of living for humanity. This meaning has been generally accepted by the International Union for the Conservation of Nature and some United Nations agencies. However, the definition requires much explanation, for example, the meaning of "quality of living." Earlier in its history conservation was regarded simply as "wise use of natural resources" or "rational use" if one preferred to avoid the implications of the word "wise."

The term *environment,* as used in this book, refers to the biosphere, the ecosystems of which it is composed, and the modifications of these brought about by human action. The *biosphere* is now defined as the thin layer of soil, rock, water, and air that surrounds the planet Earth along with the living organisms for which it provides support, and which modify it in directions that either enhance or lessen its life-supporting capacity. Some prefer the term "ecosphere" for this concept and restrict "biosphere" to life itself—but this involves separating the inseparable. We are all part of the biosphere and are supported by it, yet we are seldom aware of its presence and much of it is beyond the reach of our senses. In this lies some of the difficulty in making people aware of the reality of an environmental crisis—if they can't see, hear, smell, taste, or touch it it isn't there! Relative to the size of the earth, the biosphere is like the skin of an apple—a shallow layer of air, water, soil, and rock not much more than 15 miles deep from the bottom of the ocean to the highest point in the atmosphere where life can exist without protective devices.

Ecosystems are subdivisions of the biosphere. They consist of communities of plants, animals, and microorganisms along with the air, water, soil, or other substrate that supports them. They may be large or small—the term is flexible. Some talk about "balanced ecosystems" contained in an aquarium; others use the term to describe the tropical forests of South America. Ecosystems and the biosphere are powered by energy, most of which is derived directly or indirectly from the sun. Ecosystems may be very simple, such as a community of lichens growing on a rock in the high Arctic, or very complex, such as a specific tropical rain forest or a coral reef in tropical seas.

Natural resources is a vague term. At one time it referred to the things, or sources of energy, in the environment used by humanity—coal, iron, timber, rivers for hydropower, and the like. However, as our knowledge of the environment and our use of the planet has expanded, virtually everything on earth along with the sunlight impinging on earth has come to be considered as a natural resource. Some resources, such as the Antarctic ice cap are only potential resources, since we are not using them—but there are some who would haul the Antarctic icebergs northward to modify climates and provide urban water supplies.

In earlier conservation books a nice distinction was made between *renewable* resources and *nonrenewable* resources. The former were the living things and their derivatives, the latter, the minerals and nonliving energy resources. This was convenient, but too simple. Soils are a mixture of living and nonliving. They are renewable if properly handled, meaning that through the presence of the life on them and within them, they can be rebuilt and repaired. They are nonrenewable if handled in such a way that their fertility is exhausted or they are washed or blown away. Water is nonliving, and yet it is an inexhaustible resource—since all of the uses we make of it simply move it from one place to another. Fresh water in a particular place may be a nonrenewable resource. For example many underground reservoirs represent the accumulations of thousands of years. If we pump from them at a rapid rate they become

a

NATURAL RESOURCES

Natural resources are those forms of matter or energy considered useful or essential by human societies. They may be considered under several categories.

Inexhaustible resources. Energy from the sun (**a**) has, until recently, powered all living systems on earth. For the foreseeable future it will always be available as an energy resource; we cannot use it up. The same can be said, in a general way, for hydropower (**b**) which is derived from solar energy. For so long as the sun shines, rain will fall and water will flow downhill. Using it as a power source does not exhaust it.

b

c, d

e

Renewable resources. Forests (**c**) and all living things are renewable resources, meaning that if we balance our rate of use against their rate of growth or reproduction they can continue to renew themselves and will always be available.

Nonrenewable resources. Coal (**d**) and petroleum (**e**) are present on earth in limited quantities. When we use these resources they are destroyed. The rate at which new reserves can be formed is too slow to compensate for our rate of use. Hence, they are nonrenewable.

Recyclable resources. Many metals are not destroyed by use. The objects made from them, (**f**) and (**g**) can be melted down and the metals used again for other purposes.

f

g

exhausted. Despite all of these confusing points, it is worthwhile to make certain distinctions.

Inexhaustible resources are those such as sunlight, which will continue to pour onto the earth for as long as humanity will be around, whether we use it in certain ways or not. Water in the global sense, and air also come into this category, as also do those resources for which our foreseeable rate of use is relatively minute in relation to the supply—table salt from the ocean, for example. *Nonrenewable* resources are not regenerated or reformed in nature at rates equivalent to the rate at which we use them. Petroleum is an example. Given some millions of years, new petroleum reserves could be built up. Considering our rate of use of oil, however, petroleum is nonrenewable and will not last long. A special category of nonrenewable resources is called *recyclable* resources. These are resources, such as many metals, which are not lost or worn out by the way we use them, and can be reprocessed and used again and again. *Renewable* resources include all living things that have the capacity for reproduction and growth. As long as the rate of use is less than their rate of regeneration, and as long as their environments are kept suitable, they will go on replacing themselves. They can, therefore, be used forever without exhausting them as long as they are protected and managed. Products formed at a relatively rapid rate by living organisms are in a similar category—for example, the alcohols produced by fermentation bacteria. However, living communities are not necessarily renewable, if the way in which we use them is destructive. No living species can survive if we crop it at a rate more rapid than it can reproduce, or if we destroy the habitat on which it depends.

Ecology is the science concerned with the interrelationship among living things and with their nonliving environment. It is not a new science. The word was first used by Ernst Haeckel in 1869, but ecological studies have been carried out since antiquity, and many "primitive" peoples are first-rate practicing ecologists although they may know nothing of science.

These terms are enough to begin with—others will be explained in the chapters that follow and their definitions will be explored in greater depth.

ARRANGEMENTS The ecological basis for conservation is the first topic discussed in this book. Chapters 2 and 3 deal with ecology only. Chapter 3 examines the relationships of people to their environment throughout the lifetime of *Homo sapiens*. Some concepts within it aid in understanding situations that are described in the following chapters. Chapters 4 through 10 are concerned with ecological processes along with the human activities that affect these processes in soils, water, forests, rangelands, wildlife, and fisheries. From Chapter 11 on our concern is with the critical problems of today and tomorrow: population, energy, food, raw materials, pollution, and the organization of urban-industrial society. The final chapter examines ways out of our dilemma, along with the special problem of protecting human diversity. Those who do not wish to get involved too deeply with applied ecology or with understanding how things work in the natural environment could skip from Chapters 1 to 3 to 11 and then to the finish. However, this will lead to a rather incomplete understanding of what is happening on earth. It is better to get your feet muddy and wade right in from the beginning. People cannot survive without wild places and wild creatures to help them along. As Romain Gary has put it: "We need all the dogs, all the cats, and all the birds, and all the elephants we can find. . . . We need all the friendship we can find around us."[1]

CHAPTER REFERENCES

Leonard, George, 1972. *The transformation.* Delacorte, New York.
Odum, Eugene P., 1971. *Fundamentals of ecology.* Third edition. W. B. Saunders, Philadelphia.

LITERATURE CITED

1. Gary, Romain, 1958. *The roots of heaven.* Simon and Schuster, New York.
2. Marsh, George Perkins, 1864. *Man and nature; or, physical geography as modified by human action.* Scribners, New York.
3. Nash, Roderick, 1968. *The American environment.* Addison-Wesley, Reading, Mass.
4. Roszak, Theodore, 1972. *Where the wasteland ends. Politics and transcendence in postindustrial society.* Doubleday, New York.
5. Thoreau, Henry David, 1960 ed. *Walden or life in the woods, and On the duty of civil disobedience.* New American Library, New York.
6. UNESCO, 1970. *Use and conservation of the biosphere.* Natural Resources Research X, Unesco, Paris.
7. Watts, Alan, 1969. *The book on the taboo against knowing who you are.* Abacus ed. 1973. Sphere Books, London.

2

the
nature
of
the
environment

ECOSYSTEMS AND
COMMUNITIES

despite the present position of human dominance over the earth, people still depend totally on the interactions among other species in the biosphere for their continued existence. If one lives in a city, it is sometimes easy to forget this dependence and even to assume humanity has risen above nature. But the bread you eat comes from wheat plants formed of soil, air, and sunlight. The soil, with its hosts of microorganisms to maintain its health and fertility, was itself formed by the work of generations of green plants and animals, transforming rock and sunlight energy into the organized network of materials needed for the growth of wheat plants. The meat people demand in their diet also comes from soil materials, transformed by a great community of grassland organisms into the plant protein and carbohydrate needed to feed a steer. Beef is soil and sunlight made available to us by the work of plant communities. Like all other animals we depend on the interrelationships of living things with their physical environment.

The relationships among organisms and environment are illustrated by the concepts of biotic communities and ecosystems. A *biotic community* is an assemblage of species of plants and animals inhabiting a common area and affecting one another. Examples are everywhere—an oak woodland that forms part of a city park, the marsh separating bay from dry land, the grassy pastures on which livestock feed, a cornfield, or the rain forests of the Amazon—all are biotic communities made up of plants and animals, some large and conspicuous, some microscopic in size but major in their importance to the survival of the others. A combination of such a biotic community with the physical environment that supports it is called an *ecosystem*.

Thus the woodland community, the soil that supports it, the water in that soil or in the atmosphere, the atmosphere itself, and the sunlight that gives it life together form a woodland ecosystem. *Ecology* is considered to be the study of ecosystems to determine how they are organized, how their parts interact, and how total systems function. Ecology is the study of organisms in relation to their environment, the science concerned with interrelationships of natural systems. Since it is the interrelationships between people and their environment which are running into difficulty, ecology has been appreciated more and more. However, ecology in its strictest sense is a science, the organized pursuit of knowledge. Such knowledge can be used in ways that are morally irreproachable, but also in ways that are morally reprehensible. Ecological knowledge can be used to support environmental conservation, to maintain and enhance the human environment. It could also be used to destroy it.

The human environment is the biosphere, and the modifications within it caused by human action. The biosphere is part of the planet in which life exists and of which it forms a part. It is the surface area of the earth, made up of the lower levels of the atmosphere, the oceans, the upper surfaces of continents and islands including soil, rocks, and fresh water, and the living things inhabiting this area. In the biosphere energy from sunlight activates life processes; chemicals from air, water, and soil, are available as building blocks for living organisms.[4]

The biosphere can be considered as the sum of all the ecosystems on earth. At any one time people exist as part of a particular ecosystem, although at other times they may travel from one ecosystem to another. What happens to the biosphere and its ecosystems determines what will happen to people. It is impossible to separate individuals from the biosphere of which they form a part. The air they breathe, the water they drink, the sunlight that warms them, and the food they eat, all tie them to their immediate physical and biological environment. At any one time the human body, like that of any other animal, exists in a dynamic state of exchange with the environment—taking in or expelling gases, absorbing or giving off heat, and losing or gaining water and other chemicals. This continuous process of exchange ceases only with death, at which time a different set of environmental interactions begins. A human apart from environment is an abstraction—in reality no such being exists.

Before people became dominant on earth, they were members of a biotic community and components of an ecosystem, without having much more effect on them than any other animal species would have. In still-existing societies in remote areas of the earth, this condition remains. The dominant societies of today, however, have changed the face of the earth. Some areas have been subject to major modification, others less so, but it is probably impossible to find any ecosystem which has not been affected in some way. Nevertheless it remains useful to distinguish between the less modified, or *natural* community or ecosystem, and the highly modified, *anthropogenic* community or ecosystem. This does not mean people are not part of nature, but it does recognize our dominant role on the planet. Undoubtedly the areas subject to the most extreme modification are the major cities of the world, which often seem to exist apart from nature. This separation, however, is more apparent than real. It must be remembered that urban systems are intricately related to ecosystems on which they depend for their continued existence. They have been defined as supraecosystems, because of the degree to which they tie together what would otherwise be remote and separate ecosystems.[3] The problems of urban systems differ in degree, but not in fundamental nature, from those of other areas less influenced by people.

ENERGY TRANSFER   For a community to exist it must have energy to supply the life processes of the organisms that compose it. The principal source of energy for any biotic community is sunlight. However, one group of organisms, the green plants, makes use of sunlight energy directly for the synthesis of foodstuffs. The presence of chlorophyll in the cells of plants makes possible photosynthesis, in which light energy is used in building a plant food (glucose) from simple compounds—carbon dioxide from the air and water from the soil. From glucose, with the addition of other simple chemical compounds obtained from the soil, plants can build more complex carbohydrates, proteins, fats, and vitamins. These materials, required by animals in their diets, must come from the plant world.

The dependence of animals on plants and of plants on sunlight brings to consideration a physical law of great importance to the understanding of any ecosystem. This, the *second law of thermodynamics,* states that in any transfer of energy from one form to another, some energy always escapes from the system, usually as heat; no transfer is 100 percent effective. Always energy goes from a concentrated form useful to a system to a dilute form, in which it is not. Most transfers of energy in natural ecosystems are inefficient. In some instances, of the total amount of sunlight energy potentially available to green plants, only 1 percent will be converted finally into chemical energy tied up in foods within the plants. The remaining 99 percent escapes. Similarly, when herbivores feed on green plants and convert plant starch and protein into animal energy and protein, another high percentage of energy escapes. When carnivores feed on herbivores, there is again inefficiency in energy transfer. The limits of available energy are soon reached. Thus, in some communities, of 10,000 original calories of sunlight energy striking on green plants, only 2 calories may remain tied up in chemical energy within the body of a carnivorous animal.

The operation of the second law of thermodynamics serves to explain many of the characteristics of ecosystems. In any ecosystem the amount of green plants is limited, ultimately, by the amount of sunlight energy and the efficiency of plants in converting it to a useful form. This is a theoretical upper limit, not approached in natural ecosystems, because lesser limits are always set by shortages of required chemical elements or other factors.

In a similar way the final limit on the number of animals in an area is determined by the amount of energy available in green plants and by the efficiency of animals in converting this to a form useful for maintenance, growth, and reproduction. These relationships within an ecosystem are often illustrated in diagrammatic ways, such as the biotic pyramid, food chain, and food web (Fig. 2–1). In the *biotic pyramid* the greatest numbers of organisms, the greatest mass, and the greatest amount of food energy, are to be found in the lowest layer of organisms, the green plants. Partly because of the necessary inefficiency in energy transfer, numbers, mass, and energy decrease as you move up the pyramid. The pyramid is supported by the amount of sunlight energy received and the amounts of essential nutrients, minerals, water, and essential gases available in the soil or other supporting physical environment. In marine ecosystems the biotic-pyramid concept is less useful, since a high rate

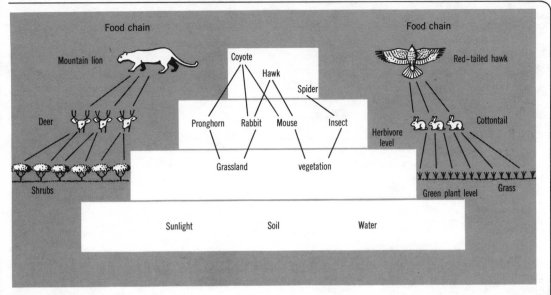

FIG. 2–1. Biotic pyramid showing portion of grassland food web.

of productivity among the floating green plants (phytoplankton) compensate for a relatively low biomass at any one time. *Food chains* are simply diagrammatic representations of the food relationships within an ecosystem. A simple example is the chain that leads from bitterbrush to mule deer to mountain lion. Bitterbrush is the green plant, or *producer,* at the base of the food chain, and is said to be at the lowest *trophic level* or energy level. The deer feeding on the bitterbrush is at the herbivore, or *primary consumer* trophic level, and the mountain lion, feeding on the deer, is at the *secondary consumer,* carnivore, trophic level. Obviously there must be more bitterbrush than deer, if the deer are to be supported entirely by it, and there also must be more deer than mountain lions, if lions are to live entirely on a diet of deer meat. Although food chains like this may be artificially separated out and studied, most food relationships of species in an ecosystem are far more complicated. In natural systems, food chains are interwoven into complex *food webs.* Thus if the simple example given is expanded, it will be seen that deer feed not only on bitterbrush but on many species of shrubs, trees, grasses and other herbs which, in turn, support not only deer but other mammals (various mice and hares, for example), birds, great numbers of insects, and other invertebrates down to a variety of microorganisms. A deer is seldom free of a whole range of external and internal parasites which are deriving energy indirectly from the green plants the deer eats—tapeworms, roundworms, flukes, bacteria and protozoa, fleas, lice, and the like. Coyotes or wildcats in addition to mountain lions may kill and eat deer. The dead green plant, deer, or lion, in turn, provides food for a great

FOOD CHAINS

At the base of any food chain are green plants which capture the energy of sunlight (**a**). At the next link in the chain (or trophic level) are herbivores which feed directly on plants, such as this goat herd in Lebanon (**b**) or prairie dogs in the American West (**c**). At the top of the chain are carnivores such as the red fox (**d**) which is shown here with a captured herbivore (cottontail rabbit).

b

c

d

variety of insect larvae, bacteria, protozoans, scavengers among birds such as ravens or vultures, scavenging mammals, all of the wide range of organisms which take the substance from a dead plant or animal and return it ultimately in chemical form to the soil, from whence it enters a new generation of plants and animals.

Despite the enormous complexity of food webs in nature, the number of layers in a biotic pyramid or links in a food chain is inevitably limited through the operation of the second law of thermodynamics. The loss of energy at each stage of energy transfer keeps biotic pyramids low and food chains short. Thus, there are no superpredators which feed exclusively on mountain lions. The expenditure of energy involved in the capture and consumption of these scarce creatures would certainly outweigh the energy to be gained. In aquatic ecosystems food chains are commonly longer than those on land—there may be several layers of predatory fish feeding on the herbivores; but even in these complex systems the inefficiency of energy transfer prevents the development of long food chains.

People, as carnivores, occupy the top layer of a biotic pyramid and the end link of a food chain. However, they can also exist as herbivores and thus lower the pyramid and shorten the food chain. In those areas of the earth where human numbers are great and productive land is limited, they cannot afford the luxury of being carnivores nor the waste of energy involved in converting plant protein to beef or mutton. In such areas they must feed on plants primarily if great numbers are to be kept alive.

Of perhaps equal importance with the limitations imposed by the second law of thermodynamics is the role played by life in conserving energy. Sunlight energy striking a bare rock or soil surface is soon lost. Much is reflected back into the air; some heats the rock or soil temporarily but is soon radiated back into the atmosphere. The earth as a whole, before life, radiated or reflected back into space an amount of energy equal to that received from the sun. In the absence of life, energy thus became degraded, i.e., dispersed through space until it was no longer capable of doing work. When green plants appeared on earth, this loss of energy was slowed down. Sunlight energy was stored in organisms in concentrated form and transferred in food chains from one to another. With the development of complex biotic communities, a living system was developed that made even greater use of the incoming solar energy and stored a part of it for the future. People have been dependent upon these stored reserves of energy. When a person eats meat, he or she obtains energy that may have been stored by plants several years before. When we cut firewood for fuel, we are obtaining energy accumulated and stored by trees for perhaps a century or more. When we burn coal or petroleum, we obtain sunlight energy stored by plant life millions of years before. We are as yet unable to store significant quantities of energy without making use of the life processes of plants and animals. When living communities are destroyed and the land made bare, the energy on which life depends is again wasted and no longer is stored for future use.

CHEMICAL REQUIREMENTS Just as each ecosystem must have a source of energy, so must it have a source of chemical building blocks or nutrients from which organisms can be constructed. In the oceans this source is seawater; on land the source is the soil. Biotic pyramids rest on an energy base of sunlight, and a chemical base of soil or seawater. Both of these sources of minerals, however, are secondary, for minerals come originally from the rocks of the earth's surface or from the atmosphere above the earth.

Rocks supply minerals to the soil slowly. Rocks break apart through weathering, the action of cold, heat, wind, and precipitation gradually cracking and shattering them into small particles. They break down more quickly through the action of organisms. Plant roots, for example, penetrate into cracks in rocks, widen them, and eventually split and separate the rock fragments. Acids released or dissolved from plant materials help the process of rock disintegration and free elements for soil formation. Organisms also help to capture elements such as nitrogen from the atmosphere and incorporate them in the soil. Nitrogen, an essential part of protein, must be present for life to exist. The cycle by which it is transferred from atmosphere to organism, to soil, and back to the atmosphere has been well studied and is illustrated in Figure 2–2. We must recognize that the atmosphere on which life depends is in itself dependent on life for the continued existence of its life-sustaining molecules.

The Russian scientist, V. I. Vernadsky, has pointed out that the biosphere holds three main components.[4] The first is *life* itself, the sum total of living matter. The second he terms *biogenic* matter. This includes all of the organic substances formed by living matter: coal, petroleum, natural gas, peat, soil humus, litter, and the like. The third, which he terms *biocosnic* matter, is represented by the minerals or chemicals formed through the interaction of life with the inorganic world. Among them, Vernadsky includes the gases of the lower layers of the atmosphere, sedimentary rocks, clay minerals, and water. Although these terms are not in general use, a gradual increasing awareness of the significance of living processes in the physics, chemistry and geology of the earth's crust has been brought about by the work of Vernadsky, and has been emphasized more recently by the Russian soil scientist V. Kovda.[4] At this point it is appropriate to consider in more detail the relationships between the earth's atmosphere and life on the earth.

Roughly 99 percent of the atmosphere consists of the two gases, nitrogen and oxygen, both of which are essential to life. The balance is made up of the equally essential carbon dioxide, water vapor, and various rare and inert gases. Nitrogen is a rare substance on earth, even though it is the dominant gas in the atmosphere. It is an essential component of all living matter, being involved in the chemical composition of the amino acids from which all plant and animal proteins are constructed. It is likely that all of the nitrogen in the atmosphere, through the operation of

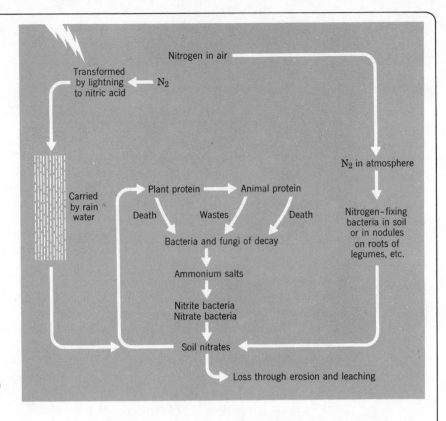

FIG. 2–2. The nitrogen cycle.

the nitrogen cycle, passes through living organisms and is returned ultimately to the atmosphere through the action of denitrifying bacteria or other processes. Even the nitrogen which escapes from the cycle to be deposited as sedimentary rock, or in the form of coal, petroleum and the like may ultimately be returned to the atmosphere through the long reaches of geological time by movements of the rocks on the earth's crust, volcanic activity, and soil formation from sedimentary rocks. The turnover rate of atmospheric nitrogen is very slow and involves many centuries. Thus, despite the steady use of nitrogen by living organisms there is little drain on the nitrogen supply and no fear of exhaustion of the nitrogen in the atmosphere.

It is a different story with oxygen. This is a highly reactive gas, unlike the relatively inert nitrogen. It is so reactive that most of it on the earth is tied up in chemical combination with other elements, such as iron oxides, and aluminum oxides. Molecular oxygen, on which life depends, exists only in the atmosphere or dissolved in water. In both places, its presence is dependent primarily on the action of green plants. Before life appeared on earth, there was little or no oxygen in the atmosphere. The first living organisms were *anaerobic* microscopic forms able to exist without free oxygen. Only when these evolved to the stage where the first photosynthetic reaction took place was molecular oxygen first released into the atmosphere. However, green plants both produce and consume oxygen. Oxygen is produced in excess in the presence of light, when photosynthesis proceeds more rapidly than respiration. In darkness, when photosynthesis cannot take place, the process of respiration burns up much of the oxygen which has been produced. During the time a plant is living, however, it is making a contribution to the atmospheric oxygen supply that exceeds its rate of use. When it ceases to live and begins to decay, various oxidative reactions take place which consume the excess oxygen the plant produced during its lifetime.

In order for oxygen to accumulate in the atmosphere, it is first necessary for green plants to produce it, and then for these plants, on dying (or for the dead bodies of the animals that consume them), to be sealed away from the processes of decay and the oxidation that accompanies them. This happens quite regularly when dead plants or animals are sealed off from the air by the accumulation of other materials on top of them. Marshes, swamps, and in particular peat bogs, accumulate great amounts of such dead plant and animal material. The sediments at the bottom of ponds, lakes, seas, and the ocean also accumulate and seal off organic materials. Thus, over the long reaches of geological time enough organic material has accumulated in a reduced state, to account for the amount of oxygen present in the atmosphere today. Much of this has gone into the formation of the deposits of fossil fuels, the coal seams, and petroleum deposits we are now mining for energy. (Some of it exists in the litter and organic humus of the soil—some in the accumulations of peat, oil shales, oil sands, etc.) However, much of it is more widely dispersed among the sedimentary rocks of the earth's surface. It is apparent that during past geological ages the rate at which plant and animal debris accumulated to form organic sediments was much faster than it is today. During recent decades there has been no observable tendency for the oxygen level of the atmosphere to increase. In fact, the fear has been that with widespread use of fossil fuels and depletion of the earth's supply of green plant life, the amount of atmospheric oxygen would decrease. In burning coal, oil, and natural gas, one is reversing the process by which the atmospheric oxygen was formed. If all organic sediments were to be oxidized, all of the accumulation of atmospheric oxygen would theoretically be consumed. However, the total amount represented by the available deposits of fossil fuels is apparently not sufficient to bring any great change in atmospheric oxygen, and during the past 60 years, the period of heaviest burning of coal and petroleum, there has been no observable decrease in atmospheric oxygen.[1,2,5]

The final atmospheric component directly related to the presence of life is carbon dioxide. Unlike oxygen, this is added to the atmosphere in considerable quantities by processes other than those directly involved with life, notably from volcanic action. The same process of photosynthesis that adds oxygen to the atmosphere removes carbon dioxide. Respiration, which removes oxygen, adds carbon dioxide. Although the total supply of carbon dioxide is relatively small, it is vital to plant growth and increases in its relative amount will stimulate plant growth where other elements are not lacking. Carbon dioxide also plays an important role in temperature regulation of the earth, since its molecules permit the passage of the shorter waves of solar radiation through the atmosphere, but interfere with the passage of the longer waves of heat radiating from the earth's surface. Consequently, changes in the amount of carbon dioxide in the atmosphere would be expected to affect the global heat balance, to make the earth either warmer or cooler. Although, human activity, in particular the consumption of fossil fuels, has not decreased the amount of oxygen in the atmosphere, it has apparently brought a noticeable increase in carbon dioxide.[2,7] The significance of this will be discussed under the subject of air pollution in Chapter 11.

SOIL FORMATION Just as the evolution of the atmosphere has been dependent on the presence of life on earth, the evolution of soil has accompanied the evolution of life—before life there was no soil—for soil is created through the action of organisms. When life is destroyed in an area, the loss of soil follows.

In an area where rocks have long been exposed to the air we can see the stages through which soil is sometimes formed. Rock surfaces, roughened and weathered, provide a foothold for primitive and hardy land plants, the *lichens* (p. 26). These exert a physical and chemical effect on the rock leading to a more rapid decomposition. Small rock particles may be accumulated and added to the dead remnants of the lichen bodies. When enough mineral and organic material has accumulated, *mosses* next invade the rock surface. These crowd out the lichens, but with their more dense growth habit and more robust plant bodies they hasten the breakdown of rock and add greater amounts of organic debris to the mixture.

Eventually a layer of materials will be formed deep enough to support the more hardy types of *annual grasses* and *forbs* (broad-leaved herbs), and these will invade and overtop the mosses. These in turn break down the rock further and add more organic material. In a forested region they are replaced by larger *perennial grasses* and *forbs;* these are replaced by *shrubs* and, finally, by *trees.* Each does its part in breaking down rock and adding organic debris to it. Joining in the process are microorganisms of various kinds, bacteria and fungi, which feed on dead plant and animal remains and eventually release from them simple mineral nutrients which may be used again to support new plant growth. Also involved are the larger burrowing animals which churn and mix rock particles together and add to the complex their own waste products and dead bodies. Eventually, with the final stage of vegetation, there has been developed that complex arrangement of minerals and living and dead organic materials which is known as mature soil.

The process of soil formation is not always the same. Few of our soils have actually developed in place from underlying parent rock. Most, the *transported soils,* are built from materials carried by wind, water, gravity, or glacial action from other areas and are broken from rock originally by the action of heat, wind, and water. Across the northern United States and sections of northern Europe and Asia the soil materials are mostly of glacial origin, built from fragments ground from underlying rocks by the action of continental glaciers during past ice ages. These have been carried hundreds of miles and deposited where the glaciers finally melted and retreated. Over wide areas in the central United States, eastern Europe and eastern Asia the soils are derived from *loess,* formed from dust particles carried over long distances by wind currents. Elsewhere, soils have been built up on wind-blown sands or from the gravels, sands, and salts deposited in stream beds or former lakes. But on glacial drifts, loess deposits, or these other sites, the process of plant invasion, breakdown, and modification of the substrate has gone on also. Where the substrate is finely divided, the lichen and moss stage may be skipped and the initial plant invasion be made by herbs, shrubs, or trees. Always, however, there is further development and change until a mature soil and a relatively stable vegetation is attained.

EROSION Just as the action of living organisms is essential for the development of soil, so it is essential if the soil is to be maintained. Throughout past ages there have been two major groups of forces at work on the earth's surface. One group of forces contributes to land raising: folding up mountain ranges, elevating plateaus, forming volcanic peaks. The other group leads to the degradation of lands, the lowering of the high lands back to sea level. These forces of degradation, or erosion, consist of gravity in combination with wind, rain, and temperature, cracking apart the rocks and carrying them to lower elevations. In the long ages before life appeared, *geological erosion* went on as a slow and unchecked process. With the development of life, however, a new force was interposed. The decomposed rocks were stopped in their movement to the sea by the countless small check dams formed from plant life. Instead of washing away, rock particles remained to form soil. But once soil is formed, it becomes highly vulnerable to a much more rapid erosion than that which wears away rocks. Without a covering of green plants and a network of plant roots to hold it in place it can be lost rapidly. When plant cover is destroyed, a few decades can see the disappearance of soils which may have been thousands of years in forming. It is this kind of *accelerated soil erosion* which is of concern to the conservationist.

BIOTIC SUCCESSION The role of plants in soil formation illustrates another process fundamental in any ecosystem and basic to much work in conservation. This is the process known as biotic succession. The way in which lichens and mosses are replaced by herbs and these by shrubs and trees as soils are being formed is an example of biotic succession. Along with the replacement and change in the types of plants, goes replacement and change in the animals dependent upon each type of plant. Biotic succession can be defined as the sequence of biotic communities which

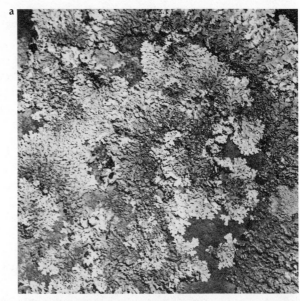

BIOTIC SUCCESSION

All ecosystems develop through successional stages, starting with *pioneer* plants or animals which can invade and colonize barren areas and moving via middle stages through *subclimax* to various kinds of *climax* communities, which are relatively stable and will persist over long periods of time if not disturbed.

Pioneer stage. (**a**) A colony of lichens colonizes a bare rock surface. **Subclimax.** (**b**) An aspen woodland. Already, dark conifers which will form the climax are to be seen. These will overtop and replace the aspens. **Fire subclimax.** (**c**) This pine forest is maintained by periodic burning. Left undisturbed it would be replaced by a hardwood forest. **Climax.** (**d**) The eastern deciduous forest shown here will persist over many centuries unless disturbed by fire, storm or human activities.

tend to succeed and replace one another in a given area over a period of time. Each community in the sequence changes the environment in such a way as to favor those species which will next take over. The starting point in any biotic succession is always a *pioneer community,* able to colonize and inhabit a bare surface. The end product in any succession is known as a *climax community.* This is a relatively stable community, able to maintain itself over long periods of time and to regenerate and replace itself without marked further change. It is usually the most complex type of community which a particular physical environment will support and makes the most efficient use of sun energy and soil materials. Climax communities represent storehouses of materials and energy accumulated over the long years of plant succession and soil formation.

Throughout the earth, wherever life can be supported, biotic succession goes on. Plants invade and colonize bare areas and are replaced in time by other groups of plants. Succession takes place on bare rock, sand, exposed alluvium in river bottoms, and in the water. Any lake or pond, unless constantly disturbed, tends to be invaded by aquatic plants which are replaced in time by partially submerged reeds and rushes and these in time by sedges and grasses. This aquatic succession is made possible by the accumulation of soil materials washed into a lake, accumulating around the bodies of plants, and being added to by dead-plant debris. Eventually, unless the process is disturbed, each lake will slowly change to a pond, the pond to a marsh, the marsh into meadow or forest.

There are two general categories of succession. One, which has been emphasized to this point, is *primary succession.* This takes place on areas that have not previously supported life. The other, more immediately important to conservation, is *secondary succession.* This takes place on areas where the original vegetation has been destroyed or disturbed but where the soil has not been lost. This process is generally familiar. A forest which has been cut down regenerates itself. The forest, if not greatly disturbed and if seed sources are available, may regenerate quickly with trees replacing trees. Usually, and particularly after a fire, there are a series of intermediate stages. A weed stage follows forest clearing. Left alone this is replaced by shrubs, then by trees and, eventually, if these have not been destroyed or the environment too greatly changed by disturbance, by the species that composed the original climax forest. The process is rapid or slow, depending upon the severity of the original disturbance. In a similar way, when a rangeland has been heavily overgrazed, the original climax grassland will go through several stages, characterized by different communities of weeds and grasses, before the climax community replaces itself. Succession tends to be an orderly and predictable process. It is a heartening process for the conservationist, who knows that with care many of our badly abused lands will repair themselves. Unfortunately, however, this process is often forgotten by conservationists. This may result in efforts to protect a successional community by excluding all disturbance (which results in its disappearance through the normal progression toward the different vegetation of the climax), or in efforts to prevent any human use of communities which can readily withstand controlled harvesting and still regenerate themselves in a short period of time.

The exploitation of biotic resources usually involves the removal and consumption of all or part of the elements that composed the climax communities of the earth. Successful conservation, or land management, often includes the manipulation of biotic succession in such a way the climax replaces itself as quickly as possible. In this way a continued high yield of resources from an area is obtained.

The lumberman is interested in obtaining the greatest yield of high-quality timber from an area. In some places, such as the redwood forests of California or the subarctic spruce forests of Eurasia, the climax forest has the greatest commercial value. Successful forest management includes a study of the way plant succession proceeds after various systems of logging and the selection of the cutting system that will lead to the most rapid regeneration of the climax. Not all high-value forests are climax, however. It is likely most of the pine forests of the world represent a subclimax stage of succession, resulting from fire or other past disturbance. Left alone they would, in time, be replaced by climax species, hardwood trees or other conifers, of lower commercial value. Studies of succession indicate pine forests are often best maintained by the controlled use of fire which removes the seedlings of the climax species and creates conditions favorable to regeneration of pine. In the longleaf pine forests of the southeastern United States, fire is now regularly employed as a management tool. In its absence, hardwood trees replace the pines.

On rangelands where climax grasses have the greatest forage value,

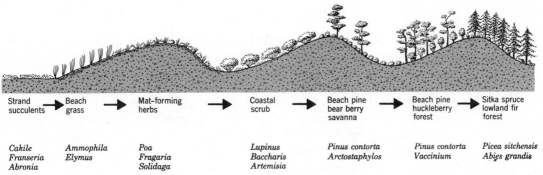

Strand succulents	Beach grass	Mat-forming herbs	Coastal scrub	Beach pine bear berry savanna	Beach pine huckleberry forest	Sitka spruce lowland fir forest
Cakile Franseria Abronia	*Ammophila Elymus*	*Poa Fragaria Solidaga*	*Lupinus Baccharis Artemisia*	*Pinus contorta Arctostaphylos*	*Pinus contorta Vaccinium*	*Picea sitchensis Abies grandis*

FIG. 2–3. Primary succession on coastal sand dunes in northern California. This progression of plant communities may occur on any site protected from disturbance for a long time. Disturbance will arrest succession or set it back. A zonation of communities from the pioneers of the strand, heavily disturbed by wind, sand, tide, and salt spray, to the more complex climax on the protected and less disturbed inner side of the dunes may often be observed.

the range manager attempts to work out grazing systems and levels of stocking which will best perpetuate the climax. Elsewhere, successional grasses may have greater value as forage, and a different system of grazing management will be needed to suppress the climax and maintain the successional forms. In wildlife management it is found that many of the valuable species of game animals are not climax forms, and hence the wildlife manager may be interested in suppression of the climax through the use of fire, cutting, or some other technique that will maintain the necessary level of disturbance. Thus, it can be seen that in many types of wild-land management a knowledge of biotic succession is essential.

The interplay of vegetation and the disturbing factors of the environment become vital also in the management of national parks, scientific reserves, or areas set aside for the protection of endangered species. Overprotection may become as lethal as no protection when the goal is to maintain a community or species that has evolved in response to the continued presence of environmental disturbance.

LIMITING FACTORS The human environment, whether in a natural state or in one greatly modified by human activity, is composed of complex arrangements of matter and energy and is maintained by the interactions that occur among them. Activity within it is ceaseless as energy and materials flow through food chains. Change is also ceaseless, whether it be the relatively rapid change represented by the growth and death of individuals and populations, by the processes of biotic succession, or the slow change represented by the evolution of new races and species of organisms. In places, we accelerate the pace of change, sometimes to our own detriment; but even in the absence of people change goes on.

In the environment, life is distinguished by growth, mobility, and reproduction, among other qualities. Every existing species tends to increase in numbers, to spread to new and suitable environments, to increase again there, and spread farther. Growth in individual size or in numbers of a population continues usually until some external factor of the environment causes it to cease, although in the human species and some others, self-imposed limitation on growth of populations may occur before external factors bring this limitation. A tree will cease to grow when water or an essential soil chemical ceases to be available in minimum quantity. A population of trees will cease to increase in numbers when the tree seeds encounter conditions unsuitable for their germination or for the growth of the new seedling. An animal population will cease to grow when there is no longer adequate food, water, and shelter for the sustenance of individuals, or where weather or other environmental factors result in conditions unsuitable to survival of individuals of that species. Whatever limits the growth in size of an individual or in numbers of a population is known as a *limiting factor* to that individual or population. The ecological principle of limiting factors is stated by E. P. Odum[6] as follows: "The presence and success of an organism or a group of organisms depends upon a complex of conditions. Any condition that approaches or exceeds the limits of tolerance is said to be a limiting condition or a limiting factor." This concept is one of the oldest in ecology and traces its origin to the chemist Justus Liebig in 1840. Liebig, who studied the effect of chemical nutrients on plant growth, first stated this concept as "growth of a plant is dependent on the amount of foodstuff which is presented to it in minimum quantity." This concept, expanded to include organisms other than plants and factors other than chemical nutrients, has been known as *the law of the minimum*.[6]

The concept of limiting factors, combined with a knowledge the earth is limited in size and in its supplies of energy and materials, leads to the obvious, but sometimes overlooked, conclusion that growth and expansion must have an end. No species, including man, can expand its population or its consumption of resources indefinitely. Any species, including man, will be better off individually if its growth is limited through its own behavior before the time when environmental limiting factors (shortages in necessities, for example) begin to take effect.

Limiting factors can be divided into two categories: physical and biological. Physical factors that limit population growth would include factors of climate and weather, the absence of water or presence of an excess of water, the availability of essential nutrients, the suitability of the terrain, and so on. Biological factors involve competition, predation, parasitism, disease, and other interactions between or within a species that are limiting to growth. In the extreme environments of the world, physical factors are generally limiting. These would include the very cold or very dry terrestrial environments or, for land organisms, the very wet environments. They also include most of the deep-water areas of the lakes and oceans of the world. Droughts, floods, unseasonable cold, extreme cold, or the absence of light or of nutrients are among the factors which limit populations in such environments. In the more optimum environments of the world (the warmer, more humid environments) biological factors more often are limiting. In such environments, complex predator-prey relationships, balances with parasites or disease organisms, and competition for light, soil minerals, or water among species with similar requirements are most frequently limiting to population growth. Thus fish populations in cold mountain lakes are most frequently limited by water temperature and the availability of chemical nutrients. Low temperatures inhibit biological activity and thus prevent the growth of plankton and of insect populations upon which the fish would feed. The low availability of chemical nutrients inhibits the growth of these organisms during the period when temperatures are suitable to growth. Fish populations are therefore small in numbers. On the other hand, in warm ponds fish populations may grow in size to a point of great abundance where competition among them not only prevents individuals from reaching large size but inhibits further growth of the population.

Limiting factors may further be classified into those whose operations are dependent upon the density (the number of individuals per unit of area) of the population and those that have no relation to density.[4] The *density-dependent* factors are those that increase in their intensity, that have greater effects, or that affect more individuals as the population increases in density. Thus the availability of food—grass, and other herbs —may be a limiting factor to the increase in numbers of domestic cattle in a pasture. The higher the density of cattle, the less grass there is per cow and the greater number of cows suffer from food shortage. By contrast, a flood sweeping through the pasture would be a *density-independent* limiting factor. It would wipe out all the cows whether there were two or a hundred in the area.

Density-dependent factors usually hold the greatest interest to students of population because of their more general and constant operation. They are usually the factors that set absolute limits to growth, that determine the number of individuals that can be supported—the *carrying capacity* of the area. They are the factors that operate to decrease the individual well-being in a population that approaches the limits or carrying capacity of its environment. In crowded human populations in many parts of the world we see such density-dependent factors in operation.

CHAPTER REFERENCES

Daubenmire, R. F., 1974. *Plants and environment.* Third edition. Wiley, New York.

Elton, Charles, 1927. *Animal ecology.* Sidgwick & Jackson, London.

Graham, Edward H., 1944. *Natural principles of land use.* Oxford, New York.

Oosting, Henry J., 1956. *The study of plant communities.* W. H. Freeman, San Francisco.

Weaver, John E., and F. E. Clements, 1938. *Plant ecology.* Second edition. McGraw-Hill, New York.

LITERATURE CITED

1. Broecker, W. S. 1970. Man's oxygen reserves. *Science,* 168: 1537–1538.
2. Cole, Lamont C. 1966. Man's ecosystem. *Bioscience.* April. pp. 243–248.
3. Fraser Darling, F., and R. F. Dasmann. 1969. The ecosystem view of human society. *Impact of Science on Society,* UNESCO, Paris; Vol. 19: 109–122.
4. Kovda, Viktor et al., 1970. Contemporary scientific concepts relating to the biosphere. (See UNESCO, 1970 in general references.)
5. Machta, L., and E. Hughes, 1970. Atmospheric oxygen in 1967 to 1970. *Science,* 168: 1582–1584.
6. Odum, E. P., 1959. *Fundamentals of ecology.* Second edition, W. B. Saunders, Philadelphia.
7. Wheeler, Fred, 1970. The global village pump. *New Scientist,* 48: 10–13.

3

the major biotic regions

o understand the complex relationships between people and environment, we must know the different kinds of environments which have provided the setting for human activities. These range from ones in which conditions for human life are near optimum, and in which humanity has thrived, to those which are marginal for human existence, and within which, even with modern technology, the numbers of people are few. In this chapter the major biotic regions are examined. These are areas between which plant and animal life, soils, and climate vary to a marked degree. They have provided settings within which human history has taken shape. Since people first appeared on earth the same general regions have been present, from arctic tundra to tropical forest. Although the boundaries of these regions have shifted as climates have changed, their general locations on earth have not changed much during human history.

In developing as a species, the human race first learned to adapt to conditions of life within the various biotic regions, avoiding those which were too rigorous. Eventually populations evolved which were able to withstand or even thrive within the more difficult biotic regions: the Eskimos of the Arctic, the Bushmen of the African deserts, the Indians of the high Andes, and the Pygmies of the Congo forests. Often these people became poorly fitted to survive elsewhere. With increasing technology and control over natural forces, people have learned to modify the biotic regions, seeking to make them more favorable to human existence. Sometimes, however, they have made them less favorable through failure to understand the natural principles under which they operate.

Over much of the earth today, new environments of agricultural or urban forms have displaced the original ecosystems. But an irrigated desert is still within a desert region, and an Arctic city must be adapted to the stringencies of Arctic life. Any major change in the environment has been, and is, accompanied by great risks, unless there is adequate understanding of ecological processes. In the past many changes were accompanied by local disasters. Today, in a heavily populated and closely knit world, we can no longer afford major failures. When we replace complex natural processes with human simplifications we must be prepared to exercise the greatest human skills in order to keep the environment healthy and productive.

There are great differences in the productivity and habitability of the various biotic regions of earth. These differences largely result from the interaction of two climatic factors, temperature and precipitation, with the geology and physiography of the earth. In the water areas of the earth, another factor, light, becomes very important. A cliff face or an active volcano will not support much life no matter how favorable the climate may be. A flat plain with an abundance of chemical nutrients will not support much life if it is too cold, too hot, or too dry. The depths of the ocean will not produce much in the way of living matter because green plants cannot grow in the absence of light.

Balances between temperature and precipitation are of significance in determining the suitability of an area for living organisms. Temperature determines the rate at which evaporation takes place, and consequently the amount of moisture which can remain in the soil available for plant growth. It also determines whether water will exist in a solid or a liquid state. The Antarctic continent and most of Greenland are relatively lifeless because they are too cold. The balance between temperature and precipitation in these places is such that both are almost completely covered by hundreds of feet of glacial ice. Although these areas have unusual scientific interest (and some potential for future use), they have as yet been little used. At the other extreme, much of the Sahara Desert is inhospitable to life because it is too hot and dry. Evaporation removes much of the rain that falls, and little falls. Only where water can be made available is it possible for such desert regions to support human populations.

In between the areas of extreme climatic or extreme physiography are a great variety of natural areas, a remarkable diversity of climates, geological formations, and biological materials. These constitute our original heritage, the diversified earth on which we evolved. Despite our accelerated dissipation of these riches, this diversity of environments remains part of the legacy that we enjoy today and can pass on to future generations. This includes the major ecosystems or biotic regions of the earth (Figs. 3–1 to 3–5).

The climax, end product of biotic succession, and the later successional stages are strongly influenced by the climate, soils, and other physical characteristics of a region. As environments vary, so does vegetation and animal life. Hence, if the major natural climax communities of the earth are mapped, the climate and soil regions and thus the major ecosystems are also mapped. A desert in Africa is characterized by vegetation, soils, and climate which more closely resemble those of a desert in South America than they do those of an equatorial forest in Africa. Tropical rain forests, too, are relatively similar between Africa, Latin America, and Asia, although the species that compose them may differ. Grasslands in North America present opportunities for human exploitation, difficulties for human occupancy, and penalties for unwise land use similar to those of grasslands in Asia.

TUNDRA In the far north of America and Eurasia is one of the more formidable biotic regions. This area, known as the tundra, is one of long winters and short summers. Winters are extremely cold; summers have moderate

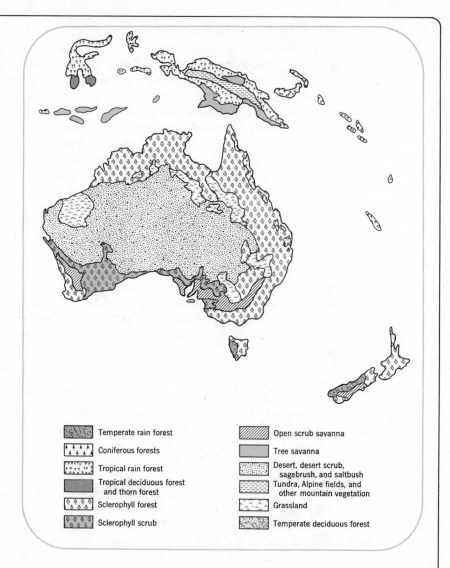

FIG. 3–1. Major biotic regions of Australasia.

Temperate rain forest

Coniferous forests

Tropical rain forest

Tropical deciduous forest and thorn forest

Sclerophyll forest

Sclerophyll scrub

Open scrub savanna

Tree savanna

Desert, desert scrub, sagebrush, and saltbush

Tundra, Alpine fields, and other mountain vegetation

Grassland

Temperate deciduous forest

to warm temperatures. Precipitation comes mostly as snow and is sufficiently low for the area to be characterized as an Arctic desert. It is preserved from desertlike qualities by the low temperatures and consequent low evaporation rates. Thus, despite the low precipitation, in summer the soils are waterlogged in surface layers. Below the surface of the ground the tundra has a layer of permanently frozen ground, the permafrost. Summers are not long enough for complete thawing to take place.

In such an environment organisms have difficulties. Plants are low growing and thus are protected from extreme cold by the winter mantle of snow. Woody plants are dwarfed or prostrate. Most of the vegetation is grass, sedge, or lichen. All of the plants are adapted to completing their life processes in the short summers: leaves must grow quickly;

flowers, fruit, and seed must be produced before the winter cold returns. Summer is a time of great activity.

Animal life is of two kinds: those active or present only in summer and those active through the year. Among the summer forms are vast numbers of migratory birds, including a high percentage of the world's waterfowl. Present also are swarms of insects, which pass the winter in egg or larval state and emerge to grow, feed, and reproduce during the period of plant growth. Many mammals also emerge from hibernation or push northward in migration from the edge of the forest to join the mass of animal life feeding on the burgeoning summer vegetation. The hardy permanent residents, musk ox, caribou, Arctic fox, wolf, polar bear, lay on layers of summer fat to last them through a winter of difficult foraging.

Only a few peoples in the past have been able to adapt themselves to the tundra. In America, the Eskimo tribes developed the cultural skills necessary for survival. Before western culture affected them they were divided into two main ecological groups: the caribou hunters, who depended on the vast herds of caribou for food and clothing, and the coastal

FIG. 3–2. Major biotic regions of Asia.

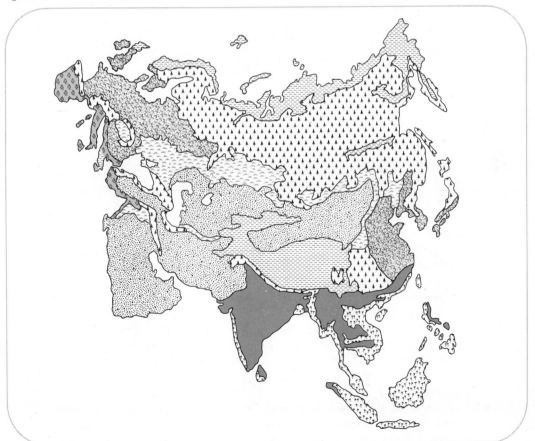

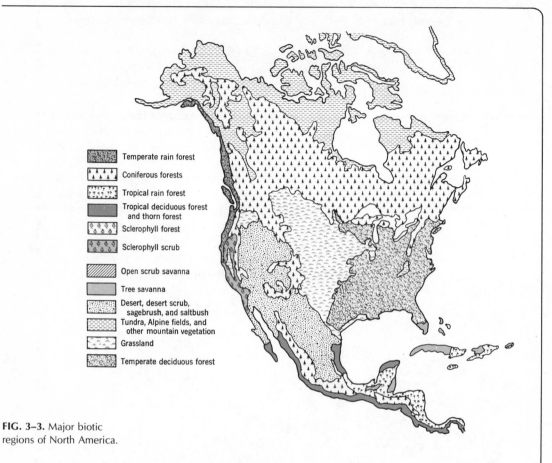

Temperate rain forest
Coniferous forests
Tropical rain forest
Tropical deciduous forest
  and thorn forest
Sclerophyll forest
Sclerophyll scrub

Open scrub savanna
Tree savanna
Desert, desert scrub,
  sagebrush, and saltbush
Tundra, Alpine fields, and
  other mountain vegetation
Grassland
Temperate deciduous forest

FIG. 3–3. Major biotic regions of North America.

dwellers, who relied on the ever-present marine life of the Arctic seas. Both groups adapted to the climate, concentrating their activities in the summer months and resisting the winter storms in weatherproof dwellings. In northern Europe, the Lapps, with their domesticated reindeer herds, also learned how to live in a tundra environment. Compared with most other biotic regions, the tundra is today less exploited and modified, although the effects of civilization are now being felt on both animal life and vegetation. Since this is a highly fragile ecosystem it is susceptible to serious damage from even minor human modifications.

The tundra ecosystem forms a circumpolar belt across North America, Europe, and Asia and reaches southward in modified form along the higher mountain ranges. It is less developed in the Southern Hemisphere, where large land masses do not occur within the appropriate latitudes.

BOREAL FOREST South from the tundra lies timberline, the northern edge of a broad belt of forest extending southward in America into the northeastern United States and in Eurasia down through Scandinavia, Russia, and

Siberia. This northern forest is characterized by evergreen, coniferous trees, mostly spruce and fir (p. 42). The region has a climate slightly warmer and with heavier precipitation than the tundra. In summer, the warmest months have enough heat to eliminate the permafrost. Without this ice barrier, tree roots can penetrate more deeply, and soils can be more fully developed.

Coniferous forest vegetation helps determine the character of the soil. The leaves and litter that fall from conifers decay slowly in the cold climate and upon decaying form acid products which are carried into the soil by rain or melting snow. This mildly acid solution dissolves and leaches out of the top layer of the soil minerals which are important for abundant plant growth. The remaining topsoil tends to be sandy, light gray or whitish in color, and relatively infertile. The deeper layers of soil, in which some of the leached minerals are deposited, become rich in iron and aluminum compounds and darker in color. Such a soil is called a *podzol*. It is of poor quality for general agricultural use.

The native animal life of this region, like that of the tundra, is seasonal

FIG. 3–4. Major biotic regions of South America.

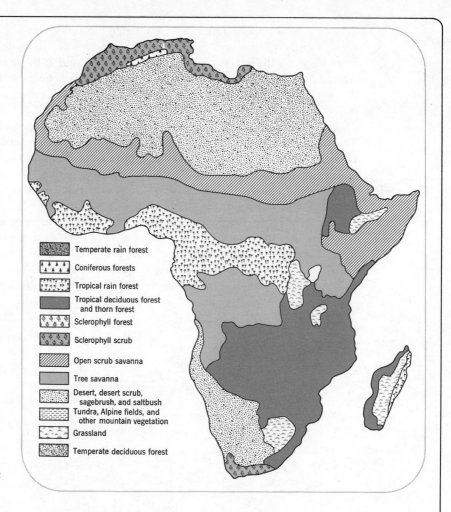

FIG. 3–5. Major biotic regions of Africa.

Legend:

- Temperate rain forest
- Coniferous forests
- Tropical rain forest
- Tropical deciduous forest and thorn forest
- Sclerophyll forest
- Sclerophyll scrub
- Open scrub savanna
- Tree savanna
- Desert, desert scrub, sagebrush, and saltbush
- Tundra, Alpine fields, and other mountain vegetation
- Grassland
- Temperate deciduous forest

in abundance. In summer, migratory birds move in to breed, and insects abound. In winter, only a few permanent residents, moose, woodland caribou, lynx, fisher, wolverine, snowshoe hare, and spruce grouse among them, remain to face the period of food scarcity.

Much of this region is sparsely inhabited. The fur trapper has led the way in settlement, followed by the lumberman. Only in restricted areas where local conditions have permitted more fertile soils to develop has agriculture been successful. Most of the inhabitants are dependent in whole or in part upon the forests for their livelihood. Forest fires, often man-caused, are an important factor. Recently, however mineral exploitation and water development have had major impacts.

The boreal-forest ecosystem, like the tundra, forms a broad transcontinental belt in North America and Eurasia, with stringers extending along the high mountain ranges to the south (p. 39). Like the tundra, and for the same reasons, it is poorly developed in the continents of the Southern

Hemisphere, although the forests of Tierra del Fuego and southern Chile have much in common with it.

DECIDUOUS FOREST   Farther south, in the eastern part of America, Central Europe, and eastern Asia one encounters a third major ecosystem, the broad-leaved deciduous forest. In this area the predominant trees are the traditionally familiar oak, maple, hickory, beech, linden, and other hardwood trees (p. 42). Unlike the northern conifers, most of these trees shed their leaves in late fall and pass the winter in a bare and dormant state.

In the deciduous forest region precipitation is relatively heavy and well distributed throughout the year. The summer rainfall and warm weather provide for abundant plant growth. In general, summers are warm and humid and winters cool to cold with heavy snowfall in the northern part of the region. Southward, as the area of cold winters is left behind, the vegetation gradually changes into the broad-leaved evergreen forest typical of the subtropics.

In primitive times the hardwood forests of America were widespread between the Atlantic and the Mississippi. However, from early times the influence of people has helped to keep portions of the forest open. Animal life was once abundant and consisted of a greater number of permanently resident species than are found further north. Characteristic of this region are the white-tailed deer, ruffed grouse, cottontail rabbit, red fox, bobwhite quail, fox squirrel, and wild turkey. All played an important role in the pioneer history of the United States.

The forest vegetation determined the soil. Temperate-zone forest litter, whether coniferous or broad-leaved, tends to form mild acids on decomposition. These acids, carried into the soil by the abundant rainfall, have a leaching effect. In the deciduous forest, however, because of the greater amounts of litter deposited and the more abundant mineral salts contained in the leaves, the results of the leaching are less severe than in the coniferous forest. There is a constant addition of organic material and basic salts to the topsoil which help to maintain its fertility. Furthermore the soils often support an abundant fauna of insects, and other invertebrates that keep nutrients in circulation and the soils well aerated. Nitrogen-fixing bacteria and other microorganisms help to keep fertility at a higher level. The luvisols or *gray-brown podsolic soils* of the northern part of the region, and the acrisols or *red and yellow podsolic soils* of the southern part are often initially fertile and readily worked when they are cleared for agriculture. Without proper care, however, they do not stand up well to continued crop production.

The deciduous forest region, more than most others, has been drastically modified by human activity. This ecosystem has seen the growth and flowering of civilization in Europe and in China. Little remains of the once extensive forests of the Far East, and in Europe they have been widely replaced by agricultural and urban lands. In the United States, considerable regrowth has taken place as marginal agricultural lands

THE WORLD'S BIOTIC REGIONS (I)

Boreal forest. (**a**) Lakeside view in Finland. **Broadleaf deciduous forest.** (**b**) An old oak forest in Germany. **Temperate rain forest.** (**c**) Redwoods in California. **Mediterranean woodland and scrub.** (**d**) Chaparral in California.

c

d

have been abandoned, but of the old forests few areas remain that have not been changed by human action.

GRASSLANDS In every continent a grassland region is to be found lying between the forest and the desert and with climates intermediate between the two. It is a region in which relatively low rainfall is normal. Summers are warm and in favorable years moist; winters are cool to cold with snow in the north and rain in the south. The rainfall, however, is erratic or cyclic. Wet cycles and dry cycles alternate. Droughts may last for several years, causing major changes in natural vegetation and even more severe changes where the land is used for grazing or agriculture.

The vegetation is dominated by grasses. Tall grasses predominate near the better watered forest border in the *prairie* community. Shorter, sod-forming grasses dominate toward the drier desert side in a region known as *steppe* (p. 50). The grasses of the climax are perennial, living for several to many years. Annual grasses, which die back to seed each year, are characteristic of disturbed areas.

The climate and grassland vegetation produce grassland soils which differ markedly from forest soils. The topsoil is usually dark in color, and rich in organic matter. Minerals are not leached out of the soil because of the more limited rainfall and the abundant humus. The subsoil is usually rich in lime, whereas forest soils are normally lime deficient. On the scale of *p*H, or acidity, grassland soils are neutral or on the alkaline side, whereas the soils of forested regions are typically acid.

Animal life of the grasslands normally includes herds of grazing animals, the bison and pronghorn of North America and the numerous antelopes of Africa and Asia being examples. Feeding on these are large carnivores, wolves and their relatives and in Africa the big cats. A variety of mice, ground-dwelling birds, and smaller predators that feed on them are to be found. The abundance of animal life reflects the richness and fertility of the soil.

Grasslands, like the deciduous forest, have long been occupied by humanity—first by hunters of the herds of big game, later by nomadic herders with flocks of sheep or cattle, and finally by farmers with their crops of cereal grains. The fertile soil has favored agriculture since the time when man developed a plow capable of turning the tough, grassland sod. There is considerable support for the idea that extensive grasslands are a result of human interaction with the climate, soil, and vegetation. Fires, caused by people, have occurred over thousands of years. These tend to favor grassland and push back the boundaries of forests.

DESERTS The dry areas of the world vary considerably in both the amount and the dependability of the rainfall that they receive. Some authorities consider all of those regions which receive an average of 10 inches of rainfall or less per year to be deserts. This includes the extremely dry areas such as the deserts of Peru and Chile, where no vegetation grows, and places such as the northern Great Basin region of the United States, where vegetation is relatively abundant.

In the United States there are two main desert regions, the high desert or Great Basin sagebrush region, which extends between the Rocky Mountains and the Sierra Nevada, and the low deserts, Mojave, Coloradan, and Sonoran deserts, which lie to the south of the Great Basin. In the Great Basin the vegetation is characterized by sagebrush and other low-growing shrubs, which form an open cover over the plains, and by the small conifers, junipers, and pinyon pines, which form an open woodland at higher elevations. The low-desert region is an area of desert scrub, where widely spaced creosote bushes are the most common vegetation, giving way in places to various species of cactus (p. 50).

In both desert regions the vegetation is drought resistant, with various adaptations to prevent or withstand water loss during the long, dry season. It is also adapted to complete its growth and reproduction during the periods when soil moisture is available.

Animal life, like plant life, is adapted to dryness. Animals avoid the heat and drought by being nocturnally active, using sheltered burrows, or remaining in cover in the hot, dry season in the vicinity of the few permanent streams and water holes. Desert rodents often have physiological adaptations which permit them to get along with a minimum of drinking water. Some receive all necessary water from their food and avoid water loss by excreting a highly concentrated urine.

The arid climate and sparse vegetation are reflected in the desert soils. With little leaching there is a minimum loss of soil minerals. With sparse vegetation there is little addition of organic material to the soil, and therefore it may be deficient in nitrogen. Where minerals are in a proper balance and not concentrated in toxic quantities, desert soils are potentially highly fertile when water can be made available.

Deserts have played an important role in human history. The geography of western Asia and North Africa is such that many of the most fertile lands are located on river bottoms surrounded by arid desert. Western civilization was born on the desert edge, and through history man has had important ecological effects on the desert. Through turning his flocks of livestock out to graze on the desert vegetation or on the grasslands at the desert edge, man has changed and modified the deserts and has spread desertlike conditions into former grassland areas.

Natural, as opposed to man-made deserts, occupy much of central and western Australia, extend in a broad band from the Sahara in Africa, through Arabia eastward to India. Smaller areas occur in southwest Africa and South America, in addition to the major North American area already described.

Abuse of the desert vegetation through overgrazing by livestock or cutting of shrubs for fuel can be extremely long lasting because the combination of high temperatures and low rainfall is unfavorable to the establishment of seedlings.

MEDITERRANEAN On most continents there is a relatively small area with a climate similar to that found around the Mediterranean Sea. Here there are winters with moderate rainfall but little snow and summers which are warm and dry. In North America this is the climate of much of California; elsewhere it is found in Chile, South Australia, South Africa, and in the sections of Europe, Asia, and Africa adjoining the Mediterranean Sea.

The most common type of vegetation in this region, although not always climax, is the dense brushfield dominated by medium-height, evergreen shrubs. This is known in California as *chaparral* and in Europe as *maquis* (p. 43). It is often interspersed with grassland, tree or shrub savanna or in more sheltered areas with broad-leaved evergreen forest. In California and the Mediterranean region, the evergreen live oaks predominate in this forest and in shrub form in the chaparral. In Australia, *Eucalyptus* forest and scrub dominates the Mediterranean biotic region.

In latitude, the Mediterranean ecosystem lies between the desert and deciduous forest, or, in the Americas and Australia, between desert and temperate rain forest. Its location in Europe has made it the setting for much of the early development of western civilization, which spread from desert river valleys to Mediterranean regions and from there to the deciduous forest.

OTHER TEMPERATE
BIOTIC REGIONS Several other important biotic regions exist in the temperate latitudes, occupying smaller areas than those previously described. One, which can be called *transition coniferous forest,* occupies a zone in the mountains lying between the southward extensions of the boreal forest and the warmer chaparral, grassland, or desert of lower elevations (Fig. 3–6). Pine trees of various species characterize the climax, or near climax, vegetation of this forest. Transition forest occurs latitudinally in some areas as a belt separating the boreal forest of spruce and fir from the deciduous forest. In the Lakes States and New England it occurs in this role.

On the northwestern coast of North America is an area of high rainfall, well distributed throughout the year, and mild temperatures—a climate of the marine west coast type. This favors the development of an unusually tall, dense, and luxuriant forest, the *temperate rain forest.* In North America, this is dominated by redwood, douglas fir, and other giant conifers (p. 43). In other continents a similar forest type is dominated by the laurel-leaved hardwood trees. Similar climates and vegetation are found in southern Chile, the South Island of New Zealand, and southeastern Australia.

TROPICAL BIOTIC
REGIONS The most favorable climate on earth for the development of the greatest variety of organic life is to be found in the rain forest region of the tropics, and in the tropics also is to be found one of the least favorable climates for life, exemplified by the virtually rainless deserts of Peru. Tropical rain forest climates have year-round rainfall, without periods when the soil dries out, and temperatures which are always favorable

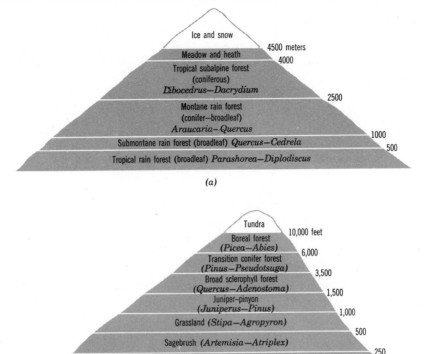

FIG. 3–6. Zonation of vegetation on mountain ranges. (a) Tropical mountains. [*Data from Richards, 1952. Genera are typical of Malayan-New Guinea region.*] (*b*) Temperate-zone mountains with vegetation typical of southwestern United States.

to a high level of plant and animal activity. There are essentially no climatic factors limiting to plant growth. The tropical rain forests are dominated by an unusual variety of broad-leaved evergreen trees—fig and mahogany may be familiar examples—of which dozens of different species often occur in a single acre and many acres may have to be searched to find a second specimen of a particular species of tree.[8]

The trees in turn support a variety of plants that can survive without contact with the soil, known as epiphytes or perched plants. Orchids, bromeliads, lianas, ferns, mosses, and lichens are in this category. Dense, climax forest has a compact, several-layered canopy which allows little light to penetrate to the ground. The forest floor, therefore, is often relatively free of undergrowth and usually supports little in the way of large animal life. The forest canopy, however, will provide a home for a diversity of birds, insects, arboreal mammals and other animals which may exceed the great diversity of plant species.

Rain forests that have been opened up, either by natural causes or human activities, quickly grow into a dense, second-growth successional forest, the "impenetrable jungle" of tropical travelers. The prevalence of such dense, second-growth jungle in today's tropics indicates the extent of human disturbance. Similar jungles occur naturally on the edges of natural clearings, such as stream courses. Since most explorers in the lowland tropics traveled by boat, their accounts of the density of the vegetation were biased by what they saw at the edge of the rivers (p. 51).

Tropical rain forest soils develop under the canopy of trees, and are enriched by the continual addition of rapidly decaying leaves and litter. The high rainfall and temperatures, however, favor rapid oxidation of organic matter and leaching of minerals from the soil in areas from which the forest has been cleared. Tropical soils therefore require careful treatment and protection if they are to be maintained in agricultural use. Many of them are poorly suited to agriculture.

Temperate zone writers, in describing the tropics, often over-emphasize the importance of the lowland rain forests, since these are the most spectacular and in many ways the most different of the various tropical communities. However, the tropics have a greater variety of biotic communities than all other areas on earth. High on tropical mountains we encounter coniferous forests resembling those of the temperate zone, oak forests similar to those in the eastern United States, as well as purely tropical vegetation such as the puña and paramo of the higher mountains, which are unlike the vegetation of temperate lands (Fig. 3–6).

In those tropical areas where a wet and dry season alternate, a different vegetation replaces the rain forest in the lowlands. This, the rain-green or monsoon forest, is deciduous, the trees shedding their leaves during the dry season. In still drier regions a thorn forest or thorn scrub will replace monsoon forest. With increasing aridity this, in turn, gives way to desert. Leslie Holdridge, working from Costa Rica, has listed 37 different major biotic communities that may occur in any tropical region that displays a wide range in rainfall and altitude.[4] Each of these communities is as distinct and recognizable as the major communities of temperate regions. Compared with the temperate zone, however, the tropics have been rarely studied. They represent a major area for future research.

Until recently, human influence on the tropics and its biota was slight. With increasing density of human populations, however, and the spread of technology, no large tropical area is any longer secure from disturbance. Without a major effort to preserve representative tropical areas, it is likely that many of the more fascinating living communities on earth will disappear before we know very much about them.

SAVANNA A glance at a vegetation map of the world (Figs. 3–1 to 3–5) will show that large areas in both tropical and temperate regions are covered by vegetation that has not thus far been described in this chapter—savanna. Savanna, sometimes known as parkland or woodland-grass in temperate countries, is vegetation consisting of scattered trees and shrubs, or groves and thickets, in an otherwise grass-covered region (p. 51). It is of natural occurrence along the boundary of forest and grassland where local differences in climate or soil favor an interspersion of vegetation. In such situations also there is normally a greater variety and abundance of animal life than is to be found in either forest or grassland.

Unlike forest or grassland there is no climate or soil that typifies savanna regions, although much savanna occurs within the region characterized by rain-green tropical forest or thorn forest. The great expanse of savanna over the surface of the earth is now believed to be caused largely by the activities of people and domestic animals. Humans seem to prefer interspersion of vegetation and create it wherever they go. Fire and grazing have been techniques used to open the forest and let the grassland enter. Grazing, irrigation, and planting are techniques for spreading woody vegetation into otherwise grassy areas.

Tropical savannas are the home of the great game herds which once roamed widely in Africa and Asia and are still to be found in areas where they have been protected. The enormous variety of wild mammals in the tropics of Africa has long attracted attention. Twenty or more species of large grazing and browsing mammals from elephants to antelope may occur in a single area, each adapted to feeding on or otherwise using different species of plants, or different kinds of vegetation. In addition to these larger creatures a variety of smaller mammals, or predators, and a profusion of species of birds and other kinds of animals will occur.[2]

AQUATIC ECOSYSTEMS
The water surfaces of the earth occupy more than 70 percent of the total world area and support a great variety of living things. However, since they are much more uniform than land areas in conditions favorable or unfavorable to life, they are not as amenable to classification. Classifications of aquatic environments are frequently based on major climatic differences, the amounts of dissolved chemicals, size and relative permanency of the body of water, and the depth of the water relative to the depth of light penetration. The greatest diversity of life is usually found on the edges or interfaces of land and water, the intertidal regions of seacoasts and estuaries, since here the widest range of physical environments will be encountered. By contrast, the open ocean is relatively homogeneous and shows much less diversity in forms of life.[7]

Classification and characteristics of aquatic environments are discussed in Chapter 11. It is worth noting at this point, however, the range in productivity of aquatic environments is as great as that encountered on lands. The open oceans have sometimes been equated with the world's deserts in supporting and producing relatively little life. Cold freshwater lakes are also relatively barren. By contrast, warm ponds and estuaries teem with life and are the aquatic counterparts of warm humid forest areas on land.

COMPLEXITY AND SIMPLICITY
The terrestrial biotic regions of the earth show the effects of climatic gradients. Tropical rainforest climates support the most complex and varied plant and animal life. However, moving out in the tropics along

a

THE WORLD'S BIOTIC REGIONS (II)

(**a**) Semiarid steppe in Oregon. (**b**) Desert in California.
(**c**) Tropical savanna in Tanzania. (**d**) Tropical rain forest in
Brazil.

b

c

d

a gradient of decreasing rainfall or increasing evaporation, one encounters communities which are less complex, and in which the numbers of species of plants and animals decrease to a low point in the tropical deserts. Similarly, moving north from the lowland rain forest climate of the tropics along a temperature gradient, we would pass through subtropical rain forests, temperate rain forests, boreal forests, and tundra. Along this line also one passes from the most complex to the least complex biotic community, and the number of species of plants and animals would also decrease along this gradient. Thus, in the boreal forests we find the single species, white spruce, as a lone dominant in great areas of Canada and Alaska.

Within each climatic region, the climax communities will represent, usually, the most complex communities the climate and geology of the region can support; but the climaxes themselves are more simple and less varied in regions where climatic or geological factors are strongly limiting.

Complexity appears to be accompanied by stability. Tropical forest communities are usually stable communities. They are relatively resistant to change. The numbers and arrangements of species within them vary little from month to month or year to year. By contrast, simple communities, whether of tundra or desert, are subject to regular and often violent changes in the relative abundance of species. The fluctuations of lemmings, a small Arctic rodent, are a legendary example of the instability of tundra populations. The changes in abundance of jackrabbits or mice in arid regions are well known. In the boreal forest, insect pests or diseases sometimes wipe out hundreds of square miles of trees. Locust plagues in dry regions do enormous damage. Similar outbreaks are rare in humid tropical communities, except where people have intervened.

People seek to simplify the complex so they can manage it. They depend for their livelihood on foods grown in artificially created, simplified ecosystems. Such simplification, however, can be dangerous, since it sets in motion all of the factors which contribute to instability in the normally simple communities of more rigorous natural environments. In the humid tropics, the presence of a great variety of naturally occurring species guarantees competition between species, predation of one species on another, parasitic relations between species, and other complicated interspecies relationships that keep each population under control and prevent any single species population from either increasing or decreasing greatly. When these interspecific controls are removed, as when a plantation of bananas, cacao, or oil palms is established, there is little to keep the pests or parasites feeding on these agricultural crops from becoming abundant. Similarly, in drier or colder regions, simplification of natural communities also permits the natural enemies of the introduced crop plants to flourish; however, climate offers some periodic control on the abundance of these species.

Plagues and pests have harried people through history, destroying crops and forcing them to engage in various forms of chemical or biological warfare in their own protection. Unless skillfully employed, however, such activities can make the situation worse, creating a more simple, less stable, more readily threatened system than the one that was endangered in the first place.[9] This subject will be discussed in more detail in Chapter 5.

BIOMASS AND PRODUCTIVITY. Gradients in complexity and stability also represent gradients in the mass of living material a particular region will support (the *biomass*), and in the amount of new living material produced each year (*productivity*). Tropical rain forests support the greatest biomass or *standing crop* of living material per acre or square mile of any naturally occurring terrestrial community. Extremely dry or cold areas, deserts and tundra, vie for the distinction of supporting the lowest standing crop of living material per land acre.

The standing crop of animal life, however, does not follow the same gradient as that of vegetation. Drier tropical savannas support a greater biomass of animal life than do the humid rain forests. Temperate zone grasslands with highly fertile soils supported, before human disturbance, a higher animal biomass than the leached soils of temperate forest areas. These differences appear related to the relative ability of the soils to produce plant proteins essential to animal nutrition. Soils in more humid areas can naturally produce a great bulk of carbohydrates, but lack the chemical balance to supply the quantity of protein per unit of area that can be supplied by the relatively unleached soils of the drier savannas or grasslands. Human populations that live away from the seacoasts in humid tropical areas have difficulty in producing their protein needs. The crop plants of the humid tropics (yams, taro, cassava, and fruit) are poor suppliers of protein.

Natural productivity varies also with the climatic and geological factors which influence complexity. The tropical rain-forest regions, with year-round growing seasons, are capable of producing more living material per acre per year than temperate forest regions where climate is seasonally limiting to plant growth. Temperate forests, however, with adequate rainfall, produce more plant material per acre than grasslands where seasonal drought restricts plant growth.

People have long had an interest in increasing productivity of plant crops and domestic animals. To some degree they have been able to improve on natural patterns through supplying nutrients, where these were in short supply, supplying water or providing shelter against climatic factors. However, the highest yield of any land-based crop in biomass gain per acre per year is in sugar cane grown in the humid tropics. In temperate regions, forest plantations are more productive in total biomass gain than are the grainfields that have replaced natural grasslands. In the Arctic, high crop production can only take place where soils and local climate can be modified, and in the desert only the presence of irrigation, which essentially creates a different local climate, makes possible abundant crop yields.

It is a law in physics that air temperature will decrease, in a stable air mass, as one moves upward in altitude. Measured in many places and averaged, or calculated from known physical relationships between temperature and pressure, it is found that temperature decreases approximately 3.5°F. for each 1000-foot increase in elevation. Thus a 10,000 foot mountain would, all other things being equal, be 35° cooler at its summit than at its base.

From this simple temperature rule one could expect a range of differences to exist in the vegetation on such a mountain. At the base there exist species requiring or tolerating warm conditions, while at the summit there are species requiring or tolerating cooler situations. Such differences can be generally observed (see Fig. 3–6 and p. 55).

However, rainfall also varies as one moves up a mountain, and this complicates the situation. Mountains stand as barriers to air movement, and winds moving in off the ocean, for example, are forced to rise over coastal mountains. As air rises, it cools, and when it cools moisture condenses and rains (or other forms of precipitation) fall. On many coastal mountains, therefore, there is a range of precipitation from moderate at low elevations to a peak at medium elevations, decreasing again to the mountain peaks. On the lee side of the mountains, where air once more descends and becomes warmer, there is commonly a "rain shadow" or dry area within which little rain falls. The vegetation on mountain ranges responds as much to these differences in precipitation as to differences in temperature. The same elevation in a mountain range may, on its coastal side, support vegetation adapted to high rainfall and humidity, and on its lee side, support desertlike vegetation.

In some tropical areas it is less the prevailing wind direction than the effect of convectional currents which determines zonation of climate and vegetation. Heated air rises and as it does so, moisture condenses. Over many tropical mountains, cloud caps form and may rest much of the time throughout the year. Within the cloud region is constant high humidity and often heavy rainfall. In response to this, and to the leaching of nutrients from the soils associated with it, a "cloud forest" will develop, vegetation particularly adapted to this climatic condition.

Variations in climate and the resulting differences in soils and vegetation in mountains have long been observed and were described by Alexander von Humboldt early in the nineteenth century. Humboldt noted the changes observed as one gained altitude in the mountains resembled those observed by going northward in latitude.[5] Still later, C. Hart Merriam the first chief of the United States Bureau of Biological Survey came out with his theory of life zones, which was based on the practical observation of zonation of vegetation in the mountains of the western United States. His observations were accurate enough, and his life zone idea is useful, although his attempt to relate zonation to temperature is oversimplified. Merriam's altitudinal and latitudinal zones corresponded, and his highest zone in altitude and latitude is the arctic-alpine, the tundra. Below that his boreal zone, with his Canadian and Hudsonian

Zonation of vegetation on Mount Hood, Oregon. Shown here are subalpine forest through timberline to the bare rock of the volcanic peak.

subdivisions, corresponds with observed changes in biota both latitudinally in North America and altitudinally in western mountains. However, in his attempts to universalize his lower life zones his system breaks down most badly, since moisture becomes far more important than temperature in determining the type of vegetation in warmer regions.[6] One of the latest attempts at vegetation classification based on temperature characteristics is that of Leslie Holdridge, working in the American tropics. His system, based on the relationship between temperature and precipitation, is much more closely in touch with reality than that of Merriam.[4]

Although the broad similarities in life zones and latitudinal zones need to be emphasized, the differences must also be stressed. The Arctic, with its enormous extremes in day length, from total daylight in summer to total darkness in winter, cannot be equated with the high altitude tropics where day length is relatively constant throughout the year, and the impact of facets of solar radiation such as the total incidence of ultraviolet light is markedly different from the Arctic. The high altitude paramo, of tropical mountains, with its predominance in some areas of forms such as giant composites of genera represented at lower elevations by daisy-like herbs, is not found in polar regions.

The realities of zonation on mountains is readily observed. The explanation, however, is complex, and still not fully understood. High mountain ecosystems, like islands, are both unique and fragile. Like oceanic islands they are isolated one from the other and each becomes a center of the evolution of new species and forms not to be found in any other place. The impact of uncontrolled human use in these areas is not only destructive but often completely irremediable. We are in serious danger of losing complete ecosystems of great value before we have begun to fully describe them or have made any real progress toward understanding them.

CHAPTER REFERENCES

Clements, F. E., 1916. *Plant succession*. Carnegie Inst. of Washington, Publ. 242.

Dansereau, Pierre, 1957. *Biogeography, an ecological perspective*. Ronald Press, New York.

Daubenmire, R. F., 1974. *Plants and environment*. Third edition. John Wiley, New York.

Elton, Charles, 1927. *Animal ecology*. Sidgwick & Jackson, London.

Graham, Edward H., 1944. *Natural principles of land use*. Oxford, New York.

Kuchler, A. W., 1964. *Potential natural vegetation of the conterminous United States*. American Geographic Society, Spec. Publ. 36, New York.

Oosting, Henry J., 1956. *The study of plant communities*. W. H. Freeman, San Francisco.

Shantz, H. L., and R. Zon, 1924. *Atlas of American agriculture*. United States Department of Agriculture, Washington, D.C.

Shelford, Victor, E., 1963. *The ecology of North America*. University of Illinois, Urbana.

Warming, E., 1909. *Oecology of plants*. Oxford, London.

Weaver, John E., and F. E. Clements, 1938. *Plant ecology*. Second edition, McGraw-Hill, New York.

LITERATURE CITED

1. Dasmann, R. F., 1968. *A different kind of country*. Macmillan, New York.
2. Fraser Darling, F., 1960. Wildlife husbandry in Africa. *Scientific American*, 203: 123–133.
3. Finch, V. C., and G. T. Trewartha, 1942. *Elements of geography, physical and cultural*. McGraw-Hill, New York.
4. Holdridge, L. R., 1947. Determination of world plant formations from simple climatic data. *Science*, 105: 367–368.
5. Humboldt, Alexander von, 1849. *Aspects of nature in different lands and different climates*. Lea & Blanchard, Philadelphia.
6. Merriam, C. Hart, 1898. *Life zones and crop zones of the United States*. United States Department of Agriculture, Biol. Survey Bull. 10, Washington, D.C.
7. Odum E. P., 1971. *Fundamentals of ecology*. Third edition, W. B. Saunders, Philadelphia.
8. Richards, P. W., 1952. *The tropical rain forest*. Cambridge University, Cambridge, England.
9. Rudd, Robert, 1964. *Pesticides and the living landscape*. University of Wisconsin, Madison, Wisconsin.

people:
from
ecosystem
to
biosphere

THE TIME SCALE °f we compare the total time people have been on earth to the duration
of recorded human history, it would appear that we have been around
for an interminable period and during most of it nothing was happening.
Then, suddenly and recently—in comparison to the whole time span of
the human species—everything has changed. This viewpoint, however,
results from the attitude of "technological busy-ness" that prevails in
the industrialized world. In truth, during the long years of human existence, people have concerned themselves with the task of becoming
human—learning how to communicate and behave with one another,
learning how to free thought and feeling for creative endeavor, and,
particularly, learning to relate to the natural world with all its intricacies
—to live with and benefit from the wild plants and animals that surrounded them. These tasks were far more difficult and important than
learning how to build a skyscraper or to fly a rocket to the moon. We
have not yet begun to reach the potential which is within each of us.
Yet many people have set aside the more important endeavors, begun
so long ago, to play with the often-dangerous toys of the technological
world.

How long *Homo sapiens* has been active on the planet is not known.
It is fairly certain the million years included in the Pleistocene or glacial
epoch encompass all truly human activity. Mankind carried out much
of its physical and social evolution during a geological epoch unusual
in the history of the earth. The glacial ages stand out as turbulent exceptions to the calm stability which has prevailed during most of geological time. They are periods of unusual climate, unusual physiography,
and abnormal instability of the earth's crust. During most of the geological eras the surface of the earth was characterized by continents of
low relief, widespread inland seas, and relatively uniform and mild
climates.[2] The diversity of ecosystems present today, and the resulting
diversity of life, was not present. The significance of ice-age geography
to human evolution was undoubtedly great. Its implications have yet to
be explored. It is difficult, however, to imagine human history against a
background of low-lying continents and uniformly mild climates. It is
equally difficult to envision the future of mankind in such a world.

For most of the story of mankind we have little record, a few fossils
here and there. Written history goes back only a few thousand years.
What we call civilization—highly developed cultures that built cities and
left remains in stone and brickwork—goes back about 6000 years. Before that we have various evidence in the ruins of old villages, cave
dwellings, camp sites, and shell mounds where human bones and imple-

ments are mixed with the remains of their plant and animal associates. From such records, through comparisons with the ways of existing human cultures, one builds up a theoretical picture of the past and can begin to trace the probable interaction of people and environment.

THE HABITAT OF PRIMITIVE PEOPLE The longest period in the story of humanity is known as the Paleolithic or Old Stone Age. During most of this period people were probably restricted in their distribution to the tropics and subtropics of Asia and Africa.[9] In the latter part of the Paleolithic, however, they spread widely over the earth. Human cultures during the Paleolithic were based on a food-gathering or collecting economy supplemented by some hunting and fishing. Dependence on wild plants and animals was complete, and the distribution of people depended on the distribution of wildlife. Late in the Paleolithic, efficient hunting cultures developed, dependent on the then-abundant herds of big game. Some believe the efficiency of human hunting was a factor causing the extinction of many of the large mammals which had survived the Pleistocene Ice Ages, but disappeared 8 to 10,000 years ago. Others believe climatic changes were more important in causing these extinctions. Perhaps interaction between a drying climate and persistent human hunting finished off the mammoths, mastodons, giant sloths, and other great beasts of the Pleistocene.

One environmental change that seems attributable to the activities of the Old Stone Age people is that resulting from human use of fire. People and fire have gone together from the earliest of times, and human campsites are characterized by the presence of hearths. Because of recent emphasis on forest conservation, many think of fire as an enemy to be guarded against. The role of fire as a destroyer has been emphasized to the point where we forget its usefulness. For primitive people fire meant warmth. It rendered otherwise unpalatable food into a tasty form. It was used as an aid to hunting, and it is still used for this purpose by hunting tribes in many lands. With fire, game animals can be driven into traps or over cliffs, or the smaller forms could be caught in it, partly burned and thus added to the larder. With the use of fire for hunting must have come the realization that fire modifies vegetation and creates successional types more favorable for human foraging than the original climax. Thus, the California Indians learned that fire in the brushfields created areas of sprouting brush on which deer preferred to feed and where they could be readily stalked and killed. Fire starting in grassland can sweep into the forest, causing a replacement of trees by shrubs which could yield berries or nuts useful for food. Also, in the forest, fire used at proper seasons and intervals can replace dense woods with grassy openings, creating that interspersion of woodland and glade which people today seem still to prefer.

It would appear that preagricultural people along with their farming successors have had major effects on the environment through burning, both deliberately and accidentally. Certain major vegetation types are now considered to be fire caused and thus probably created and maintained by human action. The tropical savanna, of which the African big game country is typical, is believed to be a product of repeated burning, which opened up the tropical deciduous forests and pushed back the edges of the more humid evergreen forests. The process of creating savanna from woodland still goes on in the tropics. Similarly, the chaparral of Mediterranean climatic regions is a fire type, which in many areas at least, is replaced by evergreen forest in the absence of burning. Some believe most of the world's grasslands are products of human use of fire.[1,25,28]

The probability that people have been modifying environments with fire since the earliest human times gives cause for thought when one seeks "natural" areas. The American scene when Europeans first arrived was one shaped by the activities of Indians over tens of thousands of

TABLE 1
The Postglacial Time Scale[a]

DATE	CLIMATIC CHANGES IN NORTHERN EUROPE	OLD WORLD CULTURAL STAGES	NEW WORLD CULTURAL STAGES
10,000 B.C.	Last glacial stage (Würm-Wisconsin ice)	Late Paleolithic hunting cultures (Cro-Magnon, etc.)	
9,000 B.C.	Retreat of the glaciers (Preboreal period, cold dry)	Mesolithic fishing, hunting, collecting cultures	
8,000 B.C.			Hunting cultures established (Folsom Man, etc.)
7,000 B.C. 6,000 B.C.		?Agricultural beginnings	
5,000 B.C.	Boreal period (Warm dry)		
4,000 B.C.	Atlantic period (warm moist)	Neolithic agriculture established and spreading	
3,000 B.C.		Beginnings of civilization (Egyptian—Sumerian)	
		Neolithic agriculture in northern Europe	

[a] Based on data from Flint (1947), Johnson (1955), Zeuner (1950), and others.

TABLE 1 (Continued)

DATE	CLIMATIC CHANGES IN NORTHERN EUROPE	OLD WORLD CULTURAL STAGES	NEW WORLD CULTURAL STAGES
3,000 B.C.			American agricultural beginnings
2,000 B.C.	Subboreal period (colder dry)	Babylonian Empire	
		Invasions: Aryans to India; Medes and Persians to S.W. Asia and Mesopotamia	
1,000 B.C.		Rise and flowering of Greek civilization	
			Early Mexican and Mayan civilizations
B.C.—A.D.	Sub-Atlantic period (cool moist)	Roman empire	
		Invasions: Goths, Huns	Decline of Mayans
		Rise of Islam	
		Norsemen to America	
1,000 A.D.		Mongol and Tartar invasions	Aztecs and Incas
		Voyages of discovery and colonization by Europe	
		Industrial revolution and modern period	
2,000 A.D.			

years. In the absence of all human interference, desirable vegetation of so-called natural types may sometimes disappear.

There is little doubt a hunting-food-gathering-fishing economy permitted the human race to thrive, to increase, and to spread over the earth. Hunter-gatherers spread from their original homeland along the tropical forest edges of Africa and Asia into all continents, following the edges of the retreating continental ice sheets, traveling from Asia to North America and reaching the southern tip of Chile more than 10,000 years ago, and traveling down the island chains from southern Asia to reach Australia and occupy that continent.

We do not know much about the ways of life of people who lived before recorded history. However, an examination of the surviving human societies who still practice a hunting-gathering way of life is revealing. Far from being a precarious existence on the edge of famine, it appears to provide economic security, much leisure, and a good level of health and well being. Studies of the San (Bushmen) of the Kalahari, of Amazonian Indians, the Hadza of Tanzania, and the Australian aborigines all support the view that, when protected from contact with outside peoples, hunter-gatherers live a highly satisfying existence and are not at all willing to give it up in favor of civilization, agriculture, or pastoralism. Characteristic of the hunter-gatherer is an intricate dynamic balance between people and wild nature—a balance in which religion and ritual play a major role.[23,30]

Obviously wild food cannot support an ever-expanding population, since hunter-gatherers require a large "home range" in which to find enough food. Overhunting would bring the decline of animal populations and must be avoided. Destruction of wild plant foods must be prevented. By one means or another, however, most surviving hunter-gatherers achieve balanced populations that do not exceed the capacity of their wild food resources. This may well be an adaptation that has come with the restriction of available territory through the pressure from other peoples. During the Paleolithic, an expanding population could always move on into new and unoccupied territory.

THE NEOLITHIC AND AGRICULTURE

ORIGINS OF DOMESTICATION

Perhaps the most important change in the history of mankind came with the domestication of plants and animals, and the rise of an agricultural way of life. No doubt some group of fishing and food-gathering people made the initial discoveries and opened up a new period in human history. This period, because it was associated with new and improved types of stone tools, is known as the Neolithic or New Stone Age. Domestication of plants was undoubtedly a gradual development. People's normal interest in food focused their attention on the plants which seemed best to provide it. Slowly they must have learned the techniques of favoring the production of these plants by fire or clearing. Eventually they acquired the idea of carrying the plants along to new sites, preparing the ground, and planting them. It seems a small change to make, but its results have affected the entire world. Through domestication people learned to channel the energy and nutrients of an ecosystem in directions of their own choosing to produce more of certain kinds of foods than the natural environment would normally supply. This permitted the growth of human populations beyond the limits set by the original ecosystem.

The earliest methods of agriculture are believed by some to be those that made use of vegetative reproduction of plants—the dividing of the parent plant through stem cuttings, or separation of the parts of a bulb, tuber, or rhizome, and the planting of these separate parts. The homeland of agriculture is thought to be the monsoon lands around the head of the Bay of Bengal in eastern India, Burma, and Thailand (Fig. 4–1).*

* Although to the writer this viewpoint of the origin of agriculture is most convincing, it is not the most widely accepted point of view. For a summary of the concept that agriculture originated with seedplanters in the lands of western Asia and northeastern Africa see Darlington (1969).

Here are to be found the wild ancestors of many cultivated plants, and here too agriculture is known to have a long and stable history.[14,26,30] Perhaps the early domestic plants were related to the present-day root crops of this region, yams, taro, and the like. In this area of alternating dry and wet tropical climate the original agriculture must have centered on wooded uplands, where the soils are light and readily worked with simple hand tools. Early agricultural practice was probably similar to that still maintained in tropical forests. A forest area would be cleared through cutting or girdling of the trees; the cleared vegetation burned; and the ashes used to fertilize the soil. In these openings, cuttings, seedlings, and tubers would be planted. Following a brief period of use, yields would start to decline, and the area would be abandoned in favor of a freshly cleared and burned plot. The original clearing would then revert to native vegetation. Such a shifting, forest-clearing system of agriculture is called today *ladang* in southeast Asia and *milpa* in tropical America.[1,13] It is well adapted to tropical forest lands, as long as the pressure of human population is low and each cleared area has time to revert to forest and have its fertility restored following agricultural use.

In the southeast Asia region the early agriculturalists are also believed to be the domesticators of animals, first the dog, later the pig, and then domestic fowls. All were household or village animals, perhaps kept as much for pets as for food. None were grazing or herding animals.[26]

From its original home, the practice of planting spread throughout the tropics of the Old World and into the Pacific islands, carried by emigrants or passed from tribe to tribe. Not all adopted it; some maintained the old food-gathering ways or kept primarily to hunting or fishing. Geographical and cultural barriers prevented a complete diffusion. Australia, for example, settled by hunters and food gatherers, remained cut off from the flow of agricultural knowledge until recent centuries. There is some reason to believe, however, the early planting practices and domestic animals spread by one route or another across the Pacific into the tropics of the Americas, for in both regions many of the customs and domesticated species are the same.[25]

SEED CROPS AND THE WESTERN WORLD[26,30] Westward from the supposed home of agriculture, in areas where the climate was too cold or dry to support the tropical root crops, the agricultural system typical of the western world had its beginnings. In this region, from western India to Ethiopia and the Mediterranean Sea, early farmers took an interest in the seed plants, particularly in the larger-seeded annual grasses. Here again the process of domestication must have been gradual. Originally various grasses were cultivated, later through selection attention was focused on the larger-seeded, harder grains, wheat and barley, which became and remain staple food crops of the western world.

In the West, as in the East, upland wooded areas probably provided the first agricultural lands. Grassland soils were too heavy and the sod

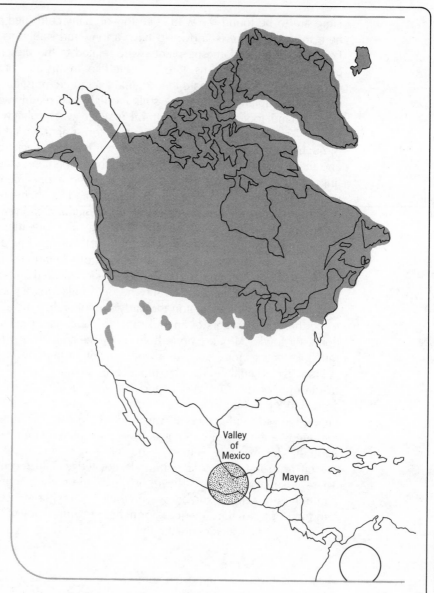

too tightly woven with a network of roots and stems to be cultivated with simple hand tools. The deep soils of the river bottoms may also have presented difficulties for early cultivation. The forest clearings in the West, in lands of Mediterranean or wooded-steppe climates, probably tended to be more permanent than those in the tropics, for the soils which develop under low rainfall are little leached and, therefore, are less quickly

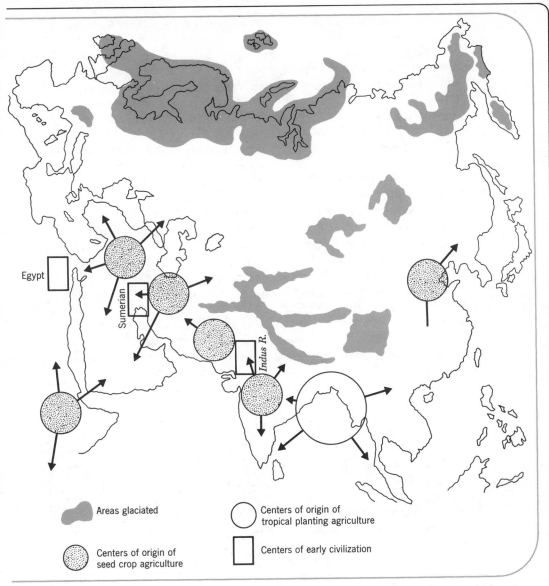

Egypt

Sumerian

Indus R.

Areas glaciated

Centers of origin of
tropical planting agriculture

Centers of origin of
seed crop agriculture

Centers of early civilization

FIG. 4–1. Relationship of areas glaciated during the Ice Ages to places in which agriculture and civilization had their beginnings [*Data from Flint (1947), Sauer (1952), and Wissman et al. (1956)*].

exhausted of fertility. The recovery of native vegetation is also more slow. Early agriculture was undoubtedly rainfall agriculture, with the planting of seed in the rainy season of early spring and the harvest in the dry, late summer or fall. The shift in emphasis in the West from vegetative planting to seed sowing brought the need for different cultivation techniques. To sow seed effectively and easily, it is expedient to lay large areas bare of native vegetation; to promote rapid growth, more intensive cultivation of the soil is helpful.

Western agriculture spread widely from its original center into other temperate and semiarid regions, northward into Europe, southward in Africa, and eastward across the steppe region of Asia to China (Fig. 4–1). In many areas an intermixture of planting and sowing developed. Thus in southeast Asia many of the planting peoples learned to use rice, a cereal grain, although it was usually planted after the seed had sprouted rather than sown as seed on the ground. Similarly, in the Mediterranean region, some plants were reproduced by cuttings or divisions of roots and tubers. By the middle of the Neolithic, agriculture was widespread throughout the Old World.

The peoples who first cultivated the cereal grains are thought to be those who first domesticated the grazing herd animals, the goat, sheep, ass, and later the cow and horse. These domestic animals, long associated with western agriculture, helped to shape its progress. With the invention of the plow, the combination of oxen and plow began to create a new agricultural pattern, the regularly plowed field, and also made possible the cultivation of the heavier soils of the river-bottom lands. In the beginnings the herd animals were closely associated with the farmlands. Abandoned croplands may have provided the early grazing land. However, in western Asia with its dry, steppe grassland and shrub-covered hills there was available a broad area well suited to providing livestock with forage. As populations increased and the agricultural lands became more intensively and permanently cultivated, it became necessary to take herds farther afield for pasturing. Eventually a pastoral way of life, separate from the farmlands, developed. The new livestock herders at first may have practiced a shifting agriculture. Later, however, they came to depend on their livestock and learned to despise the agricultural peoples. To the farmlands, they eventually returned as the barbarian, nomad conquerors.

Neolithic agriculture was a subsistence agriculture. The local fields supplied local needs, with little or no export or trading. In the better agricultural lands the former shifting tribal camps gave way to a settled, permanent village life. A close relationship formed between the new peasantry and the land permitting a high degree of land care and agricultural stability. A truly human landscape appeared for the first time on earth. Cleared fields and croplands are no part of the wild, natural scene. People for the first time obtained, through knowledge of crops and croplands, a dependable degree of control over natural forces. There was a wholeness to this Neolithic way of living that still has a strong, nostalgic appeal. Each person became familiar with all of the operations and techniques needed to support himself and his family and was not dependent on organized society to supply his needs. Admittedly, life was sometimes insecure; drought, flood, or invader could sweep over and destroy the village or its lands. Perhaps it was this insecurity which contributed to the next major development in the human story.[21]

When the Neolithic farmers began to settle in the river basins, a new way of life became possible. Here on deeper, richer soils, high crop yields could be obtained and the surpluses stored. These surpluses took away the threat of starvation and permitted time and leisure. Fewer people working on the richer soils could produce enough for all, so that some people could devote their attention to more specialized tasks. New agricultural tools were invented, and techniques of mastering the flood-waters that rose each year in the river basins were improved. With more efficient agricultural tools and the new techniques of irrigation farming, still greater yields could be produced. With water available throughout the year, more than one crop could be obtained from the land in each year. Greater yields meant more leisure and more time for specialization. Villages grew to towns and towns to cities. A new development called civilization appeared.

The cities became the homes of specialized workers freed from the necessity of tending to the land. They brought the opportunity for the farmer to trade his surplus crops for the tools or pleasures that the city could offer. With the cities also came in time a central government, temples, and palaces, armies, census takers, tax collectors, and other agencies of the state.* On the land itself this resulted in a reorganization which was to have far-reaching effects. Initially it started as a funneling of surpluses into the city to be exchanged for the products of the city. But as the power of the city grew, as armies were formed and new lands conquered, there came increasing regimentation of the peasants to provide for the support of the new agencies. Large areas were reduced to the status of agricultural colonies, which sent crops, timber, and livestock to the imperial centers. The old balance, characteristic of the village way of life, between people and resources was destroyed as increasing demands were made on the farms to provide for city populations, who had no contact with the land or realization of its needs. Emphasis on the farms changed from varied subsistence crops to specialized crops raised for sale and export and eventually to monoculture, the production of one kind of crop year after year on the same land. In return the farmers received a variety of materials they could not have produced on their farms. More important, however, the cities offered one thing the old village way of life could not offer—security. Cities brought armies to defend the lands against the sudden sweep of barbarian invaders, slaves to improve and maintain irrigation works which protected against drought and flood, and temples where the priests could intercede with stronger gods than the village could offer for protection of the lands and the people. Thus, for security and a degree of material enrichment, the old independent village way of life was sacrificed to the new organization of civilization.[27]*

* In a review of the theory of the origin of the state, Robert Carneiro has made a convincing biological case that states arose through motives that were basically coercive and aggressive. Cities and empires did not come into existence as voluntary or chance associations of people but through fear and the exercise of coercive power.[4]

It has long been a matter of surprise and concern to travelers in the homelands of western civilization that so many of the great cities and centers of ancient times are now desolate ruins located in desert lands incapable of providing for more than a few impoverished herdsmen (Fig. 4–2). It has been obvious to all who have studied the situation that the land has changed, become more desertlike, since the days of Babylon, Alexander, or imperial Rome. To document this change are some written records which describe the wealth of now impoverished lands. In other places the ruins speak for themselves; no city could be supported now where the ancient cities flourished. To account for this change in the land the idea of climatic change has been advanced.

For a time it was believed widely the glacial periods in northern Europe and Asia were accompanied by widespread pluvial periods in the now arid lands of the Asian-African desert belt. Ellsworth Huntington[16] and others have advanced the theory that the decline of civilization in parts of Asia and Africa was associated with a gradual dessication of these regions, the result of a change from a pluvial to a warmer, drier climate. That climatic changes have certainly occurred, are still taking place, and have their effects on man's use of the land can no longer be disputed.[2,28] However, the picture is by no means as simple as once was supposed. The bulk of the data now indicate there have been a great number of climatic changes in the areas of the ancient civilizations, but there has been no one-way trend toward warmer, drier climates since early historical times. Man, and not climate alone, must be held accountable for the encroachment of desert on the formerly fertile lands of the old empires (p. 72–73).

The Nile River and the Tigris-Euphrates rivers provide a contrast which throws light on the question of land deterioration in the region where western civilization began. The agricultural lands of Egypt, irrigated by the floodwaters of the Nile, have been farmed for at least 6000 years and yet remain productive. Egypt is still a densely populated center of civilization. By comparison the lands of Mesopotamia have recently supported only a fraction of their former population. Yet these lands were the first home of civilization and, since Sumerian times, supported a series of great empires. A look at the headwaters of the two river systems provides part of the answer to the differences between these regions. The headwaters of the Nile lie in the swamps of Uganda and the high mountains of Ethiopia (Fig. 4–2). Until recent times these headwaters were remote from the mainstream of Western history. Native populations and livestock numbers were kept low by the pressure of an adverse environment. The Nile has had its annual flood throughout history, fed by the monsoon rains from the Indian Ocean. It has carried a load of silt and humus which, when deposited each year on the farming lands of Egypt, has added to their fertility. However, until recent times the silt load of the Nile has been relatively light and manageable.[5]

The headwaters of the Tigris and the Euphrates lie in the highlands of Armenia, in areas which in the past have supported high populations of

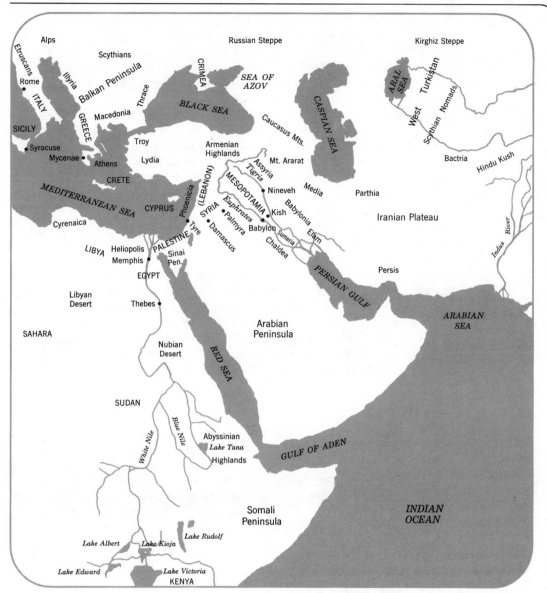

FIG. 4–2. Location of ancient civilizations in the Mediterranean and western Asian regions.

people and higher numbers of sheep and goats. They have been in the path of wave after wave of migrations of nomads from the plains of Asia. They have been subjected, therefore, to all of the pressures hillside farming and overgrazing by livestock can bring to bear. They have been deforested to provide timbers for the growing cities or to provide new grazing land for flocks and herds. The erosion that has resulted has caused an ever-increasing silt load to be carried by the Tigris and Euphrates. In Sumerian times the indications are the silt load was manageable. Subsequent empires have had an increasingly difficult task in controlling it. Armies of laborers and slaves have been kept busy keeping the irrigation canals free of silt. The silt has filled in the Persian Gulf to a distance of 180 miles out from where the rivers emptied in Sumerian times.[8] As long as strong empires centered in the lands between the two rivers, the canals were kept open. The final breakdown came with the Mongol and Tartar invasions in the thirteenth and fourteenth centuries A.D. These nomadic horsemen from Asia were interested in destroying permanently the powerful Arab states which had opposed them. They destroyed the irrigation canals and killed or carried off the inhabitants of the region. Until recently, the task of coping with silt and rebuilding the canal system was too much for the peoples who remained in the area. The silt-laden flood waters carried soil from the highlands to the sea.[8]

In the country of Lebanon is other evidence of what has happened to these lands. Here the Phoenicians founded their maritime empire and built the greatest navy of their day from the timber which grew on their mountains. On these mountains grew the famous cedars of Lebanon that helped to shape the Egyptian cities and were used in the temple of Solomon. Cutting of the timber started the trouble. Regeneration of the forest was prevented when the cleared lands were heavily grazed by goats and sheep. Only in a few protected spots do cedar groves remain, and forests of any kind are no longer extensive. Many formerly forested hills are now incredibly barren and almost devoid of soil. From their appearance it would be thought the climate was now too dry to support trees. Yet, where soil remains, in the vicinity of the ancient groves, the cedars continue to reproduce and grow.[18]

EFFECTS OF MEDITERRANEAN LAND-USE PRACTICES

Much has been written of land destruction in Mediterranean countries which cannot be reviewed here. Because the damage has been so spectacular it is well to review the causes. At the heart of the difficulty is the nature of the environment. These are lands of mediterranean scrub and forest, grassland, and desert, characterized by low rainfall, warm summer temperatures, and long dry seasons when desert winds move all but the best-protected soil. Vegetation growth and land recovery following the clearing of vegetation is slow. The soils are relatively rich in nutrients and, therefore, encourage permanent rather than shifting agriculture. To such an environment came a cereal-grain agriculture that laid bare the land for part of the year to the blowing winds and, at best, covered it with crops which offered much less protection to the soil than the native vegetation. To make matters worse, the farmers of this region developed a system intended to conserve soil moisture but which exposed the land to serious erosion. This system involved leaving an area of cropland fallow for one year out of two. During this fallow period the soil was closely cultivated but not sown to crops. Rain falling on this land in winter soaked in, and in the dry season the finely cultivated layer on top broke up the channels through which water would have evaporated from the soil and eliminated weeds which would have drawn on the soil moisture. Water loss from the deeper layers of the soil during the dry season was therefore slowed down, and extra moisture preserved in the soil. This made possible a better growth of crops in the following year when the land was again sown. Although serving some purpose in conserving soil moisture, this "dust mulch" on top of the soil led to the serious loss of soil when dry winds swept across its surface or when late rains caused heavy runoff from the fields. In general, then, the agricultural system developed in this region did not effectively prevent soil erosion. Where sloping hill lands were farmed without special precaution, soil loss would be rapid.

A second cause of land deterioration was the activities of the grazing animals. Extensive rangelands favored their spread and encouraged pastoralism as a way of life. Unfortunately the herdsmen did not learn that an area of rangeland can stand only a limited amount of grazing pressure. Continued heavy grazing by herd animals, particularly where concentrated in large numbers year after year, led to the disappearance of the plant cover and the exposure of the bare and trampled ground. Erosion followed.

Demands for more grazing land, the need for wood for fuel, and the desire for timber for ships and cities led to the cutting of the forests, the third cause of land deterioration. Regrowth of the cutover lands was prevented by heavy browsing of sprouts and seedlings by livestock and by continued cutting for fuel wood. Again the soil was left bare, and without protection it washed or blew away. Deserts spread into former scrub, forest, and steppe areas, and within the original deserts the sparse vegetation gave way to bare rock or moving dunes (p. 72–73).

It should be pointed out, however, that all was not destruction and damage in these homelands of civilization. People learned from their mistakes and began to develop systems that would correct them. The Phoenicians can be remembered for their poor management of forest and range, but they should also be remembered as people who, among their many contributions, developed the techniques of terracing hillside farm lands to prevent soil loss. Terraced farm lands in southern France, still in production today, are thought to date back to Phoenician times.[18] The Greeks, although known for poor management of flocks and forest, contributed the ideas of manuring and crop rotation to agricultural practice. The Romans, with great engineering ability, developed irrigation practices to a marked degree and made many contributions to scientific management of farming lands.[15] All of these ideas and techniques later flowed northward into Europe to form the foundation for sound land management.

CHANGES IN TROPICAL LANDS

THE TROPICAL ENVIRONMENT

Before following western agriculture into Europe and the Americas another look is needed at the area where agriculture had its beginnings, the tropics. In southeast Asia the nature of the tropical environment and the agricultural practices that developed combined to give form to a remarkably stable type of land use.

a

b

CIVILIZATION AND LAND-USE FAILURE

(**a**) Rain forest takes over where the Mayan civilization once prevailed: Tikal, Guatemala. (**b**) Old terraces which once held soil on the mountain slopes are now in ruin at Machu Picchu, Peru. (**c**) Deserts have spread where Queen Zenobia once ruled at Palmyra, Syria. (**d**) The Valley of the Nile in Egypt has remained productive despite thousands of years of agriculture.

c

d

In tropical forests the deep-rooted trees go far into the earth for their nutrients. Minerals are thus brought into the tree structures and as leaves fall or trees decay are added to the surface soil. Here the high temperatures favor rapid decay and incorporation of the organic material into the soil, where it is picked up by surface roots and returned to the vegetation. Thus soil nutrients are kept in continual circulation within the complex forest food chains.

When tropical forests are cleared and the fallen vegetation is burned, nutrients locked up in the plants are returned to the soil. Here they become exposed to two destructive forces: high temperatures which favor rapid oxidation of the organic matter and heavy rainfall which washes away the mineral salts. Thus tropical forest lands cleared for agriculture have a short life if sown to shallow-rooted crops. The remaining soil nutrients are quickly depleted, yields decline, and the land must be abandoned. Fortunately, if the area is not too badly depleted, the natural cover of deeper-rooted trees and shrubs quickly invades this abandoned land and restores the old channels for returning nutrients from deeper layers to the surface soil.

SHIFTING AND PERMANENT TROPICAL AGRICULTURE

To the tropical environment the farming practices of southeast Asia were well adapted. Clearing of the forest was seldom complete, and cover was left to screen the soils. A variety of root crops, shrubs, and trees were planted that, in turn, provided additional soil cover. Usually the crops had different ripening periods so there was no distinct harvest season followed by the exposure of bare ground. Cultivation of the soil with hand tools left no long furrows of upturned soil exposed to sun and rain. Abandonment and return to forest in the ladang system prevented permanent damage. The absence of herding and grazing animals in most areas prevented the pressure on watershed vegetation with the consequent erosion and flooding which has destroyed farmlands elsewhere. So long as populations were low in relation to the available land area, the amount of damage done through land use was negligible. However, with expanding population pressure, the continued existence of climax rain forest is threatened by the too rapid spread of forest clearing.

In many parts of the tropics shifting ladang agriculture has given way to more permanent types. These have been chiefly of two kinds: the permanent village garden and the irrigated field. In the vicinity of many of the villages the practice developed of keeping certain areas in permanent cultivation, a practice which gave a food supply close to home when travel to more distant forest clearings was restricted. Such village gardens have been carefully tended. Emphasis on a variety of crops has kept cover on the ground. Exhaustion of fertility has been prevented by the regular addition of manure from village animals and people, combined with crop remains and other plant debris. Constant care given to such gardens has kept them permanently productive despite the handicaps of tropical climate.[1,13]

The greatest yields in tropical lands, and the basis for the crop surplus which has permitted the rise of cities, have come with the farming of the deep soils of valleys and delta areas. This was made possible by the development of the hydraulic skills that permitted control of rivers and run-off waters and their use in irrigation. On these rich lands the same care and attention which made possible the permanent village garden has been given to the soil. Over thousands of years these soils have remained productive.[1,13]

Land failure in the tropics has resulted from several types of pressure. The ladang or milpa system breaks down when populations grow too rapidly. Then the land does not receive the rest and regeneration it needs. It is farmed too long and returned to again before there is time for soil damage and fertility to be repaired. Soil depletion results. This is thought to be the reason for the collapse of the Mayan civilization in the American tropics which was supported by milpa agriculture. Extensive deforestation, resulting from demands for wood for fuel or construction, also takes place in the tropics where civilizations give rise to dense populations. This is thought to be a cause for the collapse of the ancient civilization of Ceylon. Here an extensive system of irrigation reservoirs and canals was destroyed by floods and silt washed from the deforested mountains.[5] Some of the most far-reaching land damage in eastern Asia has taken place in China and India where many bad features of both western and eastern agricultural systems were inherited and combined.[18]

EUROPE AND THE NEW WORLDS

WESTERN EUROPE AND AGRICULTURAL STABILITY

At the time when the early river-basin civilizations were beginning to appear in Mediterranean lands, the first Neolithic farming peoples were becoming established in western Europe. They brought with them the cereal-grain culture of western Asia and the domestic livestock associated with it. In Europe, however, they encountered a far different environment from the homeland of seed-crop agriculture. Europe was largely covered with dense, broad-leaved forest, except for clearings made by its earlier inhabitants and some naturally open areas. The climate was humid with rainfall moderately high and well distributed throughout the year. The soils were of the deciduous-forest variety, initially fertile and easy to work. The combination of soils, climate and vegetation produced a durable environmental complex, much less subject to damage than those of the drier regions.

The usual pattern of primitive agriculture was followed in Europe. Forests were cleared, the plant debris burned, and seeds sown in the ash-enriched soil. Initially, land clearing and abandonment probably went on at a nearly equal rate, with the abandoned clearings serving for a time as grazing land. Gradually, as populations grew a more stable pattern of agriculture emerged on the better soils. With forest vegetation predominant and no extensive areas of hill range to invite flocks and herdsmen, there was initially little opportunity for the development of pastoralism apart from agriculture. Thus from early times livestock were kept close to the farm lands, and the growing of feed for the stock became as important a part of farming as the growing of food for man. The presence of livestock close to the farm meant the regular addition of manure to the soil, and with this the organic content of the soil was replenished. On lands regularly pastured a grazing-resistant group of plant species developed that was able to support a high degree of livestock pressure without soil damage. As farming progressed northward in cooler regions, the wheat and barley of Mediterranean lands were replaced to a large extent by oats and rye, better adapted to the cooler climate. These were as often raised for hay crops as for grain.[6,10]

Agriculture changed little in Europe until Roman times. With Roman conquest or influence many of the farming practices developed by the higher cultures of the Mediterranean region spread to the croplands of western Europe. They proved better adapted to the new area than to their lands of origin.

While agricultural practices were developing, the heavy forests served as a barrier against too rapid extension of farming lands. As time passed and more efficient means of clearing forest land were discovered, a relatively sophisticated and conservative type of agriculture was applied to the new land. Crop rotation, alternating cereal grain, root or leaf crop, clover or grass pasture on the same area in successive years, was widely practiced and served to maintain the soil. There developed also the practices of using plant and animal manures and of liming to reduce acidity, and other fertilizing practices that helped to maintain soil nutrients. With time came the rise of a well-established European peasantry, deeply attached to the land and attentive to its needs. The result was an unusual pattern in world land-use history. Not only was erosion and loss of soil fertility widely prevented, but to a large extent the land was actually improved through use. A stable agriculture, adapted to soil and climate, was achieved.[6,10]

With the industrial revolution came the spread of European power and influence throughout the world. Western Europe became a great industrial center, importing raw materials from other lands. The great increase in European population that followed was not, therefore, supported entirely by the products of European soils. Had this been necessary it is doubtful that the land could have been so well maintained.

SPANISH COLONIES IN AMERICA One of the regions on which Europe was to draw extensively for raw materials was the new world of the Americas. In pre-Columbian America a variety of cultural stages were to be found. In the Andes region of Peru and Columbia, the Incans had developed an advanced system of irrigation agriculture. An elaborate system of terracing conserved soil where mountain slopes were farmed. In the Valley of Mexico and elsewhere in Central and South America, civilizations had also arisen. Where these civilizations had resulted in heavy pressure on the land, there was to be found a record of agricultural failure and erosion, associated with the decline of the peoples who had caused it. In most of the Americas, however, civilization had not appeared. Many Indian tribes were still in a food-gathering stage of culture; some had become efficient hunters and fishermen; others had developed fairly effective agricultural practices. For most areas, Indian land-use practices were conservative; vegetation was modified, but soil was preserved.

Into the Americas came two mainstreams of European culture: from the Mediterranean and from western Europe. The Spanish colonizers came from a land with a long history of disregard for conservation. Spain had been unusually plagued by overgrazing. An organization of Spanish sheep raisers, the Mesta, through special concession from the crown, had for many years overrun the country. Forests had been ruthlessly cut and burned to provide additional grazing land; vast herds of sheep had moved across the plateaus and hills to create desertlike conditions in wide areas.[24] To the American mainland, Spanish livestock came with Cortez and spread from Mexico northward to the United States in the sixteenth century. The horse, escaped from domestic herds, ran wild into the plains and prairies of North and South America, where the Indians soon learned its use. Spanish livestock spread into the dry grasslands along the desert margins where they became an agent operating to extend the desert borders. In the late eighteenth century, Spanish missions were established in California, and sheep, cattle, goats, and horses began to occupy the ranges of that state.

Where Spanish livestock traveled, they brought with them a plant complex from the Mediterranean region, a variety of annual weeds and grasses. In areas of favorable climate, such as California, these exotic annuals took hold and spread widely. Aided by uncontrolled livestock numbers, drought, and overgrazing, the new annual grasses and weeds so completely occupied the grassland ranges of this region that it has been difficult to determine the nature of the original vegetation.

Spain, however, was not interested in finding a new homeland for her people but in obtaining gold, silver, and other products of value from her new colonies. Spanish colonization was restricted to local areas of favorable climate and to mining centers. Over much of Latin America, the mountainous country and the vast tropical forest, the Indians continued to live in ways little modified from pre-Columbian times. Thus, Latin America in places today presents a pattern of land use strange to North American eyes, a combination of westernized population centers, around many of which the lands have been severely damaged because of the almost complete lack of conservation practices, and remote hinterlands supporting a sparse population of primitive peoples. The hinterlands, however, are becoming less remote and the area affected by dense populations is increasing.

WESTERN EUROPE AND NORTH AMERICA North of the Spanish colonies, settlers from western Europe poured into the United States and Canada in ever-growing numbers. Seeking a homeland, not a colony, their influence on the land was to be far reaching and permanent. Before the advancing tide of Europeans the Indians retreated and shrank in numbers, eventually to be confined to reservations in the less desirable lands. With a forgotten history of land use and abuse behind them the American settlers in a short space of time repeated every mistake that man has made since the first Neolithic farmer sank a digging stick into the ground. Land destruction that had taken millennia in the lands of Asia was matched in two short centuries in America.

Through the southern states went waves of settlers, clearing and burning the forests to plant corn and tobacco or, later, cotton. Their crops made great demands on the soil and offered it little protection. Combined with careless husbandry, cotton and tobacco in particular were to leave a permanent mark on the American South. The soil was lost through erosion or impoverished through loss of fertility. This was to be reflected later in the impoverishment and malnutrition from which the people suffered. Only recently is the damage being repaired.

Farther north the early settlers accepted corn from the Indians but failed to take with it their methods of soil conservation. In the hands of westward-moving pioneers, corn planted in forest clearings led also to erosion and soil exhaustion. Fortunately, however, much of the north was settled by western Europeans skilled in farming. These people brought with them the mixed grain, clover, hog, and dairy-cattle husbandry from their homeland and found it well adapted to the similar soils and climate of the American north. With them a measure of permanent land care was provided.

Before the settler's axe much of the hardwood forest of the eastern United States disappeared. North of the hardwood belt, the white pine forests of New England and the Lake States provided the resource base on which the American lumber industry was formed. Chopping their way across the top of the nation, the white pine loggers, with the destructive fires that followed in their wake, created a desolation so impressive that the American public at last realized resources even in a new continent are not inexhaustible. With that realization, at the end of the nineteenth century, the conservation movement in America had its beginnings. The process of slowly putting back together the land that had been so quickly taken apart was under way.

OCEANIA[3,7,12,19,20] The movement of Europeans into the Americas had its parallel in other regions of the world. The islands of Oceania and the continent of Australia were opened to the western world following the voyages of Captain James Cook in 1769. Up to that time the region had been isolated from outside influences over long periods of time. Each island of any size was a small center for evolution. Each developed its own distinctive flora and fauna. Australia, the most completely isolated continent, was unlike any other place on earth in its animal and plant life. New Zealand differed greatly both from Australia and from all other islands.

The Pacific Islands had been settled, during the years from A.D. 300 to 1500 by voyagers who originated, for the most part, in southeast Asia but were later influenced by a westward moving influence from South America. These gave rise to the Polynesian peoples of the central and southern Pacific and the Melanesians of the southwest Pacific. In Australia, the Old Stone Age cultures of an isolated primitive people had endured over thousands of years. The early impact of man in this region had been essentially benign. There were some exceptions, however. In New Zealand, the giant moas, flightless birds larger than ostriches, were exterminated by the ancestors of the Maoris, soon after they settled these southern islands. In Australia, the efficient hunting peoples were undoubtedly instrumental in the extermination of some of the giant marsupial mammals, but the drying out of that continent as a result of post-Pleistocene climatic change must have been a major factor.

Island cultures and island biotas are peculiarly vulnerable to disturbance. Their life patterns were not developed under the stress of competition which has prevailed on the larger continental landmasses. Genetic combinations survived in island isolation that gave rise to traits which could not have existed under mainland competition. Resistance to the diseases and parasites of the continents was often lost in places where these factors no longer occurred in the environment.

Into these quiet Pacific lands the invaders from western Europe moved like a plague. No matter how noble their intentions, their effects were catastrophic. Introduced European animals—rats, mice, rabbits, cats, goats, sheep, and hogs—increased and multiplied to displace native species and to devastate vegetation. Introduced diseases and parasites blotted out entire populations. The island of Tahiti, the island paradise that captivated James Cook and later the mutineers of the H.M.S. *Bounty* was, in only 50 years, changed beyond recognition. Darlington believes that by the time three generations of "infection, hybridization, and selection" had occurred the population of Tahiti had changed completely.[7] The old island people with their castes and their arts no longer existed. The introduced cultures provided destructive competition with native ways, enforced by the authority of an imposed Christianity. The old ways of living with the land were forgotten.

The more benign the culture, the more mild the environment, the greater the damage. Hawaii and Tahiti, Samoa and Guam, Easter Island, and Saipan were changed completely. But the large mountainous islands of New Guinea, the Solomons and Fiji, protected by their mantle of rain forest, their swamps and rugged terrain provided better protection for the warlike Melanesians. Even the crushing effect of World War II, which devastated so many Pacific lands, only scratched the edges of New Guinea. In the hinterland, peoples held out who knew nothing of Europe, who carried on with their Paleolithic or Neolithic pastimes well into the nuclear age, the days of the cold war, and its aftermath. In recent decades colonial administrators who have lived for long years with the indigenous peoples have preferred, for the most part, to leave their cultures undisturbed. But distant governments and intergovernmental bodies, remote from the realities of island life, have decreed the necessity of "progress." It seems those who have managed to survive the brutalities and vicissitudes of Asian and European intervention thus far will be forced willy-nilly into the twentieth or twenty-first century international community. Conservationists might well wish some of these people could be left alone. It is possible they know things about life that technological man has long ago forgotten.

Australia, most secure in its isolation, in some ways was most drastically affected by the "fatal impact" of the western world.[20] But a continent is harder to subdue than an island, particularly a dry, harsh, hostile continent. In the interior deserts and in the northern savanna and scrub, aborigine tribes held out with little influence from the outside, and in time they were protected in their ways by an increasingly more enlightened government.

Initially, introduced livestock, logging, uncontrolled fire, and escaped rabbits played havoc with Australia's vegetation and animal life. Some species of the unique marsupial fauna became extinct, but most survived. Today, with Australia's beginning to take a lead in ecological research, the prospects for saving and restoring this unique continent seem better than ever before. It is not because the processes of misguided land use and of a technologically based destructiveness do not continue, but that the means for combating them grow stronger each year. Australia's conservation forces were late in evolving, but they are more soundly based in ecological knowledge than were their earlier counterparts in North America or Europe.

AFRICA[1,7,13] Perhaps to an even greater extent than Oceania, tropical Africa was for long spared the impact of advanced technological civilization. It was not because the Asians and Europeans did not know that Africa was there—it had been well known since the days of the Pharaohs—but because its environment seemed too hostile and its assets too few to be worth a serious effort at conquest or colonization. North Africa, including to some extent the Sudan and Ethiopia, lay in the mainstream of developing western civilization. The rest of Africa was not.

Agricultural ideas spread down from Egypt and out from Ethiopia to reach many of the peoples of Africa. Later tropical crops reached Madagascar from Indonesia, and they, but usually not the planting skills of southeast Asia, spread into the African tropics. Asia traded with and plundered Africa for centuries, and Arab slave traders operated in many parts of the continent long before the Europeans became involved. But over most of Africa these activities and contacts had little effect.

South Africa was colonized by the Dutch in 1652, and later by the British. The Mediterranean climatic region of South Africa was rapidly transformed by agricultural and pastoral concepts developed in Europe. It was not until late in the nineteenth century, however, that most of Africa was occupied and colonized by Europe, and even then few Europeans came to live in Africa. Scarcely a century later, European occupation of Africa came to an end, but during that century, and particularly in the years following World War II, tropical Africa was completely changed.

Plagued by diseases such as malaria and bilharzia that crippled men, and by the sleeping sickness and cattle fevers that attacked livestock, the population of Africa had remained relatively stable over many centuries. However, this balance was disturbed by European intervention. Unlike the situation in the Pacific or the Americas, the native peoples of Africa were far more resistant to the diseases of Europe than were the Europeans to the diseases of Africa. There was little of the depopulation that occurred in the New World through the spread of epidemics. On the contrary the practices of sanitation, medicine, and veterinary skills brought by the Europeans permitted a rapid growth in the population of Africa. Unfortunately, agricultural and pastoral skills did not increase to match the growth in human numbers or in the herds of cattle. Great damage to lands and resources has resulted. Africa's wildlife, once the most spectacular on earth, has been greatly diminished in numbers and variety. Africa's vegetation has been seriously damaged by fire and overgrazing. Africa's soils have been severely eroded.

Fortunately, in many of the new nations in Africa, the situation is now changing. There is a growing awareness of the problems of land use and conservation. The task of stabilizing and improving the African countryside may be well under way.

RECAPITULATION This brief summary of human history provides a framework for considering in greater detail the processes of change that have operated within the major ecosystems of the earth. Throughout history people have sought to come to terms with their environment, to obtain food, shelter, and other necessities, and to have leisure for creative work or play. At first, people were forced to adapt to nature much as any other animal would and under the same strict controls. Later, with fire and simple tools a degree of mastery was obtained and nature could be modified to some extent to yield a greater supply of wild foods. With the coming of agriculture, human control over the environment was extended. Cycles of nutrient flow and energy could be harnessed and put to work producing the materials people wished to obtain. However, any failure to adapt human techniques to the necessities of the environment would be punished by destruction of resources and the decline of the human societies involved.

Fortunately, during most of human history, people have been prevented from doing any great environmental damage by their lack of power. An early tropical farmer clearing a forest with fire and stone axes could not create the bare exposed soil which would have invited disaster. By the time more efficient tools made this possible, most peoples had learned lessons of living with tropical soils and had adapted their farming methods to them. These adaptations were reinforced by all of the rituals and ceremonies of the local religion since religion, nature, and society are closely interwoven in primitive cultures. At the worst, where

a

b

c

PEOPLE AND LAND: REGAINING THE BALANCE

Ecosystem people. (**a**) In the tropical forests of Brazil isolated Indian nations retain a hunter-gatherer way of life combined with shifting agriculture. **Peasant agriculture.** Rice culture on terraced fields in Bali (**b**) or in lowland paddies in Java (**c**) has persisted over thousands of years as a highly productive use of land. **Diversified land use.** Around the ancient neolithic rock circle at Avebury, England, a diversified pattern of field and village has persisted over centuries (**d**).

d

people were too effective for their own good, and lands were damaged, the failure was local and adjoining peoples could learn from the mistakes.

With civilization came new inventions and discoveries leading to greater environmental control. The development of transportation and food-storage facilities made possible the support of local populations over bad years when local lands had lost their productiveness. Thus the pharaohs stored food in the fat years against the coming of the lean years and the people were preserved. But a people protected against the hazards of nature could persistently misuse the land despite droughts, floods, and other signs of danger which would cause a group outside of the civilized network to perish or flee. More complete land destruction thus became a possibility. With the control of natural forces through the organization of civilization came the possibility of great enrichment, but also of much more complete failure affecting much greater areas of the earth.

From the examination of existing traditional societies and by speculation about the past, it is possible to classify people into two groups: *ecosystem people* and *biosphere people*. Until the rise of the first civilized empires, all people on earth were ecosystem people. This means they lived within one ecosystem or, at most, a few closely related ecosystems, and depended entirely on the continued functioning of those ecosystems for their survival. Their economies may have been based on hunting, fishing, and food gathering, on shifting or permanent agriculture, or on nomadic pastoralism, but in all cases their ways of life involved a close and intricate relationship between culture and nature. Religious practices and social customs formed intrinsic parts of this relationship and assured that economic activities remained in proper balance with the ecological requirements of their environment.

Biosphere people today are tied in with the global technological and economic system. This frees them from the restraints of any one particular ecosystem, since they can draw upon energy and resources from an economic network which extends throughout the entire biosphere. We need only examine the sources of the food consumed in any modern city to see that they come from virtually all of the continents and oceans of the world. Failure in any one ecosystem does not necessarily threaten the survival of the city, since it can draw more heavily on other ecosystems. This permits biosphere people to override the ecological controls in any one system and, consequently, do far greater damage than could be accomplished by a group which was totally dependent on that particular ecosystem. The biosphere network began to take shape when large areas were first brought under the control of ancient civilizations and trade routes were established across the world.

However, with earlier civilizations the amount of change or damage to the environment was limited for as long as land was exploited with hand tools or the power of domestic animals. A person clearing forest or brush land with a hand axe, or cultivating with a horse and plow has time to consider his activities and redress his mistakes. In the Old World there was time to learn to live with one's environment, to study its weather cycles and the peculiarities of its soils. Where people did not learn the lessons of the land, they disappeared, and only the desolate wastes remained. In much of the Old World, however, there is a pattern of land use which shows how people have adapted to the natural framework of their habitat, learned to avoid its dangers, and compensated for its lacks by cultural improvements. In such areas are still to be found remarkably charming human landscapes of farms and villages, pastures, and woodlands which blend with the natural scene as though a permanent part of it.

With the rise of industrial civilization the biosphere network began to be completed, and with this came the attendant dangers. Equipped with the harnessed power of rivers, coal, petroleum and the atom, armed with machines capable of doing the work of an army, industrialized man is able to shape any environment into a landscape of his own choosing and to channel its materials into an industrial network which can create for him a high degree of security and material enrichment. But with these new powers and techniques has disappeared the opportunity for long periods of adjustment to nature through small errors, small failures, and new beginnings.

The intricate balances maintained by ecosystem people throughout the world are extremely fragile when brought into contact with the biosphere cultures. Consequently, the impact of the developing biosphere culture, moving out from Europe with the voyages of discovery and colonization has brought disaster to ecosystem peoples everywhere. For example, the American Indians, dependent on their own ecosystems, could hardly hold out against those who could draw on the technology, resources, and populations of Europe in a continuing onslaught.

When the peoples of the biosphere cultures moved into the forests and fields of the new worlds and reinvaded the settled landscapes of the old, their new powers should have been tempered by the sober judgment learned over centuries of experience with the land. That they were not has been evidenced by the far-reaching destruction of both nature and human cultures. Too frequently to be observed is the new industrial landscape, raw and ugly, at odds with the environment and at war with nature. Until biosphere people, armed with powers greater than their ancestors could imagine, make use of the wisdom which ecosystem people have so painfully acquired and which their ancestors once had, they remain in peril. Like the gods of old they can make the earth into a paradise, if they so choose and if they use this wisdom, or they can destroy it.

CHAPTER REFERENCES

Clark, J. Desmond, 1959. *Prehistory of southern Africa*. Penguin, Harmondsworth.

Cole, Sonia, 1963. *The prehistory of east Africa*. New American Library, Mentor, New York.

Coon, Carlton S., 1954. *The story of man*. Alfred Knopf, New York.

Coon, Carlton S., 1962. *The origin of races*. Alfred Knopf, New York.

Darlington, C. D., 1969. *The evolution of man and society*. Simon and Schuster, New York.

Libby, W. F., 1955. *Radiocarbon dating*. University of Chicago, Chicago.

Linton, Ralph, 1955. *The tree of culture*. Alfred Knopf, New York.

Mumford, Lewis, 1956. *The transformations of man*. Collier, New York.

Osborn, Fairfield, 1953. *The limits of the earth*. Little, Brown, Boston.

Vogt, William, 1948. *Road to survival*. Wm. Sloane, New York.

LITERATURE CITED

1. Bartlett, H. H., 1956. Fire, primitive agriculture and grazing in the tropics. (see Thomas, 1956, in general references.)

2. Brooks, C. E. P. 1949. *Climate through the ages*. Ernest Benn, London.

3. Burdick, Eugene, 1961. *The blue of Capricorn*. Fawcett, Greenwich.

4. Carneiro, Robert L., 1970. A theory of the origin of the state. *Science*, 169: 733–738.

5. Dale, Tom, and V. C. Carter, 1955. *Topsoil and civilization*. Univ. Oklahoma, Norman, Oklahoma.

6. Darby, H. C., 1956. The clearing of the woodland in Europe. (see Thomas, 1956, in general references.)

7. Darlington, C. D., 1969. *The evolution of man and society*. Simon and Schuster, New York.

8. Davis, John H., 1956. The influences of man upon coast lines. (see Thomas, 1956, in general references.)

9. DeChardin, Pierre Teilhard, 1956. The antiquity and world expansion of human culture. (see Thomas, 1956, in general references.)

10. Evans, E. Esty, 1956. The ecology of peasant life in western Europe. (see Thomas, 1956, in general references.)

11. Flint, Richard F., 1947. *Glacial geology and the Pleistocene epoch*. John Wiley, New York.

12. Fosberg, F. Raymond, ed., 1963. *Man's place in the island ecosystem*. Bishop Museum Press, Honolulu.

13. Gourou, Pierre, 1966. *The tropical world*. Fourth edition, John Wiley, New York.

14. Harris, David R., 1967. New light on plant domestication and the origin of agriculture. *Geographical Review*, 57: 90–107.

15. Heichelheim, F. M., 1956. Effects of classical antiquity on the land. (see Thomas, 1956, in general references.)

16. Huntington, Ellsworth, 1907. *The pulse of Asia*. Houghton, Mifflin, Boston.

17. Johnson, Frederick, 1955. Reflections upon the significance of radiocarbon dates. (see Libby, 1955.)

18. Lowdermilk, W. C., 1953. Conquest of the land through 7,000 years. United States Department of Agriculture, Washington, D.C.

19. Melville, Herman, 1958. *Typee*. Bantam Books, New York.

20. Moorehead, Alan, 1968. *The fatal impact*. Penguin, Harmondsworth.

21. Mumford, Lewis, 1961. *The city in history*. Harcourt, Brace and World, New York.

22. Mumford, Lewis, 1966. *The myth of the machine. Technics and human development*. Harcourt, Brace and World, New York.

23. Neel, James V., 1970. Lessons from a "primitive" people. *Science*, 170: 815–822.

24. Osborn, Fairfield, 1948. *Our plundered planet.* Little, Brown, New York.

25. Sauer, Carl O., 1950. Grassland climax, fire, and man. *Jour. Range Management,* 3: 16–21.

26. Sauer, Carl O., 1952. *Agricultural origins and dispersal.* Amer. Geographical Society, New York.

27. Sauer, Carl O., 1964. The early Spanish Main. University of California, Berkeley.

28. Shapley, Harlow, ed., 1953. *Climatic change, evidence, causes and effects.* Harvard University, Cambridge, Massachusetts.

29. Stewart, Omer, 1956. Fire as the first great force employed by man. (see Thomas, 1956, in general references.)

30. Waller, Robert, 1971. Out of the garden of Eden. *New Scientist,* 2 Sept., pp. 528–530.

31. Wissman, Hermann von, H. Poech, G. Smolla, and F. Kussmaul, 1956. On the role of nature and man in changing the face of the dry belt of Asia. (see Thomas, 1956, in general references.)

32. Zeuner, F. E., 1945. *The Pleistocene period, its climate, chronology and faunal successions.* Royal Society, London.

33. Zeuner, F. E., 1950. *Dating the past, an introduction to geochronology.* Methuen, London.

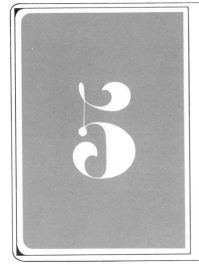

5

the
supporting
soil

n an area in the foothills north of Mexico City a story of man's relationship with the soil is written in the landscape. It was recorded by Starker Leopold in the course of his biological studies in the area.[21] The region was visited by Alexander von Humboldt in 1803. He described it as a beautiful place covered with a tall open forest of pine and oak. Only the lower slopes toward the Valley of Mexico had been cleared for agriculture at that time. But populations grew and the demand for new farming land increased. Farther and farther up the slopes the forests were cleared. First, perhaps they were cut for timber, but then the collectors of *carbon* (charcoal) came and built their little ovens to convert the remaining woody vegetation into fuel that was easily transported to the city. The cleared lands were first planted to corn or wheat, but these give poor cover to the soil on sloping ground. The rains each year would wash some of the topsoil away and leach out the minerals on which the soil's fertility depended. Finally corn would grow there no longer, but the soils continued to wash until only the barren subsoil remained. This, however, could grow maguey, the cactuslike plant raised for the fibers of its leaves. Maguey can grow on impoverished ground, but it offers scant cover. Virtually all of the soil washed down the hill until only a bare and impervious hardpan remained and the cultivation of maguey also ceased. Still a few desert-tolerant plants could grow there, and these supported the scant grazing of goats and donkeys until they too were gone. Today nothing remains except a complete wasteland. The story illustrates a process which has been repeated again and again throughout the world, an abuse of the soils on which human life depends.[35] We have learned much about the care and management of soils, but the process still continues, particularly in the tropical world where man's hope for the future slowly eroded away along with the soils that could support it.

The word "soil" is used in many different senses, and its meaning is thereby obscured. It will be used in this book to mean the thin layer on the surface of the earth formed by the interaction among the rocks of the earth's crust, sunlight, the atmosphere, and living organisms.[2] Living organisms make the difference between soil and the mineral substrate which can become soil. All true soils are the product of life, interacting with rock, air, water, and sunlight; and they, in turn, support and are maintained by life. Thus the "soils" of the moon are not soils in the sense used here, but the substrate from which soils could be formed if life were present.

Through the ages the relationship of people to the soil has been of first importance to survival. Where soil is lost civilization often goes with it.[8] Today soil is as essential for the production of food, shelter, fiber, and fuel, as it was during the Neolithic. Loss of agricultural soil through erosion has been and remains a major conservation problem.[18] Loss of soil fertility or destruction of its capacity to grow crops is almost equally serious. To maintain future production of the things we need and to provide for increasing populations, we shall need all of the knowledge and skill we can bring to bear on the art of soil conservation.

SOIL CHARACTERISTICS

Soils develop in widely different climatic regions under various kinds of plant cover and from various parent materials. Consequently, there are many distinct kinds of soils, each with its own capabilities and each presenting peculiar problems to those who must use them. One of the tasks a resource manager must face is learning ways in which soils differ and from this determining ways to keep them productive. Differences in the parent material, climate, or vegetation influence the physical characteristics of the soil, the soil chemistry, and the organic composition of the soil.

TEXTURE AND STRUCTURE

The size and physical characteristics of the various particles of which soils are composed, and the ways in which these particles are arranged are among the most important properties of soil in that they influence most other soil characteristics. Soil texture is the term that refers to the size of soil particles. The broad classes of texture range from coarse gravel at one extreme, through sand, silt, to clay at the other. The size range of particles and the way in which they are arranged in soil textural classes has been presented by the United States Department of Agriculture in the form of a pyramid in which each apex represents a different size class of soil particle (Fig. 5–1). Recognition of the differences between textural classes obviously requires either considerable effort or extensive experience.

The textural classes to be found in a soil contribute to its *structure*, a term describing the way soil particles are grouped together into larger combinations such as lumps or clods. Soil structure is dependent on the amount and kind of clay present and the amount of organic material within the soil. Clay has a large amount of surface area relative to the weight of its particle and, therefore, has the capacity to absorb water and other molecules and ions on the surface of this clay particle. These form links between the particles which give rise to aggregates. This quality of clay is familiar to the potter, who moistens dry clay and from it forms a mixture which will hold together in whatever shape he molds it. Organic particles in the soil, of the same size range as clay, have properties similar to clay—a high ability to adsorb water and link other particles together. Soils that are a mixture of clay, organic materials, and coarser substances develop an aggregated structure in which the coarse materials are joined with the fine into crumbs, nutlike aggregates, or other combinations of various sizes and shapes. Soils deficient in clay or organic materials are structureless, powdery dusts or pure sands which do not hold together. Soils too rich in clay and deficient in larger particles may form a compacted layer or soil mass which is virtually impenetrable by water or plant roots.

The structure of soil determines many of the other soil properties such as its permeability to water, its water-holding capacity, aeration, ability to supply nutrients to plants, the ease with which it can be worked with farming tools, its ability to stand up to continued cultivation, and its resistance to erosion.

SOIL WATER The water-holding capacity of a soil is one important characteristic which determines the value of the soil for agriculture or for the support of natural

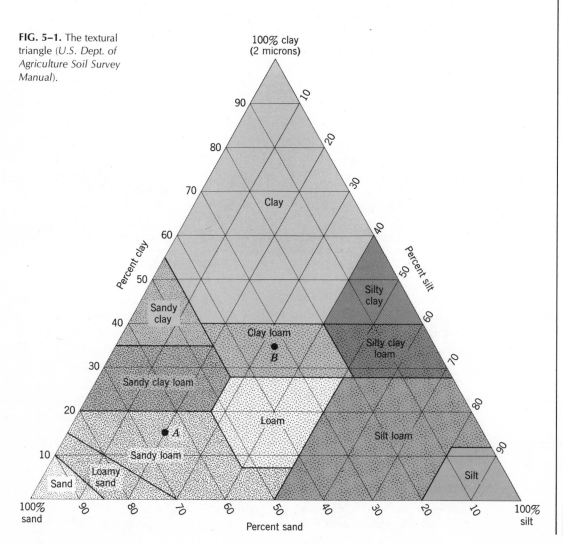

FIG. 5–1. The textural triangle (*U.S. Dept. of Agriculture Soil Survey Manual*).

vegetation. Plants not only require water, water is the solvent through which the nutrients that plants need are carried to the roots of the plant. From soil water surrounding the plant roots, nutrients may then pass through the root-cell membranes to enter the internal solution within the plant. Permanently dry soils are lifeless. Permanently waterlogged soils can support only special types of aquatic plants. Light, structure-less sands and gravels are easily penetrated by water. The air spaces between these larger soil particles provide large channels through which water rapidly sinks deep into the soil. Such soils, however, have little ability to hold water or to retain it within reach of plant roots. Sand dunes, for example, even in rainy climates, can be colonized only by drought-resistant plants or others with ability to obtain water from deep in the ground. At the other extreme, heavy clay soils which lack pores or channels are difficult for water to penetrate. Once water soaks in, however, it is slow to leave, and such soils remain moist after others have dried. Unfortunately for the plants, much water that enters clay soils is held tightly to clay particles by chemical forces. It is, therefore, unavailable to plant roots. Such tightly bound water in the soil is called *hygroscopic water*.[38]

The soil best able to hold water and supply it to plants is one that combines the qualities of pure sand or gravel and heavy clay. Such a combination is found in soils with a well-developed granular structure. Between the aggregates or crumbs of soils are channels and air spaces, and within the aggregates are smaller spaces. Water is held within the smaller channels and spaces, whereas excess water readily drains through the soil. It is the so-called *capillary* water which moves through the smaller soil channels that is most useful to plant growth in contrast with either the *hygroscopic* water or the *gravitational* water that drains through the larger soil channels. In general, soils rich in organic matter hold more water than soils low in organic material, because of the capacity of humus to absorb and hold water and because of its ability to improve the general soil structure.[38]

The ability of a soil to supply water to plants varies not only with the structure of the soil but also with the nature of its surface and the interaction between these factors and the local climate. Precipitation falling on soil must first enter it, if it is to become useful to plant roots. Soil surfaces protected with plant cover and plant litter, and penetrated by a variety of openings—from animal burrows to channels left by decayed plant roots or stems—can take on water more rapidly than bare soils, the surfaces of which tend to become compacted and sealed over by the impact of rain drops. Once water from precipitation enters the soil, some of it drains through into underground channels and becomes mostly unavailable for plant growth in that locality. That which remains in the soil is immediately subjected to evaporation. Evaporation is influenced by temperature, humidity, and wind velocity. Ten inches of rain in a cool, moist climate can keep a soil saturated throughout the year. In a warm, dry, windy climate it can evaporate almost as rapidly as it falls and will keep soils moist for only a short period. Evaporation, however, is retarded by a covering of litter on the soil, and the presence of plants above the soil, which keep the air near the soil saturated with moisture and serve also to slow down wind movement close to the soil.

An example of the way in which soil structure and, therefore, the permeability of the soil to water can be affected by cultivation has been provided by work at the Seabrook Farms in New Jersey.[31] These farms were faced with the problem of disposing of large quantities of waste water from the processing and freezing of vegetables. The water was too highly polluted with dirt and organic matter to be discharged directly into nearby streams. An effort was made, therefore, to make use of it by spraying it on the agricultural lands, where it could serve the dual purpose of irrigation and fertilization. It was found, however, that the plowed lands could not absorb the quantities of water involved. With soil structure broken down by farming, the soil pores quickly became sealed and clogged and water ceased to penetrate. The water was then sprayed on an area of previously uncultivated forest land. These forest soils, with undisturbed structure, were able to absorb 5 inches of water per 10-hour period, compared to no more than one inch on the cultivated lands. The equivalent of 600 inches of rainfall a year was sprayed on these forest soils and was absorbed. In response to this excess of water, the vegetation in the forests flourished.

AERATION Although the water relationships of soils are obviously of first importance to their ability to support plant growth, the aeration of soils is of equal importance. Plant roots engaged in respiration require a steady supply of oxygen and give off carbon dioxide. Soil organisms other than plants also require a continuing supply of oxygen. This oxygen must be able to move from the air into the soil, and carbon dioxide, in turn, must be able to move out of the soil if life is to thrive. Soils without sufficient oxygen, such as those in some marshes or at the bottoms of lakes or ponds, can support only anaerobic bacteria or other microorganisms that obtain their oxygen from the breakdown of organic materials or other complex molecules.

Heavy clay soils that are deficient in channels for drainage, and in spaces between soil particles, not only become water logged but, in consequence, become deficient in oxygen. Light sandy soils, on the other hand, are usually well aerated but are deficient in water. A well-aggregated, medium-textured soil represents the best balance between these extremes, holding air in the larger pores and spaces through which water can quickly drain.

EROSION RESISTANCE Soils with poorly developed structure readily wash or blow away through the action of water running across their surface or of wind moving loose soil particles. Under natural plant cover and with a litter layer on their surface, they will be protected against erosion. Under agricultural use, however, they become exposed. Well-aggregated soils are more erosion resistant, both because they can readily absorb water and thus reduce surface runoff, and also because the coherence of their particles resists both washing and surface blowing caused by wind.

THE SOIL PROFILE Most soils have horizons, meaning that they have more or less distinct layers. Different kinds of soil vary in the appearance and characteristics of these layers, or in other words in their soil profiles. A profile is the cross-section of a soil revealed when a trench is cut down into the ground. In mature soils, developed in place from underlying rock, the profile usually has several major layers or horizons.

At the base of the soil lies the unmodified rock or other material not yet changed by interactions with living organisms. Next, there is a layer of unconsolidated material, rock fragments, or other mineral matter not greatly modified by living organisms, although it may be broken, split, or cracked by tree roots, and in some areas will show accumulations of various soluble minerals such as gypsum or carbonates. This is known as the *C horizon* (Fig. 5–2).

The true soil begins with the *B horizon* or *subsoil*. In this, the structure of the original parent material is obliterated. It is a layer of *illuviation*, or deposition, for minerals leached out of the topsoil, and in particular it is a layer in which clays tend to accumulate. In more arid regions it will be a layer of accumulation for calcium carbonate, magnesium carbonate, gypsum (calcium sulfate), or other soluble salts.

Above the *B* horizon, the *topsoil* begins. In some soils an *E horizon* (sometimes called the *A2 horizon*) will lie immediately above the *B* horizon. This is a zone of maximum leaching or *eluviation* from which most minerals soluble in water have been washed. It is generally light colored and rich in quartz particles or other resistant minerals in the size range of sand or silt.

The *A horizon* lies next above the *E*, or in some soils is directly above the *B* horizon. This is a layer in which organic debris becomes converted into humus and mixed with mineral matter. It is also a zone of eluviation in which rainwater, commonly mixed with acids from decomposing organic material, dissolves out and carries farther down into the soil the more soluble minerals. This is also the zone for maximum concentration of soil organisms and biotic activity.

The surface of the soil is often occupied by a litter layer. This accumulation of fresh or partly decomposed organic matter, not yet formed into humus, forms the *O horizon* of the soil.

The terminology and nature of these various horizons is a basis for the classification of soils. For farm crops and most native plant growth the topsoil is the most important layer, since it is here where the nutrients essential to life are present in the most readily available form. However, deep-rooted plants continually bring up materials from the subsoil or deeper layers, add these materials to the surface of the soil when the

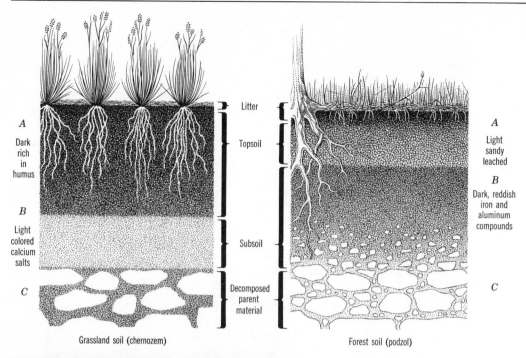

Grassland soil (chernozem)		Forest soil (podzol)

A
Dark
rich
in
humus

B
Light
colored
calcium
salts

C

Litter

Topsoil

Subsoil

Decomposed
parent
material

A
Light
sandy
leached

B
Dark, reddish
iron and
aluminum
compounds

C

FIG. 5–2. Drawings comparing profiles of forest
and grassland soil. The photo shows a profile of
grassland soil.

plants die or their leaves or twigs fall, and thus restore nutrients to the topsoil to counteract the process of leaching.

SOIL BIOTA It has already been noted that soil is the product of interaction between living organisms, the inorganic materials of the lithosphere, the atmosphere, sunlight, and water. The living components of the soil, although often inconspicuous, are vitally important to its maintenance and functioning. The variety of soil life is great, ranging from the larger burrowing mammals and other vertebrates through a variety of insects and larger invertebrates down to bacteria, fungi, and protozoa of microscopic size. Some idea of the numbers of microorganisms in the soil is provided in Table 2.[20]

TABLE 2
Abundance of
Microorganisms
in Soils[20]

Missouri corn land	648,000 nematodes per acre in top six inches of soil.
Manured soil	72,000 amoebae per gram in top inch of soil.
Saturated soil	25,280,000 bacteria per gram of topsoil.
Manured and fertilized soil	111,000 fungi per gram of topsoil, 2,920,000 actinomycetes per gram of topsoil.

Although most of the forms listed in the table are visible only under a microscope, they nevertheless add up to a considerable weight or biomass of life. The weight of bacteria alone in some soils has been estimated at one ton or more per acre.[17]

It is the conspicuous plant life growing from most soils which attracts attention, but the inconspicuous microorganisms in the soil may, at times, be far more active in producing new growth. The breakdown, decay, and subsequent recycling of the chemical constituents of organic matter is a major function played by soil life. Without such decay, minerals would be tied up in organic debris and soils would stagnate. The production of either native vegetation or crops would decline and eventually cease. Such nutrients as nitrates and phosphates are normally scarce in soils, relative to the requirements of living things, and may be tied up to a large extent in plant and animal bodies. Return of these elements to the soil through decomposition is essential if life is to continue to be supported.

In addition to their role in breakdown and decay, soil microorganisms have other functions of importance. As noted earlier, nitrogen-fixing bacteria live free in the soil and in nodules attached to the roots of various plants such as legumes. These fix atmospheric nitrogen and form the nitrates essential for plant growth. Certain soil microorganisms also have been found to produce growth-stimulating substances, plant hormones, which may be essential for maintaining vigorous plant growth.[35]

One important reason for adding organic fertilizers such as manure to the soil is the stimulation they provide for the growth and proliferation of soil microorganisms. Chemical fertilizer alone may not be sufficient for this purpose.[35]

In addition to microorganisms, the larger biotic components of the soil are also important and sometimes surprisingly abundant. The role of earthworms in churning, mixing, and processing the soil is well known. In the tropics, soil insects can be extremely active and important. For example, in one rain-forest area of the Congo it was estimated that between 20 and 25 tons of plant debris were deposited on each acre per year.[14] Yet, very little of this remained on the surface, and the litter layer was not deep. Soil insects, particularly termites, rapidly consume this plant debris as it falls to the ground. In certain tropical areas termites are both abundant and conspicuous, since some species build great mounds. Pierre Gourou has observed one area in Katanga where three giant termite mounds occur to the acre and occupy 6 percent of the area. If demolished and spread around, they could cover the acre to the depth of eight inches.[14] Elsewhere the mounds are smaller and more abundant. Even what appears to be dry and lifeless ground will spring to life following a rain, and small forests of tiny termite mounds will spring up overnight on dirt roads across the savannas of Rhodesia. In temperate-zone soils, where insect life is usually less abundant than in the tropics, it may still be impressive. In Washington in 1970 the 17-year cicadas came up from the soil to swarm in enormous flocks on trees and shrubs. Each left a hole up to one-half inch in diameter where it emerged from the soil. Ten to twenty of these per square foot could be counted in some areas.

All of these organisms, up to the size of moles, gophers, wombats, or badgers, which burrow in the soil play an important role in maintaining soil structure and fertility through the churning and mixing of the soil they carry out, the organic matter they add to it, and the role they play in the interchange and circulation of soil nutrients.

SOIL FERTILITY The fertility of a soil refers to its ability to provide essential chemical nutrients for plant growth. The mere presence of these chemicals is not adequate to make the soil fertile. They must also be present in available form, which means in solution, or capable of going into solution in the presence of water, organic acids, or other soil solvents. These essential nutrients include the ones required in large quantities by plants, the *macronutrients*, such as nitrate, phosphate, calcium, potassium, and magnesium, and also those required in minute amounts, the *micronutrients* or *trace elements*, such as copper, cobalt, zinc, or manganese. These trace elements may be poisonous to plants if present in large quantities, but in trace amounts are essential for nutrition.

The fertility of a soil is influenced by its texture, structure, and its living components. Soils with sufficient clay and humus in suitable aggregated form can hold more essential nutrients in a form available to plants than can soils that are light and sandy. However, the kind of clay is also important. In temperate-zone soils the clays are often montmorillonites in the drier regions. These are aluminum silicates in layered form in which an aluminum sheet is sandwiched between two silica sheets. They provide a high surface area which can attract and hold in loose association ions of calcium, ammonium, potassium, magnesium, and the like. These ions are readily released in the presence of hydrogen ions and enter the soil solution. Other temperate-zone clays often have similar ability to hold and to exchange nutrients with the soil solution. By contrast, in many tropical soils the clays have a low exchange capacity. An example is kaolinite. Compared to montmorillonite, this contains a higher proportion of alumina, which is bonded to silica in such a way as to provide a much smaller surface area for retention of plant nutrients. Since these tropical soils which are high in such clays are also low in humus, they not only lack natural fertility but often do not hold artificial fertilizers for long.[14,32]

Under natural undisturbed conditions, there is a constant turnover of nutrients in any area. Minerals go from soil to wild plants or animals, are returned to the soil in animal or plant wastes or remains, are liberated by soil organisms and made available for use again. In drier areas little is lost from the soil except the small amount removed by the slow processes of geological erosion or by animal or plant emigrants to other areas. In more humid areas leaching removes some minerals from the soil, but this is compensated for, in part, by minerals brought from deep in the ground by the deeper rooted trees or shrubs. When man first entered the picture, he did little to change this circulation. What was removed from the soil was returned in the form of manure or eventually by the death of man or his domestic animals.

With the advent of civilization, trade and commerce, crop plants or livestock were not used locally but were shipped away to population centers. With the development of sewage systems and various burial customs little of this organic material was returned to the soil. Thus the drain of nutrients from the soil was increased, and it was accelerated still further when erosion washed the soil itself to the sea. In some areas, soil fertility was largely exhausted. In other areas, crops continued to be grown, but the ability of these crops to provide adequate nutrition to man or animal was impaired. As a result, dietary deficiencies (shortages of vitamins, essential minerals, or proteins) developed and caused a decline in human health and in efficiency. It has been pointed out by W. A. Albrecht, for example, that the protein quality of wheat grown on the rich farmlands of Kansas declined over an eleven-year period from 1940 to 1951. In some counties the decline was as high as 8 percent, from a high of 18 or 19 percent protein in the wheat grains in 1940 to 11 or 12 percent.[1]

In the humid tropics many soils are heavily leached and their remaining nutrients are largely tied up in the organic components of their biota and are rapidly circulated through the surface soil. When they are cleared

Effects of soil fertility on yield of corn in Arkansas. The corn on the left is grown on soil enriched by the planting of lespedeza, a nitrogen-fixing crop.

for agriculture, oxidation of organic matter and leaching of chemical nutrients is accelerated. The low protein quality of crops grown on these depleted soils contributes to the widespread malnutrition in many tropical areas. The abundant and luxuriant growth of tropical plants can conceal these nutrient deficiencies, but it actually reflects an abundance of cellulose and fiber or other carbohydrates of low nutritional value.[34]

In technologically advanced countries, greater skill in soil management, the use of properly balanced combinations of fertilizers, and the direct additions of vitamins and other dietary supplements to food have now corrected dietary deficiencies to a large degree. All of these inputs to the agricultural process are, of course, reflected in the higher prices of food. Some observers have pointed out that what was once simple peasant fare, good nutritious food produced directly from fertile soil by careful husbandry, is now luxury food available only to the fortunate few.

SOIL DEVELOPMENT AND CLASSIFICATION The soil characteristics described thus far are used in classifying soils into different types and groups, the members of which can be expected to show similar properties wherever they occur. Major soil differences, related to differences in climate and vegetation, develop from the operation of various soil development processes, each of which characterizes a widespread natural region.

Thus, in cold, rainy climates, where coniferous forests grow, soils undergo a process called *podsolization*. Coniferous forests add little organic matter to the soil. The leaves and litter that fall are resistant to decay, reducer organisms are scarce in the surface soil and, consequently, there is only a slow breakdown of the needles and twigs to form a humic acid. Rainfall, percolating through this litter, becomes acidic, and since the rainfall is usually high, penetrates deep into the soil. This acidic solution, therefore, can leach most of the soil nutrients from the topsoil until it comes to consist of little but quartz sand. Some minerals, mostly iron and aluminum salts, are redeposited in the subsoil, which becomes dark colored in consequence. Many important nutrients are carried deeper or are washed away. In its extreme form, podsolization occurs under heavy coniferous forest. Most forest soils in temperate climates, however, are subjected to this development process. Where broad-leaved deciduous forests predominate the process may be compensated for to some degree. Deciduous forest litter contains basic salts and minerals, and the forest floor usually supports a rich population of reducer organisms. Consequently, humus is formed and incorporated with the topsoil to restore its fertility. Such soils are less acidic and better suited to agricultural use than podsols. Nearly all of the soils in the forested regions of North America and Eurasia can be grouped together on the basis of having undergone a similar development process, although many variations result from local differences in climate, vegetation, and substrate.[32]

In drier climates, under grassland vegetation, a different development process occurs which has been termed *calcification*. Rainfall, percolating through grass litter does not become charged with acid. Because of the relatively low precipitation, the complete leaching of minerals from the soil does not normally occur. Lime and other carbonates are dissolved from the topsoil but are redeposited in a calcified layer in the subsoil. Grasses add great amounts of organic matter to the topsoil and thus serve to replace nutrients and keep it dark and rich in humus. Calcification is best developed in grassland areas with moderate rainfall. Here the topsoil is deep and the calcified layer is well below the surface. In drier areas some calcification occurs but there is less leaching of soil materials. The topsoil may be rich in lime and basic salts but, because of the sparser vegetation, may be low in organic matter and nitrogen.[32]

In the tropics where rainfall is heavy and temperatures are high, leaching and rapid oxidation of the surface soils results in the removal of most of the nutrients. In extreme cases, even much of the silica is removed from the topsoil. The remaining soil in the *A* horizon is composed predominantly of iron oxides which, under extreme conditions, form a tough, hard layer called *laterite*. The process has therefore been called *laterization,* and the end products are variously known as *lateritic* soils, *latosols* or, more recently, *ferralsols* because of their high iron content.[32] Laterite is one of the hardest rocks known and is used for highway paving. It has been used in the past to construct such long-lived edifices as the temples of Angkor in Cambodia. When a lateritic crust forms in the tropics as a result of soil misuse, the land can be lost to cultivation permanently. Not all tropical soils, however, are subject to laterization.

An additional way of looking at soil development that helps to illustrate the "renewability" of soils and their continued usefulness under agricultural practices focuses on the natural processes to which soils are exposed throughout their existence. These processes may be grouped into three categories or "regimes": the weathering or wasting regime, the organic or cyclic regime, and the drift regime.[39]

Under the *weathering* regime the minerals from which the soils are formed are broken down to yield clay and various mineral salts or ions. The more soluble salts (e.g., sodium, chlorides, and potash) tend to wash away in any area of moderate or high rainfall, or in semiarid country they may move up with capillary water as evaporation occurs and be deposited on the soil surface. The less soluble materials, such as calcium or phosphate, are more stable, but they also move slowly from the topsoil to the subsoil or out of the soil entirely. Initially, the weathering regime favors soil fertility and plant growth through making clay and nutrients available. Over time, if it continues at a high rate because of high temperatures and rainfall, it will lead to the leaching away of most nutrients from the soil.

The *organic* regime tends to counter the weathering regime. Organic life above or in the soil not only adds carbon and nitrogen to the soil directly and incorporates solar energy within it but it also keeps minerals in circulation, holds minerals in the soil, and brings them from deeper layers back to the soil surface. It furthermore incorporates animal and plant residues in the soil. However, where oxidation and incorporation of organic materials is slowed down or arrested, as in podsolic soils, then the addition of organic acids to the soil water through partial decomposition of organic debris, can hasten the process of dissolving out and leaching away of soil nutrients.

The *drift* regime may also counter the weathering regime. This includes those processes that disturb and mix the soil: soil churning by animals, by freezing and thawing, and by shrinking or swelling, along with the erosive processes that cause the deposition of materials washed or carried by wind, water, or gravity from other areas. These processes add fresh, unweathered, materials to the soil surface with new supplies of clays and mineral salts.

The operation of these processes leads to the development of varying degrees of soil fertility and stability. Highly fertile soils in which the organic and drift regimes are operative most strongly, as in tropical volcanic soils (*andosols*) enriched periodically by ash deposit, river basin soils (*luvisols*) enriched by fertile silt deposits, and grassland *chernozem* soils, may be used for intensive agricultural purposes almost indefinitely. Moderately fertile soils in which the drift and organic regimes may partially balance the weathering regime may be exploited over long periods through careful attention to the renewal of their nutrients by fertilization. The *luvisols* (gray-brown podsolic soils) of temperate deciduous forests are an example. Finally, there are low fertility soils in which the weathering regime has been most strongly operative, or will become so when natural vegetation is cleared. These soils cannot sustain even moderate agricultural use without intensive and expensive care and management. The tropical *ferralsols* are in this category.[39]

Although the operation of broad regional processes of soil development gives rise to many similarities among the soils in any major climatic region, there are also major differences within any region. Each soil develops from a particular kind of parent material. This is acted on over time by the weather and climate of the area which may be quite different from the regional climate. Each soil will support a particular kind of vegetation and animal life which acts to modify it, and these factors, in turn, may change with time as various disturbing processes act on them. It follows, therefore, that a wide range of different kinds of soils can develop within any region which is diversified geologically or topographically, or within which different disturbing factors are operating. For example, one area might be regularly burned, changing the vegetation, whereas another might be long protected from fire. Such a wide range of soils does exist, and the task of classifying them, and of determining the purposes for which each type might best be used, has exercised the ability of soil scientists over many years. A proper classification of soils permits one to use knowledge of a particular kind of soil that has been acquired over a broad area by a great number of people for the immediate management and care of the soil in a particular place.

The basic unit of soil classification is the *soil series*.[36] This is the soil equivalent of the species in animal or plant classification. All members of a soil series will be recognizably similar, will have developed from the same kind of parent material, and will have the same characteristics and arrangements of the horizons in the soil profile. The Hugo series, for example, is a moderately acid, well-drained soil which develops under coniferous forest cover in areas with rainfall exceeding 40 inches per year. It is well adapted to growing timber and supports excellent stands of Douglas fir. It is found in areas where hard, gray Franciscan sandstone predominate. The same sandstone in lower rainfall areas and on sites less suitable for soil formation gives rise to a developmental soil series known as Maymen soil. This is shallow, rocky, and poorly suited for any use other than the support of its natural cover, chaparral.[36]

Soil series are generally grouped into higher units of classification, of which the category of *Great Soil Groups* is best known and most widely used. These tend to correspond with regional climates and vegetation.[32] A partial listing of these groups is presented for North America in Figure 5–3, using terminology still most often encountered in the literature. However, as the knowledge of soils throughout the world has grown, the older systems of classification have needed revision. It was found, for example, that the same kind of soil was often given a different name in one part of the world than that by which it was known in another, not because of language differences, but because of failure to recognize the

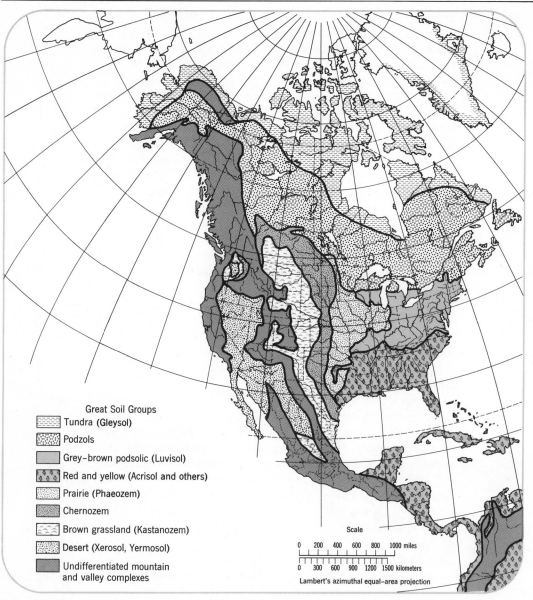

Great Soil Groups

▦ Tundra (Gleysol)

▨ Podzols

▨ Grey-brown podsolic (Luvisol)

▨ Red and yellow (Acrisol and others)

▨ Prairie (Phaeozem)

▨ Chernozem

▨ Brown grassland (Kastanozem)

▨ Desert (Xerosol, Yermosol)

▨ Undifferentiated mountain
   and valley complexes

Scale

0 200 400 600 800 1000 miles

0 300 600 900 1200 1500 kilometers

Lambert's azimuthal equal–area projection

FIG. 5–3. Distribution of zonal soil groups of North America (*adapted from Finch and Trewartha (1942) after C. E. Kellogg, Yearbook of Agriculture, 1938*).

similarity. Furthermore, other soils thought to be essentially the same throughout the world have turned out to be quite different in some areas, and to require a new terminology.[19]

In the subarctic regions of America and Eurasia it was once assumed the soils of the forested taiga would all tend to be podsolic, whereas beyond the forest boundary to the north, tundra soils (gleysols) would occur. In fact, it was found to be not that simple, because of local differences in

climate, topography, and parent material.[30] Similarly, in the tropics, soil studies have shown the early assumption that one or two great soil groups would include all of the fully developed soils of the lowland, humid tropics, does not hold up. Once again, the situation is more complex than previously expected.[24,25]

Starting in 1960, the United Nations Educational, Scientific, and Cultural Organization (UNESCO), the Food and Agricultural Organization (FAO), and the International Society of Soil Science joined together in a joint project to produce a world soil map. An internationally accepted terminology has been agreed on that permits a uniform approach to soil classification. This new terminology makes use, insofar as possible, of the older Great Soil Group terminology. Both terms are shown in Figure 5–3. It is hoped that the general acceptance of this new system will do away with the proliferation of national systems that had earlier been taking place.[9,19,39]

SOILS AND AGRICULTURE The amount of land on earth with soils well suited to agricultural use is difficult to estimate. Land surveys have yet to be carried out in many areas. Many lands are still cultivated by a shifting, tropical agriculture. It has been estimated there are 3.6 billion acres of land currently under cultivation and perhaps a total of 4½ billion acres more-or-less suitable for agricultural use.[6,7] This means there is less than one acre under cultivation for each person on earth.

For the United States, as for other technologically advanced countries, the figures are more reliable (Fig. 5.4). Of the total land area of nearly 3,676,000 square miles or 2273 million acres, somewhat less than 300 million acres or about 13 percent of the total were in harvested cropland in 1966. This was a marked decrease from previous years. In 1956, 477 million acres were classified as cropland, of which 344 million acres actually produced harvested crops. The acreage of cropland per person decreased in the United States, not just because the population increased, but because all food needs can now be met from a smaller acreage. The story of United States agriculture over the past two decades has been, in terms of production, a success story. Food production per acre has been increased enormously, and it has been possible to retire marginal lands from cultivation. Recently, however, this trend has been reversed (see Chap. 13).

A comparison of the distribution of the major soil goups with the distribution of cropland in the United States, indicates that agriculture is still largely restricted to certain soils. The chernozem, phaeozem and kastanozem grassland soils are the great centers of cereal grain production and yield the bulk of the food, not only wheat and corn for people, but grains to feed or fatten much of the nation's livestock. Similar soils elsewhere in the world are also the primary producers of cereal grains. In the tropics two general categories of soil are particularly productive, those derived from recent volcanic deposits, particularly vol-

FIG. 5–4. Land use in the United States, 1964.

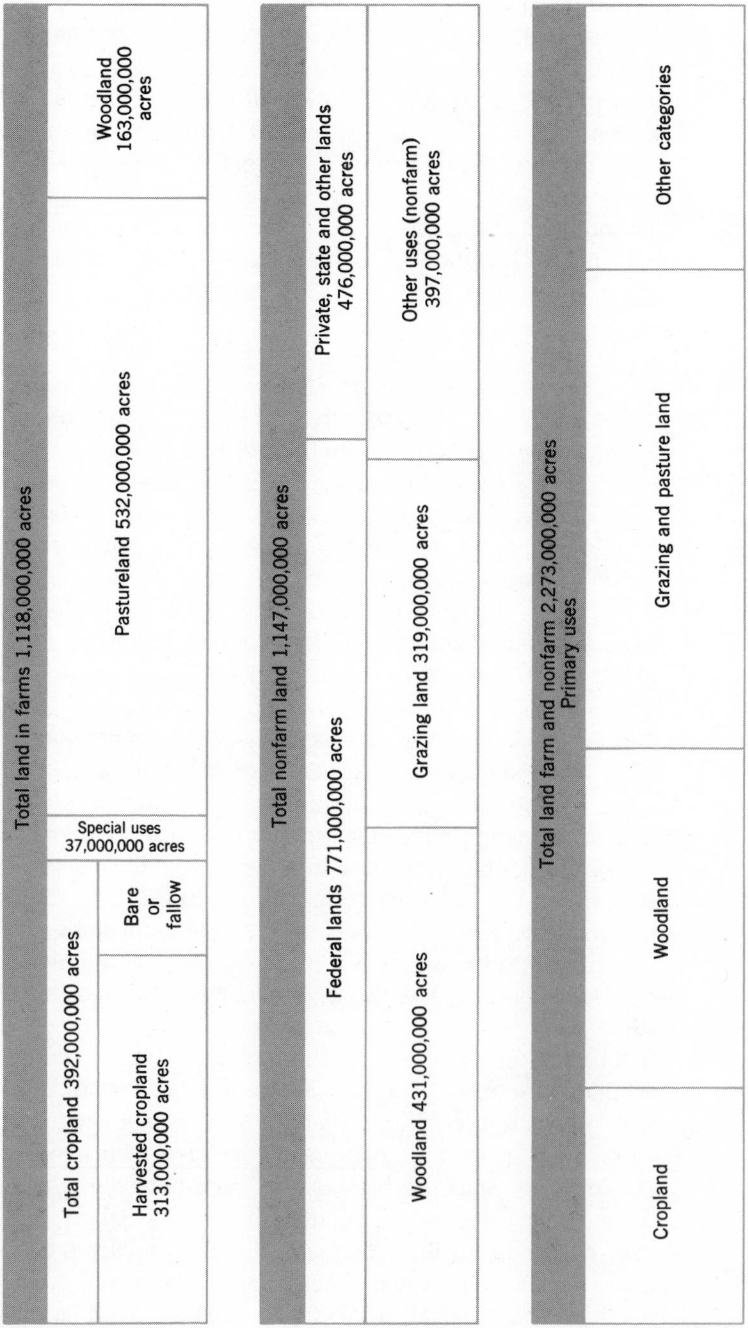

Total land in farms 1,118,000,000 acres

Woodland 163,000,000 acres

Pastureland 532,000,000 acres

Total cropland 392,000,000 acres

Special uses 37,000,000 acres

Bare or fallow

Harvested cropland 313,000,000 acres

Total nonfarm land 1,147,000,000 acres

Private, state and other lands 476,000,000 acres

Other uses (nonfarm) 397,000,000 acres

Federal lands 771,000,000 acres

Grazing land 319,000,000 acres

Woodland 431,000,000 acres

Total land farm and nonfarm 2,273,000,000 acres
Primary uses

Other categories

Grazing and pasture land

Woodland

Cropland

canic ash (andosols), and alluvial soils (fluvisols) derived from watersheds that yield an abundance of useful soil minerals. The older soils of the ancient granites and other crystalline igneous rocks of the tropics are low in fertility and yield alluvial soils low in fertility.[14] Thus the deltas of the Mekong, the Ganges, or the Nile can produce continued high yields of crops because they are enriched by silts and clays washed from the mountains of Ethiopia, or the Asian highlands. But the Zambesi, draining from the Central African plateau has no such fertile delta; nor, despite its enormous watershed, does the Amazon.[14] Most of the soils of the tropical forest country cannot produce sustained yields of crops even with the best of treatment, since they do not hold or respond well to fertilizer. At best, they are adapted to the shifting cultivation which allows them decades to recover fertility under the cover of natural vegetation.

In the temperate zone and into the subpolar regions, the highly podsolized soils are seldom cultivated, but certain soil types associated with them can be productive for dairying or for specialized crops. The less podsolized luvisols are intensively cultivated in Europe and Asia, and to a lesser degree in the United States. Similarly, some of the acrisols of the southeastern United States are successfully cultivated to yield a variety of crops. The heavily organic muck and marl soils, developed on formerly flooded lands in Florida and elsewhere in the subtropics, can be highly productive, but their productivity is gained at the expense of "soil mining," since the soils slowly disappear as their organic surfaces are exposed to the oxidizing effects of sun and air.

Desert soils (yermosols), in general, are seldom cultivated. Where irrigation can be made available, and where the proper balance of minerals exists, these soils can produce continued high yields of crops. But irrigation sometimes leads to the accumulation of alkaline or saline salts on the surface of former desert soils, brought up by high water tables or by capillary action as a result of the strong evaporative force of desert sunshine. Millions of acres of desert soils have been ruined by salinization and related processes. It can be prevented where water can be supplied in abundance, and where the excess water is drained from the soil (along with the excess minerals), and not allowed to move back upward through the soil structure.

Although it is not possible to say that agriculture has now expanded over the surface of the earth to include all of those soils most highly suitable to it, such a statement would be true with certain exceptions. There are some areas of potential high fertility and agricultural stability that have yet to be opened up and exploited, but relative to the total existing cropland on earth, these are of small extent. Efforts to expand cropland into new areas usually result only in the destruction of forests, rangelands, wilderness, or wildlife and little or no gain in total crop production. Far better results are to be obtained by using better crop varieties or better farming methods on existing farmlands. By using these improvements, production may quite easily be tripled on certain good, but poorly managed agricultural lands, and no other resources are wasted.

a

b

c

SOILS AND AGRICULTURE

During the past few decades there has
been a marked shift from a labor-
intensive, energy-conserving agriculture
to mechanized, energy-consuming
farming. This has been accompanied by
great gains in farm production, which,
however, are not necessarily due to the
use of machines or the employment of a
high-energy technology (see Chapter 12
for an analysis).
(a) Labor-intensive farming in the
Ukraine. (b) Peasant farm near Smolensk.
(c) Mechanized wheat harvesting in
Washington.

In relation to the future of agriculture and the soil, it is instructive to review the past since, regrettably, many of the old mistakes are being repeated today. The history of agricultural use in the United States is particularly instructive.

AGRICULTURE AND FOREST SOILS The objective of agriculture is to convert the nutrient materials of the soil into agricultural crops. Cultivation of the soil is intended to facilitate this process. Through plowing and harrowing the farmer breaks up the soil surface and the larger soil chunks, making it easier for the planting of seed and for the germinating seedlings to obtain water, air, and nutrients. In his initial cultivation also he removes competing natural vegetation or weeds and thus channels soil materials in the one direction of crop production. Through generations of experience, farmers have found the best soil structure for the production of most crops is one in which the soil is worked into relatively small crumbs and easily penetrated by water and plant roots. Cultivation aims at producing this condition.

Western agriculture in the long history of its development in the brown forest soils of Europe, became characterized by those practices suited to produce the best possible agricultural structure in forest soils. It will be recalled that these soils are characterized by a layer of leaf litter and debris, a relatively leached topsoil, and a darker-colored subsoil in which the materials leached from the topsoil are deposited. Shallow cultivation does little for these soils. Deep plowing, however, tends to mix together the litter and humus, the light topsoil, and the deep mineral and clay-rich subsoil. The resulting mixture is a stable, less erodible soil complex, with a better structure than the original forest topsoil.[18] The addition of lime, which reduces acidity, and manure, which adds nitrogen and organic compounds, further improves the structure. With care and with the standard European practices of crop rotation, cultivation can continue to improve these soils. Without this care and particularly under a system of farming based on the continued production, year after year, of a single cash crop, the structure of the soil breaks down, the soil nutrients leach out, crop yields decline, and eventually the soil becomes exhausted. If the soil lies on sloping ground, rainfall removes much of it by erosion once the structure is destroyed. When the eastern United States was settled, the European immigrants who were capable farmers continued their well-suited agricultural practices on the new lands. Where the settlers were poor farmers or interested only in production of cash crops for quick profit, the forest soils were depleted.

AGRICULTURE AND GRASSLAND SOILS When the wave of settlement reached the grassland belt of soils, an entirely different set of conditions were encountered. The grassland soils naturally possessed the structure which cultivation over the years produced in forest soils.[18] In their natural state they were resistant to erosion and slow to lose fertility. Because of this, many of the practices used on forest soils were gradually dropped. The new soils of the West gave continued high yields, year after year, of corn or wheat with little crop rotation. Liming and fertilization seemed unnecessary. So long as farm animals were used to pull the agricultural machinery, a certain amount of crop rotation took place to provide hay for the farm livestock, and manure was added to the soil. However, with the advent of farm machinery even these elementary soil-preserving practices were abandoned. Monoculture, emphasizing high-value, high-yield grain crops in the northern plains and cotton in the southern plains, became the rule.

Despite their depth, excellent structure, and fertility, the grassland soils were not inexhaustible. Under natural conditions they were continually restored by additions of vast quantities of organic material from grass roots and stems and the droppings and remains of grassland animals, and they were maintained in structure by the mechanical action of grass roots and the burrowing of animals. Under continuous cultivation all of the factors that originally contributed toward building the soil were removed. Gradually soil structure has broken down and with it the capacity of the soil to absorb and hold water. Dry spells, which under natural conditions did little damage, became severe when the soils failed to take on and hold the rain that did fall. Yields began to decline as natural sources of nitrogen, organic materials, and mineral nutrients were removed. Farming in this region reached its lowest ebb during the decade of the 1930's.

THE DUST BOWL In the better watered grassland soils of the East, the damage has not been so severe as that which accompanied the westward march of agriculture. In the brown soils of the arid Great Plains the most serious difficulties arose. The Great Plains region has been subjected throughout history to periodic droughts.[29] The dry, hot areas of the southern Great Plains in particular have been plagued by long spells of below-average rainfall. Under their natural cover of short, sod-forming grasses, the droughts did little lasting damage. In the 1880's, however, the first wave of settlers moved into the southern Great Plains during a period of relatively high rainfall and lush growth. In 1890 a severe drought hit the plains and persisted for the better part of the decade. Many of the early settlers gave up and moved on to better farming lands elsewhere. In the late 1890's the rains returned, and the area again looked green and productive. A new wave of settlers arrived, plowed the plains, and planted the rich, brown soil to wheat.

In 1910 there was another dry spell and more damage. On the farm lands with bare soil exposed and soil structure broken down by cultivation, dust began to blow. An extensive area was damaged, and again many farmers gave up and moved on. In 1914 there was a great demand for wheat as the grain belt of Europe was ravaged by war. With high wheat prices, previously abandoned land looked like a good investment. Returning rains further improved the outlook. All of the land now judged suitable for agriculture was plowed, and in addition an estimated 6 million acres which should not have been plowed were put into wheat production. High rainfall and good times remained in the southern Great Plains until 1931.

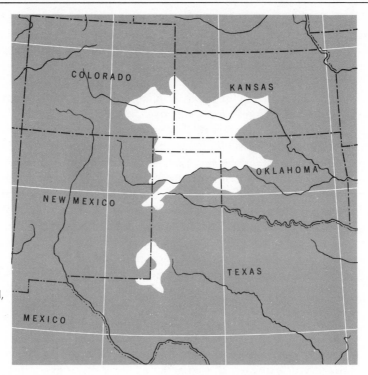

FIG. 5–5. The Dust Bowl, showing areas of severe wind erosion (*Soil Conservation Service, U.S. Department of Agriculture*).

In 1931 the nation was in the grip of a severe economic depression. In 1931, also, drought returned to the plains. Accentuated by previous damage to soil structure, the new drought surpassed all previous ones in severity. In the fall of 1933 began the series of dust storms which gave to the region a new name, the Dust Bowl (Fig. 5–5). Dust blew across the continent, darkened the skies, reddened the sunsets, and made the plains region almost uninhabitable in spots for man or livestock. Millions of acres of farms were damaged, with an estimated loss of topsoil ranging between 2 and 12 inches in places. Drifting dunes moved over farms, burying roads, fences, and even dwellings. A mass exodus of farmers, ruined by drought and unable to find work, streamed from Oklahoma, Kansas, Texas, and adjoining areas and moved west to California or east into city bread lines. It was a period of misery and privation difficult to match in American history.

Drought, dust, and despair did what countless written and spoken words by soil scientists had failed to accomplish—it brought the nation to an awareness of the need for soil conservation. In 1935, in Washington, the Soil Conservation Service was created. The federal government and state legislatures soon passed enabling legislation which permitted the forming of soil-conservation districts. In these districts the Soil Conservation Service provided the aid and technical knowledge which farmers needed to put sound land-use principles into effect. In the Dust Bowl the process was begun of putting land back into grass where the plow should never have been used. On soil types better suited to farming, the use of conservation techniques was started.

In the 1940's the rains came again. Through efforts on the part of farmers and with the help of state and federal governments, many farms were restored to productivity. For a time it looked as though the Dust Bowl was a thing of the past, as though we had finally learned the lesson of conservation. But the 1940's also brought world war. In 1941 the German Wehrmacht swept across the rich, wheat lands of the Ukraine and brought the retaliatory measures of "scorched earth" and "lend lease." Grain from America went overseas to feed the allied armies and peoples, and grain prices in America went up. Economics and patriotism were mixed in the drive which sent the plow biting deep into millions of new acres of plains grassland. The armies were fed, the Nazi war machine was broken, and the war-starved peoples of Europe were supplied. But in 1950 drought returned.

The drought of the 1950's set a new record in severity. Again the dust storms arose from eroded farms and overgrazed ranges. Crops failed, and farmers gave up trying. An emergency was proclaimed, and federal aid funds were poured into the area. That the conditions of the 1930's did not return was due in part to the generally high level of national prosperity. Farmers could afford to support their homes by working in factories in nearby cities. The land-ownership pattern had also changed. The family-sized farms that failed in the 1930's have been incorporated to an increasing extent into larger units. Fewer people were on the land to stand the brunt of the drought. In 1957 a second consequence of land misuse was felt throughout the Southwest. The rains returned, but not as gentle, life-restoring showers. Torrential downpours fell on the dust-blown eroded lands of the southern plains. Rivers swelled to flood proportions and poured over towns and cities, carrying with them the soil from once

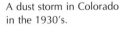
A dust storm in Colorado in the 1930's.

TABLE 3
Cropping Systems
and Soil Erosion

TABLE 3

CROPPING SYSTEM OR CULTURAL TREATMENT	AVERAGE ANNUAL LOSS OF SOIL PER ACRE (TONS)	PERCENTAGE OF TOTAL RAINFALL RUNNING OFF THE LAND
Bare, cultivated, no crop	41.0	30
Continuous corn	19.7	29
Continuous wheat	10.1	23
Rotation: corn, wheat, clover	2.7	14
Continuous bluegrass	0.3	12

Average of 14-years measurements of runoff and erosion at Missouri Experiment Station, Columbia. (Soil type: Shelby loam; length of slope: 90.75 feet; degree of slope: 3.68 percent. From *Cropping systems in relation to erosion control*, by M. F. Miller, Missouri Agric. Exp. Sta. Bul. 366, 1936. (Adapted from Jacks & White, 1939, p. 111.)

productive grassland ranges. Once again in the 1970's drought returned and ended the expectation that the United States could provide the world with all the grain needed to stave off hunger.

The Soil Conservation Service estimated in 1955 that, at least, 14 million acres in the Great Plains currently under cultivation should be returned to grass. It was pointed out that more than three-fourths of the plains cropland could be kept in crops but only if soil- and water-conservation measures were used.[29]

The Dust Bowl was an object lesson on the effects of erosion. We have had many such lessons, from the dongas of South Africa to the gullies of South Carolina. We have had scientific studies of erosion on many soils and in many areas. The results of two such studies in California and Missouri, tell their own story and show what happens when prairie is changed to cornland or left fallow, or when land is unprotected by conservation farming practices (Tables 3, 4). Erosion remains a major prob-

TABLE 4 Effect of Cover and Conservation Treatment on Erosion Loss from a Heavy 3-day Rain Storm

AVERAGE DEPTH OF EROSION (INCHES)	EROSION PROTECTION PROVIDED				NO EROSION PROTECTION PROVIDED			
	COVER CROP	BASIN LIST-ING	TER-RACES	NATIVE COVER (GRASS BRUSH)	GRAIN	VOLUN-TEER COVER	BARE	CULTIVATED (FALLOW, ORCHARD, VINEYARD)
	Percentage of area in each type of treatment that was eroded to the indicated depths, from survey of 5 areas							
No erosion	88	69	12	53	30	37	4	0
⅛ to ⅜	11	31	84	37	58	37	62	45
¾ to 1½	1	0	4	8	12	21	15	42
3	0	0	0	2	0	5	19	13
Area in acres	32,515	788	5,614	41,160	12,119	15,376	18,495	15,705

Source. Adapted from Bamesberger, 1939, SCS publication, p. 7.

lem, from the wind erosion which brings the dust storm or the spectacular gully erosion, to the less noticeable sheet erosion which each year removes a thin film of topsoil from farms until finally all of the topsoil has gone, and the farmer is left pouring fertilizers and dollars into barren subsoil.

SOIL CONSERVATION — The most important step in soil conservation is first to hold the soil in place. If the soil remains, its other qualities can be improved. If it has washed or blown away, nothing more can be done. There are many ways of preventing erosion which can be summed up in one term: intelligent land use. In detail, they can be broken down into two major categories: mechanical or engineering methods, and biological methods.

ENGINEERING METHODS — Of the engineering techniques, the first and most basic is to adapt cultivation to the contours of the land. The square field and the straight-plowed furrow have a place only on flat land. Unfortunately, our land-subdivision system has favored the square or rectangular field, and our past plowing practices have favored the straight furrow for economy of effort (p. 122). It is now generally realized, if not always practiced, that when sloping ground must be cultivated cultivation should follow the contour of the land. *Contour plowing* is a first step toward keeping soil from washing downhill. When the furrows follow the contour of a slope, each furrow acts as a check dam and reservoir to prevent water from following its normal course downhill (p. 122). Excess runoff can be accommodated in grassed-over waterways or natural drainage channels.

Where slopes are greater and the danger of soil loss higher, contour cultivation needs to be supplemented by *terracing*. The flat terraces of the Far East or the old Incan lands are not suited to the farm machinery of today. In their place a broad-based contour terrace has been developed that permits contour cultivation (p. 123). Behind the terrace a channel forms, which should usually be maintained in sod. This leads excess water into diversion ditches or channels that permit adequate drainage.

If erosion in the form of sheet erosion, wind erosion, or rill erosion (the incipient beginnings of gullies) is present, contour treatment of the land will help to halt it. Where gullies have cut into the land, however, they must be reclaimed. In the absence of reclamation, gullies work up hill, biting deeper into otherwise well-managed farm land. Mechanical methods of gully control involving damming are a first step. Usually, biological methods of revegetation must also be applied (p. 117). In some instances old gullies have been dammed and converted into farm ponds.

BIOLOGICAL METHODS — Biological methods of erosion control are those making primary use of organisms rather than of tools and mechanical equipment. These methods are an attempt to provide through the manipulation of domesticated plants the same degree of soil protection formerly provided by natural vegetation. One biological method of erosion control on sloping ground

EROSION

Wind erosion. (**a**) Deserts spread on the Sahara margin when wind erosion follows overgrazing. **Water erosion.** (**b**) Gullies grow and spread, threatening the remaining wheat fields. (**c**) Severe gullying from water runoff in Iowa. (**d**) The same area following gully stabilization measures.

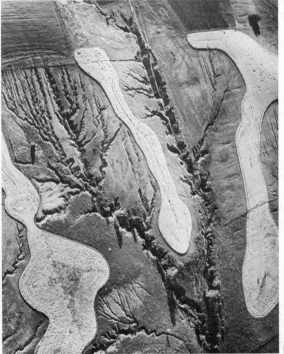

c

d

is *strip cropping,* the alternation of grain or other crops which give little soil protection with strips of close-grown leaf crops or grass sod, which give more adequate protection (p. 123). Where grass or legume strips are alternated with crops, the soil structure, organic content, and nitrogen content may also be improved. Strip cropping is often combined with contour cultivation, or where necessary, terracing.

Where wind erosion has proved serious, shelter belts are useful. Such shelter belts consist of plantings of shrubs and trees in windbreaking barriers along the windward edges of croplands (p. 122). During the conservation-conscious days of the late 1930's, shelter belts were widely planted across the Great Plains to break the wind velocity.

One of the most important factors to consider in preventing water erosion is the destructive force of rain drops. Rain falling on bare soil breaks up structure and bounces soil particles high in the air. These are caught by water running over the ground and are carried down hill. Without the impact of rain drops on the soil, runoff removes surface particles only. With rain drops new particles are continually being broken loose and added to the soil carried away. Natural vegetation and ground litter break the force of rain and prevent its impact on the bare soil. Many crop plants, however, do not provide this protection. One method, therefore, of preventing erosion is to keep crop litter and crop residues on the surface of the ground instead of turning them under in plowing. Special subsurface tillers have been developed which break up and loosen the soil without turning under the litter. Where this is not sufficient, the direct addition of mulches or plant remains to cover the soil surface may provide the necessary protection.

Crop rotation, where it involves the alternation of soil-conserving crops, such as legumes or grass, with other crops also serves as an effective measure of erosion control, both through giving more complete protection during the period when the grasses or legumes are present and through improving the soil structure. Manuring and the use of other organic wastes also help in preventing erosion through improvement of soil structure.

MAINTAINING SOIL FERTILITY The final step in soil conservation to be discussed is the maintenance of soil fertility. A decrease in soil fertility may be masked by increased crop yields brought about by improved varieties of crop plants.[13] A high yield per acre may mean a much greater output of carbohydrates per acre but can disguise a reduced output of proteins, vitamins, and essential minerals.[1] Measured in terms of energy units (calories) produced, the increased yields are comforting. But man does not live by calories alone and is selling himself short if increased yields do not mean increased nutrition.

Many studies have now been carried out to show the effects of soil fertility on wild and experimental animals. Crops grown on more fertile soil, although similar in appearance, give higher growth rates, stronger bones, and increased reproductive rates when fed to animals than those from less fertile soils. A greater number of animals per acre and a greater average body weight per individual can be supported on fertile soils.[22] Experiments show that a lack of nutritional balance, such as a decrease in calcium relative to potassium or calcium relative to phosphorus, can have serious effects on animal nutrition, even where total plant growth is not affected. The absence of a single trace element such as cobalt once rendered large areas of range in Australia useless for livestock production. Addition of minute amounts of this element through a top-dressing of fertilizer has brought this range into livestock production.

Vitamin, mineral, and protein deficiencies where severe enough to take the form of human deficiency diseases are easily recognized. Where they simply add to a general, slow decline in health and vitality, they are less apparent. It is nevertheless a sufficiently serious matter for every citizen, no matter how far he may be removed from the land, to concern himself with the conservation practices which produced the food that he buys.

Many of the techniques described above are also of value in maintaining soil fertility. Techniques that maintain soil structure also prevent the excessive leaching of soil nutrients. Crop rotation, the planting of legumes and grass, and the addition of animal manures and plant remains to the soil are valuable techniques. The balanced use of chemical fertilizers, based on careful study of soil chemistry and soil needs, can help to compensate for the drain from agricultural crops. In extreme cases, complete rest from crop production under some type of soil-restoring cover may be necessary.

The techniques of conservation farming cannot be described adequately in a textbook of environmental conservation. Each piece of land is different and has its own peculiar problems. For most farmers in the United States, however, technical advice and knowledge is readily available through the offices of the Soil Conservation Service or the county farm advisers maintained by the state land-grant colleges and universities. Ignorance is now rarely an adequate excuse for the misuse of land.

LAND CLASSIFICATION AND USE   The first step toward sound land use and soil conservation is land classification. Throughout the world, marginal-land farmers have attempted to squeeze a living from lands not suited to commercial crop production and have ruined the lands in the process. Elsewhere in areas otherwise suited to farming, the agricultural machinery is too often run over acres that were best put to some other use. Such areas are poor producers and can serve as focal points for damage that will spread later to the better lands. With proper classification of lands, such misuse can be avoided.

In an effort to see that land is treated according to its capabilities, the Soil Conservation Service has worked out a detailed land-classification system.[15,16,37] This takes into account the soil types, slope and drainage of the land, the erodibility and rockiness of the soil, and all other factors which influence the capability of the land. Although the complete system is elaborate, its principal features are shown in modified form in Table 5. In soil-conservation districts, the Soil Conservation Service is prepared to work out a land classification and use plan for each farmer who requests it (p. 121). Outside of the soil-conservation districts, other

TABLE 5
Land-capability Classification

LAND CLASS	LAND-CAPABILITY AND USE PRECAUTIONS	PRIMARY USES	SECONDARY USES
	Group I. Lands Suitable for Cultivation		
I.	Excellent land, flat, well drained. Suited to agriculture with no special precautions other than good farming practice.	Agriculture	Recreation Wildlife Pasture
II.	Good land with minor limitations such as slight slope, sandy soils, or poor drainage. Suited to agriculture with precautions such as contour farming, strip cropping, drainage, etc.	Agriculture Pasture	Recreation Wildlife
III.	Moderately good land with important limitations caused by soil, slope, or drainage. Requires long rotation with soil-building crops, contouring or terracing, strip cropping or drainage, etc.	Agriculture Pasture Watershed	Recreation Wildlife Urban-industrial
IV.	Fair land with severe limitations caused by soil, slope or drainage. Suited only to occasional or limited cultivation.	Pasture Tree crops Agriculture Urban-industrial	Recreation Wildlife Watershed
	Group II. Lands Not Suitable for Cultivation		
V.	Land suited to forestry or grazing without special precautions other than normal good management.	Forestry Range Watershed	Recreation Wildlife
VI.	Suited to forestry or grazing with minor limitations caused by danger from erosion, shallow soils, etc. Requires careful management.	Forestry Range Watershed Urban-industrial	Recreation Wildlife
VII.	Suited to grazing or forestry with major limitations caused by slope, low rainfall, soil, etc. Use must be limited, and extreme care taken.	Watershed Recreation Wildlife Forestry Range Urban-industrial	
VIII.	Unsuited to grazing or forestry because of absence of soil, steep slopes, extreme dryness or wetness.	Recreation Wildlife Watershed Urban-industrial	

Source. Modified from land-classification system of U.S. Soil Conservation Service, Department of Agriculture. (From Wohletz and Dolder, 1952.)
Note: The Use columns in particular depart from the usual SCS form.

CLASS VII LAND

CLASS VIII LAND

CLASS VII LAND

CLASS VI LAND

CLASS IV LAND

CLASS II LAND

CLASS V LAND

CLASS I LAND

CLASS III LAND

Land classified according to capabilities.

agencies such as the Agricultural Extension Services are usually willing to perform a similar service or to provide the information on which such a system can be based. With a classification worked out, the farmer not only can put his best lands to work but also knows what conservation measures are required to maintain all of his lands in top condition.

LAND ZONING AND ENVIRONMENTAL CONSERVATION[40]

A second step in conservation planning follows after land classification and becomes a community responsibility. This step is land zoning, supported by adequate legislation, to prevent the misuse of land. Anyone familiar with the population expansion in the state of California or in the urbanized area of the East Coast following World War II has seen the consequences which follow on lack of zoning and planning. There is a normal tendency for cities to expand along lines of least resistance into lands, level and clear of heavy vegetation, on which housing or industrial construction can be carried out at minimum cost. Such lands, unfortunately, are usually also the high-value farmlands. City lots can always compete in price, if not in real value, with agricultural use of the same land. City taxes, extended to farm land, can force the most resistant farmer out of business. Industries, airports, and superhighways are all equally effective at forcing the farmer off his land. Into the orange groves of the Los Angeles basin and the cherry orchards of the Santa Clara Valley, suburban housing has moved like a crop-destroying blight. Fruit growing and crop production is forced into marginal areas of less suit-

a

SOIL CONSERVATION

(**a**) Shelter belts in the Middle West to reduce wind erosion. (**b**) Contour cultivation. (**c**) Strip cropping. (**d**) Terraced farmland.

b

c

d

able soil. That the houses might more attractively and fittingly be built on lands poorly suited to agriculture is a form of common sense difficult to hear when "money talks." Some states have taken steps to protect farmlands from urbanization and forest lands from misguided farming efforts by laws that encourage the assessment of land according to its use rather than its value if sold for real estate development, that give other forms of tax relief to farmers who choose to keep their lands in productive agriculture, and that encourage counties to zone according to land capability.[40] In most instances, however, local zoning has not held up against severe economic pressure, and it is difficult to keep a man farming the land when by selling to a developer he could make more than he might expect in ten or more years of farming effort. Whether better effects would be achieved were the state governments to take zoning power from local communities is debatable. To date, direct land purchase by the state or local government, purchase of development rights, or purchase with leaseback to a lessee who will use the land for the desired purpose have been the principal methods which have proved effective in controlling land use. Much, therefore, remains to be done to guarantee that lands will be used in accordance with the best planning principles. In England, where the situation has been particularly severe, a National Town and Country Planning Act was adopted after World War II. This gave the national government restrictive control over land use, and was the instrument used in accomplishing the establishment of a green belt around London and of new towns located beyond the green belt. However, even this has not been entirely effective, and Great Britain still suffers from urban-industrial encroachment into agricultural lands and other open space.

A final step toward the planning of conservation on agricultural and other lands must be the realization that we can no longer afford single-purpose use of extensive areas. Croplands of good quality must be reserved primarily for crop production. Such farming use of these primary agricultural lands necessarily rules out for much of the year most other land uses. However, even the best farming region has lands not suited to crop production, for example, roadways, streamsides, rock outcrops, and steep slopes. If the entire landscape is to be considered in an environmental approach to conservation, these waste areas need attention and development also. Properly cared for they can provide recreation space, retreats for wildlife, sources of timber and range forage, or simply add to rural beauty. Uncared for they become garbage dumps or sources of disruption of the whole land complex. If rural living is to remain a part of the American scene, its quality must be considered. The elements that once lent a wholeness to rural life, firmly established in our national background and culture, must be retained or regained. Rural factories grinding out cash crops at the expense of human values may feed an excess of people but cannot provide the qualities that make life worthwhile.

CHAPTER REFERENCES

Bennett, Hugh H., 1955. *Elements of soil conservation.* McGraw-Hill, New York.

Dale, Tom, and V. G. Carter, 1955. *Topsoil and civilization.* University of Oklahoma Press, Norman, Oklahoma.

Graham, Edward H., 1944. *Natural principles of land use.* Oxford, New York.

Jacks, G. V., 1954. *Soil.* Philosophical Library, New York.

Oosting, Henry J., 1956. *The study of plant communities.* W. H. Freeman, San Francisco.

UNESCO, 1970. *Use and conservation of the biosphere.* Natural Resources Research X, UNESCO, Paris.

United States Department of Agriculture, 1957. *Soil.* The yearbook of agriculture, Washington, D.C.

Woodbury, Angus M., 1954. *Principles of general ecology.* Blakiston, New York.

LITERATURE CITED

1. Albrecht, William A., 1956. Physical, chemical and biochemical changes in the soil community. (See Thomas, 1956.)

2. Aubert, G., F. Fournier, and V. Rozanov, 1970. *Soils and the maintenance of their fertility as factors affecting the choice of use of land. Use and conservation of the biosphere.* Natural Resources Research X, UNESCO, Paris.

3. Bamesberger, John G., 1939. *Erosion losses from a 3-day California storm.* United States Department of Agriculture Soil Conservation Service.

4. Bartelli, Lindo, 1966. General soil maps—a study of landscapes. *Jour. Soil and Water Conservation,* 21: 3–6.

5. Bennett, Hugh H., 1955. *Elements of soil conservation.* McGraw-Hill, New York.

6. Borgstrom, Georg, 1965. *The hungry planet.* Macmillan, New York.

7. Brown, Lester R., and E. P. Eckholm, 1974. *By bread alone.* Praeger, New York.

8. Dale, Tom, and V. G. Carter, 1955. *Topsoil and civilization.* University of Oklahoma Press, Norman, Oklahoma.

9. D'Hoore, J. L., 1964. *La carte des sols d'Afrique au 1/5.000.000. Mémoire explicatif.* Commission de Coopération Technique en Afrique, Lagos, Nigeria.

10. Ellis, B. S., 1947. A guide to some Rhodesian soils. *Rhodesian Agricultural Journal,* 44 (3): 197–210.

11. Finch, V. C., and G. T. Trewartna, 1942. *Elements of geography, Physical and cultural.* McGraw-Hill, New York.

12. Fournier, F., 1963. The soils of Africa. *A review of the natural resources of the African continent,* pp. 221–248. Unesco. Natural Resources Research—1. UNESCO, Paris.

13. Fraser Darling, Frank, 1955. *West highland survey: an essay in human ecology.* Oxford University Press, Oxford.

14. Gourou, Pierre, 1966. *The tropical world.* Wiley, New York. Fourth edition.

15. Graham, Edward H., 1944. *Natural principles of land use.* Oxford, New York.

16. Hockensmith, R. D., and J. G. Steele, 1943. *Classifying land for conservation farming.* United States Department of Agriculture, Farmer's Bull., 1853, Washington, D.C.

17. Jacks, G. V., 1954. *Soil.* Philosophical Library, New York.

18. Jacks, G. V., and R. O. Whyte, 1939. *Vanishing lands.* Doubleday, Doran, New York.

19. Kovda, V. A., 1965. The need for international cooperation in soil science. *Nature and Resources,* 1 (3): 10–16, UNESCO, Paris.
20. Leopold, A. Starker, 1959. *Wildlife of Mexico.* University of California Press, Berkeley.
21. Leopold, Luna B., 1956. Land use and sediment yield. (See Thomas, 1956.)
22. Nagel, Werner O., ed., 1952. *Wildlife and the soil.* Missouri Conservation Comm., Jefferson City, Missouri.
23. Oosting, Henry J., 1956. *The study of plant communities.* W. H. Freeman, San Francisco.
24. Richards, P. W., 1961. The types of vegetation of the humid tropics in relation to the soil. *Tropical soils and vegetation,* pp. 15–20. Humid tropics research. UNESCO, Paris.
25. Richards, P. W., 1952. *The tropical rain forest.* Cambridge University, Cambridge, U. K.
26. Shantz, H. L., and R. Zon, 1924. *Atlas of American agriculture.* United States Department of Agriculture, Washington, D.C.
27. Smith, F. B. et al., 1967. *Principal soil areas of Florida. A supplement to the general soil map.* University of Florida, Agricultural Experiment Station, Bull. 717.
28. Snyder, J. H., 1966. New program for agricultural land use stabilization: the California land conservation act of 1965. *Land economics,* 42: 29–41.
29. Soil Conservation Service, 1955. *Facts about wind erosion and dust storms on the Great Plains.* Leaflet 394. United States Department of Agriculture, Washington, D.C.
30. Tedrow, J. C. F., 1970. Soils of the subarctic regions. *Ecology of the subarctic regions.* Ecology and Conservation, 1; UNESCO, Paris.
31. Thornthwaite, C. W., 1956. The modification of rural microclimates. (See Thomas, 1956.)
32. United States Department of Agriculture, 1957. *Soil.* The yearbook of agriculture. Washington.
33. United States Department of Agriculture and Department of Housing and Urban Development, 1967. *Soil, water, and suburbia.* Washington, D.C.
34. Vogt, William, 1948. *Road to survival.* Wm. Sloane, New York.
35. Waksman, Selman A., 1952. *Soil microbiology.* Wiley, New York.
36. Wieslander, A., and R. Earl Storie, 1952. The vegetation-soil survey in California and its use in the management of wild lands for yield of timber, forage, and water. *Jour. Forestry,* 50: 521–526.
37. Wohletz, L., and E. Dolder, 1952. *Know California's land.* California Department of Natural Resources, Sacramento, California.
38. Woodbury, Angus M., 1954. *Principles of general ecology.* Blakiston, New York.
39. Wright, A. C. S., and J. Bennema, 1965. *The soil resources of Latin America.* World Soil Resources Reports, 18. FAO, Rome.
40. Zimmerman, G. K., 1966. Meeting urbanization and resource pressures in rural America. *Trans. North American Wildlife Conference,* Wildlife Management Institute, Washington, D.C.

6

civilization and water

Water has the peculiar quality of being an inexhaustible natural resource which is nevertheless in short supply. In the broad sense there is not and in the foreseeable future will not be a water shortage. Water in the oceans, the atmosphere, and falling on the land is more than adequate to meet all human needs now and in times to come. However, water of usable quantity and quality, present in the right place at the right time, is not inexhaustible. It is a renewable resource, but one for which in many areas of the world the demand is far greater than the supply. Water shortages are becoming increasingly a problem of western civilization. In earlier times people first looked to the water supply before attempting to settle in an area. Modern man too often settles in a desert and demands that water be brought to him, or he settles in a floodplain and demands that water be kept away.

The rise of civilization came with the ability to manage the floods and irrigation waters of the river basins of the Old World. Western industrial civilization, more than any preceding it, demands water. Industries engaged in processing raw materials require vast quantities of water for their functioning, and could not grow or be maintained without the ability to obtain these quantities from streams or underground water sources. Cities could not have reached their present size without drawing water from distant hills and mountains, the watersheds from which rainfall drains into the lakes and rivers. If our ability to manage water falls short, the entire framework of civilized life is threatened.

THE LOS ANGELES STORY An example of the unbalanced distribution of population and water supply characteristic of the western world is provided by the coastal plain of southern California. Here on one-eighth the area of California live more than half the people. Los Angeles alone is the second largest city in the United States. The warm, dry mediterranean climate, with its prospects for outdoor living throughout the year, the miles of bathing beaches and recreational grounds, and the employment offered by industry have attracted people from afar. Early in the twentieth century the motion-picture industry moved to the Los Angeles area, attracted by the clear air and the climate conditions favorable for year-round open-air photography. The air is no longer clear, but the industry remains in a diminished state. Aircraft and other industries, since attracted to the region, have provided employment for the people and have, in turn, attracted more people.

The same climate which brings people to southern California does not bring water. The rainfall may be between 10 and 20 inches annually, on the average, over most of the coastal plain and only reaches a more adequate 30 to 40 inches in restricted areas of the higher coastal mountains. The rainfall is erratic, dry cycles alternating with wet, and much of the annual rainfall may come in a few gully-washing storms. The area receives less than 1.5 percent of the state's total water. By contrast the sparsely peopled northwest coast of California receives more than 38 percent of the total rainfall.[10]

Water problems are not new in southern California and cannot be related entirely to misuse of the land. Between 1769, when the Spanish first arrived, and 1955 there were an estimated 25 major floods, alternating with long periods of drought and crop failure.[17] In the late nineteenth century an effort was made to bring the local water supply under reasonable control through the construction of dams and aqueducts and through the placing of timber and brush-covered mountains in federal forest reserves for the protection of the watershed cover. Underground water supplies were tapped by drilling numerous deep wells.

By the early 1900's it was realized local water supplies were inadequate for the growing population. Los Angeles city began to reach out for water, first to the Sierra Nevada in the north. After much controversy with the local residents, Los Angeles obtained control of the Owens River watershed, draining the east slope of the Sierra 250 miles away. A great aqueduct carried the first water from this region to Los Angeles in 1913. With further population growth, this supply proved inadequate, and the city reached farther north to tap the Mono Lake watershed in the period between 1934 and 1940. Realizing that even this supply would be insufficient, Los Angeles next looked to the waters draining from the western slopes of the Rocky Mountains into the Colorado River. In 1933 work was begun to impound the Colorado at Parker Dam, 155 miles south of Hoover Dam (p. 137), and to carry this water across the desert 242 miles to Lake Matthews in southern California.[17,29]

Other southern California cities and communities, faced with similar problems, have engaged in equally heroic efforts. In all, an estimated sum of more than 7000 million dollars has been spent in an attempt to solve California's water problems. Yet they are not solved. With ever-growing populations, southern California has had to look still further afield. In 1951 a project was approved to bring water from Feather River in the north Sierra Nevada through some 567 miles of conduits to the south. As part of the California state water plan the Feather, the Trinity, and other northern rivers are being tapped to provide water for urban populations and irrigation farming in the drier southern regions of the state. However, the end is not in sight as yet, and plans exist for channeling water from the Columbia River southward.

In many places throughout the United States, similar water problems have developed. Good farming soils, good industrial sites, and centers for trade or commerce often fail to coincide with dependable year-round water supplies. Populations grow and water demands increase.

The alternative to bringing water over great distances to these areas could lie in locating industry and in encouraging people to settle in areas where water is abundant, while limiting growth in areas where it is scarce. This approach, however, has not been seriously tried in the United States.

THE HYDROLOGIC CYCLE Water-conservation problems are unusually complex and are too often approached with simple solutions which are ineffective or even disastrous. The conservation of water requires the best efforts of those concerned with the conservation of all biotic resources and also draws on the specialized knowledge of hydrologists, geologists, and engineers to an extent that few other renewable resources require. To begin to understand the nature of the problems it is necessary to examine the hydrologic cycle (Fig. 6–1), the cycle through which water moves from ocean to atmosphere to land and back to the oceans, and to consider the many and complex uses to which it may be put along the way.

The source of most of the rain which falls on the land ultimately is the ocean. Air masses lying long over the seas pick up large quantities of water through evaporation. When they move inward over the conti-

FIG. 6–1. The hydrologic cycle.

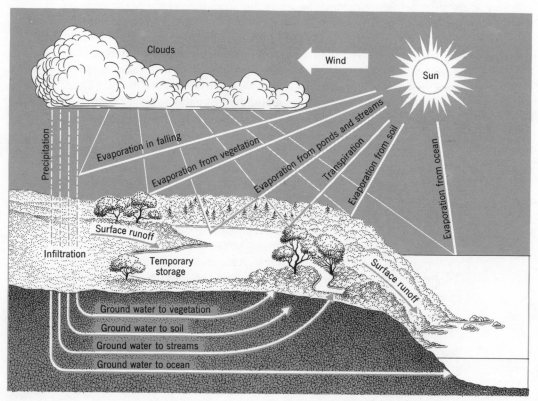

nents, much of this water falls out as precipitation. The movement of air masses, which to a large extent controls climate and weather, is and probably will remain a natural phenomenon over which man has little or no control. The timing and distribution of rainfall may be affected in the future by human activities as techniques for inducing precipitation are improved; however, it is likely dry climates will remain dry and man will remain unable to squeeze water from a dry air mass. Indeed, the ecological consequences of any massive attempt at weather control are so enormous and potentially dangerous that the writer hopes that we will move slowly in this direction and only after the most rigorous research. We cannot afford the kinds of blunders we have already made in the use of atomic energy or in the careless application of pesticides to the land.

When water first reaches the ground in mountain areas in the form of rain, snow, sleet, hail, or surface condensation, it becomes useful to man. Falling on areas covered with natural vegetation it provides the soil water from which forests and range grasses must grow. Combined in vegetation it provides timber or forage for livestock or wildlife. The excess, running off the surface or sinking in the ground to reappear in springs or as base flow in streams, again becomes useful, providing drinking water for livestock and game and habitats for fish and aquatic life. Meanwhile much is returned to the air by evaporation from vegetation, soil, streams, lakes, or rivers, and by transpiration from the vegetation of the area, and this is returned once more to the ground in further precipitation in other areas. Another portion has gone deep into the ground and has moved downhill slowly through aquifers—underground strata of porous rock or sediments not yet consolidated into rock. This groundwater may later reappear as base flow into streams, lakes, or ponds, maintaining the flow or level of these bodies of water during the dry season when surface runoff is no longer available. Groundwater may also travel further to lie under the valleys, perhaps to keep their soils saturated and give rise to meadow or marsh or perhaps to lie deeper and provide soil water in the dry seasons or feed the deeper-rooted plants. The depth to which it is necessary to go to find saturated ground is known as the depth to the *water table*. Water tables in the lowlands are maintained by water seeping into the ground in the hills and mountains. Still other quantities of groundwater may remain for long periods in underground storage, until tapped by wells.

Water falling on farmland follows a similar course. Sinking into the soil, it provides the water from which crops are made. In the process much is transpired or evaporated back into the air. If the amount of rainfall is great and the ground porous, some water sinks through to add to underground supplies. Some will run off to add to stream flow and eventually will reach the ocean.

In the larger rivers and streams, water can supply transportation for people and their products. It also provides for additional fisheries and, everywhere it lies in quantity, water provides recreation. People have

TABLE 6
Where the Water Is:
Distribution in the
Biosphere[32]

LOCATION	VOLUME IN CUBIC MILES	PERCENTAGE OF TOTAL
Oceans	317,000,000	97.2
Glaciers and ice caps	7,000,000	2.1
Groundwater	2,000,000	0.6
Saltwater lakes and inland seas	25,000	0.01
Freshwater lakes	30,000	0.01
Soil water	16,000	0.01
Atmosphere	3,100	—
Stream beds	300	—
Total	326,000,000	100.00

Note: It has been estimated by Vernadsky that an additional amount of water approximately equal to that in the oceans may be bound in chemical or physical combinations in the rocks of the earth's crust.

always been attracted to stream or lakeside for rest and pleasure. They may seek only the scenery and beauty the water provides; they may seek the joys of fishing; or perhaps swimming, boating, and related sports will attract them. Where the water in the biosphere is located at any one time is indicated in Table 6. The rate at which it moves in the cycle is shown in Table 7.

With the growth of civilization the course of waters has been changed from the simple original pattern. Water running from the mountains in streams is impounded behind dams. From here it may be led into irrigation canals to provide water for dry but otherwise fertile lands on which crops can be grown. It may be diverted into aqueducts and carried to meet the needs of towns and cities, or it may be used to provide electric power.

Water that reaches population centers is put to greatest use. It must first meet the living needs of the people, to provide drinking, cooking, and washing water. It is used to suppress city fires, to wash down streets, and to water lawns and gardens. It provides a means of disposing of waste products, from sewage to the vast quantities of waste created by industry. It must be used in industrial production, the processing of foods, the milling of timber, and the manufacture of countless products used by humanity.

Excess water must also be coped with. Dams and levees are constructed to reduce floods. Drainage ditches and canals are built to remove excess waters from otherwise adequate farming lands.

Most who deplore the demands made by civilization on water supplies are still not willing to forego the benefits that civilization has brought. Yet the problems have become severe. Each portion of the hydrologic cycle and each use that we make of the water present us with new dilemmas. That these dilemmas result from the way in which we have organized our societies more than from the way nature has organized the water cycle is a truth yet to be widely appreciated.

TABLE 7
How the Water Flows:
Movement in the
Cycle[18]

	GAIN (CUBIC KILOMETERS)	LOSS (CUBIC KILOMETERS)
OCEANS		
Gain		
From precipitation	411,600	
From runoff	37,300	
Loss		
From evaporation		448,900
CONTINENTS: PERIPHERAL AREAS		
Gain		
From precipitation	101,000	
Loss		
From runoff		37,300
From evaporation		63,700
CONTINENTS: LANDLOCKED AREAS		
Gain		
From precipitation	7,400	
Loss		
From evaporation		7,400

WATER NEEDS
AND PROBLEMS

URBAN
WATER SUPPLIES

Water that reaches a city should be clean and pure. Water that leaves a city is often dangerously contaminated. The provision of adequate supplies can be difficult; the disposal of wastes is sometimes more difficult. These are generalizations which need qualification. In much of the heavily populated part of the world today the water that reaches a city is often contaminated and the water leaving it is even more contaminated. The more technologically advanced cities have installed elaborate water-purifying plants for removing the various pollutants from water and for rendering it reasonably safe for human consumption. In less advanced areas the people take their chances and pay the costs in health. However, few people, except those living high on the watersheds, or in unpopulated areas, have the privilege of drinking "new" water, fresh from the air or from the ground and uncontaminated by previous use. For most city dwellers the water used has been used before —it has gone through somebody's kidneys or somebody's industries before reaching the urban water supply.

Water uses can be classified as consumptive or nonconsumptive. Consumptive uses lead to direct loss of water from the useful part of the hydrological cycle, either through evaporation, or through incorporation of it in some other substance such as animal or plant tissues or industrial products. Most urban-industrial uses are relatively nonconsumptive. Thus Kalinin and Bykov have estimated one-sixth of the water used for domestic purposes and one-tenth used for industrial purposes is consumed. The rest is restored to streams or underground storage for further use, although at the present time usually in a contaminated state.[18]

The amount of water used in urban-industrial processes is large. Landsberg has calculated for 1964 that each urban resident in the United States used 110 gallons of water per day.[20] Of this, 60 gallons was used in the home for gardening, air cooling, laundry, cooking, bathing, washing, and drinking (the latter amounting to 1 gallon per day). An additional 26 gallons per day were used in restaurants or offices and 25 gallons were used for community services such as fire suppression, street cleaning, parks, and the like. For 1970 Eisenbud reports the per capita use of water in New York to be 150 gallons per day.[12] Industries, however, use much greater amounts. Borgstrom has therefore calculated the average person in the United States uses 1500 to 2000 gallons per day, primarily in domestic and industrial processes.[3] This does not account for the amounts used in agriculture or in the production of wild vegetation and animal life. He quotes Soviet estimates that any person in a modern, technological society requires 720 gallons of water per day. The demands of industry are considerable. It takes 30 to 60 tons of water to refine one ton of petroleum; 900 to 1000 tons to produce one ton of newsprint, and 2500 to 3000 tons to produce a ton of synthetic rubber.[32] Power production through use of fossil fuels, in thermal electric power plants, uses more water than any other category of use except irrigation. However, the water requirements, for cooling purposes, of the new nuclear power plants are far greater (see Table 8).

The extent to which a city will go to meet its domestic and industrial water needs has been exemplified by Los Angeles. Other problems which may be encountered in the drier parts of the world are pointed up by the experience of another California city, Santa Barbara. Santa Barbara is built on a narrow, coastal plain backed up by high, chaparral-covered mountains. From early days it has had difficulty in obtaining water. In 1920, Gibraltar Dam was built on the Santa Ynez River in the mountains behind the city, and water from the reservoir was carried through the mountains in a tunnel four miles long (p. 136). Shortly after the dam was built it became obvious the reservoir was filling with silt and losing its storage capacity. To stop silting, two additional dams, Mono and Caliente, were built upstream (p. 136). Within two years their reservoirs were completely filled with silt and debris. In 1946 to 1947 siltation had reduced the capacity of Gibraltar reservoir to one-half, and it was nec-

TABLE 8
Expected World
Demands for Water:
2000 A.D.[18]

| FORM OF USE | WATER REQUIRED (CUBIC KILOMETERS) | |
	TOTAL	AMOUNT LOST IN USE (EVAPORATION)
Irrigation	7,000	4,800
Domestic	600	100
Industrial	1,700	170
Dilution of wastes	9,000	—
Other	400	400
Total	18,700	5,470
Total available supply: 37,300 cubic kilometers.		

essary to build the dam higher. In 1948 a severe water shortage hit the city and caused great restrictions and inconvenience. To obtain additional supplies a new and larger dam, Cachuma Dam, has been completed on the Santa Ynez River below Gibraltar Dam.[17] The expense of all of this construction has been considerable, and yet no permanent solution has been achieved if population and industrial growth are to continue.

The Santa Barbara problem is one shared by many arid regions. The watershed cover in the mountains is highly inflammable. Despite extreme efforts at protection, including the closing of the entire watershed to public use during the dry season, fires start and sweep over vast acreage. Burned over slopes erode badly, and the resulting debris fills reservoirs (p. 137).

Thus the provision of adequate water to a city involves the careful management of vegetation in sometimes distant mountains. Such watershed management must include the prevention of erosion with consequent siltation and also the provision of optimum quantities of usable water. Natural vegetation, while maintaining soil, preventing erosion, and regulating runoff from watersheds, can also be a source of much water loss through water transpired from leaf surfaces. Some transpiration is an unavoidable cost of the protection and other values vegetation provides. However, there is much difference in the amounts of water transpired by different types of vegetation. Replacement of one type by another could be one way to increase water yields from a watershed without loss of benefits provided by well-covered hillsides. Where the natural vegetation, like chaparral, is highly inflammable, the danger of fire and resulting erosion loss could be minimized where it could be replaced by a less inflammable type. The danger in such management, however, comes when one set of values such as high water yield is placed above all others such as timber, forage, wildlife, and recreation values which may contribute to an enrichment of the lives of people in the area concerned.

In the humid eastern United States it was once thought any serious water crisis would be unlikely. In the early 1960's, however, New York and other eastern seaboard cities faced water shortages which only partially could be blamed on a series of below-average rainfall years. Mostly the water problem was the result of blundering in the management of water to a degree that seemed to reflect a serious inability to plan for the future. At the worst of the drought, the Hudson River continued to flow past New York City, much as before. Its water, however, was too dangerously and heavily polluted to be considered for the city water supply, since the means for purifying it had not been installed, and the possibility of bringing any quick control to pollution was remote. New York used over a billion gallons of water per day but, since it had long been believed water would remain abundant, there was no control over individual use. New Yorkers paid a flat rate for water and the amount used was not metered. Furthermore, the aqueducts and mains

WATER AND WATERSHEDS

(**a**) Gibraltar reservoir near Santa Barbara. The steep, chaparral-covered slopes erode readily when fire removes the vegetation. (**b**) Mono reservoir near Santa Barbara. This dam was built to stop silt from flowing into Gibraltar reservoir. In this 1938 picture the area behind the dam had completely silted in. (**c**) In this 1949 picture the old reservoir site had grown an open woodland. (**d**) Before a brush fire burned the area in the southern California mountains enclosed by the dotted line, a single storm drain handled the runoff in this orchard. (**e**) Following the fire in 1941, runoff from a light rain filled the orchard with debris. (**f**) Hoover Dam on the Colorado River, part of the system that provides Los Angeles with water.

d

e

f

that supplied water to the city were found initially to be wasting water through numerous leaks.[12,15,22]

South from New York in the nation's capital, the drought forced Washingtonians to take a hard look at the Potomac. It was found to be seriously polluted and flowing at a dangerously low level. It was unsafe for swimming and could be made safe for urban use only after expensive purification. A major campaign to clean up the Potomac was initiated by the federal government with a view to having a river fit for recreational use. Even Rock Creek, flowing through the capital's famous Rock Creek Park, was so polluted from seepage from septic tanks and other sources that it was unsafe for children to wade in. By 1970, water pollution control had become a major national issue to which Congress and the Administration were devoting major attention. It was realized that an expenditure of 40 billion dollars over a ten-year period might be required to bring the nation's rivers back to, not their original purity, but a reasonably clean condition.

To meet urban-industrial water requirements in semiarid and arid lands today, a variety of approaches may be required. Manipulation of vegetation on the watersheds is one that has already been discussed. However, to be available at need, water must be stored in some way, and surface reservoirs have been the usual approach to this problem. Such reservoirs, however, suffer from siltation, which cuts down their useful life and storage capacity, from pollution of their waters, and from serious problems of evaporation that can remove a high percentage of their water. Some success in retarding siltation and pollution has been achieved, although in very few places, as a result of careful management and regulation of use in the watersheds. Evaporation losses have been reduced by the use of films of heavy alcohols such as hexadecanol, which are floated on the surface of the reservoir. For small ponds, these films can be quite effective, but for large reservoirs, subject to mixing and churning by wind, they are relatively ineffective. Attempts have also been made to increase water yields and to cut down on siltation by sealing off the soil on small watersheds by the use of asphalt, plastic sheets, silicone resins, or even rubber sheets. As yet, these efforts have been confined to small areas, but they do produce remarkable results. The only problem is that virtually all other values in the lands of the watershed are sacrificed to the single purpose of water production. This seldom can be justified.

An approach to urban water storage that has high merit is the one that makes use of underground reservoirs. Water is allowed to soak or is pumped into natural aquifers beneath the ground, and is held in these permeable layers of rock or of alluvial materials. Most natural underground supplies, in areas of high water demand, have been depleted. Indeed, excessive pumping of underground water has in some areas caused a sinking of the land surface and in coastal regions has often led to an invasion of the aquifers by saltwater from the sea. Recharging aquifers by pumping in freshwater, during times of high rainfall and runoff, or by holding runoff where it can soak into the aquifers through permeable soil, not only restores the underground supplies but is a way of keeping water where it will not be subject to siltation or evaporation, and where, with care, it can be kept free from pollution.

WASTE DISPOSAL The disposal of sewage and other wastes produced by human activities is a problem which has confronted the human race since populations first concentrated in towns and cities. Satisfactory solutions were seldom attained. Conditions in ancient Rome have been described by Lewis Mumford. Despite the engineering skills of the Romans and their inclination toward plumbing, most people lived under highly unsanitary conditions, and some of their refuse dumps were still highly obnoxious when excavated more than 1000 years later.[28] Nevertheless neither Rome nor any other ancient city had much effect on the total environment. The quantity of water, air, and land available to dilute and break down waste products was sufficient to rule out any more than local pollution problems.

Sir Arthur Bryant has described the conditions of pollution in London during the seventeenth to nineteenth centuries.[4] The small streets and byways and the streams which drained through the city were often stinking and foul. Yet the Thames flow was sufficient to dilute the wastes, and it was not until relatively recently that it became too polluted for salmon or for swimming. However, it was also not much more than a century ago that sanitary sewers began to be used extensively to carry urban wastes into watercourses. Many cities had sewers before them, but these were storm drains intended to prevent flooding rather than for the disposal of wastes. It was not until 1855 that the first comprehensive sanitary sewer system was constructed in the United States, in Chicago.[1]

Motivation toward the construction of sanitary sewers was provided to a large degree by the prevalence of disease. Diarrhea and dysentery, typhoid fever, and cholera, all transmitted by human wastes, were notorious killers up until relatively recent times and remain so in areas where sanitation is inadequate. However, the water dispersal of wastes, and more particularly the purification of urban water supplies have done much to remove these diseases as serious causes of death in industrialized countries.[1]

The initial gains obtained by water disposal of wastes continued only so long as the supply of water was relatively large in relation to the numbers of peoples and industries—that is so long as dilution was great and the water was sufficiently well-oxygenated to enable biological decomposition of wastes to proceed normally. However, certain disadvantages appeared initially—organic matter carried down the stream was lost to the land, and in many areas soil fertility and structure had been maintained through the return of these manures to the soil. As time passed and populations grew, the load of waste materials in the streams and other water bodies began to exceed the capacity of water to disperse, dilute, or to provide the means for breaking down these materials. New health problems developed from polluted waters. The recreational value of these waters disappeared—they were ugly, odoriferous, and unpleasant to be near. Furthermore the excess of nutrients provided to these waters created a condition known as *accelerated eutrophication*— meaning an excessive enrichment by such nutrients as nitrates and phosphates. This disrupted biological balances, causing undesirable "blooms" of algae that on dying placed an excessive demand on the oxygen supply of the water. Oxygen deficient or anaerobic conditions developed in which only anaerobic forms of life could exist.

To meet these difficulties, cities installed sewage-disposal plants. In them the solid organic matter is separated from the liquid through various washing, skimming, and settling processes. These solids, when processed, disinfected, and dried have potential value as fertilizer. However, the great reliance of agriculture on inorganic chemical fertilizer, because of its relatively low cost and the ease with which it is applied, has limited the demand for treated organic solids from sewage. Furthermore the liquid effluent, still highly charged with nutrient materials, must be disposed of. In a few instances, cities have used this effluent for industrial processes. In the city of Baltimore, for example, sewage effluent water has been piped to the steel mills of the Bethlehem Steel Company. There it has been used in large quantities in the manufacturing and processing of steel.[41] By this method the normally high water demand of the steel mills has been reduced and a pollution problem alleviated. In general, this sensible approach has not been followed because of the relatively high initial cost for piping and pumping the wastes.

Disposal of wastes from canning and food-processing industries presents difficulties similar to the ones of sewage disposal in that high concentrations of organic matter are carried in the waste waters. Lumber mills and other industries also have waterborne wastes that are highly charged with organic materials and that can cause serious stream pollution. One effective means of disposing of these wastes was described in the previous chapter when the Seabrook Farms problem was discussed.[38] Similar disposal techniques have been used at State College, Pennsylvania, St. Charles City, Maryland, and in other areas. Such land disposal, however, is seldom feasible in large urban-industrial areas. Ways for concentrating and removing wastes, and of finding uses for them (*recycling*) must be found.[12]

Mills, mines, chemical industries, tanneries, and other industrial concerns often have waste waters containing highly toxic or objectionable chemicals which can render large streams unfit for any further use. Some pulp mills, which may have highly toxic wastes, have devised recirculating systems whereby the waste water is processed, the chemicals reclaimed for further use, and the water rendered pure enough for reuse. These systems, although expensive to install, cut down on the freshwater requirements of the mill and make it possible to operate where water supplies are limited. Similar processes can now be considered completely essential for all polluting industries. Yet they are slow to take effect. The extent of the danger which can result from the failure to act is exemplified in the mercury story.

In 1953, people in the vicinity of the city of Minamata in Japan fell ill from a mysterious disease. Before it could be identified, 105 had either died or were seriously incapacitated, their nervous systems badly damaged. Mercury poisoning had long been known but had not been expected here. Nevertheless, the cause of the trouble was mercury which was dumped into the water by a large chemical factory, passing then through food chains and becoming concentrated in the bodies of fish on which many of the local people relied for their protein.[26] In the mid-1960's, mercury poisoning was identified in Sweden and dangerous concentrations of mercury were found in freshwater fish. The source here proved to be primarily pulp mills, which had been treating their logs with a mercuric compound to prevent fungal growth and damage to the wood. This came through in the pulp-mill effluent and became involved in the concentrating mechanisms of aquatic food chains. The Swedes took drastic action, closing down fisheries and forcing the pulp mills to seek new means for protecting their logs. But few other countries took notice.

In the late 1960's and early 1970's mercury was found to be widespread in North American waters—pulp-mill chemicals, agricultural seed dressings, and a variety of other mercury sources were identified, and vigorous action was taken to close down on obvious polluters. But in 1971 the world was shocked by the discovery of high levels of contamination in tuna and swordfish products. Tuna and swordfish feed across the open oceans on other fish which feed on the floating oceanic plankton. For these fish to be contaminated meant clearly that mercury, like DDT, had become a global pollutant and would have to be tackled at the international level. No longer could it be considered in local terms to be handled by the efforts of a city or a county.

Thus, during the 1960's and increasingly into the 1970's, it had become obvious that all previous efforts at water pollution control had been inadequate. People were disturbed to hear that a Great Lake, Lake Erie, was dying from excessive eutrophication.[16,39] Yet it was to be expected. Lake Erie absorbs the wastes from the factories of Detroit, Toledo, Cleveland, Erie, Buffalo, and other cities, and the sewage from an even greater range of towns. Much of this has received little or no treatment. In addition, the runoff, laden with pesticides and excess fertilizer from a great area of midwestern farmland, spilled into the lake. Lake Erie lost its normal complement of aquatic life, supported great algal blooms, had a growing percentage of oxygen-deficient water inhabited only by anaerobic organisms. Niagara Falls, over which Lake Erie drains, had become the nation's most spectacular sewer outfall. Yet Lake Erie was only one of many problems.

Lake Tahoe, high in the Sierra Nevada, faced a sewage problem brought about by a combination of unrestricted growth and an initial complete lack of attention to sewage treatment. Lake Geneva, once a clear, blue lake in the Swiss mountains, was clear and blue no longer, but polluted from sewage. Even remote Lake Baikal in Siberia, unique for its distinctive aquatic fauna, was threatened by the effluent from new Soviet pulp mills. It was obvious, world over, that despite the brave words of earlier years, most factories, socialist or capitalist, had not installed recirculating or waste-reclaiming systems; most communities had not provided adequate sewage-treatment systems and siltation, from accelerated erosion, was still going on at a disturbingly high rate.

In the United States, congressional and administrative action was taken by the federal government, and equivalent moves were made by most states and many cities. In 1966 water pollution control was moved from the Department of Health, Education, and Welfare to the Department of the Interior, in recognition that it was a general environmental problem and not primarily one involving human health. Then, because of the belief that it was being insufficiently emphasized at the urban level, a new Environmental Protection Agency was established in 1970 with a responsibility for the control of all forms of pollution. A bill passed in 1965, the Clean Rivers Act, required all states to develop water quality standards, subject to federal approval, in order to restore the nation's rivers and streams. In 1966, Congress appropriated 3.6 billion dollars for the development of waste treatment facilities. Each year more and more money has been directed toward these ends. New York City alone has appropriated 2 billion dollars toward the alleviation of pollution.[12] In effect the average citizen must pay more for the clean water he once considered free and part of his heritage. He is paying for lack of foresight, for the cost of doing the job right many years ago would have been only a fraction of the cost of changing a system built to provide short-term benefits at the expense of long-term costs.

On the international level all industrialized countries have been forced to face the same problems as the United States. This has led to many new conferences and programs. Unfortunately, many developing countries in Asia, Africa, and Latin America, feeling less involved in pollution problems, have shown a willingness to accept pollution as part of the price of development, and have welcomed those industries fleeing from the increasing environmental controls of the technologically advanced countries. Such an attitude shifts the location of the problem but guarantees it will continue to grow more severe on a global scale.

WATERPOWER That running water could be put to work was discovered early. Stream flow was used first to turn simple water wheels which turned stones to grind grain or which dumped water into flumes to be carried elsewhere. Later, with the discovery of electricity, the rivers were further harnessed. Simple water wheels were replaced by rapidly spinning turbines, generating electric power to do work a hundred miles away.

The need for waterpower, in addition to the needs for municipal water supplies, irrigation waters, and flood control, has spurred on the building of dams. Furthermore the sale of electric power from federally constructed water projects to private power companies or to municipalities has helped to pay, in part, the costs of dam construction. Water has an advantage over the fossil fuels (coal, petroleum, and natural gas) as a source of power because it is a renewable resource. It has the disadvantage that the possibilities for its development are limited. Compared to the total energy requirements of the United States, the amount of power provided by hydroelectric installations is small, approximately 1 percent of the total. Future development of hydroelectric sites will not greatly increase the percentage contribution of waterpower to total energy needs. Locally, however, waterpower is highly important, and without it many industries could not have been developed in their present location, and many communities might lack electricity.

The sale of waterpower, however, has provided an economic justification for the construction of projects which might otherwise appear less feasible. In 1966, for example, the Bureau of Reclamation proposed two dams, Marble Canyon and Bridge Canyon, be constructed in the Grand Canyon.[30] These would have detracted not only from the wild quality of one of the nation's most important scenic resources, but would have backed water into the area of Grand Canyon protected by the National Park Service. The sole justification for these dams was the production and sale of hydroelectric power for income to be balanced against the cost of other facilities, designed to bring irrigation water to central Arizona. Fortunately, an outcry from conservation organizations caused the Department of the Interior in 1967 to withdraw its plans for these dams.

Perhaps one of the greatest "boondoggles" proposed under the justification of hydropower production has been the Rampart Dam on the Yukon River in Alaska.[36] This immense structure, to be built at a cost of over a billion dollars in the Yukon wilderness, would have flooded 8 million acres of land and have done almost incalculable damage to fish and wildlife resources. It would have generated an excess of power beyond any foreseeable needs within Alaska. Fortunately a study sponsored by the National Resources Council and conducted under the leadership of Stephen Spurr of the University of Michigan, revealed the high costs and doubtful benefits of this project before plans for it had become too far advanced. It was shown that Alaska's power needs could be met by smaller dams closer to its centers of population.[35]

On a worldwide basis, the future development of hydroelectric power sources would provide only a fraction of anticipated power needs, because many lands lack the combination of elevated lands and fast-flowing rivers needed for hydroelectric development. Yet for many countries and areas, which have not yet developed their waterpower potential and are poorly endowed with coal and petroleum, such development can bring gains in living standards. Unfortunately, what appears to be in part the "prestige" value of tall hydroelectric dams and the availability of great quantities of electric power has led some countries to make a disproportionate effort toward their construction. Egypt's High Aswan

Dam has its primary justification for irrigation, but power yield is also important. Serious environmental problems have resulted from its construction, including erosion of agricultural lands in the Nile Delta, decline of Eastern Mediterranean Fisheries, and an increase in waterborne disease.[27] In Rhodesia, Kariba Dam brought environmental problems both before and after its construction—the displacement of native peoples, the need for an internationally supported rescue effort to save the wildlife, the rapid spread of water weeds, the consequent failure of the fisheries to develop in the manner expected, and others.[27] Ghana's Volta Dam, completed in 1964, provides power for the development of the aluminum industry, but has brought accompanying environmental problems of considerable consequence, including the displacement of peoples and the spread of the disease, "river blindness," to an increasing number of people.[21] The Ivory Coast now is building a 100-million-dollar dam, the Kossou, on the Bandama River.[37] This will displace 100 thousand people and, undoubtedly, will bring a spread of waterborne diseases, for dubious gains in power and irrigation. One is inclined to question, whenever a major dam and reservoir is proposed, whether or not the same development ends could not be reached in some way less destructive to the environment. The role of waterpower in the world energy picture will be further discussed in Chapter 12.

IRRIGATION Throughout the drier parts of the world there is a great demand for water to be used in irrigation of farming lands. To provide such water highly expensive dams and water-diversion projects have been built and are being built in many places. In general, areas with less than 20 inches of rainfall annually can be farmed only at a risk of crop failure unless irrigation water is available. There are complicating factors, such as temperature and evaporation rates and the regularity and dependability of the rainfall, which make farming successful in some areas with less than 20 inches of rain, but these are exceptions. The soils in the drier lands, because of the low rainfall, are relatively unleached and therefore rich in surface materials. Where water can be made available in quantities sufficient for washing out excessive accumulations of salts, even the soils in dry, desert lands can become highly productive.

One of the most successful irrigation projects in the United States is the Imperial Valley of southern California. Here, some 500,000 acres were brought into cultivation through the private and doubtfully legal construction of the all-American canal from the Colorado River which provided the necessary water. Because of the warm climate, crops can be grown in seasons when they are unavailable elsewhere in cooler areas, and subtropical crops such as dates and citrus fruits can be produced in quantity.[17] Other areas throughout the southwestern United States have also been brought into production. Their value is high, yet their benefits and costs need careful study.

In 1960 the total area of irrigated farmland in the United States amounted to 33 million acres. Of this, more than 30 million acres were in the 17 western states. The remainder consisted largely of lands supplementally irrigated to increase crop yields where the rainfall was otherwise adequate. The U.S. Bureau of Reclamation has estimated an additional 12 million acres in the West can be brought under irrigation. This would make a total of slightly over 42 million irrigated acres in the West, compared to nearly 190 million acres being dry-farmed. The expected increases in population over the next few decades could require a further expansion in agriculture if needs are to be met at present standards. Yet it must be faced that the cost of irrigating new land is extremely high and that water used for this purpose is no longer available for other uses. Gains in new agricultural acreage must then be met by losses in other areas toward which our effort might equally well be directed.

Successful irrigation of dry land requires the continual exercise of skill and vigilance. The irrigation system of Egypt in preindustrial times was, for the most part, successful because it was based on a relatively simple plan, involved the use of an excess of water, and took advantage of the natural drainage system established when the Nile River subsided within its banks at the end of the flood season. The irrigation system in Mesopotamia failed because it was a complex system requiring a high degree of human control and likely to go wrong when human society became disorganized. Furthermore, the distribution of relatively limited amounts of water through canals exposed it to an illness that has plagued all irrigation efforts—the salinization of the soil.[11] This occurs when water tables are raised or when water moves upward through the soil by capillary action in response to evaporation from the soil's surface. As water evaporates, it is converted into vapor and leaves behind on the surface the salts dissolved within it.

When water is abundant and the conditions of drainage are favorable, the excess of salts is leached from the soil and carried away by subsurface drainage. When water is scarce or drainage is impaired, the movement of salts is upward; they accumulate on the soil surface, and eventually form surface layers in such quantities the soil becomes unsuited for anything except salt-tolerant plants.

Roger Revelle has described the problems which developed in West Pakistan.[33] Here the British performed a major task of land transformation in the valley of the Indus River. What was once desert was changed into highly productive irrigated land through the construction of a series of barrages (low dams) which diverted Indus water into an intricate system of irrigation canals. About 23 million irrigated acres were brought into production and, in the early part of this century, Pakistan produced a surplus of food. Soon, however, trouble developed. No shortage of water was involved but, instead, the reverse. Because of inadequate drainage the water table was raised to a point where some areas were virtually drowned out. With the high water table and rapid surface evaporation, salts were deposited on the surface and made the soil unsuitable for crops. By the 1960's Pakistan's population had grown and its lands were going out of production. In place of food surpluses, there

a

b

c

d

WATER USES AND PROBLEMS

(**a**) Mechanized, highly fertilized farming systems require a much greater input of water throughout the growing season. Here corn crops are irrigated by a sprinkler system. (**b**) Moving Colorado River water westward to irrigate the Imperial Valley resulted in the refilling of the Salton Sea. Here the Alamo River, a drainage ditch from the Imperial Valley, empties into the Salton Sea. (**c**) Efforts to bring more fresh water to dry areas has led to the building of desalinization plants such as this test facility near San Diego. (**d**) Efforts to prevent excess water from flooding farmlands, such as this one in Pennsylvania, or cities has led to the building of expensive dams and other flood control structures.

were major food scarcities. The problems are not irremediable, but the cure is expensive. The irrigation canals must be sealed so they do not leak water and raise water tables in the areas through which they pass. Drainage canals must be established to move off the excess water. An abundance of water must be provided to leach out the excess salts which can then be carried off in the drainage canals.

This same type of problem is common to all irrigated areas. In some places, where excess water and drainage could not be provided, it has forced land abandonment. However, even where drainage is handled well and salinization is under control, the problem remains of where to put the drainage water. At this stage in human history, agricultural drainage water is far from being an innocuous substance. Generally, it is loaded with excess pesticides, herbicides, and other agricultural chemicals in addition to the great quantities of minerals leached from the fields. Dumped into a river, it can make the water unsuited for further irrigation downstream. Dumped into a bay, a lake, or an estuary, it can cause the difficulties associated with eutrophication plus those which are caused by the accumulation of toxic chemicals in food chains.

It is increasingly obvious that the difficulties associated with irrigation should give pause to individuals who view it as an easy way out of the world's food dilemma. Unfortunately, however, the demand for higher and higher production to match ever-growing human numbers favors a willingness to ignore the risks.

EXCESS WATER The spread of man over the face of the earth has been accompanied since early times by his attempts to settle in areas where an excess of water was a problem. Low-lying seacoast lands, marshlands, and alluvial plains have attracted him as potential agricultural or urban sites. In each such area he has sought ways to dispose of the surplus water. One of his most heroic efforts in this direction has been the reclamation of land from the sea in the lowlands of the Netherlands and Belgium. Here an elaborate system of dikes, drains, and pumps has been put to work to reclaim over a million acres of land for urban and agricultural use from the Zuider Zee.[9,25]

In the United States reclamation of marsh lands has long seemed a good way to bring new areas into agricultural use. Drainage of marshes has in some instances succeeded in providing first-class farming land. In other instances unfavorable consequences of marsh drainage have become obvious. Marshes, through providing areas of storage and later slow release of excess water, can be of great value in regulating stream flow and preventing floods, in increasing the quantity of groundwater and in keeping water tables high, and in providing a habitat for vast numbers of waterfowl and other wildlife. Drainage not only has brought wildlife destruction but also has contributed to increased floods and lowered water tables. In many cases the damage has overbalanced the gains.

One of the worst examples of a conflict between drainage projects and other environmental values has been in southern Florida. Here irreplaceable natural areas are being sacrificed to bring additional land into housing or agriculture by drainage and the impoundment of water.[19] However, over much of the eastern seaboard the same process may be observed.

Unfortunately, coastal marshes and swamps are frequently regarded as wasteland to be drained or filled in for "useful" purposes. Yet, repeatedly, studies have shown them to be some of the most highly productive ecosystems on earth. Not only do they support great quantities of waterfowl and have high recreational value, they have a key role to play in aquatic food chains, providing nutrients on which coastal and oceanic fisheries may depend, and often providing shelter for young or larval stages of species which later move out and contribute to the richness of ocean fisheries. The pink shrimp fishery of the Gulf of Mexico is an example. This multi-million-dollar fishery is dependent on the "nursery" function of the mangrove swamps of the Everglades, estuarine regions where the developing shrimp spend a critical part of their life cycle before moving as adults into open marine waters.

Where man has settled in the floodplains of rivers he has run the risk of being drowned out. In ancient Egypt man learned to live with the Nile floodwaters, allowing them to rise each year, deposit their thin layer of silt, and retreat once more to the river channel.[8] In America we have seldom adopted this reasonable way of living with nature but have, instead, sought to control and confine the rivers. Such control has brought gains in increased crop yields, has permitted the building of cities and residences on the floodplains and, in general, has permitted more intensive land utilization, but at a cost.

Along the lower Mississippi and other major river systems, one method of controlling floods has been to build levees which keep the river in a restricted channel. The normal tendency of the river is to rise over its banks in flood time and often to deposit silt on the flooded areas. Confined by levees, the silt load may still be deposited but within the river channel. Each year the river may build its bed higher, and the next year's flood is consequently raised. To meet this threat, levees have been built higher until finally in some areas the river, confined by levees, flows well above the rooftops of cities and towns along its bank. Sooner or later comes the big flood the levees cannot hold, and the results are disastrous. In a spectacular flood in 1852 the Yellow River in China broke through such elevated levees, took millions of lives, and found a new channel to the sea.[25] Along the Mississippi Valley similar catastrophes, but with less loss of life, have happened in much more recent times. In the great California floods of 1955 the Feather River poured through a levee break to do millions of dollars in damage and take many lives in Yuba City. In 1965, hurricanes and high water combined to send water over the Mississippi River levees in New Orleans and do millions of dollars worth of damage. To prevent this type of damage, spillways and bypasses are built along with a levee system to allow excess floodwaters to pour out through channels across bottom lands, which can otherwise be used at nonflood times for agricultural purposes. However, even with these devices, levees break, and flood damage still takes place.

To give further flood control the tendency in the United States has been to emphasize large multiple-purpose dams. These dams, when built in a suitable location, can reduce floods as well as provide water for power, irrigation, and other uses. There are few conservation questions, however, about which more controversy has raged than the question of the value of these multiple-purpose dams. The most elaborate series of dams in the country thus far has been built along the Tennessee River, under the jurisdiction of the Tennessee Valley Authority. These have converted much of the river into a chain of freshwater lakes. The TVA has provided flood control, irrigation water, electric power, navigation, and water for domestic and industrial use through the dams built as part of a project to restore the badly eroded lands and to reorganize the damaged economy of the Tennessee River watersheds.[6] The TVA has served as a model for many other nations and yet has been the target of more criticism than most other government agencies have received, in part because it was considered to represent a major federal intrusion into an area which had been previously the domain of private enterprise, but more recently because it has been a cause of destructive strip mining and air pollution.

Along the Missouri, the Columbia, and the Colorado, series of dams and reservoirs have grown to provide flood control, power, irrigation, or these and other functions in combination. Virtually every river in California has been dammed or will be under the state water plan. As a nation we seem committed, perhaps somewhat unwittingly, to the principle that dams are worthwhile and, since they channel federal funds and employment into local areas, it is seldom politically desirable for local congressmen to oppose them.

Objections to the big dams on our river systems are many, and some of them have been discussed previously. However, dams are expensive. They flood lands at the reservoir site; they lose water through evaporation from the reservoirs; they destroy fisheries. Wilderness, wildlife, and recreational values are often sacrificed to dam construction. Dams may catch water heavily laden with silt. This silt normally settles to the bottom of the reservoir, and silt-free water is released at the outlet. Such silt-free water often has unanticipated damaging effects on the stream channel below the dam, scouring and eroding the river banks and picking up a new silt load which is then deposited in some previously silt-free area.[23,24] In addition, siltation of the reservoir may threaten the life of the structure and, in some instances, may result in the creation of a new alluvial plain at the former reservoir site. Water storage in reservoirs, with the consequent decrease in stream flow, can cause invasion of saltwater in delta areas, creating new problems for agriculture in these regions.

It must be realized also that large dams do not prevent downstream floods. Each dam is built with a certain reservoir capacity and, with the realization that under certain known flood conditions, floodwaters will be in excess of what the reservoir can hold. Complete flood prevention, if it could be accomplished, would be so costly it is not even contemplated for any major drainage area. At best, dams are planned to hold back floodwaters up to a certain rate of flow and to minimize damage from floods which exceed that rate. Yet, because they control most floods, dams encourage development on floodplains thus partially protected. In consequence, when floods do occur the damage far exceeds what might have been expected had no dam been present.[19]

Opponents of large dams indicate the same objectives can be accomplished at less expense by "stopping floods where they start" at the headwaters of streams. There is something to be said for this point of view. Under natural conditions of forest and grassland vegetation, soils in the watersheds of streams were protected by a spongelike layer of litter and humus, and the structure of these soils favored water penetration and retention rather than runoff. Destructive use of headwater lands has increased the amount of runoff and in many areas has increased the frequency and severity of floods. Attention to proper conservation use of headwater lands would cut down on flood danger. Thus, along the Wasatch Front in Utah, heavy summer rains in 1923 and 1930 caused severe flooding in many areas. In two adjacent canyons, however, the flood picture was quite different. Both watersheds received equally heavy rain, yet the watershed of Parrish Canyon produced severe floods, whereas the adjacent Centerville Canyon produced little or no flooding. Investigation showed the Parrish Canyon watershed was heavily overgrazed; whereas the Centerville Canyon watershed was protected from excessive grazing. With this realization, the Parrish Canyon watershed was brought under protection from heavy grazing and fires, and the vegetation was restored. This has prevented further flood damage.[7] A dam in Parrish Canyon would not have helped. With the excessive erosion taking place it would soon have filled with silt, and the flood damage would have gone on. In this area the answer to floods was protection of the watershed.

In southern California in 1933 a chaparral fire burned seven square miles of land in the San Gabriel Mountains. In the following winter a severe rainstorm occurred, and it was followed by a flood which caused an estimated 5 million dollars worth of damage. The flood issued from the burned-over watershed and had a peak flow estimated at 1000 second-feet per square mile. Nearby unburned watersheds that received the same amount of rainfall had peak flows measured between 20 and 60 second-feet per square mile and experienced little damage. In this area, vegetation protection rather than dams is the way to prevent such floods.[7]

To demonstrate the effectiveness of watershed management as a means toward flood control, the Soil Conservation Service has undertaken a series of watershed projects aimed at stopping floods high in the drainage basins, preventing erosion and siltation, and also providing a better quality of land use. To date, these efforts have met with considerable success in some directions. Lands have been improved and made more productive and stable. Erosion has been cut down, and with this the silt load of streams has been decreased in some areas. Small local floods have been eliminated, and larger floods reduced to some extent. Flood damage to lands located in the upper watershed has been greatly reduced. However, land management practices alone have not accomplished all of these objectives. Flood control is still provided in part by dams but, in these projects, by many small dams on tributary streams (p. 155). In the aggregate these small dams are expensive and can be subjected to many of the criticisms also directed against the large downstream dams. Furthermore against certain types of floods they are ineffective.[23] For example, in December 1955, heavy general rains fell for many days over much of northern and central California. Nearly every stream and tributary reached flood stage, and the major rivers poured into many cities and towns and inundated vast areas of agricultural land. In all, the damage was measurable only in hundreds of millions of dollars. Watershed treatment and small upstream dams would not have controlled these floods, although they would have alleviated much flood damage. However, the severity of the floods was reduced by the presence of the giant multiple-purpose dams at Folsom and Shasta. Such heavy rains as this can saturate the best-managed soils and can exceed the water-holding capacity of the best-treated drainage basin.

It must be realized that long before civilization appeared on the scene there were floods and that regardless of how much land-use practices are improved and whether we build small dams or large, floods will still occur. There is no single panacea to flood problems. In some places large dams alleviate flood damage; in others they are ineffective, and watershed management offers most promise. Lands must be preserved, and erosion must be prevented for reasons other than flood control. However, as long as we continue to build high-value structures, subject to damage by flooding, in areas where floodwaters naturally accumulate, we will continue to experience damage from floods. To control this damage we seem committed to spend somewhat fantastic sums of money for dams and levees, upstream and down, but we cannot economically eliminate this damage so long as cities and industries remain on the floodplain. Under these circumstances, it seems reasonable to consider an alternative. Areas subjected to frequent flooding can be zoned to prevent their use for purposes which might involve excessive loss of property or life when floods occur. Such zoning can prevent the construction of additional structures in these areas. Outright purchase and removal of existing structures by government agencies would be less expensive than the efforts now directed toward flood control. Such lands could then be devoted to other uses less likely to be adversely affected by floods. Such floodplain zoning has been tried on a small scale in a few areas, but on the larger scene it has not yet received adequate consideration.

The possibility has been suggested also that, in place of spending money for flood control, governments should offer flood insurance to those using areas subject to flood damage. The cost of the insurance to the floodplain user could be adjusted to the type of use and the likelihood damage will be experienced. Such insurance costs would effectively prevent certain types of use for land subject to frequent flooding.[5,19,23,40]

NAVIGATION Another major use of water is for transportation—the movement of goods and people. During the early history of civilization, water transportation was generally cheaper, more efficient, and faster than land-borne transport. The balance shifted with the coming of the railways and shifted even further with the development of rapid highway and air travel. Nevertheless the importance of water for transportation remains, particularly with materials which are bulky, required in quantity, but for which speed of transport is not vital. Furthermore, navigation on water provides a satisfying form of recreation of growing importance. The use of water bodies for navigation is entirely nonconsumptive and should not necessarily involve any impairment of their quality. However, the maintenance of navigation channels frequently involves dredging or other modification of waterways, and this can have an impact on aquatic life and its productivity. The disruptive effect of waterborne transportation on natural or wild areas is often considerable. Increasingly, also, the presence of waterborne transportation adds to water pollution. These problems will be discussed in other chapters of this book.

RECREATION Water-based recreation is now big business in America. In many places— Reston, Virginia, and Columbia, Maryland, are examples—new towns and communities are planned around artificially created bodies of water in the expectation they will make the site more attractive to the prospective home buyer. Waterfront property has become a scarce and expensive commodity. The costs of new dams and reservoirs are partially justified on the basis of the recreation use they will attract. In a survey of America's outdoor recreation preferences, the water-based sports of swimming, fishing, boating, ice skating, water skiing, canoeing, and sailing ranked in the top twenty pursuits.[31] There is no doubt the demand for access to recreation water is high and growing (see Chapter 11).

The need for natural bodies of water, untouched by development of any kind, is also great. Natural streams, lakes, and seashores which can be maintained in a near-primeval condition have become scarce in America, and have a value not only to those seeking a high quality of outdoor recreation but also for the study of hydrology, ecology, and other environmental sciences. These areas form needed reference points for comparison with those areas man has changed (Chapter 16).

There is a tendency in water development projects to underestimate the value of an untouched stream or other body of water and to overemphasize the benefits in irrigation, urban water, power, or other quantifiable benefits to justify the construction of engineering facilities. Unless this practice can be reversed, America stands to lose much that is priceless and irreplaceable in outdoor resources.

SOME FUTURE PROSPECTS   During the decades since World War II the growing demand for water has brought an increasing investment in research and development aimed at extracting freshwater from the sea. Such a source of freshwater could not only spare remote watersheds from development but would make it possible for seacoast cities and islands to become independent of other water sources.

The feasibility of desalting water is related to the salinity of the water and the desired purity of the product. Seawater, because of its high salinity, 35 to 36 parts of salt per thousand, is far more difficult to purify than is brackish water of a much lower salinity. It is easier to purify water to a level equivalent to hard freshwater, with a salinity of perhaps 0.3 parts per thousand than it is to carry the process farther and achieve soft water with a salinity of 0.06 parts per thousand. Consequently the greatest successes, from an economic viewpoint, have come from the desalinization of brackish water rather than seawater. Nevertheless the desalting of seawater to produce urban drinking water is now past the theoretical stage and is being practiced in many areas.

Buckeye, Arizona, a town with a 1960 population of 2300, became the first American community to obtain is water supply from the desalting of brackish water. Its desalting plant produced 650,000 gallons of water per day at a cost of less than a dollar per thousand gallons.[22] Later, Port Mansfield, Texas developed a plant which yielded 250,000 gallons per day. A large desalting plant was established in San Diego, California in the early 1960's and later was moved to Guantanamo Bay, Cuba, where it produces a million gallons of water per day. In the Virgin Islands a seawater distillation plant yields 275,000 gallons per day at a cost of a $1 per 1000 gallons. A still larger seawater plant in Kuwait, Arabia, using natural gas for power, yields 9 million gallons of water per day. In 1966 there were 200 desalting plants in operation around the world.[22,39]

There is no doubt the desalting of ocean and brackish water holds great hope for supplying future water needs. However, there are problems to be overcome. A proposed Southern California plant, for example, would yield 23,000 tons of salt per day from seawater. This would include not only common sodium chloride but also many minerals of potentially high value, but at present the greatest challenge may lie in the disposal of the salt. Where nuclear energy is used to operate desalting plants, the safe disposal of atomic waste products presents another problem, as well as the more serious risks associated with breakdown of the power plant itself.[13] The use of solar energy, directly, for desalting water needs more careful study (see Chapter 12).

It is unlikely the desalting of seawater will be practical for producing the major amounts of water needed for irrigation. Arizona, for example, pumps 5 billion gallons of water per day from underground storage areas, but uses 4.7 billion of these gallons in irrigation alone, with all other needs supplied from the remaining 0.3 billion gallons. In federal irrigation projects the cost of water to the user is far less than the actual cost of delivering the water. The irrigation farmer is thus subsidized, indirectly. It is unlikely the cost of desalted seawater will ever be within reach of the farmer. Furthermore, since seawater is available only at sea level it would be necessary to pump it, at a still higher power cost, in order to deliver it to irrigation projects located inland. The biggest hope for irrigation may lie in the desalting of brackish water located in inland sources or underground. Seawater is most likely to continue as a source for seacoast urban-industrial water supply.[22,39]

Despite the promise of desalinization, efforts to develop new sources of freshwater may be expected to continue. The most massive water development scheme yet proposed has been brought forward by the Parsons engineering firm of Los Angeles. This is the North American Water and Power Alliance (NAWAPA). It would tap the rivers of nothern Canada and Alaska, pump water southward into a storage area in the Rocky Mountain trench of Canada, and deliver it as needed as far south as Mexico for a cost estimated at 100 billion dollars.[34] Obviously such a plan would reorganize the western countryside, have massive effects on environment, and destroy great wilderness and wildlife areas. Wallace Stegner has described it as being potentially a "boondoggle visible from Mars, a project to make Rampart Dam look like something created in a sandbox."[36]

Regardless of what we do, the ultimate answer to water problems lies in population limitation. We could move water down the continent and irrigate all our deserts to provide more water and more food for more people. The people would then not have wild country or desert wilderness, but they would still have a population problem and growing water needs. We could, on the other hand, limit population growth at some point where we would have enough food, enough water, and enough wild country to satisfy anyone. We still have the choice.

WATER CONSERVATION— RECAPITULATION In this chapter we took an overall view of water conservation, looking from the top down, for the most part. Problems look different when viewed from the national or international level than when examined from the ground locally, and it has perhaps been the greatest failing of technological civilization that it shifts the point of view and responsibility upward and destroys local initiative.

For example, if we accept that a person in a modern, technological society requires 720 gallons of water per day,[31] and then multiply that by one million people, we have a problem for government of finding 720 million gallons of water per day for a population of a large city. However, in an area with an annual rainfall of 36 inches, a collecting surface of 100 square feet could gather 300 cubic feet, or roughly 2400 gallons of water a year. One person will not drink more than 365 gallons of water a year. A house with 2000 square feet of roof-collecting surface could harvest 6000 cubic feet or 48,000 gallons of water in a year—enough to provide 130 gallons of water a day. The practice of collecting rainwater from rooftops and running it into household storage tanks was once common, and still is in some areas, and has been used as a means for supplying most household water needs. However, reliance on massive water developments and regional supply systems has caused people to give up such do-it-yourself practices and has changed a non-problem into a national problem.

Similarly, the problems of disposing of sewage and other wastes can be either a national dilemma, or the same "waste" can be a local asset. Such devices as the Swedish "Clivus" toilet use very little water and produce as end products solid materials which can be composted for farm or garden use. A step further along the line is the "biogas" or methane-generating unit, which has been extensively used in India, and to a lesser extent elsewhere. This requires also a much lower water input than in conventional western septic tank or mass-sewage-disposal systems. It produces as a benefit, not only methane gas which can be used for heating or cooling, but also fertilizers for farms and gardens. It requires a greater input of organic wastes than one household can supply, but becomes practical where several households along with farm and garden wastes can be fed in.[2] This will be discussed further when we consider energy, but is another example of how problems are generated through the way societies are organized. China has probably done more than most nations toward eliminating the whole concept of "waste," through making maximum use of all materials at a local level. Waste in China is considered to be a resource they have not yet learned to use.

Mass agribusiness, which now dominates farm production in the United States, requires massive developments to provide irrigation water and other inputs. Growing food, which is the purpose of much of this activity, can often be carried out far more effectively by using local resources and substituting a high level of human care and careful management for those outside inputs which would otherwise have to be purchased or supplied. Evenari and his co-workers in Israel have investigated the past practices of the Nabatean civilization which managed to support itself in the Negev Desert where rainfall is less than 5 inches a year.[14] By improving on the rainfall-collecting and water-use systems developed by this culture, such desert areas are again producing crops, without massive import of water from outside sources. A high level of labor investment and human skill is necessary to make the desert bloom, but in today's world there is no scarcity of "surplus" human labor, displaced from the land and unable to find employment in cities. Further discussion of this problem is found in Chapter 16.

One cannot pretend all problems of water management and conservation can be met by paying greater attention to local human efforts to solve local problems. New York's water problems will not be solved by putting in roof collectors. It is certain, however, that many water conservation problems would be alleviated and some would disappear if individuals would once again assume greater responsibility for their own welfare, and if small communities would work together to find local solutions to their difficulties. We have gone much too far toward mass organizations, government or private, assuming responsibilities for supplying all things to all people.[34]

Shifting now to the more global viewpoint of water conservation, we must see to it that water-conservation plans are fitted into an overall pattern of environmental conservation and not treated in isolation. They must always include attention to proper land conservation in watershed areas. Better soil conservation on farming lands will lead to better use of soil water, better storage of soil water, increased filtration to subsurface water supplies, and a lessened demand for irrigation water. Through soil conservation, erosion can be slowed to a tolerable rate, and problems of downstream siltation reduced. Better land use in forest and range areas brings increased water filtration, stabilized runoff, and improved year-round water yields. Each region must take responsibility for its own watersheds, streams and rivers. Individuals, communities, municipalities and industries must be held responsible for reducing water pollution to tolerable levels.

All needs for flood control, irrigation, electric power and municipal water cannot be met by sound land management and local initiative— at least not the way societies are organized today. State and federal governments necessarily become involved in the broader issues. Yet the expenditure of great sums of money for somewhat doubtful gains in flood control, irrigation, or hydropower cannot continue. Each day decisions made on the use of water involve the sacrifice of one value for the enhancement of another. Too often the values sacrificed are those which make life worth living for many people, and the values enhanced are those which increase profits for the few.

CHAPTER REFERENCES

Colman, E. A., 1953. *Vegetation and watershed management.* Ronald Press, New York.

Dale, Tom, and V. G. Carter, 1955. *Topsoil and civilization.* University of Oklahoma, Norman, Oklahoma.

Kittredge, Joseph, 1948. *Forest influences.* McGraw-Hill, New York.

Kuenen, P. H., 1956. *Realms of water.* John Wiley, New York.

Leopold, Luna B., and T. Maddock, Jr., 1954. *The flood control controversy.* Ronald Press, New York.

Milton, John, and M. T. Farvar, eds., 1971. *The careless technology.* Doubleday-Natural History Press, New York.

Nadeau, Remi A., 1950. *The water seekers.* Doubleday, New York.

National Academy of Sciences—National Research Council, 1966. *Alternatives in water management.* Publ. 1408. Washington, D.C.

National Academy of Sciences—National Research Council, 1966. *Waste management and control.* Publ. 1400, Washington, D.C. *Saturday Review,* October 23, 1965.

Zon, Raphael, 1927. *Forests and water in the light of scientific investigation.* Appendix 5. Final report of national waterways commission. Senate Document 469, 62nd Congress, 2nd Session, Washington, D.C.

LITERATURE CITED

1. Banks, A. L., and J. A. Hislop, 1956. Sanitation practices and disease control in extending and improving areas for human habitation. (See Thomas, 1956, in general references.)

2. Bell, C., S. Boulter, D. Dunlop, and P. Keiller, 1973. *Methane: fuel of the future.* Singer, Bottisham, U.K.

3. Borgstrom, Georg, 1965. *The hungry planet.* Macmillan, New York.

4. Bryant, Sir Arthur, 1968. *Set in a silver sea.* Doubleday, Garden City, New York.

5. Burton, Ian, and R. W. Kates, 1964. The perception of natural hazards in resource management. *Natural Resources Journal,* 3: 412–441.

6. Clapp, Gordon R., 1955. *The TVA, an approach to the development of a region.* University of Chicago, Chicago.

7. Colman, E. A., 1953. *Vegetation and watershed management.* Ronald Press, New York.

8. Dale, Tom, and V. G. Carter, 1955. *Topsoil and civilization.* University of Oklahoma, Norman, Oklahoma.

9. Davis, John H., 1956. Influences of man upon coastlines. (See Thomas, 1956, in general references.)

10. Dolder, Edward F., 1954. Water—California's lifeblood. *Conservation—concern for tomorrow.* Calif. State Dept. Educ. Bull., pp. 45–63.

11. Eaton, F. M., 1949. Irrigation agriculture along the Nile and the Euphrates. *Scientific Monthly,* 48: 33–42.

12. Eisenbud, Merrill, 1970. Environmental protection in the city of New York. *Science,* 170: 706–712.

13. Ellis, Cecil B., 1954. *Fresh water from the ocean for cities, industry, and irrigation.* Ronald Press, New York.

14. Evenari, M., 1974. Desert farmers: ancient and modern. *Natural History,* 83: 42–49

15. Gordon, Mitchell, 1965. *Sick cities.* Penguin, Baltimore.

16. Hill, Gladwin, 1965. The great and dirty lakes. *Saturday Review,* Oct. 23, pp. 32–34.

17. Hutchinson, Wallace I., 1956. *Water for millions.* Forest Service, United States Department of Agriculture, San Francisco.

18. Kalanin, G. P., and V. D. Bykov, 1969. The world's water resources, present and future. *Impact of Science on Society,* Unesco, 19: 135–150.

19. Kates, Robert W., 1964. *Hazard and choice perception in flood plain management.* University of Chicago, Department of Geographical Research, Paper 78, Chicago.

20. Landsberg, H. H., 1964. *Natural resources for U.S. growth.* Johns Hopkins, Baltimore, 260 pp.

21. Lawson, G. W., 1970. Lessons of the Volta—a new man-made lake. *Biological Conservation,* 2: 90–96.

22. Lear, John, 1965. The crisis in water. What brought it on? *Saturday Review,* October 23, pp. 24–28, 78–80.

23. Leopold, Luna B., and T. Maddock, Jr., 1954. *The flood control controversy.* Ronald Press, New York.

24. Leopold, Luna B., and W. B. Langbein, 1960. *A primer on water.* Geological Survey, United States Department of Interior, Washington, D.C.

25. Lowdermilk, W. C., 1953. *Conquest of the land through 7,000 years.* United States Department of Agriculture, Washington, D.C.

26. Marx, Wesley, 1967. *The frail ocean.* Sierra Club—Ballantine, New York.

27. Milton, John, and M. T. Farvar, eds., 1971. *The careless technology.* Doubleday—Natural History, New York.

28. Mumford, Lewis, 1961. *The city in history.* Harcourt, Brace and World, New York.

29. Nadeau, Remi A., 1950. *The water seekers.* Doubleday, New York.

30. Nash, Hugh, 1966. Storm over the Grand Canyon. *Parks and Recreation,* June, pp. 497–500.

31. Outdoor Recreation Resources Review Commission, 1962. *Outdoor recreation for America.* Washington, D.C.

32. Pereira, H. C. et al., 1970. Water resources problems: present and future requirements for life. (See UNESCO, 1970, in general references.)

33. Revelle, Roger, 1966. Salt, water and civilization. *Food and civilization.* Voice of America Forum Lectures, U.S. Information Agency, Washington, pp. 83–104.

34. Schumacher, E. F., 1973. *Small is beautiful. Economics as if people mattered.* Harper Torchbooks, New York.

35. Spurr, Stephen H. et al., 1966. *Rampart Dam and the economic development of Alaska.* University of Michigan, Ann Arbor.

36. Stegner, Wallace, 1965. Myths of the western dam. *Saturday Review,* October 23, pp. 29–31.

37. Sterling, Claire, 1971. Environmental problems face a new super-dam. *Washington Post,* January 11.

38. Thornthwaite, C. W., 1956. The modification of rural microclimates. (See Thomas, 1956, in general references.)

39. *Time,* 1965. Hydrology. A question of birthright. October 1, pp. 70–79.

40. White, Gilbert F., 1964. *Choice of adjustment to floods.* University of Chicago Department of Geological Research, Paper 93.

41. Wittfogel, Karl, 1956. The hydraulic civilizations. (See Thomas, 1956, in general references.)

forests
and
timber

$\mathbb{M}$an has proved surprisingly illiterate in reading the lessons of history. Perhaps this is because, blinded by the glare of immediate profits, he sees the pages of the past as blank. Whatever the cause, the results are a discouraging repetition of mistakes. This has been true particularly with respect to man's treatment of the forests. Properly managed, forests can enrich human life in a variety of ways which are both material and psychological. Poorly managed, they can be a source for the disruption of the environment of an entire region. However, through the centuries we have seen a pattern repeated. The misuse of axe or saw, of fire or grazing, causes forest destruction. This leads to disruption of watersheds, to the erosion or loss of fertility of soils, to siltation and flooding in stream valleys, and to loss of the continued productivity of the land on which man must depend. Yet, the process goes on. In Africa, Asia, and Latin America the tropical forests disappear at a rate approaching the catastrophic. Even in countries where forestry is an old and well-established profession the pressures toward single-purpose management of the land threatens the existence of the life-enriching diversity which has characterized forest lands in the past.

ECOLOGICAL CONDITIONS Compared to other forms of vegetation, forests have a high degree of complexity and diversity. Even the northern forests (where a few species of trees dominate great areas) support a variety of other plants at the shrub or ground level, and a diverse biota within the soil. All of these species interact with their environment and with each other, and we have yet to unravel all of their specific roles and their relative importance to the forest system. In the tropical forests the diversity has already been emphasized. Not only are there many layers of trees rooted in the ground but there are the great number of epiphytes, plants growing on plants, ranging from simple algae to the strangler figs that encompass and in time replace their host trees.[21]

Perhaps the most striking characteristic of the dominant trees in forest vegetation is their longevity. Even the transient successional forms, the birches or aspens that occupy the land for a time following a fire, are long-lived by human standards, whereas some of the conifers live for millennia—a European yew for more than 2000 years, redwoods for more than 1000, the giant sequoias for more than 3000,[16] bristlecone pine, growing at the limits of tree growth in western America, for more than 4000 years and, in the arid Hoggar Mountains of the Algerian

Sahara, a Mediterranean cypress (*Cupressus dupreziana*) has lived for 4700 years.[9]

Diversity and longevity bring difficulties for management of forests. The human mind is ill at ease with problems which present too many variables, and we have traditionally preferred to simplify things down to "manageable proportions." Yet the greatest challenge to environmental management and conservation is the challenge of diversity, and the new computer technology could be used to solve these complex problems. Still, the approach has been and continues to be one of simplification, and simplification sets in motion all of the forces of instability examined earlier in this book.

We prefer to manage biotic resources in such a way that they produce a sustained yield, producing a new crop each year equivalent to or greater than the one harvested the year before. With certain types of relatively fast-growing forest, this sustained yield principle has been successfully used, and it can apply anywhere to the production of wood. Yet we are deceiving ourselves if we talk of the sustained yield of *forests* which have taken centuries or millennia to develop. It would be possible to manage ancient forests on a long-term cycle so that there would always be ancient forests—but people do not like to order their economic affairs with a view to the centuries or millennia. Perhaps they really do not expect the human race to last that long. Perhaps they are right.

People were not originally forest animals and are seldom at home in the forests. It is true that there are forest peoples who have learned over the course of human evolution to adapt to forest ways, but the dominant tribes who have taken over the earth have come from more open lands, and when they have occupied the forest they have cleared it. Their attitude toward the forest has been one of the invader and aggressor. Part of the reason for our general failure to adapt to forest life lies in the nature of forest vegetation. Forests are great storehouses of carbohydrate, and in particular cellulose. But they are not great producers of accessible protein.[11] Ground-feeding animals that depend on grazing and browsing are always scarce in comparison to their relatives that live in more open lands simply because the nutritional quality of the accessible vegetation is inadequate.[2] The successful forest animals live in, on, or within the trees. In the rich tropical forests the nutrients are largely locked up in the forest vegetation and not in the soils. Protein deficiency has plagued people who use tropical forest lands. They can grow an abundance of starchy food, but to find protein they must be ingenious.

THE STATUS
OF FORESTS
Throughout the world it has been estimated that there are approximately 3800 million hectares of forest of all kinds.[5] This is a generous estimate and includes certain types of savanna and shrubland. It has been stated that this represents approximately one-half of the original forested area of the world.[16] However, forest in the broad sense, still covers approximately 30 percent of the land surface of the earth. Wherever people have

settled in great numbers, forests have tended to disappear. The extent of change has been most marked in western and southern Europe, northern Africa, and western Asia. Through trial and error, people have selected those forest soils most suited to other purposes such as growing agricultural crops or pastures. In general, forests remain in those areas least suited to other uses.[16]

If we regard forests as sources of wood useful for commercial purposes, we find that approximately 60 percent of the world's total forest area is considered productive in this sense—the amount varying from 50 percent in the less developed countries of the world to 80 percent in the more developed countries.[5] The extent to which these forests are used for the production of wood products has been increasing over the years. Thus in 1950 the value of world production of wood, plywood and related panel boards, pulp and other wood products was 24 billion dollars.[6] By 1968 this had increased to almost 46 billion dollars. The total removals of wood from commercially exploited forests in 1959 was 1900 million cubic meters. By 1968 this had increased to 2126 million cubic meters.[6] This is by no means a sustained-yield production of wood. In many parts of the world this harvest has simply been forest "mining." After the woodcutters go through, the land is taken up for temporary cultivation, pasturage, or other uses, and its productive capacity is impaired. Wherever old-growth forest is being exploited, the cut is far in excess of growth. Of the total wood cut, nearly 45 percent is used for fuel and not for manufacture or construction. In less-developed countries, this percentage increases to nearly 80 percent.[6]

Of the world forest total, approximately 75 million hectares are reported to be protected in some kind of forest reserve within which commercial harvesting of trees is prohibited.[5] This represents approximately 2 percent of the world's forest area. The percentage varies among the continents, but not greatly.

When the colonists came to America, the United States was one of the richest forest areas in the world (Fig. 7–1). It has been estimated there were over 1000 million acres of forest in the United States, with over 8000 billion board feet of potential saw timber.[13] But to the early settler the forest was a nuisance, its limited value as a source of fuel and construction timbers was outweighed by the fact it occupied land wanted for his crops and grazing. The old, traditional fear of the dark woods as a dwelling place for real or imagined enemies was aggravated by the Indian wars, when hostile raiders swept from the forest cover into the settled lands. Great areas of hardwood forest, which would be worth a fortune today, vanished, therefore, without contributing a single piece of furniture or a finished board.

With the increase in population and the need for wood for ships and cities, enterprising people were attracted by the value of the soft, easily worked, but strong and durable wood of the white pines, which grew in a belt separating the cold, northern spruce forests from the southern hardwoods. We know now these pine forests were an historical accident,

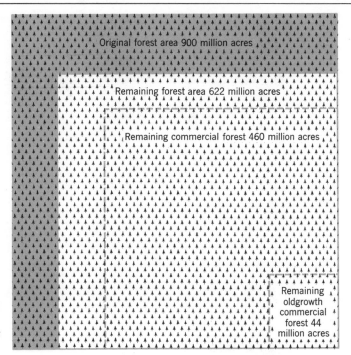

FIG. 7–1. Changes in forest areas in the United States from settlement to 1952 (*source: U.S. Forest Service*).

successional forests grown up following some widespread catastrophe, perhaps fire or hurricanes, which had swept through the northern United States in the fifteenth century.[3,20] However, they were available for easy exploitation at the time when the surge of colonists into the prairie states created a major demand for timber. In the early nineteenth century white pine logging on a commercial basis began, centering in the New England states. The management practices used, if they can be called such, have been summed up as "cut out and get out." The future was little thought of when the supply of timber in relation to the number of people seemed limitless, and there was always more "out West." As the readily accessible forests dwindled, the center of the white pine industry shifted from Maine to New York to Pennsylvania and finally in 1870 to the great forests of Wisconsin and Minnesota.[22] With the destruction of the forests in the Lake States came the finish of the eastern white pine as a major commercial species, and the attention of the industry shifted to other species. Following on the heels of the loggers came fire (p. 177). The logging practices left much slash and debris on the ground; the rolling topography of the Lake States provided few natural barriers to fire. Fire starting in cutover areas can generate enough heat to leap to the tree crowns where, carried by the wind, it can spread at horrifying speed, almost impossible to escape or to control.

In October 1871, a fire started near Peshtigo, Wisconsin that swept over more than a million acres, burned out numerous towns and settlements, and killed 1500 people. In 1894 two major fires in Wisconsin

a

b

c

FOREST VALUES

Forests are more than just timber and cannot be valued only in terms of wood production. Forests hold mountains together. They enrich the human spirit.
(**a**) Old beech forest in Belgium.
(**b**) Ancient bristle cone pine in California's White Mountains—not a renewable resource. (**c**) Tropical rainforest in Guinea—its values cannot be measured in commodity production.

and Minnesota burned hundreds of thousands of acres, killed more than 700 people, and wiped out many towns. In 1918, a spark from an engine at a lumber mill in Minnesota started a fire that burned out Cloquet, a town with 12,000 inhabitants, swept over a large sector of country, and was stopped only at the outskirts of the city of Duluth. Four hundred people were killed, and timber and property worth 30 million dollars were destroyed. These and many other fires during the same period finished off the damage that logging had begun. The virgin pine forests of the Lake States dwindled to a few scattered remnants, and in their place a scrubby growth of birch and aspen took over.

Between 1900 and 1910 the lumber industry in the South occupied the center of the scene. Here the emphasis was on the hard, southern yellow pines. These trees, spreading from the area originally forested, had sprung up on abandoned and depleted fields left as the wave of cotton and tobacco planters moved west. Fast growing, quickly regenerating after logging, and favored by limited burning, the southern pine forests have proved highly resistant to destruction, and the South remains today the center of pine-timber production.

At the same time the southern pine industry was beginning to boom, the attention of other lumbermen shifted to the West. Here, the stands of Douglas fir in the Pacific Northwest represented an immense storehouse of timber. In 1905 the state of Washington took the lead as the chief lumber-producing state, and has held it since. By the time the logging boom reached the West, however, sufficient force had been generated by the newly organized conservation movement to prevent the outright destruction that other areas had experienced. In forestry, this first took shape with the growth of federal concern over the hitherto unmanaged public lands. From the federal lead, the idea of conservation gradually spread to the large lumber companies. Left with no new worlds to conquer, these organizations realized the necessity of managing their own lands for permanent production. However, the original large wave of forest destruction has continued in numerous small ripples, represented by the smaller logging concerns with no lands of their own, which have moved through the woods country devastating remaining areas not brought under federal or forest-industry ownership. Many of these operators, as well as the major companies too hemmed in by conservation laws in their homeland, have now moved into the forested lands of the developing countries of the world, hoping to repeat there the process of quick profits which mean prolonged devastation.

FOREST CONSERVATION AND MANAGEMENT

FEDERAL FORESTRY

The growth of federal forestry in the United States is associated with the name of Gifford Pinchot, one of America's first professional foresters. He and other leaders were interested in bringing to a halt the "mining" of forests and in treating the forests as renewable resources capable of being both used and preserved for the future. Starting in 1891, President Harrison was enabled by Congress to withdraw federal lands from the general public domain and set them aside as forest reserves—Yellowstone Timberland Reserve, surrounding Yellowstone Park, was the first. With the election of Theodore Roosevelt as President, a naturalist and outdoorsman became chief executive. With the advice of Pinchot and others, Roosevelt managed to add a large new area to the forest-reserve system and to bring it to a total of 148 million acres by the end of his terms in office (Fig. 7–2). At the same time, he realized these forests need not be "reserved" but could be used under careful forestry practices as permanent sources of timber. With their names changed to "National Forests," the old reserves were transferred to a new agency, the United States Forest Service, which was placed in the Department of Agriculture. Under the leadership of Gifford Pinchot, as the first Chief Forester, the Forest Service undertook the task of bringing management for use to the National Forests.

The brand of forest conservation exemplified in the National Forest system can be summarized as follows: (1) *Sustained yield,* the concept that timber harvest and growth must be balanced over a period of time so that forest yield will be continued into perpetuity. This leads to some popular misconceptions in its practice. When a mature forest is being cut, almost any degree of cutting represents an excess over growth. However, if management is planned so that abundant reproduction takes place, fast-growing young stands soon balance the rate of cutting. (2) *Multiple use,* the principle that the National Forests serve a variety of purposes and not just the single purpose of providing wood products. Grazing, wildlife, recreation, soil conservation and, perhaps most important, watershed conservation are among legitimate forest uses, the ideal being to serve the community and nation in as many ways as possible. Although often receiving only lip service for lack of money or other reasons, this concept is one of great value for the future. (3) The general ideal of *"the greatest good for the greatest number in the long run"* has been intended to guide Forest Service policy. The emphasis is here placed on the "long run" to avoid the short-term, high-profit philosophy which has influenced so many other activities in this nation.

The development of the Forest Service and its methods for managing National Forests have not followed any straight or easy path. Although the initial withdrawal of National Forests from the public domain occasioned some opposition from individuals who sought the ultimate disposition of all federal land into private hands, and from those who were interested in the resources of National Forest lands, there was comparatively little pressure from the timber industries on the Forest Service during the early years of its history. The timber industries were busy cutting on their own lands, and most companies had little interest in federal timber. The National Forests were, in truth, forest reserves, with their timber stands protected from exploitation. Following World War II, however, the timber stands on private lands were depleted, and industry found a growing market for timber products. The Forest Service began increasingly to open up its lands to cutting on long-prepared management

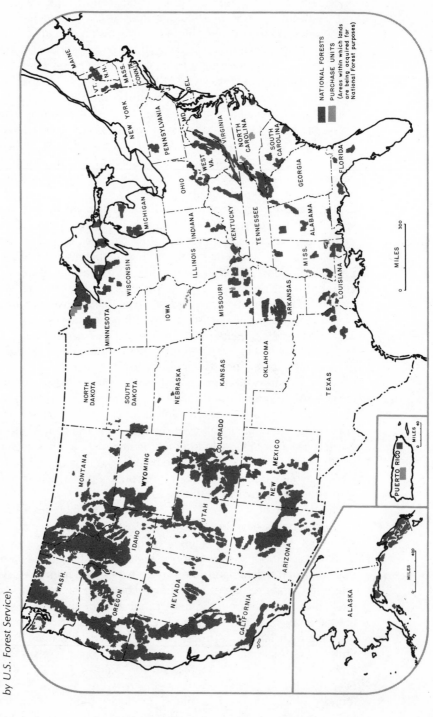

FIG. 7–2. National forests of the United States (map by U.S. Forest Service).

plans. But demand continued to grow and industries resented the restrictions enforced by the Forest Service to protect other resources and timber crops. Pressure was mounted to get the National Forests into "full production," meaning essentially to allow quick harvesting of the remaining old-growth timber.[18] In some regions the Forest Service accelerated its cutting program, to an extent that many believed was detrimental to other forest values and contrary to the principle of multiple use.

The concept of "multiple use" was long established in Forest Service administrative policy. In 1964, the passage of the Multiple Use Act by Congress provided a legal basis for the policy and extended it further to include the lands administered by the Bureau of Land Management in the Department of the Interior. Nevertheless, the concept was more recognized in words than in deeds. To quote Michael Frome:[18]

The National Forest Development Program, a 10-year project of the Forest Service, was intended to cover the period of 1963 to 1972. During the years of 1963 to 1970 the proposed level of spending for "timber sales and management" was fulfilled by Congress to 95 percent of the total. Other phases, however, did not fare as well: planned "reforestation and stand improvement," "recreation-public use," "wildlife habitat management," and "soil and water management" were financed at levels of only 40 percent, 45 percent, 62 percent, and 52 percent, respectively. Then came the 1971 budget, for which the administration proposed an increase of $5,000,000 in timber sales and management to a total of $52,000,000—more than twice as much as for all other forest land uses combined.

Those who have followed the history of the Forest Service know funds were forthcoming for protection against fire, insects, or disease and for the sale and management of timber, but were rarely available for the other purposes for which the National Forests were presumed to exist. However, more trouble was to come. In 1970 a National Timber Supply Bill was introduced in Congress that would have established timber production as the "primary use" over 97 million acres of National Forest land. All other forest values would receive scant attention. Fortunately, conservation organizations all over the nation were in opposition, and the bill did not reach the floor of Congress. However in 1964, Congress established a Public Land Law Review Commission to study the laws and policies affecting the present use and the future of public lands. When the report of this commission was finally delivered in 1970, it advanced the concept of "dominant use" to apply to those areas of the National Forests deemed particularly valuable for timber production, and recommended they be managed to "maximize net dollar returns." A federal corporation was proposed to handle these dominant-use forest areas, thus essentially removing them from normal Forest Service control. Again a congressional battle with conservation interests in opposition to exploitative interests was inevitable, and is continuing.[18]

As noted earlier, even the principle of "sustained yield" is subject to criticism in its operation. Ideally viewed the concept means forests should be managed to produce a sustained flow of forest products at some near optimum level. These forest products include clear water, wildlife, fisheries, recreational space, and livestock forage, as well as timber. In practice, the concept is applied too often to a sustained yield of timber and no commitment is made to maintain forests in their natural state, or in a state suited to the sustained production of their other products of value.

FOREST MANAGEMENT There are many ways to manage forests, and one is to leave them alone. This is the obvious approach in areas where one wishes to follow the course of events as they would occur without human interference, and is appropriate to various reserves to be discussed in Chapter 9. Usually, however, one wishes to use a forest for some other purpose, and some degree of change within the forest ecosystem is deemed desirable. If one is concerned primarily with the protection of watersheds to insure good infiltration of water to underground aquifers, and a high sustained yield of water to streams with a minimum of siltation, it may be desirable to maintain a virtually undisturbed forest cover. However, if water yield is a principle objective and is to take precedence over all other uses, it may be important to modify the vegetation, to replace those species which transpire more water with others that are less water demanding. Trees are heavy users of water, in most instances, in comparison with grasses, and certain species of trees transpire more water than others.[16] If the objective were to maintain a maximum diversity of native species, offering a maximum number of ecological niches to wildlife, one would institute a management system favoring a wide variety of successional stages of forest growth in balance with areas of climax vegetation. Within the latter, one would be particularly careful to maintain old trees, dead trees, and fallen trees, since these provide a habitat for particular kinds of animals. A forest to be managed for public recreation may be kept more open than one managed for other purposes, to allow easy access and scenic vistas, as well as a variety of habitats for wildlife.

Management for timber production, as an important or primary objective, also can involve many different approaches. Trees grow faster and produce more cellulose per acre when young than when mature. If the need is for pulpwood or wood chips, or for firewood, then maximum areas will be kept in young forest reproduction and trees will be cut before their growth begins to slacken off with approaching maturity. However, if the need is for high quality lumber, then a maximum area devoted to mature trees will be required. For certain species, only the very old trees produce the higher quality lumber. The redwood lumber that has traditionally reached the market from California forests is the product of old trees. Youngsters only a century or two of age do not produce it.

One of the oldest forms of silviculture (tree culture) is *coppicing*. In this, mature trees having the capacity to sprout from their stumps are cut back. Sprouts come up in abundance, are allowed to grow to the required size, and are then harvested. The stump will then produce additional sprouts and the process is repeated. Oaks, ashes, chestnut, alder, and other hardwoods will sprout in this way. The products of coppices were used for poles, firewood, charcoal, and other special uses. A modified coppice system was known as *coppice with standards*. In this some single-stem, tall trees (standards) were left to provide shade for the coppices and to produce ship's timbers. Coppicing is no longer widely used, although it has value wherever needs for small wood products exist.[16]

Where a sustained yield of wood is expected, it is important to carry out a forest survey and inventory as a first stage of management. In this the volume of timber in an area is determined, broken down by location, species, age classes, condition of trees, and other criteria. When this is available, a management plan may be worked out, usually involving a system of rotation cutting, to enable a regular harvest and to provide for regular growth to replace the trees that are cut. Where mechanical equipment must be moved about to reach trees and to haul them out of the forest after they are cut, a network of roads must be planned and constructed before logging actually takes place. Skills and care taken in locating and constructing roads to avoid erosion or other forms of forest damage is as important to forest perpetuation as other aspects of the activity.

Three basic systems of cutting are now in use in forests managed for timber: clear cutting, shelterwood cutting, and selective cutting.[16] The first is particularly appropriate to forests in which the trees are of relatively uniform age and are made up of commercially useful species. All the trees are cut from a block or strip, leaving open ground. The debris and litter left after logging may also be removed, burned, or concentrated, and the ground left suitable for seedling growth. If the trees in uncut blocks or strips can provide an abundant supply of seeds, no artificial planting may be required. Otherwise the area may be reseeded or planted to nursery-grown seedlings.

Selective cutting is particularly appropriate to forests of mixed age classes or containing several species of unequal commercial value. Mature trees of the desired species are harvested. Young trees are left to grow to maturity. Great care must be taken not to damage the trees left in the process of removing the ones to be cut.

Shelterwood cutting is intermediate between the above two systems. In this, part of the tree stand is removed in the initial cutting, and in particular those trees of poor form or quality are taken out. This is essentially a thinning operation that opens up the forest floor to light. The best quality trees are left to cast seed and provide shelter for the growing seedlings. After a good seed crop has been distributed, a heavier cut is made of the remaining trees, leaving some to provide shelter. In a third stage after seedlings are well established, the remaining mature trees are removed.

In all of these systems, the yield from the forest must be balanced against ecological requirements and economic conditions. Cutting will be less when market conditions are poor, and heavier when good market conditions exist, but in no case should the existence of good markets permit deviations from the system to the degree that growth and reproduction are seriously reduced.

Systems of clear cutting commonly leave ugly and unnatural openings in a forest, particularly where operators insist on following straight lines or contours and leave sharp lines of demarcation between the cutover and unlogged forest. Where forest debris, including major parts of the tree not wanted as saw logs, is left on the ground, the results are unattractive. Systems of selection or shelterwood cutting leave a more natural appearance to the forest and are preferred by those who favor multiple use and wish to use forests for outdoor recreation. Clear cutting is also more likely to encourage erosion, and it may leave stream beds choked with debris following logging. Nevertheless, some types of forest do not regenerate well following selective cutting, since the seedlings may thrive best on soil from which the debris and litter have been removed and which is exposed to full sunlight. Careful forest management requires a balancing of all of the various values obtainable from the forest and the selection of systems that will perpetuate them. Care for forest regeneration is equally important with skills used in forest cutting and timber removal if the forest is to be maintained. In intensively managed forests, trees may be thinned and pruned to obtain the best growth and highest yield. Diseased and damaged trees may be removed and dense stands of young trees opened up. Lower branches may be taken off to improve lumber quality. In the forest of many age classes and species, some form of cropping can be going on at all times and a steady income can, theoretically at least, be produced.

Prevention of waste is another important part of good timber management. Full utilization of a tree for lumber is not possible, but remnant parts may have value for other uses (Fig. 7–3). The development of the pulp industry, producing paper and other products, and the plastics industry, based on cellulose, has created a demand for almost the entire tree. Recent developments in these industries have made possible the use of many species of trees previously not utilized and, in fact, almost any kind of cellulose can now be used in one or another forest-based industry.

FOREST PROTECTION Individuals who manage forests to obtain a sustained yield of wood or for maintenance of other values have long been concerned with preventing or suppressing those factors in the environment which are destructive to forests. These factors are many. Fire has received the most publicity and prominence but is easily surpassed in its effects by forest diseases, forest insects and, at times, by damage by vertebrate animals, floods, avalanches, hurricanes, storms, or other unusual weather conditions. All of these are natural and have been operative for as long as forests have been on earth. None can necessarily be classified as "problems" in themselves. They become problems because of the values people place on certain areas of forests, and their consequent desire to maintain these areas in a particular state.

The effect of fire and the role fire plays in forest ecology can be considered to vary along a climatic gradient. The highly humid forests such as tropical and some temperate rain forests are virtually fireproof in their natural state. Although man has used fire to open up or clear these forests, he can burn only by cutting the vegetation and allowing it to dry and then by taking advantage of brief dry periods in the generally humid weather. The extremely dry forests at the arid end of the climatic gradient are dry enough to carry fire at any time. However, because they are slow growing and produce relatively little plant debris they may not accumulate enough fuel at the surface of the ground to carry a fire. When they do burn, however, they are slow to recover, and may be permanently replaced by vegetation more suited to arid conditions.

Those forests most suited to fire grow in climates with a pronounced dry season but also with enough rainfall to permit abundant plant growth. In such areas, fire has been a constant factor in forest history, and forests are to some degree conditioned to its presence. Fires may start from lightning, in the absence of man. However, man has been around a long time and has been using and misusing fire for a good share of that time. Thorn forest and monsoon forest alternate with savanna in accordance with the prevalence of fires. Pine forests, redwood forests, and mediterranean sclerophyll forests are all adapted in varying degrees to fire. Redwoods, for example, have an unusually tough and fire-resistant bark. When they do burn they have the capacity to sprout vigorously from what appear initially to be blackened and lifeless trunks.

FIG. 7–3. Waste of wood in harvesting and milling (*data from U.S. Forest Service*).

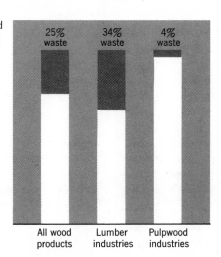

All wood products

Lumber industries

Pulpwood industries

25% waste

34% waste

4% waste

a

b

c

d

FOREST MANAGEMENT AND PROTECTION

(**a**) Fires may move from the ground, up tree trunks to become devastating crown fires. (**b**) Repeated burning changed this forest to low-value brush. (**c**) Controlled burning can reduce the danger of wild fires through removal of fuel and may help to maintain certain types of forest in a productive condition. (**d**) In block cutting, seed trees are left to favor regeneration. (**e**) Early clear-cut-and-burn logging brought ruined landscapes. (**f**) In selective cutting in western pine forests, younger trees are left to produce a new crop. (**g**) An intensively managed forest in Sweden.

e

f

g

During the early development of forestry in the United States as well as in many other countries a decision was made to protect forests as completely as possible against fire. Although this decision was difficult to carry out, skill in the prevention, detection, and suppression of forest fires was gradually developed, and many areas of forest were protected for long periods of time. Unfortunately, this policy had unanticipated effects. Litter accumulated on the ground in quantities that would not have built up in the absence of human intervention. Dense stands of tree reproduction and brush grew wherever light penetrated the canopy. When a fire eventually entered such a protected forest it was a different kind of fire than what would have occurred under natural conditions. Generating intense heat from the abundance of fuel it could quickly change from a ground to a "crown" fire sweeping through the woods at a terrifying rate of speed. Under some circumstances, fire "storms" develop, devastating great areas and impossible to suppress until all fuel has been consumed or rainstorms have saturated the ground.

Gradually a shift in attitude toward fire has occurred. Prescribed burning is now used more and more widely as a forest management tool. In this practice, fires are started at a time of year when they will burn slowly and will not generate intense heat. They are used to thin the layer of forest litter and open stands of brush and young trees. A forest managed by fire in this way can be made secure against devastating wildfires.

During recent decades, however, the prevention and suppression of wildfires has remained and certainly, for sometime to come, will remain a major burden for forest protection agencies. It has not been unusual in the United States to lose a billion board feet of timber to fires in a single year. Acreage burned annually is in the millions, and expenditures for fire protection are generally in excess of 100 million dollars a year.[7,8]

Disease has been less-publicized, but much more destructive than fire. In the United States in 1962, for example, fires burned 1.3 billion board feet of timber, disease knocked out 3.8 billion board feet, and forest insects killed 5.4 billion board feet.[8] All of this was saw timber, trees of a species and size suitable for logging. Disease-and-insect-killed timber is commonly salvaged by logging, but much is not used, and management plans are impaired. Among the more spectacular forest diseases in the United States have been chestnut blight, blister rust, and Dutch elm disease. All are caused by parasitic fungi. Chestnut blight, introduced accidentally from the Orient early in the twentieth century quickly spread through the eastern hardwood forests. Within a short time it had almost completely eliminated the once abundant and highly valued chestnut tree. No effective way of controlling this disease has yet been found. Fortunately, other species of chestnuts are resistant, and it has not done equivalent damage in other continents. White-pine-blister rust was accidentally introduced from Germany. It has prevented the eastern white pine from becoming reestablished in areas from which it was eliminated by fire and logging. It has spread into forests of western white pine and sugar pine and has done great damage. Since this fungus must spend part of its development cycle on gooseberry or current bushes (*Ribes* spp.), it can be controlled through the laborious process of eliminating these plants from the vicinity of white pine or sugar pine forests. The Dutch elm disease is carried from tree to tree by insects. It threatens the elm-tree component of America's deciduous forests.

Thus far the best hope for controlling diseases lies in sound forestry practices, including the removal of trees likely to become infected and the prevention of injury to young trees. Encouraging forest diversity is the best forest insurance. Disease spreads more quickly and has greater effect where one species of tree dominates the ground in closely ranked stands. Interspersion of species allows for slower spread and easier control. If one species is lost, others remain to fill the gaps and maintain the forest.

Insect pests represent the most serious threat other than people to forests; and because of human reaction to them, a serious threat to entire ecosystems. Daniel Janzen has pointed out that a plant has three major external defenses against herbivores. (1) Weather inimical to the insects or other plant-eaters; (2) predators and parasites that feed on the herbivores and at times control their numbers; and finally (3) forest diversity with scattering and interspersion of individuals of a species.[12] In temperate zone forests, management practices that cut down on species diversity remove the third defense and interfere with the second. Weather, however, remains a controlling factor, so that insect outbreaks are periodic and do not take a constant toll. In tropical forests, diversity provides a high degree of protection, and there is an unusual variety of predators and parasites for any insect that feeds on plants. However, the first factor is not operative. Weather is always favorable to outbreaks of any kind of species. Hence, when tropical forests are simplified into single-species plantations, all of the defenses against herbivorous enemies are removed, or seriously reduced.

Insect pests particularly destructive in Northern Hemisphere forests include the spruce budworm, which at times sweeps through northern forests with devastating effects, the larch sawfly that can destroy great areas of larch or tamarack, the pine weevil that attacks those white pines which escape blister rust, and the pinebark beetle which devastates forests of ponderosa pine in the western United States.

With insects as well as disease, sound management aimed at maintaining healthy, vigorous trees, good soil conditions, and the maximum diversity commensurable with the goals of management provides the best protection. Where this fails, expensive special control measures must be employed. However, the practice of using DDT and its relatives can only be condemned, since it has effects that ramify through the ecosystem. Such pesticides fail in the long run to control pests. But they succeed too well in reducing populations of species preying on the pests. Since these pesticides accumulate in food chains, they destroy great numbers of animals. The ideal pesticide to control insect pests would be one highly toxic to the pest, but to nothing else. In the absence of this ideal, balanced chemical controls, using the least dangerous pesticides, become essential at times, where good management and biological control have not succeeded.

TIMBER SUPPLY
AND DEMAND In the United States the existing forest area represents approximately three-fourths of the original forest area. The balance has been converted to agriculture, pasture, or urban-industrial uses. There is still a great store of timber. Approximately one-half billion acres of land are rated as commercial forest—land capable of producing commercial wood products now or in the near future and not withdrawn from commercial use in parks or reserves. More than 90 percent of the area is covered by second growth forest, or in some parts of the country by forest succession even farther removed from the primeval forest which first supported logging. It is, however, somewhat optimistic to classify as commercial forest areas which are in the hands of private owners not primarily interested in timber production—the farm forests, suburban forests, and forests growing on residential or recreational holdings. Much of this may never be used for the growing of wood products (Fig. 7–4). Only 40 percent of commercial forest land is in federal, state, or timber company hands and, therefore, likely to remain in timber production.[8]

Timber production figures for the United States are presented in Table 9, with those for Canada for comparison.[6] Canada possesses a much larger forest area, but much is in boreal forest of low productivity, and large areas are still relatively inaccessible to commercial harvest. In addition to the 316 million cubic meters of wood produced, the United States had a net balance of imports over exports amounting to approximately 6 million cubic meters. The United States produced 33 million metric tons of pulp and more than 40 million metric tons of paper and paperboard. In addition, however, it imported a net of approximately 6 million metric tons of pulp and paper.

TABLE 9
Forest Production in
the United States and
Canada, 1967[6]

PRODUCTS	UNITED STATES	CANADA
	(Thousands of cubic meters)	
Sawlogs	191,160	63,325
Mine timbers	991	130
Pulpwood	88,500	37,681
Other industrial wood	13,594	1,600
Total industrial wood	294,245	102,736
Fuel wood	21,948	4,836
Total production	316,193	107,572

Processed wood products, 1967

	(Thousands of metric tons)	
Pulp	33,258	14,435
Paper	40,578	10,316
Newsprint	2,245	7,432

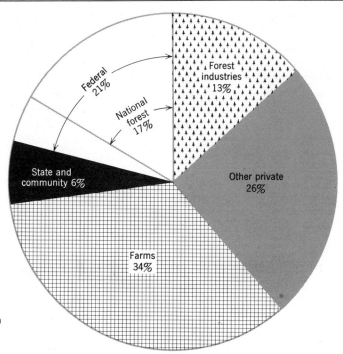

FIG. 7–4. Ownership of commercial forest land in the United States (*data from U.S. Forest Service*).

North America, including only the United States and Canada, leads all other continents and regions in the production of wood products. The United States, however, in addition to being one of the greatest timber producers, leads also in consumption. Particularly in the consumption of paper the United States is far ahead of other nations. Thus the average consumption of newsprint was approximately 41 metric tons per 1000 people. The nearest rival was Sweden which consumed 36 metric tons per 1000 people.[6] Anyone who has compared the giant-sized United States newspapers with the small ones produced by most other countries can understand the reason. It has been estimated that the Sunday edition of *The New York Times* for one year requires 125,000 tons of newsprint, which requires the annual growth from 1250 square miles of Canadian forest land.[4] The wasteful consumption of paper, and the problems that result from the disposal of paper wastes have led to increased interest and activity in recycling or reusing paper.

In 1962 the Forest Service made various predictions about supply and demand in relation to wood and wood products in the United States. There has been no reason to revise these estimates markedly. In that year the United States consumed 12 billion cubic feet of wood, and this represented an increasing per capita demand. Assuming some increase in demand and the expected increase in population it was predicted that by A.D. 2000 we would require 21 billion cubic feet of wood.[8,15] Between now and A.D. 2000, we can expect no increase in forest acreage but, instead, a decrease. There is little reason to believe we can command an increasing share of the world's timber exports, since demand in other countries is likely to grow more rapidly than in the United States. Some gains can be expected from better management of existing commercial forest lands, and major gains could come if the owners of small forest tracts could be encouraged to practice forestry.[19,20]

Nevertheless, the more sensible approach to a potential shortage of wood is hardly to bend every effort, and sacrifice other values, to make each forest acre produce more and more boards and pulp. Rather, it is to cut down on our present wasteful approach to timber usage, both at the production end by getting more out of each tree cut, and at the consumption end by using wood products for worthwhile purposes and paying major attention to reuse and recycling.

FORESTRY IN OTHER COUNTRIES

Outside of the United States the nations of the world represent all extremes in forest resources and forestry practices. Canada is most like the United States, and its situation has already been considered. It is a timber-exporting country and likely to remain in this category for some time to come. Particularly favorable to the practice of forestry is its land ownership pattern. Over 90 percent of its commercial forest land is in federal or provincial ownership.[23]

Europe has led the world in the development of forest science and forest management. This has resulted partly from the drastic reduction which took place in its total forest area as land was cleared for agriculture or other more intensive uses. Although most of Europe was once forested, only 29 percent is forested today, and much of this is in Scandinavia. In Great Britain, which was once largely forested, only slightly more than 7 percent of the land is now in forest. In France only 20 percent remains in forest.[5] In 1664, the realization that forests were rapidly disappearing caused John Evelyn, one of the founders of the Royal Society of London, to recommend the establishment of forestry as a science and as a concern of the Royal Society. Shortly thereafter Colbert, minister to Louis XIV of France, produced the *French Forest Ordinance of 1669* in which sound forestry and land management rules were promulgated.[10] Gifford Pinchot learned his forestry at the French forestry school at Nancy, and most of the pioneer foresters in America were influenced by French and German forestry concepts.

The total forested areas in Europe, outside of the USSR, is 138 million hectares compared to 710 million in North America. However, the total production from European forests in 1968 was 309 million cubic meters compared to 445 million from North America.[5,6] The yield per hectare, therefore, was nearly four times greater in Europe than in North America. The difference reflects the intensity of care and the skill in management.[14] Trends in forest management in Germany are of particular interest. After 1840, German foresters engaged in a highly artificial form of forest management. Forests were clear-cut and replanted to the species of trees that were in greatest demand, mostly to pure stands of spruce and pine. It was believed by doing this the highest yields could be obtained from each acre without wasting soil productivity on growing "weed" trees or brush. The former broad-leaved and mixed broad-leaved and coniferous forests were replaced by uniform, even-aged stands of conifers. In time it was found that the continued production of these single-species forests damaged the soil through increasing the rate of podsolization and by breaking down the circulatory system of soil minerals. Losses to insects, diseases, and storms increased. Then the second and third generations of pure spruce and pine began to decline in yield per acre as both growth rate and timber quality fell off. In consequence, after 1918, there was a swing in Germany back toward a more natural type of forest. Mixed forests were planted, as comparable as possible to the original forests of the area. Clear cutting was replaced by selective cutting, using logging methods which did as little damage as possible to the remaining stands of trees. Under this system of management, known as *Dauerwald*, yields have increased and forest lands have been improved.[14]

In Switzerland, most forest land belongs to the communes or the cantons, but management rules have been laid down by federal law and affect all forest owners. Clear cutting is not allowed nor can forest land be converted to other uses without federal permission. Great Britain, in an effort to restore the productivity of land and to reduce its reliance on imports, has instituted a major reforestation program. Areas of the Scottish highlands long ago depleted of trees and then burned and grazed into ruin, are now once again supporting healthy stands of Scots pine.

Southern Hemisphere countries such as Australia, New Zealand, and South Africa were deficient in conifers originally and faced the need to import most of the softwood timber required for construction. To remedy this situation, extensive coniferous plantings over millions of acres have been undertaken, relying particularly on California's Monterey Pine. In Australia, great areas of native *Eucalyptus* forest have been cleared to make way for pine monocultures. Such plantations are depressing to anyone but a wood producer, but initially, at least, they have produced high yields in a remarkably short space of time. Whether these yields will continue or the German experience will be repeated remains to be seen. It must be recognized, however, that such plantations are most comparable to agricultural croplands and represent a sacrifice of wild land values to commodity production.[16,17]

By far the greatest of the world reserves of timber lie in the tropics. South America in particular leads all other continents in forest acreage, and much of this is still little utilized. But the tropics are a depressing region for those who hope to see forest land remain in forest cover. The techniques for managing rain-forest land for sustained and profitable forest production, and for controlling land use to prevent the conversion of forest into short-term exploitative farming and pastoralism have not been widely applied.[12,22]

Long before forests were regarded as commercial resources, they were of great value. These values remain even in areas where the need for wood products is high. Forests hold the land together and keep water cycles functioning. They are regulators of the atmosphere and areas where people can go for recreation and renewal of spirit. They are the homes for the greatest diversity of plant and animal species which can be found in any region on earth.

Planning for sound forest management requires the recognition of all forest values. In some places and some times it is necessary to emphasize one value over others—wood or water may take precedence. Over any broad region, however, we cannot afford to sacrifice too many forest values. Perhaps the lesson of environmental conservation is to recognize forests are far more than trees. In our concern to see more trees, we must not lose sight of the forest.

CHAPTER REFERENCES

Department of Agriculture, 1949. *Trees.* Yearbook of Agriculture, Washington, D.C.

Forest Service, 1965. *Timber trends in the United States.* Forest Research Report 17, Washington, D.C.

Haden Guest, S. et al., eds., 1956. *World geography of forest resources.* Ronald Press, New York.

Ovington, J. D., 1965. *Woodlands.* English Universities Press, London.

Pyles, Hamilton, K., 1970. *What's ahead for our public lands?* Natural Resources Council of America, Washington, D.C.

LITERATURE CITED

1. Albrecht, W. A., 1957. Soil fertility and biotic geography. *Geographical Review,* 47: 86–105.
2. Bourliere, F., 1962. The uniqueness of the African big-game fauna. *African Wildlife,* 16: 95–100.
3. Curtis, John T., 1956. The modification of mid-latitude grasslands and forests by man. (See Thomas, 1956, in general references.)
4. Department of Agriculture, 1949. *Trees.* Yearbook of Agriculture, Washington, D.C.
5. Food and Agricultural Organization of the United Nations, 1963. *World forest inventory.* FAO, Rome.
6. ———, 1969. *Yearbook of forest products.* FAO, Rome.
7. Forest Service, 1956. *Timber resource review fact sheets.* Washington, D.C.
8. ———, 1965. *Timber trends in the United States.* Washington, D.C.
9. Gabriel, Alfons, 1969. The geography of the Sahara. *Sahara,* G. P. Putnam's Sons, New York, pp. 10–65.
10. Glacken, Clarence, 1967. *Traces on the Rhodian shore.* University of California, Berkeley.
11. Gourou, Pierre, 1966. *The tropical world.* Wiley, New York, fourth edition.
12. Janzen, Daniel, 1970. The unexploited tropics. *Bull. Ecological Society of America,* 51: 4–7.
13. Josephson, H. R., and D. Hair, 1956. The United States. In Haden Guest et al., above.

14. Lowenthal, David, 1956. Western Europe. In Haden Guest et al., above.

15. McArdle, Richard E., 1955. *Timber resources for America's future*. United States Forest Service, Washington, D.C.

16. Ovington, J. D., 1965. *Woodlands*. English Universities Press, London.

17. Peace, T. R., 1961. The dangerous concept of the natural forest. *Advancement of Science*, 17: 448–455.

18. Pyles, Hamilton K., 1970. *What's ahead for our public lands?* Natural Resources Council of America, Washington, D.C.

19. Quinney, D. N., 1964. Small private forest landownership in the United States—individual and social perception. *Natural Resources Journal*, 3: 379–393.

20. Raup, Hugh M., 1964. Some problems in ecological theory and their relation to conservation. *Journal of Ecology*, 52: 19–28.

21. Richards, P. W., 1952. *The tropical rain forest*. Cambridge University, Cambridge, England.

22. Rostlund, Erhard, 1956. The outlook for the world's forests and their chief products. In Haden Guest et al., above.

23. Tunstell, George, 1956. Canada. In Haden Guest et al., above.

8

rangelands
and
livestock

omestication of livestock brought opportunity and danger to humanity. The opportunity lay in the possibility for material enrichment through use of lands too arid for farm or forest. The danger materialized in the disastrous consequences of overgrazing in lands of western Asia, Africa, and Mediterranean Europe. Grasslands and dry shrub vegetation, in their native state, provide little food or products of commercial value. To become economically useful native vegetation can be converted into animal protein through the agency of wildlife or domestic grazing animals. In America, grasslands were used in prehistoric times as a source of meat and hides from native big game—buffalo, pronghorn, and elk. With the coming of Europeans, wild livestock were rapidly replaced by domestic cattle and sheep. Still later, better-watered sections of grasslands were plowed into farmlands for cereal-grain production. Farther west, however, in drier regions, grassland and shrub ranges have continued as grazing lands.

THE RANGE
LIVESTOCK
INDUSTRY IN THE
UNITED STATES

BEGINNINGS

The first livestock probably reached America when the Norsemen landed in Vinland in the eleventh century. Neither the Vikings nor their livestock survived.[30] It was not until the time of Columbus when livestock were again brought to the Americas, and it was probably Cortez who first brought cattle and sheep to the mainland of North America in the early sixteenth century. Livestock spread rapidly under Spanish methods of handling. Cattle and sheep came to New Mexico in the sixteenth and seventeenth centuries, and spread through California in the latter part of the eighteenth century.[33] The horse must have escaped from Spanish missions and settlements in the seventeenth century, for by 1680 the Pueblo and Apache Indians had the horse, by the 1750's the horse had reached Montana, and before 1800 Canada. The feral mustang and Indian pony played an interesting role in the history of the American West.[35]

The livestock industry in the United States has had its most colorful history in the area known as the western range, the arid grassland, sagebrush, and scrub country lying westward of the 100th meridian, which bisects North Dakota and runs southward through Dodge City, Kansas. It should not be imagined, however, that the western range supports most of the livestock in the United States. The area east of the 100th meridian supports far more beef and dairy cattle than the area to the west, and it is only in sheep numbers that the West has a slight edge.[28] The livestock business had its beginnings in the eastern United States with animals brought from Europe by early colonists. From early colonial times livestock were pastured in forest clearings along the westward fringes of agricultural lands. From here the animals were moved back into farm fields and pastures for fattening and from there to market in towns and cities. As agriculture spread westward, the pastoral fringe of land moved ahead of it until the prairie states were reached.[8]

In the eastern United States, livestock had a profound influence on vegetation. With grazing pressure native grasses and forbs were displaced from pastures and fields. In their place came a mixture of exotics which had followed the settlers from Europe. The most important of these was Kentucky bluegrass, a perennial which has followed agriculture and pasturing throughout its long history in Eurasia and which helped to stabilize the pasture lands of western Europe.[7] Bluegrass is an excellent forage grass for livestock and well able to hold up under heavy grazing. With its aid the soils on eastern pastures were held in place and their condition improved.

TEXAS CATTLE While livestock were gradually spreading with the American colonies, a major center of stock raising had grown up in the Spanish domain of Texas. Spanish land grants were liberal and favored the establishment of large ranches needed for the maintenance of a range livestock industry. The cattle in this region were the Texas longhorns, a breed originally developed in Spain, long legged, rangy, hardy, and well suited to foraging in a half-wild condition on the open range (p. 192). When Texas entered the Union there was little change in land-ownership policy. Texas retained ownership of public lands within its boundaries and continued to follow the Spanish practice of disposing of them to encourage range livestock production. As a result the livestock business thrived. With abundant grassland range and little need for hay or pasture land, costs of operation for cattlemen in Texas were low. Markets were difficult to reach, and many cattle were butchered for hides and tallow. Nevertheless, stock raising remained profitable. In the 1840's trail herds of Texas cattle were driven to market in Louisiana and later to Ohio. With the California gold rush, a number of drives of Texas cattle to California were carried out.[8]

In 1860 Texas is estimated to have held more than 4½ million cattle. Following the Civil War, a greatly expanded market for beef led to the series of trail drives of Texas cattle immortalized in western song and story. Most of the cattle trails were developed to meet shipping points on the new railroads that were being built westward in the 1860's. These shipping points, Abilene, Newton, Dodge City, and others, soon developed into the wild and lawless cow towns of western legend. During the 20-year period between 1865 and 1885 an estimated 5½ million head of cattle were driven northward from Texas, some to market, others to stock the newly opening rangelands to the north.[8]

The settlement of the grassland ranges in the central and northern prairies and plains was retarded for a time by the Plains Indians. A few pioneer stockmen established ranches in the North in early times. However, the biggest expansion took place in the 1870's, as the Indians were subdued and the herds of bison on which they had depended reduced and finally eliminated. In 1870 it is estimated that there were between 4 and 5 million cattle in the seventeen western states; by 1890 there were over 26½ million.[8]

SHEEPHERDING Sheep brought to New Mexico in the sixteenth century were to form the basis for the sheep industry in the West. In the seventeenth and eighteenth centuries sheep ranches were established in New Mexico, Texas, Arizona, and California. Along with cattle, sheep spread westward in front of American colonists from the eastern seaboard.[33] However, the greatest expansion of the sheep business in the plains and prairie states took place after the cattlemen were well established. The extent of this expansion is indicated by the figures for 1850 when there were 514,000 sheep in the West and 1890 when the numbers had reached 20 million. The greatest increase in the northern plains came in the 1880's when cattle numbers were beginning to decline. Wyoming carried 309,000 sheep in 1886 and over 2,600,000 in 1900, during which period the number of cattle declined by half a million. In Montana there was little increase in cattle between 1886 and 1900, but sheep increased from somewhat less than 1 million to over 3½ million.[8]

In California sheep spread with Spanish missions, *ranchos,* and later with American settlers. Great bands of sheep were moved westward to stock California in early days—more than a half million between 1852 to 1857,[23] and later equally vast bands moved eastward to stock ranges of the Great Basin states. Many early sheepmen in California used to carry on the old Spanish practice of nomadic or migratory sheep grazing. One route regularly followed took the sheepherders up the east side of the Sierra Nevada, across the high passes of the central mountains, and back southward along the western slopes.[33] The numbers of sheep on these long drives were large, and the damage has been made memorable in the writings of John Muir, who described the devastation in the Yosemite region, and in the findings of later surveys which described the almost complete destruction of ground vegetation in the Mt. Whitney region.[21,34] The spread of sheep in the West did not take place without arousing bitter feelings among the cattlemen. Cattlemen, with established home ranches, particularly resented the passage of migratory bands of sheep across ranges, using forage they had hoped to reserve for their own cattle. The bitterness broke out into the open cattle-sheep wars in some areas.

PUBLIC LANDS AND LIVESTOCK The history of livestock in the West cannot be understood without considering the land-disposal policy of the federal government. As a result of numerous transactions, the United States government had obtained claim to approximately 1½ billion acres of land within the boundaries of the contiguous United States (Fig. 8–1). The policy of the government

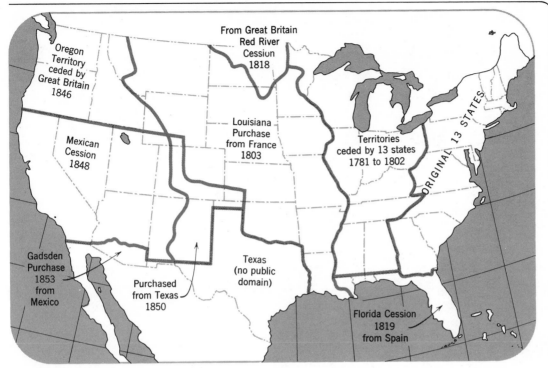

FIG. 8–1. The original public domain of the United States (*source: Bureau of Land Management, 1968*[4]).

Map labels:
- Oregon Territory ceded by Great Britain 1846
- From Great Britain Red River Cession 1818
- Mexican Cession 1848
- Louisiana Purchase from France 1803
- Territories ceded by 13 states 1781 to 1802
- ORIGINAL 13 STATES
- Gadsden Purchase 1853 from Mexico
- Purchased from Texas 1850
- Texas (no public domain)
- Florida Cession 1819 from Spain

was to dispose of these lands as rapidly as possible. The philosophy of Thomas Jefferson has dominated land-disposal policies. He believed lands should be used to encourage settlement and development of the nation and thus to strengthen it against its enemies rather than sold for immediate gain to the treasury (Fig. 8–2). A variety of acts were passed by Congress providing for the sale or homesteading of federal land. Noteworthy was the Homestead Act of 1862, which provided title to 160 acres of land, free of charge, to legitimate settlers after 5 years of residence on the land. The 160-acre limitation proved to be a major difficulty. In the farming lands of the East, 160 acres is more than adequate to support a family. In the arid West, where agriculture is not possible, 160 acres is insufficient for the raising of livestock. The acreage limitation, for the West, was later raised to 320 and then to 640 acres in 1916. However, even 640 acres does not provide adequate space for commercial stock raising. Much unfortunate publicity about farming opportunities in the West, accompanying the passage of the various homestead acts, encouraged settlers to cultivate land which should never have been plowed. Ultimately this led to failure and land abandonment but not without hardship to both land and settler.[8]

When the livestock industry expanded into the West, it moved into federal land. In favorable locations, stockmen established headquarters and attempted to obtain for themselves adequate range for their livestock.

c

THE WESTERN RANGE

(**a**) Cattle on an Oregon range. (**b**) Texas longhorns. (**c**) The cowboy tradition—moving out Herefords in Idaho. By 1890 there were more than 26 million cattle on the western range. (**d**) Sheep survived where cattle died, also in Idaho. From 1850 to 1890 sheep on the western range increased fortyfold to 20 million.

d

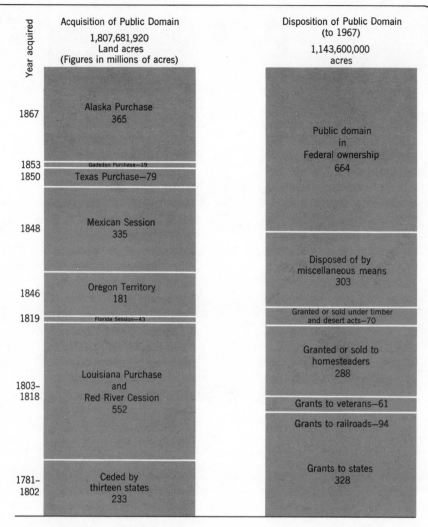

Year acquired	Acquisition of Public Domain 1,807,681,920 Land acres (Figures in millions of acres)	Disposition of Public Domain (to 1967) 1,143,600,000 acres
1867	Alaska Purchase 365	Public domain in Federal ownership 664
1853	Gadsden Purchase—19	
1850	Texas Purchase—79	
1848	Mexican Session 335	
		Disposed of by miscellaneous means 303
1846	Oregon Territory 181	
1819	Florida Session—43	Granted or sold under timber and desert acts—70
		Granted or sold to homesteaders 288
1803– 1818	Louisiana Purchase and Red River Cession 552	Grants to veterans—61
		Grants to railroads—94
1781– 1802	Ceded by thirteen states 233	Grants to states 328

FIG. 8–2. Additions to and disposals of the public domain to 1967.

The limitations of the Homestead Act were evaded in various ways: by having friends or relations take up homesteads on adjoining areas and eventually dispose of them to the central ranch owner or by homesteading land in the areas where water was available and thus obtaining use of the surrounding, drier ranges. By one device or another, many ranch owners obtained title to considerable areas of land. Still, many were dependent on unpatented federal land, the public domain, for a large part of their range forage.[8]

The invention of barbed wire in the middle 1870's brought a measure of stability to western grazing lands by making it economically feasible to fence off areas of private range and thus exclude the migratory herder, or trespassing livestock. Some ranchers, however, undertook to fence in large areas of public domain as well and had to be restrained from this by federal order. In the absence of fencing, ranch owners decided to respect each others rights to graze certain areas of public land and joined together to exclude trespassers.[8]

With the establishment of the forest reserves in 1891 and the National Forest system in 1905, additional stability was brought to western grazing lands. The land removed from the public domain and reserved as National Forest included much valuable mountain grazing land. Initially, misunderstandings led to efforts to eliminate livestock from forest reserves. Later, however, local stockmen were allowed grazing privileges on National Forest land, being charged a nominal fee per head of livestock grazed. Difficulties arose when the Forest Service attempted to improve National Forest ranges by restricting livestock numbers or seasons when grazing was permitted. Many stockmen resented what they believed to be unwarranted government interference with their rights.[33]

After the National Forests were established, much federal land still remained as unreserved public domain. Much of this was suitable for grazing. In 1934 the Taylor Grazing Act was passed by Congress as a measure to bring this federal range under proper management. Eighty million acres of public domain land were placed into grazing districts to be managed jointly by the federal government and committees of local stockmen. The Grazing Service was established to administer the new grazing districts. From the start, however, it was handicapped by the opposition of stockmen, who resented interference with long-established practices, and by lack of support from other federal agencies. In 1946 its functions were taken over by the Bureau of Land Management, which since that time has had responsibility for both the Taylor grazing districts and the other unreserved public-domain lands. This agency has responsibility over 160 million acres of federal land in western grazing districts and has been attempting to restore them to productivity (Fig. 8–3).

Since the 1880's western stockmen with access to federal land have been dissatisfied with its administration. Since the time when they were ordered to remove all fences from public-domain land, they have attempted to bring pressure to bear on Congress to make it possible for them to obtain outright leases of federal land for grazing purposes. Grazing privileges on National Forests and the more liberal grazing allowances on Taylor grazing lands have not been sufficient to satisfy those who want permanent grazing rights. Stockmen's associations, with a powerful lobby in Washington, have brought pressure in many sessions of Congress to have grazing lands removed from the jurisdiction of the Forest Service and other federal agencies and turned over to the use of cattle and sheep interests.

The 1970 report of the Public Land Law Review Commission reflects an effort in this direction, recommending the "dominant-use" principle as a means for giving livestock grazing priority above all other uses on certain lands, and recommending the disposal of certain lands to livestock owners.[25]

The westward movement of agricultural settlement rapidly cut down on the amount of land available for grazing. Originally the rich chernozems, prairie soils, and the deeper brown soils of the plains states supported range livestock. Early livestock owners in the northern grasslands once found forage so abundant and nutritious that cattle could thrive on it throughout the year. Some reported cattle were able to gain weight on natural feed during the winter and become fat enough for market in early spring.[8] But as the better soils were taken by farmers, livestock were

FIG. 8–3. Public lands and administrative agencies, 1967.[4]

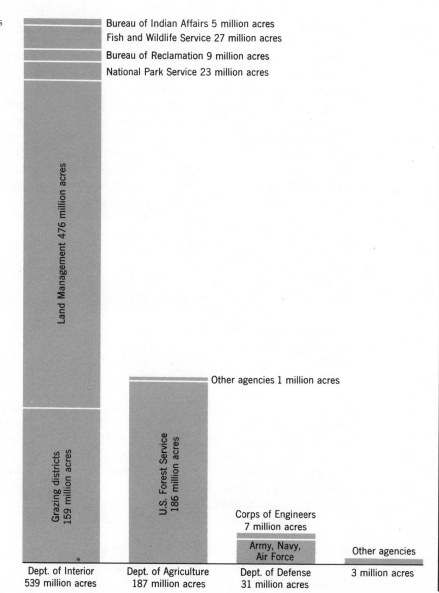

Bureau of Indian Affairs 5 million acres
Fish and Wildlife Service 27 million acres
Bureau of Reclamation 9 million acres
National Park Service 23 million acres

Land Management 476 million acres

Other agencies 1 million acres

Grazing districts 159 million acres

U.S. Forest Service 186 million acres

Corps of Engineers 7 million acres

Army, Navy, Air Force

Other agencies

Dept. of Interior 539 million acres

Dept. of Agriculture 187 million acres

Dept. of Defense 31 million acres

3 million acres

forced into drier lands and less fertile upland soils. This, combined with deterioration of the vegetation, made it no longer possible to carry livestock through the year on natural forage. Furthermore the market for grass-fed beef began to decline as the cornbelt states were settled and corn-fed cattle were shipped to market. A relationship developed between western cattle owners and the mixed farm-livestock economy of the corn belt. Cattle were shipped young from the western range, fattened to market age on corn and other forage, and moved to market. This practice, in turn, led to a change in the type of cattle in the West. The hardy Texas longhorns could thrive on rough range forage but failed to fatten into choice beef in the corn lot. They were gradually replaced on the western ranges through shipment of other breeds from the East—Herefords mainly, but also Aberdeen-Angus, Shorthorns, and others. The newer cattle breeds required more care and were less able to fend for themselves. The rancher with a permanent establishment and available hay or irrigated pasture lands was favored over the older type who depended entirely on native forage.[8] Western sheepmen, primarily interested in wool production, were less dependent on the farming states. The Merino sheep, a wool breed, came with the Spanish and for long remained the preferred sheep. Later, a new Merino-type sheep, the Rambouillet from France, became popular for wool production. In the farming states, generally, the emphasis shifted from wool to mutton breeds as the industry became established.[33]

Severe winters, drought, and the uncertain market conditions of the late 1880's and the 1890's put an end to the great expansion of the livestock industry. During this expansion the western United States was settled, but at a high cost to the nation. This cost was revealed in the first general survey of the western range carried out by the Forest Service in the early 1930's.[13] This survey showed that the original capacity of the native range vegetation to support livestock had been cut in half during the few decades that the range had been grazed. The original capacity of the native vegetation was estimated at 22½ million animal units (1 animal unit equals 1 cow or horse or 5 sheep or goats). As a result of overstocking by livestock the vegetation had deteriorated to the point where in 1930 the range capacity was only 10.8 million animal units. However, in 1930 the western range was still carrying 17.3 million animal units instead of the 10.8 million that it could have supported without further damage. The damage was therefore continuing. If stocking were reduced to a level below the range capacity, it would take approximately 100 years to restore the ranges to their original condition. In about 60 years of use, therefore, enough damage had been done to require a century to repair.

The survey also found that of the 728 million acres of range in the West, 589 million acres were suffering from serious erosion, thus both reducing their future productivity and adding to the silt load of the streams. Only about 95 million acres were found in satisfactory condition, and these, for the most part, were either privately owned or National Forest lands. The lands in the worst condition were the public domain, the no-man's lands of the West that had received neither administration nor care.[13] This Forest Service report was received with great distaste by stockmen, who admitted local overgrazing but denied the widespread severity of the damage and labeled the report as seriously biased.[3,25,33] However, both sides would admit that much was needed to restore or build up the grazing capacity of western rangelands.

Factors which have contributed to overgrazing of rangelands are several. First, in the early days, was ignorance. Stockmen from the East, inheritors of European traditions, were familiar with livestock management on well-watered pasture lands. They had no experience with the arid West, where the capacity of the land to support livestock is often extremely low. The Spanish, experienced with arid ranges, had learned mostly how to exploit them, not how to conserve them. As permanent ranches were established and men settled down to the business of earning a living on a long-term basis, some proved to be good observers and managers. They learned to recognize the better forage plants and the conditions that favored them and handled their livestock accordingly. Through practical, trial-and-error management they developed systems that later-day scientific range managers were to adopt or modify. Others, less capable or more handicapped by economic or environmental circumstance, failed to learn the lessons and continued to try to carry more livestock than the range would support.

Climate has been, and remains, a cause of range damage, although it is often blamed for man's mistakes. Droughts are normal on western ranges, and grazing capacity fluctuates with wet years and dry. A range properly stocked for a high rainfall year, may be dangerously overstocked if drought follows. With dry years, livestock numbers must be reduced, or supplemental feed in the form of hay or food concentrates must be purchased to carry them without pressure on range forage. However, a widespread drought often brings falling market prices and higher prices for hay or grain. If the rancher is short of cash, there is a strong temptation to try and hold excessive numbers of livestock in the hopes that better conditions will return. Damage always results.

Economic factors contribute to range damage. High prices for beef, mutton, or wool encourage heavy stocking; falling prices make it difficult to dispose of animals without great financial loss. Ranchers, like others, are in business to make money.

RANGE ECOLOGY AND MANAGEMENT

CARRYING CAPACITY

Much range damage has occurred because of failure to realize that each area of range has a carrying capacity. This can be defined as the number of animals which can be carried on it and kept in good condition without damage to the range forage. Carrying capacity depends on the soil and climate, the type of native vegetation, and the ability of the vegetation to hold up under grazing. It varies from one site to another, being high in well-watered areas with deep soil and extremely low on rocky, arid ranges.

Grass can stand only a limited amount of grazing pressure. Each perennial grass plant produces each year a certain surplus of growth which can be safely grazed without injury to the plant. Each plant also has a *metabolic reserve,* a certain minimum area of leaves and stems needed to carry out the necessary photosynthesis to build and store foods in the crown or root system. Annual grasses, which die each year and regenerate from seed the following year, could theoretically be cropped off to the roots once seed has been cast without damage to future generations. Actually, with annuals as well as perennials a certain minimum amount of leafage and stem must be left on the ground to provide soil protection and a more favorable bed in which seeds will germinate. The number of animals to be carried safely on the range depends, therefore, on the surplus of leafage and stems put on by vegetation. If too many animals are held, not only the surplus is eaten but also the reserve portions of the plant. If this process is repeated for long plants weaken and die.[12]

Species of range plants differ greatly in their ability to withstand use. The taller grasses of climax vegetation of the prairies are not able to withstand heavy grazing. Under heavy cropping they disappear, and their place is taken by more resistant, often sod-forming, grasses, which

FIG. 8–4. Growth forms of grasses: (a) annual; (b) sod forming; (c) bunch.

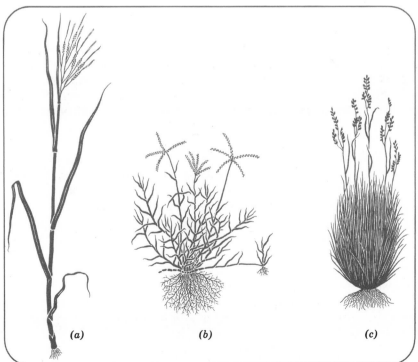

(a) (b) (c)

TABLE 10
Successional Changes
with Grazing and
Protection on the
North American
Prairie[32]

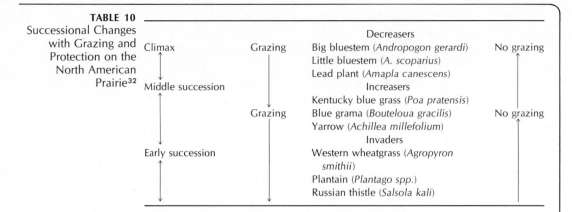

		Decreasers	
Climax	Grazing	Big bluestem (*Andropogon gerardi*)	No grazing
		Little bluestem (*A. scoparius*)	
		Lead plant (*Amapla canescens*)	
Middle succession		Increasers	
		Kentucky blue grass (*Poa pratensis*)	
	Grazing	Blue grama (*Bouteloua gracilis*)	No grazing
		Yarrow (*Achillea millefolium*)	
		Invaders	
Early succession		Western wheatgrass (*Agropyron smithii*)	
		Plantain (*Plantago spp.*)	
		Russian thistle (*Salsola kali*)	

have leaves and stems that grow more nearly horizontal to the ground surface and are, therefore, less easily cropped (Fig. 8–4). With continued heavy use even these sod-forming grasses disappear. On the resultant bare ground, relatively unpalatable weeds of various kinds seed in. If the range is protected from fire, woody plants of less palatable varieties will move into former grassland areas.[6]

In a widely used classification, put forward by Dyksterhuis,[11] range plants are placed into three categories: *decreasers,* the tall climax grasses, nutritious and highly preferred by livestock, which decrease in number under moderate grazing; *increasers,* species also present in the climax but in a lesser amount or subordinate position. They are often sod formers and are also nutritious and eaten well by livestock but better able to stand up to grazing use. These species increase in number or in space occupied as the tall climax grasses diminish. With very heavy grazing pressure, even the increasers are killed out, and their place is taken by *invaders,* native or exotic weeds or woody plants of low forage value, little used by livestock and generally not as well adapted to maintaining or holding the soil as the original vegetation. Proper range management includes maintaining a balance on the range between increasers and decreasers and keeping the invaders to a minimum (Table 10).

In terms of plant succession, overgrazing leads to a replacement of climax species or species high on the successional scale by plants low on the successional scale or pioneer species. Conversely, absence of grazing pressure if the damage is not too great will usually allow successional processes to operate and permit climax species to regain the ground.

RANGE CONDITION AND TREND   Range managers are trained to judge ranges on the basis of *condition,* which on many range types is simply a way of measuring the extent to which a range has departed from a climax stage toward lower successional stages as a result of grazing use, and *range trend,* which determines whether under existing conditions of management the range is returning toward a climax condition or deteriorating further.

In the Soil Conservation Service system, five classes of range condition are recognized, varying between excellent and very poor[17] (p. 204). An example of the criteria used is provided in Table 11. Notice that in the bottom row of this table the acres required per animal unit month, that is, the acres needed to support one cow or five sheep for one month, vary between 0.75 for a range in excellent condition and more than

TABLE 11
A Range Condition Score Sheet

FACTORS EVALUATED	EXCELLENT	GOOD	FAIR	POOR	VERY POOR
1. Relative potential forage yield (in percent)	90–100	75–90	50–75	25–50	0–25
2. Important desirable forage plants (percentage of ground surface covered by each species): Wild oats, *Avena* spp. Soft chess, *Bromus mollis* Calif. bunchgrass, *Stipa pulchra* Cutleaf filaree, *Erodium cicutarium* Bur clover, *Medicago hispida*, etc.	85–100	65–85	35–65	10–35	0–10
			"DECREASERS"		
3. Less desirable forage plants (percentage of ground covered): Ripgut brome, *Bromus rigidus* Annual fescue, *Festuca megalura* Foxtail, *Hordeum murinum* Yarrow, *Achillea millefolium* Blue dicks, *Brodiaea capitata*, etc.	0–15	10–30	15–50	25–65	40–90
			"INCREASERS"		
4. Undesirable forage plants: Medusahead grass, *Elymus caput-medusae* Nitgrass, *Gastridium ventricosum* Star thistle, *Centaurea melitensis* Dwarf plantain, *Plantago erecta* Tarweed, *Hemizonia* spp., etc.	0–15	5–20	10–40	25–75	40–100
			"INVADERS"		
5. Plant residue or litter per acre	Abundant	Adequate	Moderate	Scarce	Very scarce
6. Erosion	None	None to slight	Slight to moderate	Moderate to severe	Severe
7. Acres per animal unit month	.75–1	1–2	2–3	3–5	5 plus

Source. For California Annual Grass Range in North-Central California. Adapted from Grover (1945).

5.0 for a range in very poor condition. Obviously then, a rancher who keeps his ranges close to excellent condition will be able to carry more livestock and make greater profits than a rancher who allows his ranges to deteriorate. It should be remembered, however, that range condition is a measure of the degree to which a particular type of range approaches its maximum potential yield of forage. It is something quite apart from range and soil type. Thus, a well-watered prairie range with tall climax grasses on deep soil, rated in excellent condition, would have a higher carrying capacity than a range in excellent condition in the desert grassland region of the Southwest.

RANGE PESTS Although it is true in general that in the absence of grazing or with a reduction in livestock numbers ranges will improve in condition, there are many exceptions. Some of the invaders that occupy depleted ranges are not native plants and occupy no place in normal successional processes. Under some circumstances these invaders will continue to hold the ground even when the range is completely protected. Normal successional processes are halted, and the cover of exotics is said to form a *disturbance climax.* Thus, in California, the exotic grasses and weeds which arrived with the Spanish now form a disturbance climax that maintains itself. Studies at the San Joaquin Experimental Range in California have shown that even with complete protection from grazing over a long period of years, native perennial grasses do not replace the exotics. Elsewhere in the West, large areas of rangeland have been covered by a blanket of cheat grass (*Bromus tectorum*) which has completely replaced the original vegetation.[19] Both its soil-holding ability and forage value are low compared to the native grasses, but it maintains itself effectively even in the absence of grazing.

In Pacific Coast states the poisonous Klamath weed has invaded overgrazed ranges, and for a long period seemed impossible to control. Finally a species of beetle, which feeds only on Klamath weed, was introduced from Australia and has proved to be an effective agent of control. Unfortunately the beetle does not tolerate the disturbance in the vicinity of roads and highways. Here a fringe of Klamath weed persists, ready to reinvade when beetle numbers decline. Beetle and weed thus live in a precarious balance.

Along with an invasion of weeds following overgrazing comes an invasion of animal pests. Under climax conditions in grasslands a variety of rodents and other types of animals live without creating serious problems. When low successional weeds replace the climax, a different group of animal species also moves in and usually increases in numbers. The kangaroo rat (*Dipodomys*), jack rabbits (*Lepus*), and ground squirrels (*Citellus*) are among the range invaders. Vast amounts of money and time have been spent on their control, often under the theory that the rodents were the cause rather than an effect of range damage. However, numerous studies have shown that the most effective means of control is a barbed-wire fence, which keeps out livestock. When grazing is excluded, and grass grows tall and dense, ground squirrels, jack rabbits, and kangaroo rats must either move out or perish.[16,20]

Range management would be relatively simple if all that were needed to solve range problems was a simple reduction in livestock numbers. Unfortunately, the problem is much more complex. Livestock, like wild animals, have behavior patterns of their own, which often lead to actions quite contrary to the rancher's desires. An annual grass range of 10,000 acres in good condition could theoretically carry 800 head of cattle for a 6-month grazing period without any damage to range forage. Yet, such a range with 800 head could also show signs of serious overgrazing. The difficulty is livestock of their own accord do not distribute themselves evenly over a range and graze every acre equally. There is a normal tendency to concentrate and spend much time around watering places. Similarly, livestock like salt and will congregate in the vicinity of salting grounds. The topography will also influence their distribution. Level ground will usually receive heavier cattle use than slopes. Even on an area of level range, cattle may prefer to graze in one place in preference to others. Minor soil differences, resulting in better tasting or more nutritious forage can attract livestock to one area instead of another. Habit is also a strong factor. The result is that on the theoretical 10,000-acre range, areas the livestock prefer may be overgrazed, whereas other areas will remain untouched. Proper range management must take this into account. Fencing, although expensive, is an essential tool. With fences, livestock can be moved from one area to another and kept in each until the forage is properly utilized. Where fencing is not practical, good results sometimes can be obtained by the strategic location of salting grounds and watering places. The location of salt blocks near the water hole is usually an indication of careless range management.

Choice of livestock is another important factor in range management. Some breeds are better adapted for one range than another. Sheep normally do better on steep-hill ranges than cattle and are better adapted to ranges where forbs and shrubs predominate over grasses. Sheep breeds which band closely together require a herder and must be kept moving to avoid range damage. Where predatory animals are common or where ranges are unfenced, these breeds are preferred. On fenced ranges where there is little danger from predators, the breeds of sheep which tend to scatter rather than band together will usually give more even utilization of the range.

To restore damaged ranges, a reduction in stocking is often needed, and sometimes that is all that is required. In some instances, however, a reduction is not the answer but, instead, a difference in the method of handling livestock. Thus, if it is desired to shift the vegetation from fast-growing, early-maturing annual grasses to slower-growing, later-maturing perennials, it may be desirable to graze an area heavily early in the season, thus preventing the early-maturing species from setting seed. The

RANGE CONDITION AND MANAGEMENT

(**a**) Fencing is an essential tool for controlling livestock. (**b**) Excessive overgrazing around waterholes is often an indication of poor management of livestock. (**c**) Nebraska prairie in excellent condition. (**d**) Oregon rangeland in very poor condition.

c

d

livestock are then removed to another pasture until the later-maturing species have time to mature and cast seed. The stock may then be returned to the area, to moderately graze the desirable species and to trample the seed into the ground. Such a system, of course, requires the rancher to have enough feed elsewhere to carry the stock during the period when the desired grass species are maturing. A variety of similar systems have been devised to meet various problems of range management. All of the answers are not yet known, but we know enough now to do a much better job of range management than is being done.

RANGE PROBLEMS IN OTHER COUNTRIES Throughout the world, in prairie, steppe, pampas, and veld, ranges are still being damaged and deserts are encroaching on formerly useful land. The more productive ranges with high carrying capacities usually receive adequate care, but the more arid and marginal rangelands are frequently exploited with little apparent concern for the future. Abuse of rangelands carries not only the consequences of lowered carrying capacity and a diminished economic return from the land but affects all other natural resources as well. In some areas a valuable wildlife resource is destroyed to make room for livestock; the range is then damaged so that it is no longer suited for either wildlife or livestock. Such damaged areas are a source of erosion and disruption of watersheds, which can, in turn, affect still wider areas than those originally damaged.

In many areas of Africa among pastoral peoples, cattle have a traditional social value that far exceeds any market value that they may have. Traditionally, the worth of a person has been measured by the number of cattle he owns. The animals are killed and eaten only on ceremonial occasions and are not regarded as a source of meat, although their milk is used. Under such circumstances the usual incentives for animal husbandry or for careful management of range and pasture are lacking. Under primitive circumstances, livestock numbers were limited by predators and a variety of other natural causes. With civilization, however, many of these limiting factors have been removed and numbers of livestock have increased rapidly. With this has come widespread overgrazing and severe erosion. Large areas of Africa in the past have been rendered uninhabitable to cattle by the presence of the tsetse fly, some forms of which carry human sleeping sickness, but which more commonly carries the livestock disease *nagana*, fatal to cattle. Efforts to extend grazing land through elimination of the tsetse fly have involved bush clearing and the use of insecticides. However, since wild species of African game serve as hosts for the tsetse fly, campaigns have been directed against the wild game, and hundreds of thousands of head of spectacular and valuable wild mammals have been slaughtered in the name of fly control. Ironically, more recent studies have shown that the game animals being removed have a higher economic value and produce more meat than the livestock with which they are replaced (Chapter 9). The most economically efficient utilization of the dry, rough rangelands of Africa in the future will probably prove to be some combination of use by existing domestic breeds and species of grazing and browsing mammals that are at present wild.[9,10]

In India, as in Africa, the noneconomic value of cattle has handicapped range-management progress. The cow, introduced by the invading Aryans over 3000 years ago, is an object of religious veneration to many Hindus. Sacred cows, unrestricted and unconfined, damage both range and agricultural lands. India is a country that normally would support forest. But over much of the peninsula, forests have been completely eliminated to make room for grazing or cropland. Overgrazing, combined with gathering of vegetation for fuel, has done further damage so that, in an area that would have supported productive vegetation, barren desert exists and is spreading. George Schaller has stated:

India had an estimated 204 million cattle and buffalo and 94 million goats and sheep in 1956, of which 21 million of the former and 13 million of the latter grazed exclusively in the forests (Venkataramany, 1961). Livestock is permitted to graze without restrictions in virtually all forests and most sanctuaries, and serious damage to the vegetation culminating in widespread erosion is common particularly in the thorn and deciduous forests.[29]

Efforts on the part of the government to reduce the numbers of cattle have caused riots and the threat of political upheaval.

In the Middle East and the Saharan region, deserts have been spreading and becoming more barren through overgrazing. Writing of Iraq, Bryan and Springfield[1] have described the virtual elimination of vegetation from the rangelands. Larson has described devastation in the Libyan desert, and sees no hope for range improvement until such time as the numbers of livestock moved about by nomads can be brought under some control.[18]

In 1971 many of the nations which share land on the southern edge of the Sahara Desert joined in requesting United Nations assistance toward halting the southern march of the Sahara. Yet, in virtually all places where a southern extension of the desert has been observed the cause is the same—failure to control the numbers and distribution of livestock. Planting, reseeding, water development, and virtually every other available means toward improvement of range and livestock are bound to fail unless this control can be exerted. Indeed, most development efforts that have been attempted in this region have aggravated the problem rather than cured it. Water development in areas previously protected from livestock use because of the lack of water brings destruction of these in addition to the destruction of the ones previously grazed.

Australia has been a world leader in the management of pastures in

a

b

THE WORLD SITUATION

(**a**) Some see hope for the future in new domestic species adapted to extreme environments, as reindeer are adapted to the Arctic tundra of Sweden. (**b**) Cattle are not valued everywhere only for meat and hides: sacred cows in India. (**c**) Domestic llamas in Peru are well adapted to life in the high Andes Mountains. (**d**) Along the desert edge in Africa and Arabia, overgrazing and range destruction has led to an advance of the desert into formerly productive lands.

c

d

its better watered lands but, in the semiarid lands of the interior, range-lands have been allowed to deteriorate extensively. The presence of exotic pests has handicapped range improvements in many areas. At one time the prickly pear cactus, introduced from Mexico for livestock feed, overran millions of acres of range, forming dense, impenetrable thickets. All efforts at control failed until a biological method was attempted. An insect enemy of the prickly pear was brought in, which fed on and destroyed the cactus. Its extent was thus reduced to manageable proportions. In 1928 and 1930, several million eggs of the *Cactoblastis* moth were brought from Argentina and the larvae hatched out in prickly pear territory. By 1933 the last big area of prickly pear had been cleared out.[9,24,26]

The introduction of the European rabbit to Australia greatly aggravated range problems. Originally brought in by those who felt nostalgic for the rabbit hunting of the Old World, the rabbit spread rapidly throughout much of temperate Australia. Free from the predators and other limiting factors of its homeland, it had no difficulty displacing the native, marsupial mammals. On the arid ranges of the interior the combination of sheep and rabbit grazing was more than the vegetation could withstand. Drifting sand dunes and blowing dust marked the eastward march of the desert into the already narrow belt of productive land. Great sums of money were spent on rabbit control. A fence was built completely across the border between New South Wales and Queensland in hope of confining the rabbit. The effort failed.[24] A new answer was then sought, a biological one. Myxomatosis, a virus disease endemic among cottontails in South America, but fatal to the European rabbit, was introduced. Spread from one rabbit colony to another by mosquitoes, it proved to be initially highly effective in reducing the rabbit population. Undoubtedly tens of millions of rabbits died. Rangelands, held back by rabbit grazing, began to recover. But the rabbit did not disappear. Here and there rabbits survived, apparently disease-resistant, and these are building up a new strain of hardier rabbits against which some new, more virulent strain of the disease will undoubtedly be applied.[27]

With rabbits temporarily under control, their place on the arid lands was taken by the native kangaroos, the red kangaroo in the steppe, the grey kangaroo in the scrub, the wallaroo or euro in Western Australia. A war against kangaroos was underway before the war against rabbits had ceased. Arid lands are unstable ecosystems. Further simplication of their biota from grazing pressure of domestic livestock increases their instability.

It would be possible to go on for pages, reciting stories of successes and failures in managing rangelands. It is enough, perhaps, to emphasize that, throughout the world, livestock have a place in balanced land use. With increasing populations in an already meat-hungry world, this place will grow in importance. It becomes urgent therefore to institute effective range management in all lands, before rangelands are pushed downhill on the successional scale to a point of no return.

CHAPTER
REFERENCES

Burcham, Lee T., 1957. *California range land.* California Division of Forestry, Sacramento.

Forest Service, 1936. *The western range, a great but neglected natural resource.* Senate Document 199, Washington, D.C.

Heady, Harold F., 1960. *Range management in East Africa.* Kenya Department of Agriculture and E.A.A.F.R.O., Nairobi, Kenya.

Humphrey, Robert R., 1962. *Range ecology.* Ronald Press, New York.

Sampson, Arthur W., 1952. *Range management principles and practice.* John Wiley, New York.

Stoddart, L. A., and A. D. Smith, 1955. *Range management.* McGraw-Hill, New York.

LITERATURE
CITED

1. Bryan, H. M., and H. W. Springfield, 1955. Range management in Iraq—findings, plans, and accomplishment. *Jour. Range Management,* 8: 249–256.
2. Buechner, Helmut K., 1950. Life history, ecology, and range use of the pronghorn antelope in Trans-Pecos, Texas. *Amer. Midland Naturalist,* 43: 257–354.
3. Burcham, Lee T., 1957. *California range land.* California Division of Forestry, Sacramento.
4. Bureau of Land Management, 1968. *Public land statistics 1968.* United States Department of the Interior, Washington, D.C.
5. Clark, A. H., 1956. The impact of exotic invasion on the remaining New World mid-latitude grasslands. (See Thomas, 1956, in general references.)
6. Cook, O. F., 1908. *Change of vegetation on the south Texas prairie.* Bureau of Plant Industry, Washington, D.C.
7. Curtis, John T., 1965. The modification of mid-latitude grasslands and forests by man. (See Thomas, 1956, in general references.)
8. Dale, E. E., 1930. *The range cattle industry.* University of Oklahoma, Norman, Oklahoma.
9. Dasmann, R. F., 1963. *The last horizon.* Macmillan, New York.
10. ———, 1964. *African game ranching.* Pergamon, Oxford.
11. Dyksterhuis, E. J., 1949. Condition and management of range land based on quantitative ecology. *Jour. Range Management,* 2: 104–115.
12. Ellison, Lincoln, 1954. Subalpine vegetation of the Wasatch Plateau, Utah. *Ecological Monographs,* 24: 89–184.
13. Forest Service, 1936. *The western range.* Senate Doc. 199, Washington, D.C.
14. Fraser Darling, F., 1955. Pastoralism in relation to populations of men and animals. *The numbers of man and animals.* Oliver and Boyd, Edinburgh, pp. 121–129.
15. ———, 1956. Man's ecological dominance through domesticated animals on wild lands. (See Thomas, 1956, in general references.)
16. Graham, Edward H., 1944. *Natural principles of land use.* Oxford, New York.
17. Grover, D. I., 1945. *Range condition, a classification of the annual forage type.* Soil Conservation Service, Washington, D.C.
18. Larson, F. D., 1957. Problems of population pressure upon the desert range. *Jour. Range Management,* 10: 160–161.
19. Leopold, Aldo, 1949. *A sand county almanac.* Oxford, New York.
20. Linsdale, Jean M., 1946. *The California ground squirrel.* University of California, Berkeley.
21. Longhurst, W., A. S. Leopold, and R. F. Dasmann, 1952. *A survey of Cali-*

fornia deer herds, their ranges and management problems. California Department of Fish and Game, Game Bull., 6.

22. Malin, James C., 1956. The grassland of North America: its occupance and the challenge of continuous reappraisals. (See Thomas, 1956, in general references.)

23. Miller, Robert F., 1942. *Sheep production in California.* Agricultural Extension Service, University of California, Berkeley.

24. Pick, Jock H., 1944. *Australia's dying heart.* Melbourne University, Melbourne.

25. Pyles, Hamilton K., 1970. *What's ahead for our public lands?* Natural Resources Council of America, Washington, D.C.

26. Ratcliffe, Francis, 1947. *Flying fox and drifting sand.* Angus and Robertson, Sydney.

27. ———, 1959. The rabbit in Australia. *Monog. Biol.,* 8: 545–564.

28. Sampson, Arthur W., 1952. *Range management principles and practice.* Wiley, New York.

29. Schaller, George, 1967. *The deer and the tiger.* University of Chicago, Chicago.

30. Towne, Charles W., and E. N. Wentworth, 1955. *Cattle and men.* University of Oklahoma, Norman, Oklahoma.

31. Tribe, Derek et al., 1970. Animal ecology, animal husbandry and effective wildlife management. (See Unesco, 1970, in general references.)

32. Weaver, J. E., 1954. *North American prairie.* Johnson, Lincoln, Nebraska.

33. Wentworth, E. N., 1948. *America's sheep trails.* Iowa State University, Ames, Iowa.

34. Wolfe, L. M., ed., 1938. *John of the mountains; the unpublished journals of John Muir.* Houghton Mifflin, Boston.

35. Wyman, Walker P., 1945. *The wild horse of the west.* Caxton, Caldwell, Idaho.

9

wild
creatures,
wild
places

CONSERVATION BEGINNINGS ⌈here is no area of conservation with a longer history in America than ⌊wildlife conservation. From early times, colonists became concerned with the dwindling numbers of wild animals and took measures to pre-

DEPLETION serve them. Laws intended to protect game appeared on the books as early as the seventeenth century.[10] But to the pioneers cutting a swath through the American wilderness, conservation laws meant little. Species after species of wild animals decreased in numbers or disappeared. Leading the list of vanished species is the passenger pigeon, once present in flocks that darkened the skies. About its passing, Aldo Leopold has written:[16]

There will always be pigeons in books and in museums, but these are effigies and images, dead to all hardships and to all delights. Book pigeons cannot dive out of a cloud to make the deer run for cover, or clap their wings in thunderous applause of mast-laden woods. Book pigeons cannot breakfast on new-mown wheat in Minnesota, and dine on blueberries in Canada. They know no urge of seasons; they feel no kiss of sun, no lash of wind and weather. They live forever by not living at all.

In the West the bison saw the march of progress. In herds numbering in millions they roamed the grasslands from Canada to Mexico. For generations they had supported hundreds of thousands of Plains Indians, and uncounted wolves, coyotes, and bears. But a market for meat and hides, the buffalo rifle, and the westward-moving railways brought their doom. A few carefully guarded herds in parks and refuges are survivors. Perhaps the near extermination of the buffalo was part of a concealed national policy to subdue the Indians, perhaps not. At any rate, with the buffalo went the last hopes of the Indian tribes. Soon after the Indians were vanquished, the prairie itself mostly disappeared with its biota.

Still farther west the path of progress crossed the trail of the grizzly bear of California. The Spanish *vaqueros* had hunted the grizzlies, even testing their courage and skill by capturing them and later matching them in combat with their range bulls. With less color but more dogged persistence, the settlers who followed the lure of gold westward, hunted the grizzlies down. By the start of the twentieth century, hope for the California species was finished, and in the following two decades the last few survivors were destroyed by persons whose names, in this connection, are best forgotten.[10]

At the start of the twentieth century, despite volumes of paper conservation laws and the passionate pleas of conservationists, wildlife in North America had reached a low ebb.[11] The hope of most naturalists was that, somehow, in refuges and reserves and through carefully enforced laws, we could preserve the remnants of once vast wildlife populations. Few foresaw the change that was to come, although at the time the forces which would bring the change were already at work.

RESTORATION Wildlife occupies the position of belonging to everybody and, therefore, under the earlier interpretation, of belonging to nobody. The ownership of other resources usually goes with the land, and it has been the responsibility of the landowner to preserve or destroy them as he sees fit. But the title to wildlife does not go with the land. Centuries of British tradition, under which wildlife belonged to the Crown, led to the American concept that wildlife belonged to the American equivalent of the Crown, the sovereign people.[9] However, it was a long time before the people, through their representatives in the state governments, assumed their responsibility. There are many turning points in the history of wildlife conservation in America, but a significant one came in 1878 when California and New Hampshire first established fish and game commissions, charged with the duty of conserving wildlife.[15] Soon the other states followed.

The establishment of agencies concerned with wildlife conservation gave hope the many game-preservation laws already on the books would be taken seriously. A further step in this direction was taken in 1887 when Michigan, Minnesota, and Wisconsin went into the business of hiring permanent salaried game wardens to enforce the game laws.[15] These early game wardens had a difficult task, for the pioneer spirit tolerated little interference with traditional rights to hunt and fish. In the backwoods, if a game warden were to be shot, nobody knew who pulled the trigger. But, gradually, respect for law and order and interest in game preservation became more widespread. The warden's job was made easier.

The amount of protection offered to wild animals through enforced game laws has grown steadily. First, hunting seasons were set with a view to protecting game during the breeding seasons and at other times when they were most vulnerable. Then the means by which game could be taken were limited, with the more obvious methods of mass destruction outlawed. Bag limits, restricting the number of animals a single hunter could take, were passed to prevent the wagon loads of game which early hunters used to cart away. Hunting for the market was outlawed in many states and was mostly stopped when the federal government entered the game-protection struggle through the newly formed Bureau of Biological Survey (now U.S. Fish and Wildlife Service). For species of little value for meat or sport, complete protection became the rule, with the result that by the early twentieth century most wild animals classified as neither game, predators, nor pests were added to the protected lists. For game, additional protection came with the institution of wildlife refuges, intended as resting areas or breeding grounds, from which game could issue forth to restock hunted lands.

The idea of protection for game spread from the limitations placed on human hunting to that of eliminating the natural foes of game, the predatory animals. It seemed a simple rule, to the biologically uninformed, that, if a coyote ate quail, fewer coyotes would mean more quail. Predator-control practices spread from the simple hunting and trapping of predators by private individuals to the participation of county, state, and federal governments. Hunters, trappers, and poisoners were hired to conduct a ceaseless war against those animals which, like man himself, preferred meat.

As game departments became better endowed financially, the idea spread that, where nature had failed, man should do the job. When protection from hunting and predators failed to increase game, artificial propagation of game appeared to be the answer. It seemed to make sense that game should be produced on farms, reared to a size when they could shift for themselves, and then released in depleted habitats. Among the native game, quail, cottontails, deer, and other species, were reared on game farms, hauled about the country by wagon, train, or truck, and released in what appeared to be suitable locations. Interest of the game farmers shifted early to exotic species. The ring-necked pheasant, native of eastern Asia, was well adapted to life of agricultural lands, where native game failed to thrive. Reared on game farms, and later introduced throughout America, it spread to become the country's number one upland game bird. Similarly, the Hungarian partridge and the Chukar partridge were introduced and liberated from game farms to become permanent additions to the wildlife of America. But for every success, there were countless failures, when the liberated game failed to survive. To balance the record, some introductions were too successful; the English sparrow and starling were added to the list of urban and agricultural pests.

DASMANN   ED

With all of these conservation efforts and sometimes in spite of them, some kinds of wildlife began to increase. To these the game conservationists "pointed with pride," as proof that their methods produced results. But, at the same time, other species on which equal or greater efforts were lavished, continued to decrease to the point of extinction. And to further confound the picture, species regarded as pests, predators, and enemies of man and game in many instances increased more rapidly than the carefully protected game animals, despite countless dollars and man-hours of effort spent toward their eradication. We can now evaluate these apparent paradoxes and the worth of early game-conservation measures in the light of new ecological knowledge.

ECOLOGICAL IDEAS

THE KAIBAB STORY

In northern Arizona, in the Grand Canyon country, lives a herd of Rocky Mountain mule deer which has achieved international fame. Here in the Kaibab National Forest the deer are not different in appearance from their relatives elsewhere in the West. What distinguished them was their phenomenal rate of increase and equally rapid decline several decades ago. They were one of the first American wildlife populations to put on a demonstration of what has since been called a population *irruption*. Thus they achieved a measure of immortality in conservation annals.

Before 1906 there were not many deer in the Kaibab country. Nobody knows how many, for sure, but the best guesses say about 4000 animals. Supported in part by this deer population was an abundant population of predatory animals, plains wolves and coyotes, mountain lions and bobcats, and some bears. Sharing the range with them were sheep and cattle in addition to various other wild animals. In 1906, President Theodore Roosevelt, acting in the name of wildlife conservation, proclaimed the Kaibab region a federal game refuge. To make room for more game, the livestock were moved out. To allow the game to increase, trappers were put to work removing the predatory animals. Operating with great efficiency these men exterminated the wolf and greatly reduced the numbers of other predators.

Without further livestock competition for forage, with complete protection from hunting, and with few remaining natural enemies, the deer population responded. At first the forest rangers and others noted with satisfaction a healthy increase in the number of deer. Soon, a different note was sounded in the Forest Service reports. There were deer everywhere. Tourists could count hundreds in a short walk. Shrubs began to take on a heavily hedged appearance, as though overefficient gardeners had been pruning them. On the aspen trees a browse line was noticed, with all the leaves and small twigs removed as high as a deer could reach. Next, timber-tree reproduction began to suffer and to be killed out from heavy deer browsing. Forest Service reports sounded a warning and requested the deer population be reduced in numbers.

Elsewhere in the country, conservationists and sportsmen were waging

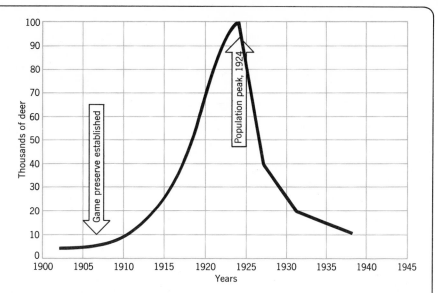

FIG. 9–1. The Kaibab deer irruption (*from Rasmussen, 1941*).

what they sometimes thought was a losing battle to save wildlife from extinction. The idea that there could be too many deer, anywhere, was strange and frankly unbelieveable. The Forest Service reports were ignored, even by the game department of Arizona. Meanwhile, the Forest Service was becoming desperate in its efforts to prevent forest damage and what seemed to be inevitable mass starvation for the deer herd, and they attempted to initiate a large-scale hunt to eliminate the excess deer. A wrangle about the rights of the federal government over wildlife as opposed to states' rights developed and went to the high courts of the land. While the controversy went on the deer problem solved itself, the deer died.

Between 1906 and 1924 it is estimated that the Kaibab deer herd had increased from 4000 to 100,000 animals (Fig. 9–1). Between 1924 and 1930, 80,000 deer died from starvation. Between 1930 and 1939 further die-offs reduced the herd by another 10,000.[30]

SOME POPULATION DYNAMICS

The Kaibab example taught some people that protection for wildlife can be carried too far. It demonstrated to game biologists some facts about animal populations which have since been confirmed by numerous studies. One basic fact is that most animals have high reproductive rates. Given favorable conditions an animal population can multiply rapidly. In nature a balance is reached between reproductive capacity and the drains on the population by all of the many factors that bring loss. The number of animals present at any one time depends on the balance between two forces: the *biotic potential*, or maximum rate at which a species can increase if unchecked, and the *environmental resistance* (Fig. 9–2), the sum of all the forces that cause death or lower reproductive gains. If the environmental resistance is lowered, in one way or another, animal populations increase. If a species, such as the Kaibab deer, is

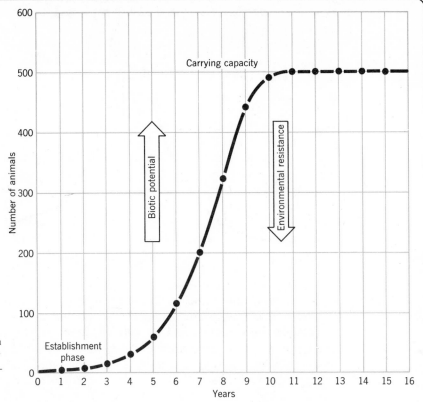

FIG. 9–2. Theoretical population growth curve showing the increase in a deer population in a new environment with a carrying capacity for 500 animals.

freed from natural checks by a great expansion in its habitat or reduction in the numbers and kinds of enemies, it can increase for a time at a rate determined only by its maximum reproductive ability.

Every habitat, for wildlife as well as for domestic livestock, has its *carrying capacity,* which sets firm limits on population increase. No wild-animal population can be maintained permanently at a level above the carrying capacity, which is determined by the available food, cover, water, and other essentials for life. Yet each year, a population at carrying capacity will produce young. This crop of young will represent, therefore, an excess above what the environment can support. Either the young must perish or older animals must die to make a place for them. The annual crop of young, therefore, represents a surplus number of animals that cannot be maintained by the environment (Fig. 9–3). This surplus each year may, in theory, safely be harvested by man, without in any way decreasing the numbers of animals the environment will maintain.[15] If man does not harvest it, natural causes will bring about the reduction. However, the surplus also provide food for all the predators, scavengers, and decomposers. It is part of the fuel for the ecosystem—and if totally removed by man, the ecosystem will change.

The carrying capacity for any species in a complex, climax environment may be relatively stable from year to year and, consequently, the number of animals will not change greatly. If the environment is generally favorable for the support of a great variety of animal species, then there will be predators, parasites, diseases, and competitors present in numbers adequate to remove the excess produced annually by one species population. In the more simplified environments in cold or dry ecosystems, carrying capacity can be expected to fluctuate greatly. Following wet years in an arid region an abundance of plant life may be produced and provide a high carrying capacity for a species such as the Chukar partridge which will build up to a high population level. However, in such areas, dry years follow wet and, at such times, the carrying capacity for most species may drop to an extremely low level. Thus we see great fluctuations in the numbers of animals that inhabit arid regions, and we cannot count on any particular level of abundance being maintained.[4]

In successional environments the carrying capacity changes from year to year in a direction either favorable or unfavorable to a particular species. Thus the habitat may absorb the annual surplus of young produced during the time when succession is proceeding in a direction favorable to that species. However, once a turning point is reached and plant succession is no longer in a direction favorable to the animal species, carrying capacity will decline in each succeeding year and die-offs in the population will follow.

FIG. 9–3. The annual fluctuation in a deer population and the "shootable surplus."

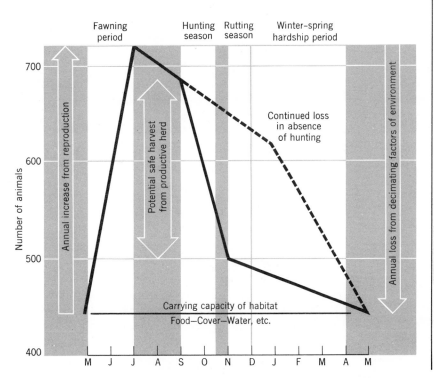

CHANGING ABUNDANCE

(**a**) The bison have survived the march of ''progress'' and are again abundant. (**b**) Caribou, seen here on Alaskan tundra, decline in number as fires burn over their wintering ranges in the boreal forest. (**c**) But the same fires bring in successional vegetation on which moose thrive. (**d**) and (**e**) With reasonable protection, species can survive as with the seabird colony on Isla Roza, Mexico and the European red deer.

c

d

e

Among the various kinds of animals, some species in some environments appear to control their own numbers. These are the *territorial* animals. A *territory* is now generally considered to be an area inhabited by an individual or group of animals of a given species and maintained for the more or less exclusive use of that individual or group. Other individuals or groups are excluded either by direct aggression toward them, or by various behavioral devices that lead to mutual respect of each other's territories. Some animals (the robin, for example) maintain territories during the breeding season but then come together in large flocks for migration and the winter. Other animals, the wren-tit for example, maintain territories throughout the year. Some species, such as many of the colonial-nesting seabirds, have territories which consist only of the immediate area surrounding the nest. Others, such as the California quail, include within their territory feeding, nesting, roosting, and escape cover. The roe deer, in some environments, maintains a territory for the exclusive use of the single family group. The wolf maintains a pack territory within which all members of the pack may breed and rear their young. In all species that are territorial, this form of behavior results in spacing of individuals and thus a limitation of the numbers of individuals permitted within a particular environment. Excess individuals, unable to find a suitable territory, are driven out or otherwise are forced to move out from the particular area.[4,22]

Among nonterritorial animals, some appear to be controlled in numbers by various predators or by some combination of predation, parasites, and disease so that their numbers remain fairly stable as long as their natural enemies are present. If the enemies are removed by man's activities or by some natural catastrophe, then populations of such species may increase for a time to high levels before other environmental factors, food shortage, lack of cover, adverse weather, and the like, operate to cause a decline in their numbers. Many of the smaller game animals, quail, pheasants, cottontails, tree squirrels, appear to have their overall levels of abundance controlled in these varied ways. Those which are to some degree territorial assist through their own behavior the operation of other limiting factors in their environment. The animals that cannot *find* suitable territories become more vulnerable to predation, adverse weather, or other causes of death.[4]

Among animals such as the mule deer or white-tailed deer, territorial behavior is at best weakly developed. Where natural enemies are reasonably abundant, they can exercise some control over numbers. Where man has removed most natural enemies, however, these species soon begin to increase to a point where they press on the food supply of their environment. Thus the Kaibab deer increased to a level beyond the carrying capacity of their area, overbrowsed and destroyed the shrubs and other food plants on which they depended, and thus ultimately crashed to a much lower level than might have been maintained if their numbers had been controlled by man.

HABITAT NEEDS A major task of wildlife management, if we are to have wildlife at all, is creation or maintenance of suitable wildlife habitats. Habitat needs vary for each species. Failure to understand these needs has led to many mistakes. A study carried out in British Columbia helps illustrate this point.

R. Y. Edwards has told the story of Wells Gray Park and its caribou herd.[6] Before 1926 this was a primitive area, of high, glacier-topped mountains, breaking off southward to foothills and valleys. The valley floor and lower mountain slopes were covered with a dense, humid, cedar-hemlock forest. At higher elevations this was replaced by a drier, boreal forest of spruce and fir, breaking way at about 7000 feet into alpine tundra. On dry, south slopes at lower elevations was a forest of Douglas fir, with grassy openings.

The original animal life was varied but without excessive numbers of any one species. The mountain caribou were the most spectacular animals present. They wintered in the damp cedar-hemlock forest, where they fed on the abundant supply of lichens which grew there, and in summer traveled to the higher tundra and spruce-fir forest. There were a few mountain goats at higher elevations and a small number of mule deer that wintered in the dry, Douglas fir forest and grassland. A few mountain lions and coyotes followed the deer. Small numbers of black and grizzly bears were present, as were wolverines and martens in the heavy forest. Beaver were well distributed but not abundant.

In 1926, the scene changed. A fire started in the Douglas fir forest and spread northward along the river valleys sweeping into the cedar-hemlock forest. The fire was intense and destroyed the humus of the forest floor, and even burned out the large stumps of trees. Over 200 square miles of forest were destroyed. After the 1926 fire, another 80 square miles burned in 1930 to 1931 and another 100 in 1940. Together these fires reduced the great extent of climax forest to early successional stages. On the burned area fireweeds and willow invaded, followed by birch and aspen. A completely new habitat was created, with a much simplified type of vegetation. In this habitat a different type of animal life was favored, not the rich abundance of many species which had been present but great numbers of a few adapted species.

Deer became numerous in the burn, and with the increase in deer the mountain lion and coyote increased also. White-footed mice and ground squirrels invaded the burn and increased to high levels. Beaver and black bear, favored by the successional growth, increased and thrived. Most strikingly, moose, previously unknown in the area, colonized it four years after the first fire. Favored by the abundant willow, birch, and aspen browse, they became numerous. With the moose, timber wolves invaded the area. By contrast, all of the species that had been favored by the climax forest growth decreased. Most striking was the decrease in the caribou. The decline started in 1926, was noted with alarm by 1935, and was accentuated by the 1940 fire. In the early 1950's only a small remnant of the caribou herds existed, and these animals were to be found in winter in the three small remaining patches of mature, cedar-hemlock forest. They were absent from the burn. With the fire had gone the dense cover and abundant growth of lichens and other climax plants on which they had depended for food.

Throughout North America, the decrease in numbers of caribou in recent decades has been a matter of concern to wildlife conservationists. In Alaska and Canada the barren-ground caribou of the tundra have declined in numbers.[1,17] The woodland caribou has vanished from the forests of the northeastern United States and has decreased greatly in Canada. Wolves have been blamed for the decrease, climate has been blamed, competition with moose and deer has been blamed. It is now generally recognized, however, that the basic cause is fire or fire plus logging. Fire has destroyed the lichen-covered forest over great areas of caribou range. With the climax forest the caribou have gone. At the same time the great increase in moose in both Canada and Alaska has caused comment. Fire, with the successional growth of willow, birch, and aspen, is a basic cause. Conservation efforts aimed at decreasing losses from hunting or eliminating predation by wolves have had little effect on numbers of moose or caribou. Habitat is the controlling factor.[17]

If the list of wildlife species now extinct or threatened with extinction is examined, it will be found that a high percentage of these species are like the mountain caribou. They are wilderness animals, dependent on the maintenance of climax or near-climax habitat conditions. The now-rare fur bearers of the United States, the marten, wolverine, and fisher, appear to be among these forms. They are now scarce in most areas of their former range, despite almost complete protection from hunting or trapping. For such wilderness animals it is now apparent maintenance or restoration of their numbers depends, with our present knowledge, on maintenance of extensive wilderness areas in which they can survive. As we learn more of their habitat requirements, we may be able to single out those special features which favor their survival and, through management, to increase these habitat features. Until then protection of wilderness is the only answer.

The species of wildlife that form the bulk of our huntable game populations and those which have become pests of farmlands, forest lands, and rangelands are the successional forms. They have been favored by our use, and misuse, of the land and have exercised their biotic potentials in expanding into newly created habitats left by fire, loggers, or excessive numbers of sheep and cattle.

Looking at the wildlife situation now through the eyes of ecologists, we can easily see the importance of habitat and the capacity of game populations to expand when habitat is provided. Yet through the long years of effort toward wildlife conservation, these facts were not obvious.

THE ROLE OF PROTECTION   Protection from hunting once seemed to be all that was needed to bring game back to previous levels of abundance. We know now all of the protection in the world cannot lead a game population to increase when the habitat is not adequate. For wilderness animals, strict protection from hunting or trapping is required if they are to remain in the few remaining areas where they survive. But protection will not increase them; for that, we need more wilderness.

Waterfowl, while not climax species, have been hard hit by the expansion of settlement. Their migratory habits and tendency to congregate in large flocks have made them particularly vulnerable to hunting. Veritable armies of duck hunters set forth each year in pursuit of waterfowl. Without rigidly enforced game laws, the numbers of ducks, geese, and swans would soon be reduced to the vanishing point. Many waterfowl breed in the pothole country of the Canadian prairie and the still largely undisturbed tundra of the Arctic. From breeding grounds they migrate along well-defined routes, or flyways, to wintering grounds in the southern United States or Central or South America (Fig. 9–4). Those wintering in the United States have been affected by the drainage and reclamation of formerly extensive marsh or slough areas. In California, a major wintering ground for the Pacific flyway, high land values have resulted in the drainage of much of the former winter habitat. Flocks of geese and ducks concentrate on the few remaining water areas and move out to feed on rice, barley fields, and truck gardens, causing extensive damage. Management has attempted to provide, through land purchase and development, more extensive wintering grounds and feeding areas apart from the croplands.

Drainage and urban development have removed large areas of marsh along the East and Gulf coasts, wintering grounds for birds of the Atlantic, Mississippi, and Central flyways. Some of these birds are also affected by the disappearance of breeding grounds. The ducks and geese of the Mississippi flyway breed in large part in the marshes and potholes of the North Central United States and Canada. The great land-reclamation program of the federal government in the early decades of this cen-

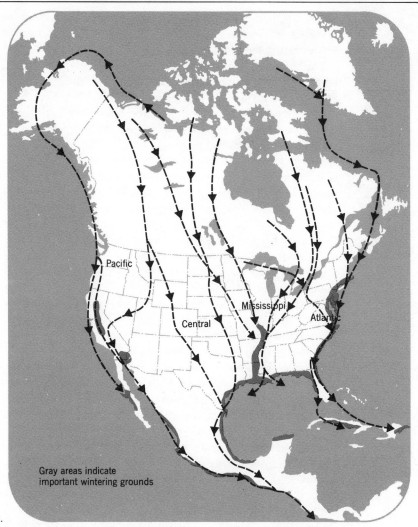

Pacific

Mississippi

Atlantic

Central

Gray areas indicate
important wintering grounds

FIG. 9–4. The waterfowl
flyways of North America.

tury led to the drainage of many important breeding areas. Waterfowl-
conservation measures have included reflooding of formerly drained
marshes, where these are of low agricultural value. Rigid protection
from excessive hunting remains important if waterfowl are to be preserved, but protection alone will bring no great increase in numbers.
The habitat holds the key to increase. Further development of breeding,
resting, and wintering areas is needed to bring the great flocks of former
years back to the flyways.

With the great bulk of our now-abundant game animals, protection
has been carried too far. We have created what is almost an excess of
the successional type of habitat in which most game animals thrive. Into
this habitat, quail and grouse, deer and rabbits, pheasants and doves
have expanded. With a minimum of protection their numbers could be

maintained, and their annual increases could provide recreation for many. But the public has been sold on the idea of protection and it is difficult to convince them that there can be too much of it. This has been most obvious with the deer, which have increased to the level of becoming a pest of forest land, rangeland and farmland in many areas of the country. With deer, early in wildlife-conservation history, hunting was restricted to the male sex only. This was done with the realization that under normal levels of hunting enough bucks would survive for reproductive purposes. The female animals, protected from hunting, could produce enough young to permit the population to increase. The law protecting does was a measure to provide for population growth, not a measure of chivalry. However, a tradition has grown among sportsmen to the point that the doe deer has been elevated to the position of "America's sacred cow." Some simple mathematical calculations will show that removal of part of the bucks each year will never keep a deer population from increasing. Yet, it has been extremely difficult to obtain the necessary changes in hunting laws essential if excess deer populations and the consequent die-offs are to be prevented.[21]

More so than protection from hunting, the importance of predator control has been oversold to the public by zealous conservationists. It is difficult to find records of any serious studies which show where predator control has accomplished anything of value. Where livestock are concerned, it can be a different matter. Major predators may have to be thinned out where sheep are to be run free on the range. Smaller predators can be an expensive nuisance when overly abundant in farming areas. But where game alone is involved, predators are part of the ecological balance. Predators help to remove the annual increase and thus to keep populations from overrunning the food supply of their habitat. Predators help to eliminate the old, and sick, and weak from a population and make room for younger and more vigorous animals. And above all predators have a place in a balanced biota, as part of the natural scene. Their recreational value and aesthetic worth is immense. Wildlife to be worth preserving should be wild, and to remain wild it should be rich and varied, with predators as well as prey. If wildlife management is to concentrate on the sheer production of meat, eliminating all that conflicts with or feeds on the cherished herbivores, it becomes then only another form of animal husbandry, a useful and profitable pursuit, but lacking those qualities associated with the word "wild."

AN ENVIRONMENTAL APPROACH We have passed through two major phases in wildlife conservation in America. Initially, preservation and restocking dominated thinking. This led to confusion and bafflement when carefully protected species declined or liberated animals from game farms failed to survive. Next we moved into the age of the wildlife specialist, when emphasis on habitat management and population dynamics led to some spectacular gains and to a greatly widened understanding. But this period has also been the age of the hunting-license buyer, the hunter who demands an ever-increasing supply of those species he prefers to shoot. Using the new techniques, the game specialist has been able to produce great crops of deer, pheasants, or ducks but at a cost. In dollars alone this cost is excessive. Game departments are supported entirely by income from hunting-license fees. Too often the sportsman who buys a three-dollar license expects to shoot a brace of pen-raised pheasants that cost five dollars for the game department to produce and still get his deer, ducks, and quail shooting thrown into the bargain.[18] Sometimes, also, the gain in shootable game has been at the expense of other natural resources. Increasingly it has been at the expense of wildlife itself, neglected or destroyed in the effort to increase numbers of already too abundant game.

It is necessary to reexamine basic thinking about wildlife problems and to enter a new era of wildlife conservation, of the conservation of balanced biotas in place of specialized concentration on increasing numbers of huntable game. It should be an era in which the needs of the people as a whole, for natural environments with abundant and varied animal life, are given precedence over the wants of the hunter.

In the past, wildlife has been relegated in the thinking of conservation workers in other specialties to those land areas not suited for more economically valuable products. The Class VIII land of the soil conservationist has been called wildlife land. We realize now that wildlife, like all life, requires deep, rich soils and does poorly on areas where soil nutrients are lacking.[26] If wildlife is to remain abundant, it must be fitted into farm plans, range plans, and forest plans. Only a small percentage of our lands can reasonably be reserved for wildlife alone. However, it is *wildlife* which must be fitted into land-use plans, not an unhealthy monoculture of a favored game species. The hunters of the future must pay for this in decreased game bags. They must also pay in higher costs, for in most parts of the country game is produced on private lands. Money is still the main incentive for encouraging private production, whether the production be of machines, corn, or pheasants.[18] The shootable crop of currently favored game animals will be smaller as game are fitted back into a balanced biota. But for the hunter who seeks a type of recreation which is not found in taverns or on skeet ranges, the rewards of being active on wild or well-managed lands which have a rich and varied animal life should far outweigh the decrease in hunting take.

A BROADER VIEW North America has, to a marked extent, led the way in wildlife conservation on wild lands. Although we still have problems with threatened species and natural areas (see Chapter 11), wildlife conservation has been generally successful, and the skills of wildlife management have been developed to a high degree. Elsewhere in the world, however, such success is rare. Wildlife is being decimated by the same combination of destructive forces which were operative in nineteenth-century America, aided by the extreme pressure of human populations on the habitat that still remains.

Europe, with a long tradition of wildlife conservation, has gone farther in some respects than have the United States and Canada. The European emphasis has been on the intensive production of game on limited areas. In many European countries, responsibility for wildlife rests with the landowner. Those who take an interest have often done a creditable job; those who have had no interest in wildlife have done poorly. Despite the density of population in most European countries, the more popular animals have been maintained on private estates and sometimes on public land in fair numbers. Away from farm and urban areas, in forests and mountains, the numbers and variety of wild animals are often quite high. Although there has been in the past a trend toward the extermination of predators, the wolf and bear still remain in the mountains of the Balkans and in northern forests. Considerable success has been achieved with saving and restoring some species which were once on the point of vanishing. Thus the European bison has been maintained in the forests of Bialowicza in Poland, despite the hazards and devastation caused by two world wars in that general region.[39]

In the Soviet Union the protection and management of wildlife has made enormous strides in recent decades, and Soviet wildlife scientists are now among the world's leaders. Despite the practical orientation of Marxist political philosophy the preservation of wildlife for aesthetic, recreational, and scientific values is well accepted. The economic exploitation of wildlife resources, however, has been developed to a degree exceeding any efforts in North America, and progress has been made in the domestication of wild species such as the African eland. One of the most spectacular successes has been in the preservation and commercial use of the saiga antelope, a species that once abounded on the steppes of Eurasia but was reduced to near extinction in the early decades of this century. Under management it once more numbers in the millions and yields quantities of meat and hide for the market through sustained-yield cropping.[2]

South from the USSR the lands of Asia present one of the more discouraging spectacles for wildlife conservation. The situation in India, once a land that could equal Africa in the scenes presented by great herds and flocks of wild animal life, is representative. George Schaller has summarized the information on the primitive abundance and present scarcity of large mammals in India. Where once elephant, rhino, buffalo, lions, tigers, and many kinds of deer and antelope roamed in great numbers, extinction, near-extinction, and scarcity are now the rule. Much of the damage has occurred in recent decades. Indiscriminate slaughter, direct shooting campaigns aimed at protecting crops, and a general inattention to protective game laws have been involved. Most serious, however, has been the continued and growing pressure of people and livestock on the remaining wildlife habitat.[32]

a

c

b

WILDLIFE RESTORATION

(**a**) The wild turkey, once seriously threatened, has been restored to abundance by protection, habitat management and restocking. (**b**) The trumpeter swan has been brought back to a secure population level by protective measures. (**c**) Rated as "dangerous to man" the grizzly bear holds on in national parks such as Yellowstone and Glacier, despite the efforts of those who want all dangerous animals destroyed. (**d**) Long feared and hated because of false ideas, the wolf is now becoming a popular animal and its future in North America is becoming more secure.

d

By contrast, the situation in Africa is more hopeful. Here are the world's greatest existing wildlife resources and here not long ago was the bleakest prospect for future conservation. Fortunately, many of the governments of Africa, despite economic difficulties and political turmoil, have recognized the value of wildlife and have taken steps to protect it. The economic impact of tourism in East Africa has been a marked factor leading to effective wildlife preservation. A major attraction to the tourist from Europe or America has been the sight of game herds roaming wild in the East African national parks.[12] In southern Africa the protection of wildlife in national parks has a long history and, more recently, the management of wild animals outside of parks has proceeded on a rational basis. The commercial production of wildlife on ranches for sale as meat, hides, and other by-products is now well established. Springbuck and blesbuck have replaced sheep on many South African farms; mixed game ranching has proved more profitable than cattle ranching in areas of Rhodesia.[3,34]

Although conditions for wildlife vary enormously around the world, in most areas wildlife has been neglected. Where population pressure is great and resources are few, there has been little room for wildlife conservation. Lee Talbot, after a survey of world wildlife problems, has stated that wildlife can be used as an index to the condition of the biotic resources of an area.[33] Where wildlife is abundant, other renewable resources are usually well preserved. A scarcity of wildlife accompanies destructive exploitation of resources with all of its unfortunate consequences.

Where wildlife still remains, it is essential to take early steps toward conservation and management. With present rates of human population increase it is unlikely that any area will remain unaffected for long. It would be unfortunate if future generations were denied first-hand knowledge of the variety of wild animals that have accompanied and influenced humans throughout their evolution and spread over the earth. There is an increasing feeling also that wild land and wildlife may be strangely important for the preservation of humanity. With the unbridled growth of technological civilization, with its regimentation, specialization, and tensions, the pressures on the human spirit grow more intense. Until a more sane way of life can be achieved, we need a refuge, a place for escape from artificiality and confinement, where we can come to grips with our own still-primitive self. So long as wild places and animals are preserved, a sanctuary for people remains.

VANISHING HERITAGE   In any discussion of environmental conservation it is natural to emphasize the issues of direct and present concern to most people, in particular those factors with an immediate bearing on human survival. Yet, to do so is to create a false impression of relative priorities, because some of the more important aspects of conservation have little relation to our quantitative needs, no obvious or immediate bearing on human survival, and are scarcely known to most people. Yet, if they are not attended, and soon, the long-term chances for human survival may be impaired, and the quality of life will be damaged. There is far more to conservation than the efficient and sustained production of species or things of economic value. There are qualities of the environment that must be considered without reference to any increment that they might add to the gross national product, or to any fluctuation that they might create in the indices of economic growth. There is a need in the human environment for wild nature, untouched or little modified by human activities. There is a need also to maintain the physical records of our cultural past if we are to better evaluate the prospects for the future. A heritage of diversity exists on earth, natural and man-made, which we cannot afford to lose.

We must recognize the value of nature in itself, apart from any value it may have for future exploitation. A need exists to protect areas only for the purpose of having them available for future knowledge about the natural world. There is a need to set aside natural communities solely for the quiet, aesthetic appreciation some people may gain by viewing them. There is also a need to set aside other places only for the sake of the wild creatures who live, unstudied and unpraised, within them. There is room on earth for all such areas and purposes. We must be prepared to grant the right of existence to species other than man, without being threatened by the obvious truth that our own survival may ultimately depend on them.

Those who are already convinced hardly need further arguments about the value of nature. Those who are not convinced, and their numbers are legion, include many who hold the future of the biosphere in their hands—legislators, planners, and the decision makers of industry and government. It is necessary to try to convince them.

THE VALUE OF WILD SPECIES

"PRACTICAL VALUES"

The rhesus monkey has probably been on earth as long as man himself. Since man and monkey came into contact, the monkey has been viewed as a pest or a pet or as something to eat, depending on which person was viewing it. In the twentieth century, however, the monkey became an important medical ally of man. As an experimental animal it has made possible major advances in biology and medicine, including knowledge about human blood groups, which has permitted the survival of many people who might otherwise have died. We could have survived without the monkey, but the monkey has increased our welfare. In the nineteenth century, however, a practical man might well have asked "What good are monkeys?" Few could have given him a convincing reason why monkeys should be preserved.

In the early years of this century, *Penicillium* was a nuisance mold on bread. Nobody could have convinced a congressman that this genus of molds should be saved, even after Alexander Fleming in 1929 discovered it had an antibiotic effect on bacteria. But the many soldiers who did not die in World War II because of the availability of penicillin and the millions of people since then who have been saved by it or its various antibiotic descendants should be willing to vote for the preservation of "useless" species.

The list of previously wild species which have suddenly made major contributions to human survival and well-being is long: from the wild grasses that were to become corn and wheat, the wild mammals who were to become our domestic animals, on through to the sea urchin and the house mouse. We do not know what previously unnoticed creature, living perhaps in some rain forest or at the bottom of the sea, may hold the key to protection against some disease or environmental predicament that besets mankind. The value of saving wild things as a sort of "life insurance" for humanity should be obvious.

The wild species of this earth represent a reservoir of genetic materials. Each species is irreplaceable, we cannot create it again if it is lost. Each is a storehouse of genetic information we cannot afford to lose, since we cannot predict or in any way foresee the ways in which this information may someday prove valuable.

It is comparatively easy to maintain an awareness of the relative abundance and distribution of the larger or more conspicuous species of plants or animals. We have a fairly good idea of the number of rhinos and elephants on earth, and of the acreage of old-growth redwood trees. It is impossible to keep track of the presence or abundance of the great variety of small and inconspicuous creatures. We don't know if some species, once described and studied, still exist. However, each species exists as part of some ecosystem or natural community. As long as representative areas of the earth's different kinds of communities and ecosystems are preserved, we have a strong likelihood of maintaining those species that comprise them. It becomes important, therefore, not only to give attention to the preservation of these species of which we are aware but to preserve an adequate representation of the different kinds of environments and communities on earth.

A community or ecosystem can in itself make a contribution to our knowledge that none of the individual species within it can do. Through studies of the structure and functioning of ecosystems that have not been modified, we gain a better understanding of those that we have modified and are using to practical ends. If small areas of intact vegetation had not been preserved in the mountains of Lebanon we might never have guessed that trees could still grow there, and the process of reforestation might not yet have started. The existence of natural communities in Africa made possible the studies of the economic values of wild mammals and the relative advantages these have as meat producers compared to domestic livestock breeds. The existence of undisturbed watersheds makes possible the study of the role of vegetation and soils in water yield and flood control that could not be carried out were such intact ecosystems not available.

The presence of natural areas in a region can further be of benefit through maintaining the stability of lands that are used for direct commodity production. In part this can be through contributions to the stability of watersheds, in part through contributions to overall biotic diversity. There is a distinct need for comparative studies of *long-term* yields from areas of diversified biota compared to simplified or monocultural areas. Thus far our emphasis has been on short-term gains.

AESTHETIC AND ETHICAL VALUES

There is no general agreement on the meaning of beauty, but there is widespread agreement on the nature of ugliness. Most people prefer a beautiful environment to an ugly one, and most would agree that a major element of environmental beauty is contributed by the natural scene, either in itself or in some blend with the man-made.

The contribution of natural areas and wild species to the aesthetic quality of the environment is obvious. The untouched wild land provides an opportunity for us to contemplate and enjoy a portion of the world as it once was. Wild species enrich the quality of those lands that we are using. A city park without wild birds is a sterile place. Farming lands from which all wild things are removed are little better than rural factories.

One cannot state the degree to which we are dependent on some contact with wild nature and natural environments. Although we are becoming increasingly an urban people, this is a recent phenomenon, and there is no evidence by which we can judge what kind of people would be produced after many generations of separation from a more natural world. We are after all a wild species, only recently separated from environments that were mostly wild. Our behavior was conditioned by life in the wilderness, and later for thousands of years in rural villages and fields. The extent to which people flee the cities to seek outdoor recreation whenever the opportunity is presented may itself be an indication of our need to have contact with environments not entirely shaped by man.

We go to great lengths throughout much of the world to preserve monuments and historical sites that tell us of our past accomplishments and cultural heritage. The difficulties of being without history have been faced by many of the developing nations of the world, where the oral traditions once passed on by the tribal elders have been forgotten and written records are few. But there is also a need to preserve the environments in which history took shape. A person who has not seen wild country can hardly appreciate the experiences of his ancestors.

Perhaps even higher than the values which have been discussed are the ethical reasons for preserving wild nature. These vary from culture to culture. In America they have been stated by many people from Henry Thoreau to Aldo Leopold.[16,35] Perhaps Leopold's concept of an extension of ethics from people to land states adequately the philosophical issue involved. Do we concede a right of coexistence to the other species which have evolved with us on earth, or do we insist on our prerogative to kill and destroy anything that stands in the way of our immediate and assumed material well-being? Some would insist along with Walter Lowdermilk on the need for an 11th commandment, concerned with conservation;[23] but considering how inadequately we observe the other ten it seems adding another would give little further protection to wild creatures.

To the followers of some religions, forms of Hinduism and Buddhism for example, life is sacred and one avoids taking it. Such a restriction, however, has been applied only to animal life and not to the vegetation that supports it. Without habitat, animals do not last long, despite religious protection. In the Western tradition the concept of a "reverence for life" has been a strong feature of the philosophy of Albert Schweitzer and of St. Francis of Assisi.

One cannot legislate religion or ethics, or force people to assume a sense of responsibility for their fellow beings. Neither can one force an appreciation for beauty. One can only hope such feelings toward the human environment will grow. Meanwhile, to convince the Philistines, it may be necessary to fall back on harder economic weapons. Recreation and tourism are part of this arsenal.

THE DEMAND FOR RECREATION Following World War II, as national prosperity soared to new levels and leisure time for Americans became more abundant, it became clear a new industry of major national significance had arisen, the outdoor recreation industry. Although related to the old area of conservation, recreation provided a new banner under which groups not previously interested in conservation could rally. Furthermore, recreational needs and wants could be quantified, expressed in terms of man-hours or recreation days, or assigned dollar values based on actual cash expenditures.

The increasing national interest in recreation was given focus with the creation of the Outdoor Recreation Resources Review Commission and, in particular, with the publication of its report in 1962.[28] New facts were revealed on recreation demands by the general public, new data were presented on the availability of recreational space and facilities, and new questions were raised, such as: Why do people do what they do, and would they rather do something else?

THE OUTDOOR RECREATION RESOURCES REVIEW[28] The major recommendations of the recreation commission fell into five categories:

1. Establishment of a national outdoor recreation policy.
2. Establishment of guidelines for the management of outdoor recreation resources.
3. Improvement of outdoor recreation programs to meet increasing need.
4. Establishment of the Bureau of Outdoor Recreation in the Federal Government.
5. A federal grants-in-aid program to the states.

Congress responded favorably to the report and in essence the government accepted the statement that "It shall be the national policy, through the conservation and wise use of resources, to preserve, develop, and make accessible to all American people such quantity and quality of outdoor recreation as will be necessary and desirable for individual enjoyment and to assure the physical, cultural, and spiritual benefits of outdoor recreation." The commission report specified further the role of the federal government to be:

1. Preservation of scenic areas, natural wonders, primitive areas, and historic sites of national significance.
2. Management of federal lands for the broadest possible recreation benefit consistent with other essential uses.
3. Cooperation with the states through technical and financial assistance.
4. Promotion of interstate arrangements, including federal participation where necessary.
5. Assumption of vigorous, cooperative leadership in a nationwide recreation effort.

In 1962 the Bureau of Outdoor Recreation was established within the Department of the Interior. In 1964 the federal grants-in-aid program was assured with passage of the Land and Water Conservation Fund Act. This permitted the charging of fees to users of national parks and other federal recreation lands, with the money to go into the federal fund. The fund would also receive money from the sale of federal real property and from taxes on motorboat fuels. The fund would provide money to the states on a 50–50 matching basis for recreation planning, land acquisition, and land development for recreation. To receive federal funds, however, the states were required to submit to the Bureau of Outdoor Recreation a suitable recreation plan, before money could be used for land acquisition or development. Thus overall planning to meet outdoor recreation needs was provided.

The recreation commission further recommended as guidelines for management the classification of lands into six categories of outdoor recreation resources:

Class I. High-density recreation areas.
Class II. General outdoor recreation areas.
Class III. Natural environmental areas.
Class IV. Unique natural areas.
Class V. Primitive areas.
Class VI. Historic and cultural sites.

Through such a classification it was hoped to guarantee not only the provision of mass-recreation facilities but also the reservation of wild and remote natural areas for the highest quality of outdoor recreation. Hopefully, if the needs of the many could be met close to home, the remote areas could be preserved for the use of those who really preferred and appreciated their qualities.

RECREATION ACTIVITIES[28] In its analysis of American outdoor recreation activities the commission found pleasure driving ranked first, walking for pleasure second, and the playing of outdoor games or sports third, in a tally of the average number of days spent per person each year. Water-based activities of all kinds, from swimming to skin-diving, ranked high. Activities that, by their nature, were related to wild country or natural areas (for example, nature walks, hunting, hiking, mountain climbing) did not rank as highly as those activities that required only open space or water space for their exercise. The American people were revealed as having a high demand for outdoor recreation but not necessarily a high demand for those forms of recreation based on wild country. Nevertheless, because of the lack of more generalized mass recreation facilities, the pressure on wild country was enormous. The need for development of recreational space in or near the cities to meet the daily or weekend recreational demand was stressed by the committee.

Of the various categories of state and federal outdoor recreation land, the state parks received the greatest number of visits (nearly 255 million in 1960), national parks received nearly 80 million visits, and national forests nearly 93 million visits. The greater pressure on state parks reflects their location closer to the major urban centers of population. To the Easterner in particular, the national forests and parks are often far from home and require a major vacation trip if they are to be visited. State parks can be reached easily in an afternoon or weekend.

Unfortunately, statistics can be misleading, and there is some cause to wonder whether both state and federal recreation agencies are not misled by the statistics provided by recreation surveys. Thus statistics on the preference of people for automobile driving leads to the expansion of highways and, in particular, to a scenic highway program, since these are apparently what the people want. People drive, however, for a variety of reasons: because they know how, have a car, can afford to operate it, because it gets them away from their usual environment, and brings the family together, while providing some degree of privacy from other people. In driving they see different areas, get to know new places, have the opportunity to enjoy whatever roadside beauty is available. Many people also get considerable pleasure out of the sheer ownership and operation of a motor vehicle. But people may also drive because there is nothing else to do within easy reach that they know how to do, how to appreciate, or can afford to do. Given an equal choice between driving and skiing, which is relatively low on the list of preferences, and assuming an area was available (along with skiing lessons, skis and other equipment), and that the person could equally afford skiing, there is little doubt skiing would climb much higher on the list of activities among younger or more active people.

Relatively few people go on nature walks or hike in wild country compared to those who drive or walk about the city. But the comparison is again open to question. Few people have been taught anything about nature or how to appreciate wild country. Few people have the same opportunity to participate, therefore, in activities that include a personal involvement with wild nature, as in activities that involve only a motor car and a road.

Should we spend federal and state funds more for building highways and swimming pools, because these are what people will use, or should we spend the money for building the skills and appreciation needed for better use of wilder and more natural environments? There are those who say we must not make value judgments about recreation, that nobody can say that a hike in the wilderness or the operation of a sailing craft on the ocean is a higher form of recreation than driving a car or sitting by a swimming pool. However, we are accustomed to making such value judgments, and we do not spend federal money to build bigger and better equivalents of Las Vegas, even though gambling is a highly popular form of recreation. Undoubtedly, those who understand the values of wilderness, the skills of skiing or sailing, or the adventure of hunting are in a better position to make judgments about them than those who know of these things only from seeing them on television.

OTHER NATIONS The demand for outdoor recreation in other nations appears to vary with their state of urbanization and technology. People who live year-round in the country are inclined to go to town for their vacation. They make daily use of the open space around them, but often view this activity as part of the daily routine rather than as recreation. People who do not have enough to eat are little inclined to seek recreation. Consequently, the apparent internal demand for outdoor recreation space in most of the developing nations is small. The potential demand, however, as the circumstances of the people improve is probably great. It would be easy for these countries to save open space now when the demand is small. It may be quite difficult to obtain space for recreation in the future when the demand is great.

In Japan, for example, with increasing prosperity, the demand for recreation has grown enormously. The nation has a respectable national park system, but the parks are overcrowded. Millions of visitors seek them out during vacation and on weekend trips and, to an American, almost unbelievable numbers of people toil up the mountain trails and climb the high peaks. Still greater numbers crowd the available beaches. The weekend journey from Tokyo to Mount Fuji is a nightmare to one who is used only to a New York level of overcrowding. Similar conditions prevail in European countries, and there has been an increasing flow of European tourists to recreation areas abroad.

In England there has been a long tradition of using the countryside for hiking, cycling, riding, shooting, and other outdoor activities. With increasing prosperity, outdoor space has become crowded. The Nature

Conservancy, a government agency, has done an excellent job of establishing and preserving a system of national parks and other outdoor areas, but it has been a difficult struggle, since pressure on lands for other uses has also been increasing.

The interest of people in the wealthier nations in preserving and in visiting the natural treasures and outdoor resources of the developing nations has been an unexpected boon to the economies of some of these countries. In Kenya, for example, tourism is a major industry and the principal source of foreign currency. Throughout East Africa, it has had an economic impact far greater than was expected when these nations were first independent. Nevertheless, the support for the preservation of outdoor recreational space in developing nations must come, to a large extent, from outside their boundaries until such time as the economic welfare of their own peoples has improved. This is a contribution which must be made by those who understand the value to all mankind that these recreational resources represent.

STEPS TOWARD PRESERVATION

THE NATIONAL PARK SYSTEM

America, through its national park system, has in many ways led and set an example for the rest of the world in setting aside extensive natural areas to be preserved in a primitive condition. Although the roots of the ideas of natural area reserves go far back into the past, the first beginnings of the American park system came in the 1860's when Yosemite Valley in California was set aside as a reserve.[31,36] The credit for this must go in large degree to Frederick Law Olmsted, the designer of New York's Central Park. Having visited Yosemite and having been impressed with its grandeur he managed, with the assistance of others, to persuade Congress to pass a bill preserving Yosemite Valley "for public use, resort and recreation." This occurred in 1864, with the Civil War still raging. Since no federal organization existed to accommodate such a reserve, it was ceded to the state of California to become the first state park. Under state control, however, it suffered from extensive mismanagement, and the area above the valley of Yosemite was subjected to extreme abuse from excessive grazing. John Muir, California naturalist and founder of the Sierra Club, led the fight to have Yosemite proclaimed a national park and placed under army protection. In 1890, partial success was achieved as the Yosemite watershed was proclaimed a national park. It was not until 1905, however, with the intervention of Theodore Roosevelt, that Yosemite Valley was removed from state jurisdiction to become part of Yosemite National Park.[36]

While the Yosemite battle was going on, Judge Cornelius Hedges and several other explorers visited an area of incomparable beauty in the mountains of northwest Wyoming. Impressed by the grandeur of this region of geysers, hot springs, waterfalls, lakes, and mountains, they worked to have the area set aside for the future enjoyment of the American people. In 1872, with little debate or understanding of what was happening, Congress passed a bill that President Grant signed into law, proclaiming the Yellowstone region as America's first national park, to be administered by the Secretary of the Interior. The beginning of a system that now includes much of America's finest and most scenic country was achieved.[36]

Into the national park system, however, was built contradictions that were ultimately to cause trouble. Yellowstone was designated as a "pleasuring ground" for people. Public recreation was stressed when Yosemite Valley was first reserved. In the background, however, was the belief that the natural values which were the focus of this public use must be fully preserved. In 1916, when an agency was finally formed within the Department of the Interior, the National Park Service under the leadership of Stephen Mather, the congressional act stated the need to conserve the scenery and wildlife in such a way that they would be "unimpaired for the enjoyment of future generations." The parks thus had a dual purpose, to preserve nature and to make it available for public enjoyment. These two purposes have come into conflict. In the 1970's the Park Service is in the process of designating, within the national parks, areas to be protected against people, to be maintained as wilderness or natural reserves.

WILDERNESS PRESERVATION A second step was taken toward the preservation of natural areas when in 1929 the United States Forest Service recognized the importance of designating certain portions of the national forest system as "primitive areas," to be maintained free from development or disturbance. In this act they were following the leadership of such men as Aldo Leopold and Robert Marshall, who believed there was a need to maintain large wilderness areas to which men could go and live under primitive conditions and experience a completely natural environment, remote from civilization and its adjuncts.[5]

Further protection for Forest Service primitive areas came in 1939 when some of the more scenic and spectacular regions were designated as wilderness areas. However, these administrative decisions on the part of the Department of Agriculture did not give the protection to wilderness that many who were strong believers in wilderness thought necessary. Consequently, a drive began to give full legal protection to wilderness by having Congress designate a National Wilderness System, from which all forms of development would be restricted—roadless areas, within which only primitive means of transportation would be permitted—areas within which vegetation and animal life would continue to exist in an undisturbed state.

The Outdoor Recreation Resources Review Commission studied the wilderness resource of America and in its 1962 report recommended Congress enact legislation designating, for permanent preservation, a national system of wilderness areas.[28] In the course of this study it was revealed there were only 64 large wilderness areas, over 100,000 acres

a

b

c

d

NATIONAL PARKS AND OUTDOOR RECREATION

National parks, at their best, protect undisturbed areas of
wild nature and secure them for the future. Much of the
justification used to finance the national park system,
however, is based on the role they play in attracting tourism
to a region, or in meeting popular demand for outdoor
recreation. Conservation and mass tourism may conflict
within a national park.
(a) The future of the cheetah is not secure. It appears safe,
for the moment, in Africa's national parks but is vulnerable to
disturbance from tourism. (b) Although sailing is not incompatible with nature protection, the provision of roads,
marinas or other facilities can be disruptive to other national
park values. (c) Rocky Mountains National Park—maintaining
wilderness values near the Denver metropolis. (d) Ski
schools and other elaborate developments for skiiers belong
in recreation areas, not in wilderness regions. (e) Great
Smoky Mountain National Park—here wilderness values
have been restored following a long period of human
settlement.

e

in size, remaining in the contiguous United States. The total area in such large wilderness tracts was 28 million acres. Most of these, fortunately, were on federal lands, but under the jurisdiction of a number of separate agencies.[20]

After long debate in Congress, in 1964 a Wilderness Act was finally passed establishing a national wilderness system, but designating as part of the system only the wilderness areas and smaller wild areas that had already been designated by the United States Forest Service. Provision was made for the addition of other appropriate areas to the system after future study and review.[28] Wilderness hearings are still being held throughout the United States with a view to including within the wilderness system the still wild areas in national parks, wildlife refuges, and other areas of public land, including those Forest Service primitive areas that had not been designated as wild or wilderness areas before the bill was enacted. Only nine million acres were included in the wilderness system established by the 1964 act.[5,28]

United States
Wilderness Areas 1974

ADMINISTERING AGENCY	TOTAL ACREAGE	NUMBER OF UNITS AND ACREAGE PROTECTED IN NATIONAL WILDERNESS PRESERVATION SYSTEM	NUMBER OF UNITS AND ACREAGE AWAITING CONGRESSIONAL APPROVAL	POTENTIAL TOTAL UNITS AND ACREAGE IN SYSTEM
Forest Service	187,225,000	65. 10,741,000	22. 3,881,000	87. 14,622,000
Fish & Wildlife Service	32,500,000	22. 103,000	80. 10,750,000	102. 10,894,000
National Park Service	30,000,000	4. 201,000	56. 16,862,000	60. 17,063,000
Totals	249,725,000	91. 11,045,000	158. 31,492,955	249. 42,538,000

SMALL NATURAL AREAS Further steps toward the preservation of natural areas, including many of smaller size than could logically be included in the wilderness system, are being taken by both government and private organizations. Among the latter, the Nature Conservancy and the National Audubon Society have been leaders in the purchase and preservation of important wild areas that had been in private ownership.

In 1959, in discussions between the International Council of Scientific Unions and the International Union of Biological Sciences, it was agreed that it would be worthwhile to establish an International Biological Program to study certain urgent biological problems as part of a joint world effort. A committee was established to study the problem. In 1963 the International Council agreed to establish an international program (IBP) to study the "Biological Basis of Productivity and Human Welfare."

Among the various activities of IBP it was recognized that the establishment of protection over a system of natural reserves for scientific study was of great importance, since many of the more interesting biotic communities were rapidly disappearing in the face of population growth and development. A subcommittee to develop a program for conservation of natural environments was therefore established.

The IBP has given further stimulus to a program to designate and to protect natural areas for scientific study. Such areas have been reserved in suitable locations on federal lands, and it is expected that a national system of natural areas will result, to be added to an international register of natural areas designated primarily for scientific study.

The struggle to retain bits and pieces of the old, wild America is well advanced, but can hardly be considered a victory. Each area gained must still be held against the encroachment of those who would develop it for mass public use and those who wish to extract some resource that it contains. There is still a job to be done in designating, within the wilderness system, a special category of protection to be extended to large blocks of undisturbed land needed for the study of extensive communities containing far-ranging species of animal life. The International Union for the Conservation of Nature has provided a special title for such areas, Strict Nature Reserves, not to be used even for wilderness recreation if this will interfere with the long-term preservation of the natural biota. There are few areas in the United States that fit this category, although some national parks and portions of others meet the necessary criteria.[14]

Perhaps most disturbing is the continued onslaught against areas supposedly set aside "for all time." The drive to build dams that would flood part of the national park area of Grand Canyon is an example. The struggle to obtain needed water for the Everglades National Park, in the face of urban and agricultural requirements that each year grow larger, is an even more desperate situation. Efforts to set aside new national parks, such as the Redwood National Park in California, encountered opposition from the private interests involved and from local governments which feel their tax base threatened by any extension of federal ownership.[5]

RARE AND ENDANGERED SPECIES

Although the United States is a world leader in wildlife management, the emphasis of this profession has been directed toward producing game for the hunter rather than the protection and restoration of animals not available for sport. Early in history, some species (the passenger pigeon, Carolina parakeet, heath hen, and California grizzly among them) became extinct. Today many species are rare and in a highly endangered status. Other once-abundant species are decreasing for reasons not understood.[7,13]

A concern for endangered species has led to acceptance of responsibility over them by the United States Fish and Wildlife Service, and active interest and protection by private groups such as the Audubon

a

b

THREATENED SPECIES

Critically endangered. (a) The Arabian oryx has been rescued, but now survives only in captivity. Some day it may be restored to the wild. **Critically endangered. (b)** Pushed to near-extinction, the once-abundant California condor shows little tendency to increase despite complete protection. **Endangered. (c)** The mountain gorilla depends on the continued protection of those African reserves where it still can exist. **Threatened. (d)** Continued persecution by hide hunters

d

e

threatens most species of alligators and crocodiles. **Threatened.**
Although still numerous in national parks, such species as
lions (**e**) and the black rhino (**f**) are unlikely to survive
outside of such totally protected areas.

f

societies. For some, strict protection from hunting or other disturbance seems the only measure needed to bring back populations. For others, habitat restoration is essential. The establishment of a Federal Wildlife Refuge system, starting with the Pelican Island in Florida in 1903, and since extended to 300 refuges by 1967, has been an important step.[7]

Good success has been achieved with some species. The trumpeter swan, once near extinction, is now relatively secure. The sea otter of the Pacific Coast, once thought to be extinct, is once more abundant. The Key deer of southern Florida is, for the present at least, secure. The wild turkey and the Alaskan fur seal are now abundant, although they were not long ago considered endangered.

Among the many species for which special protection is still required are the California condor, black-footed ferret, ivory-billed woodpecker, whooping crane, grizzly bear, Everglades kite, Hawaiian geese, Florida panther, timber wolf, and red wolf. Continued vigilance is extended over the small remnant populations of condors, cranes, and Hawaiian geese. Equal vigilance must also be extended to other species if they are to remain on this earth.

WORLD VIEW As in most areas of environmental conservation the prospects for preservation of natural environments and wild species are far less promising in most of the world than they are in the United States. The critical nature of the problem has been brought into focus by such organizations as the International Union for the Conservation of Nature, which starting in 1966 has published Red Data Books which list hundreds of rare and endangered species over the world.[13] The International Biological Program has helped focus world attention on the need to set aside areas of undisturbed vegetation and animal life for future scientific study, and IUCN is helping to carry out this activity.

Perhaps the situation in underdeveloped countries is best exemplified by consideration of Peru. A survey of the Peruvian interior in the 1960's, intended to locate an area to be designated as a national park, found only two areas in the entire Amazonian headwaters region that were at all satisfactory. Over most of this rain forest the influence of shifting cultivation, exploitation of timber, commercial hunting of animals for furs or meat, and other activities had seriously interfered with the native biota. Of the two areas, one located on the Manu River northeast of Cuzco had remained undisturbed only because of a small, but highly warlike, group of Indians who had kept all strangers out. The other, located around the Cutibireni River, northwest of Cuzco, was satisfactory in many respects, but appeared to be lacking in animal life, perhaps as a result of continued hunting.[29]

The situation in the Philippine Islands is even more critical. Although national parks have been proclaimed, they have not been protected. Lumbering and other activities threatened to destroy all remaining natural areas of significant size in the islands. Throughout Asia and Latin

America, with a few exceptions, similar problems prevail. National parks often exist on paper, but receive no effective protection in the field. The pressure of population, of people living on the edge of poverty in lands with little technological development, threatens environments in areas that were not long ago considered far remote from any likely disturbance.[14]

The IUCN maintains The United Nations List of National Parks with data on the size, nature, and status of management for each park. The list is impressive, but the reality much less so.[14] For too many countries, national parks exist only so long as there is no real interest in their exploitation. Once they stand in the way of development, they disappear. How far should one go in attempts to convince people who do not care, to protect something they know nothing about?

In an attempt to find some better way to preserve the outstanding wild areas of the world, Russell E. Train, then president of the Conservation Foundation, proposed the creation of a World Heritage Trust. This could channel private and public money toward an effort to purchase and provide adequate protection for outstanding examples of the world's wild country and wildlife. The idea has been developed over several years, and currently it will be an arrangement, under UNESCO, by which nations may dedicate their outstanding natural areas or cultural sites to the long-range benefit of mankind as part of a World Heritage system. In return, apart from the prestige and publicity, they would receive assistance from a World Heritage Fund in achieving or maintaining proper standards of protection and management.

There are great numbers of proposals at both the national and international level to do something about the problems of the Human Environment. In 1970 at its General Conference, UNESCO approved a program known as Man and the Biosphere, intended to initiate and coordinate international research aimed at discovering the information essential for the proper conservation and management of the world's living resources. Many of the projects designed for this program could do much toward maintaining the heritage of wild nature.[37] In 1970, the International Council of Scientific Unions (ICSU) launched a new program under the aegis of SCOPE (Special Committee on Problems of the Environment) intended, among other activities, to provide for a worldwide system of monitoring the changes in the environment caused by human activity. All of these programs have great potential importance. None of them as yet has received any significant amount of financial support. None of them can operate without adequate money.

Among all of the potential programs for conservation, the ones directed toward the preservation of wild species and biotic communities require the highest priority in any planning. The time in which this job can be accomplished is critically short. Failure to act will mean an irrevocable change in the human environment. We shall never be able to remedy this loss.

c

d

A WORLD HERITAGE

An international convention ratified in 1975 by governments will create a world-heritage system of outstanding protected natural and cultural areas. Some obvious candidates for such a system are shown. (**a**) Angkor in Cambodia. (**b**) The Galápagos Islands of Ecuador. (**c**) Machu Picchu in Peru. (**d**) The Acropolis in Athens.

CHAPTER
REFERENCES

Allen, Durward, 1954. *Our wildlife legacy.* Funk and Wagnalls, New York.

Clawson, Marion, 1963. *Land and water for recreation.* Rand McNally, Chicago.

Dasmann, R. F., 1964. *Wildlife biology.* Wiley, New York.

Douglas, William O., 1965. *A wilderness bill of rights.* Little, Brown, Boston.

Elton, Charles, 1927. *Animal ecology.* Sidgwick and Jackson, London.

Fosberg, R. R., ed., 1963. *Man's place in the island ecosystem.* Bishop Museum, Honolulu.

Fraser Darling, Frank, and Noel Eichhorn, 1969. *Man and nature in the national parks.* Conservation Foundation, Washington.

————, 1970. *Wilderness and plenty.* Houghton Mifflin, Boston.

Graham, Edward H., 1947. *The land and wildlife.* Oxford, New York.

Leopold, Aldo, 1933. *Game management.* Scribners, New York.

LITERATURE
CITED

1. Banfield, A. W., 1951. *The barren-ground caribou.* Canada Dept. of Resources and Development, Ottawa.

2. Bannikov, A. G., 1962. *Exploitation of the saiga antelope in the USSR.* Proc. Institute of Biology, London.

3. Dasmann, R. F., 1964. *African game ranching.* Pergamon, Oxford.

4. ————, 1964. *Wildlife biology.* Wiley, New York.

5. ————, 1968. *A different kind of country.* Macmillan, New York.

6. Edwards, R. Y., 1954. Fire and the decline of a mountain caribou herd. *Jour. Wildlife Management,* 18: 521–526.

7. Fish and Wildlife Service, 1965. *Survival or surrender for endangered wildlife.* Department of Interior, Washington.

8. Fraser Darling, Frank, and John Milton, 1966. *The future environments of North America.* Natural History, New York.

9. Graham, E. S., 1947. *The land and wildlife.* Oxford, New York.

10. Grinnell, J., J. Dixon, and J. Linsdale, 1937. *The fur-bearing mammals of California.* University of California, Berkeley, 2 vol.

11. Hornaday, W. T., 1913. *Our vanishing wildlife.* Scribners, New York.

12. IUCN, 1963. *Conservation of nature and natural resources in modern African states.* IUCN Publ., New Series, no. 1, Morges, Switzerland.

13. ————, 1966–1974. *Red Data Book.* Morges, Switzerland.

14. ————, 1975. *United Nations List of National Parks and equivalent reserves.* IUCN, Morges, Switzerland.

15. Leopold, Aldo, 1933. *Game management.* Scribners, New York.

16. ————, 1949. *A sand county almanac.* Oxford, New York.

17. Leopold, A. Starker, and F. F. Darling, 1953. *Wildlife in Alaska.* Ronald Press, New York.

18. Leopold, A. Starker, 1956. Hunting for the masses—can game departments supply it? *Proc. 36th Annual Conference,* Western Association of State Game and Fish Commissioners.

19. Leopold, A. Starker, et al., 1963. Wildlife management in the national parks. *Transactions,* North American Wildlife and Natural Resources Conference.

20. Leydet, Francois, ed., 1963. *Tomorrow's wilderness.* Sierra Club, San Francisco.

21. Longhurst, W., A. S. Leopold, and R. F. Dasmann, 1952. *A survey of California deer herds, their ranges and management problems.* Calif. Department of Fish and Game, Game Bull. 6.

22. Lorenz, Konrad, 1963. *On aggression.* Harcourt, Brace, New York.

23. Lowdermilk, W. C., 1953. *Conquest of the land through 7,000 years.* Soil Conservation Service, Washington.
24. Mumford, Lewis, 1966. *The myth of the machine.* Harcourt, Brace and World, New York.
25. Nadel, Michael, ed., 1964. A handbook on the wilderness act. *Living Wilderness,* vol. 86.
26. Nagel, W. O., ed., 1952. *Wildlife and the soil.* Missouri Conservation Commission, Jefferson City.
27. Odum, Eugene P., 1959. *Fundamentals of ecology.* W. B. Saunders, Philadelphia.
28. Outdoor Recreation Resources Review Commission, 1962. *Outdoor recreation for America.* Gov't Printing Office, Washington.
29. Pan American Union, 1965. *The Cutibireni national park: a pilot project in the selva of Peru.* PAU, Washington.
30. Rasmussen, D. I., 1941. Biotic communities of the Kaibab Plateau. *Ecological Monographs,* 3: 229–275.
31. Russell, Carl P., 1957. *One hundred years in Yosemite.* Yosemite Natural History Association, Yosemite.
32. Schaller, George, 1967. *The deer and the tiger. A study of wildlife in India.* University of Chicago, Chicago.
33. Talbot, Lee M., 1957. The lions of Gir: wildlife management problems of Asia. *Transactions,* 22nd North American Wildlife Conference, pp. 570–579.
34. ———, 1966. *Wild animals as a source of food.* Bureau Sport Fisheries and Wildlife, Washington.
35. Thoreau, Henry David, 1961. *Walden.* Holt, Rinehart and Winston, New York.
36. Udall, Stewart L., 1963. *The quiet crisis.* Holt, Rinehart and Winston, New York.
37. UNESCO, 1970. *Use and conservation of the biosphere.* Natural Resources Research, 10, UNESCO, Paris.
38. Yocom, C. F., and R. F. Dasmann, 1957. *The Pacific coastal wildlife region.* Naturegraph, Healdsburg, Calif.
39. Zabinski, J., 1961. A propos du bison d'Europe. *La terre et la vie,* 1: 113–115.

10

the aquatic environment

People are land animals and their interest and attention over the millenia of history have been directed toward the lands of the earth. The oceans, seas, bays, great lakes, and rivers have been often regarded simply as the spaces between the lands—to be crossed as quickly as possible in going from one land area to another. Consequently the continents are well known, whereas the oceans and other waters have been little known. We forget, therefore, their great extent and importance. All of the continents fitted together could be placed in the space occupied by the Pacific Ocean, and there would be room left over. More than 70 percent of the earth is covered by oceans and seas. Of the remaining area a high percentage is covered by rivers, streams, lakes, ponds, swamps, and marshes. Furthermore, the continent of Antarctica, the island of Greenland, and extensive mountain areas of other continents are covered by glacial ice. If all of this melted, as it has in past interglacial ages, the water area of the world would be greatly extended.

Boundaries between land and water—the shorelines of the world—have always held a special attraction for people. Today they are under great pressure from those who wish to exploit their resources, and from those who seek to use them as living space or recreation areas. Also, with growing populations, human dependence on the seas as a source of food and other materials has increased. With this comes the need for greater understanding of aquatic environments.

GENERAL CHARACTERISTICS

Water is an unusual substance despite its abundance in the biosphere. Its characteristics make it highly suitable both as a medium in which life exists and as a component of living substance. All of the minerals and gases required by life are soluble in water and, passing through water, can be absorbed by living cells. Water has a high specific heat, meaning it takes a relatively large application of energy to raise its temperature, and once heated, it is slow to cool. Thus the aquatic environment is buffered against rapid temperature changes that occur in terrestrial environments. Furthermore, water reaches its maximum density at 4° C., four degrees above its freezing point. Water approaching the freezing point, therefore, is lighter and moves to the surface of water bodies. On freezing, water takes on a crystalline structure, and as ice, floats on the surface of liquid water, providing insulation against further temperature reduction underneath. Thus, with the exception of small bodies of water, aquatic environments provide protection against freezing for the organisms that occupy them. Furthermore, in comparison to other environments, aquatic environments are relatively uniform, and the organisms within them are sheltered against physical and chemical changes to a degree that most terrestrial organisms are not. This relative uniformity, however, makes it difficult to arrange the neat classifications of aquatic habitats and biotic communities that one is accustomed to in the terrestrial environment. Also, within any one aquatic ecosystem, food chains and webs become more complicated than those that are generally encountered on land.

Despite their complexity, aquatic ecosystems have the same basic components as those of dry land. Energy comes from sunlight. Chemicals enter the water either from the atmosphere or from the lithosphere; in particular, from the soils that surround the water body and form its *basin*. Green plants are the principal producers. Of these, the most important are the floating green plants, or plankton—commonly of microscopic size and made up, for the most part, of green algae, blue-green algae, and bacteria. The plant plankton, or *phytoplankton,* provides food for the floating animal populations of the water, also mostly of microscopic size. These, the *zooplankton,* provide food for larger organisms that in turn lead up through the food chains to tunas, sharks, or billfish or the large carnivorous invertebrates. Reducer organisms play an important role and range from the scavengers which feed on and break apart carcasses to the bacteria that finally convert organic materials into their mineral components.

Among the chemical limiting factors in water, the amount of dissolved oxygen is particularly important. Cold water holds more oxygen than warm. Oxygen must enter water either directly from the atmosphere through diffusion or physical mixing, or through the action of photosynthesis. It follows, therefore, that the surface layers of water, which are readily penetrated by light and can consequently support green plants, or which are in direct contact with the air, are well oxygenated, whereas deeper layers to which light cannot penetrate and in which the decay of dead organisms most commonly takes place, may have low supplies of oxygen. Were it not for the factor of mixing, and of overturns of surface and deeper water as a result of turbulence and the movement of currents, there would be continual oxygen exhaustion in these deeper, unlighted layers.

Also of importance among chemical limiting factors are the supplies of nitrates and phosphates. Where overabundant, they can cause excessive "blooms" of plankton which, on decay, exhausts the supply of oxygen. In many lakes and throughout most of the surface water of the oceans, however, these chemicals may be relatively scarce and in consequence the amount of life that can be supported is limited.

Life originated in the oceans, and animal life is adjusted to the salinities of ocean water which are reflected in the composition of blood and other body fluids. The greatest abundance of aquatic life is still to be found in the oceans. Relatively few species have adapted to the more rigorous freshwater environments of the earth, or to inland salt lakes.

A detailed classification of marine environments would not be useful in this text. It is worthwhile, however, to consider certain differences among these environments. One factor of importance is light penetration. Sunlight can reach depths of 400 feet in the oceans, but it usually reaches less than 180 feet.[18] The depth of light penetration is influenced by the amount of dissolved or floating substances in the water. Where nutrients, and consequently life, is abundant, light penetration is limited. Where the ocean is relatively sterile and consequently clean, light penetration reaches a maximum.

The lighted zone of the oceans is known as the *euphotic zone*. Within this all of the phytoplankton exist. Where the ocean floor is within reach of sunlight, attached plants—the *benthon* as distinct from plankton—are able to grow. These may be of great abundance and sometimes, as in the case of the giant kelp, reach enormous size. That part of the euphotic zone normally confined to continental shelfs and the shallower waters surrounding islands is called the *neritic* or green water zone, as distinct from the *pelagic* or blue water zone of the open ocean. Below the lighted pelagic zone is the dark, intermediate layer of the ocean, known as the *bathyal* zone. Here may live a great variety of organisms that depend for their existence either on the downward "rain" of dead plant or animal materials from the euphotic zone above, or else on diurnal or periodic forays upward to feed within pelagic waters. Some species, and many of the whales are in this category, move freely between zones. Far below the lighted zone of the oceans, at depths of more than 2000 meters where pressure is enormous and food is necessarily limited is the *abyssal* zone. Here in the deepest parts of the oceans life still exists, dependent on the rain of nutrient materials from the lighted zone above. In the great chasms or oceanic troughs these depths may reach to 30,000 feet or more. Only specialized creatures can exist in such deeps, and their abundance can never be great.[15]

The topography of the oceans leads to another separate means for classifying ocean environments. Each continent is a block of lighter, largely acidic rock, floating on heavier, basic rock that forms both the floor of the oceans and the basement of the continents. Under present conditions of world climate, when glaciers occur but are not extensive, large areas of each continent are flooded by the oceans. These areas, the *continental shelfs,* extend varying distances out from land to a maximum depth of approximately 200 meters. Beyond these shelfs, the continental margin plunges off steeply into the area of confluence between continental rocks and those of the deep ocean floor. The area of steep descent is known as the *continental slope*. Continental shelfs represent areas where, in the neritic zone, attached vegetation can grow. They are also the areas which receive the maximum input of nutrients flowing into the oceans from streams and rivers. Consequently most of them support a relatively great abundance of life (Fig. 10–1).

Beyond the continental shelf the ocean floor extends as a generally

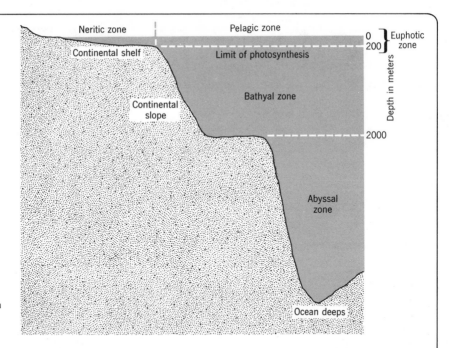

FIG. 10–1. Zonation in the ocean (*data from Odum, 1959*).

flat surface over long distances. It is interrupted in places, however, by the results of volcanic activity in the form of islands or submerged sea mounts. Elsewhere, oceanic rises, such as the mid-Atlantic ridge or various island chains, are oceanic mountain ranges formed by the upward thrusting of segments of the earth's crust. Where these extend upward to the euphotic zone they may support an abundance of life. In places, the ocean floor is further broken by deep chasms of oceanic deeps. These, too, are associated with areas of earth movement and volcanic activity.

The greatest variety of aquatic life is to be found in the neritic or coastal zone where the waters of the ocean mix with those flowing from land, and where marine environments give way to dry-land habitats. This is the region where tidal action is to be most readily observed.

The tides are caused by the gravitational attraction between the sun, the moon, and the earth. Water bodies, being free to move, respond to these gravitational forces more than do land masses. In consequence, as a result of the spinning of the earth on its axis, there will be, at least, one period each day when the waters of the ocean are raised to a peak by the gravitational pull of the moon (or moon and sun together), and another when they are contracted to a low point by the absence of such a force. Each separate body of water develops its own tidal rhythm in response to these varying forces. Along the Pacific Coast of North America there are two periods of high tide each day, and two of low. In other areas there may be a single high and low tide in each 24-hour period.

a

THE COASTAL ZONE

(**a**) The intertidal zone. In this meeting place between land and sea a great diversity of marine life is to be found. Sandy beaches, mud flats or rock out-croppings each support a distinct group of marine organisms. (**b**) Mangroves line the estuaries of tropical coasts and provide a nursery ground for many marine animals which spend their adult life at sea. In addition, they support a specialized biota which is largely restricted to the mangrove habitat. (**c**) Life in the coastal zone reaches its greatest diversity in the coral reefs of shallow tropical seas.

b

c

The effect of tidal movements is to expose a section of the coastal (or littoral) region to the air at times of low tide, and to flood it with water when tides are high. Organisms living in this *intertidal* zone must be able to resist dessication during the periods when they are exposed to air, and to tolerate immersion in marine saline waters during the rest of the day. Those living high in the intertidal zone are seldom covered by water; those occupying the lower levels are rarely exposed to air. The very highest area is not covered by tidal water, but is soaked each day by the splash from waves.[18]

These influences create a wide variety of intertidal animal and plant communities. In the upper zone live creatures such as the periwinkle, certain limpets and barnacles. In the lower zone live eel grasses or turtle grasses, sea palms, and animals such as abalones. In between one finds an enormous variety of invertebrate animals and algae that can establish themselves on rocks or can grow in mud. Further differences are interposed by the nature of the substrate. Rocky shores will support one group of species, sandy beaches another, mud flats a third, and so on. Still greater variety is interposed where freshwaters enter the oceans. In this, the *estuarine* region, is to be found enormous complexity, and high productivity. To a remarkable degree, the life of the broad oceans is dependent on the continued functioning of the estuarine region.[18]

The ability of organisms to occupy the estuaries depends on their ability to withstand salinities which diminish from the oceans into freshwater, and which fluctuate both with the outpouring of freshwater from streams and rivers and also with the inland movement of salt water in response to tidal fluctuations. Zonation of plants and animals in estuaries reflects their tolerance to decreased and fluctuating salinities. Here one may trace possible pathways over which the evolution of freshwater species occurred in past aeons, just as one may trace, along the rocky intertidal zone, pathways by which certain organisms evolved from an aquatic to a terrestrial existence.

It follows from the above classification that the productivity of marine environments is highly variable. Coastal and estuarine zones are inclined toward high productivity, since they receive a constant replenishment of nutrients from the dry land. By contrast, productivity away from shores is dependent on other factors. In any open area of ocean water, as the distance from the influence of continental sources of nutrients increased, one might expect a continually diminishing productivity. Nitrates, for example, would enter from the atmosphere both directly and through the activities of nitrogen-fixing microorganisms. The input of most other nutrients depends on their rate of deposition from air currents—winds that had swept them off eroding land in continental areas. These nutrients are taken up quickly by phytoplankton, pass through food chains to larger organisms, and eventually are carried downward out of the euphotic zone on the death of these organisms. There is in consequence a steady drain of nutrients from the upper, productive layers of water down into unlighted lower layers. Were this to continue unabated the productivity of the upper layers would be low and entirely related to the input of nutrients from the air.

Fortunately for life in the oceans such a downward drain does not continue unabated. In any large body of water, currents, both vertical and horizontal, develop. They serve to move and mix water. In all the oceans, surface currents develop in response to the rotation of the earth and movement of the atmosphere. These result in counterclockwise flows of water in the Southern Hemisphere, and clockwise flows in the Northern

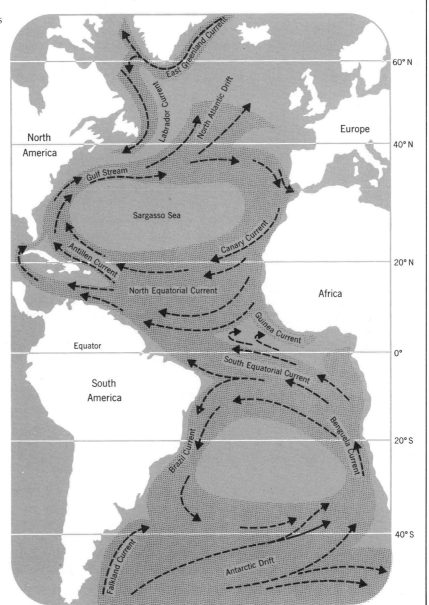

FIG. 10–2. Major currents of the Atlantic Ocean. These currents carry nutrients from areas of upwelling to other parts of the ocean.

Hemisphere (Fig. 10–2). Interruptions of these flows by islands and continents, and interactions between the major oceans lead to complicated surface currents that move water from one part of an ocean to another and, thus, lead to a considerable degree of surface mixing. Adding to the effects of these surface currents are vertical movements of water. Cold water, being more dense, sinks to the bottom; warm water, being lighter, rises to the surface. In the tropics surface water is heated; in the polar regions in winter it is drastically cooled. Polar water, consequently, sinks and moves in ocean basins toward the tropics, where it replaces the warm, light water which moves toward the poles. A degree of vertical mixing of water therefore takes place along the edges of the polar ice caps and also in equatorial regions. This brings nutrients from deep water to the surface and restores the fertility of surface waters. Polar and equatorial regions are often highly productive.[10,15]

Along the western coast of continents, in the trade wind zone, there are relatively constant winds blowing offshore that push the surface waters away from the land. This outwardly moving surface water is replaced by an *upwelling* from deeper, colder layers. This upwelling brings nutrients from the deeper parts of the ocean and restores surface productivity. Thus, one of the most highly productive areas in the ocean is on the western coast of South America in Chile and Peru. Here, because of the outward movement of the trade winds there is virtually no rain or runoff of water from the land. Yet the strong upwelling brings high fertility to the surface waters. A cold, northward moving current, the Humboldt Current, carries these nutrient-rich waters up the South American coast into equatorial regions where they move offshore into the tropical ocean, adding to its productivity. The coasts of Chile and Peru are noted for their fisheries and for great numbers of seabirds that depend on the fish produced in the Humboldt Current. Deposition of seabird faeces, guano, on the offshore rocks and islands of Peru, have made them, in the past, one of the world's great sources of nitrate fertilizer.[3]

As a result of the variations in input from continental sources and the enrichment of surface waters by mixing and upwelling, the productivity of the oceans varies enormously. The central portions of the major oceans, such as the Sargasso Sea in the mid-Atlantic, are notoriously unproductive and have been compared to terrestrial deserts. By contrast, the areas of Antarctic mixing, and such upwelling areas as the Peruvian and California coasts, are highly productive.[10,15]

MARINE FISHERIES Human exploration of the oceans undoubtedly began with the intertidal zones. A variety of palatable and nutritious species are found there, including clams, oysters, crabs, and lobsters as well as a variety of fish. In time people learned to put out from shore in boats and exploit the fisheries along the continental shelves—the herring, cod, haddock, and plaice of the North Sea and the sardines and mackerel of the Mediterranean. As long as the numbers of people were few and the boats and gear used for fishing were primitive, their influence on fish populations was minor. Now, with the growth of technology and numbers of people, this situation has changed. Human capabilities for overfishing and exhausting oceanic resources are now well developed. However, the concept of overfishing needs some examination.

Fish, and most other aquatic animals, have a high biotic potential. Thousands of eggs are laid by each female. Although few of these eggs usually survive because of predation and unfavorable environmental conditions, the capacity for rapid growth of a population is readily expressed. People enter the marine environment as one of many oceanic predators. Usually their efforts are directed toward the capture of the larger, more mature members of a species population. Fishing is motivated either by a desire for food, for profit, or for sport. It is rarely profitable from any of these viewpoints to expend the effort necessary to pursue the last surviving members of a species. When a fishery no longer yields a good profit, commercial fishing ceases, whereas the take of a sport fisherman becomes random and incidental when fish populations are low. In consequence fishing alone is not likely to cause the extermination of a marine fish species, except under unusual conditions. Unfortunately, fishing operates in combination with a great number of other factors in marine ecosystems, and when fishing reinforces other adverse environmental factors, serious problems can develop. The example of the California sardine fishery is illustrative.

THE SARDINE STORY[6,10,21] Management of ocean fisheries is plagued by the difficulties of finding facts about animal populations which cannot easily be counted or watched as they go through their life cycles. It is faced by the mysteries of a highly complex and little understood oceanic environment. To date, fisheries management in ocean waters has been largely a research endeavor, a continuing attempt to find the basic information on which a sound management program can be based. When this is discovered and the fishing industry convinced of the necessity for management, laws can be passed and agreements made which will help to perpetuate fish resources. Until then, we will continue to face crises such as the one that has confronted the sardine-fishing industry of the Pacific (Fig. 10–3).

In 1936–1937, along the Pacific Coast of North America between San Diego and British Columbia a total of nearly 800,000 tons of Pacific sardines were landed. The sardine industry had risen to the point where it was the first-ranking fishery in North America in pounds of fish caught and the third-ranking commercial fishery in value of catch, surpassed only by tuna and salmon. The value of the take was in excess of 10 million dollars annually. The sardine found its way to market in many forms, as bait for fishermen, as the familiar canned sardine, as dog food, oil, and fertilizer. Nevertheless by 1953–1954, the catch of sardines had fallen to a total of 4460 tons (Fig. 10–3). Sardine-fishing fleets were sold for other uses; canneries and reduction plants were idle. The failure of the sardine fishery illustrates many of the questions that puzzle those

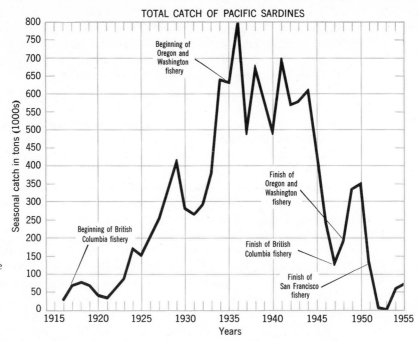

FIG. 10–3. Rise and fall of the sardine fishery of the North American Pacific coast. Since the date shown, until 1970, there has been no recovery (*data from California Department of Fish and Game, 1957*).

who depend on the resources of the sea for a livelihood and biologists who seek to maintain those resources.

The sardine fishery in the Pacific began during World War I in California, with a catch of over 27,000 tons reported in 1916–1917. In succeeding years it spread northward to the waters off Oregon, Washington, and British Columbia. Soon it supported a major fishing fleet and processing industry. In 1924 the catch jumped to 174,000 tons and continued upward to its peak in 1936–1937. The fishing fleet grew to 300 vessels, each taking 100 to 200 tons of fish per day of fishing. After 1936 the take remained at a fairly high level until 1944. Biologists, however, could see that trouble was developing long before the total catch started to decline. Under heavy fishing the older fish were removed from the population, and the annual take began to depend on the yield of younger fish. The average catch per boat and per night of fishing declined. This was masked by more boats putting out to sea and fishing longer, so that the total catch held up. The symptoms of trouble caused biologists to attempt to regulate the fishing industry in order to balance the annual catch against the productivity of the population. These efforts were not successful.

The first fishery to fail was in Canadian waters. Between 1945 to 1946 and 1947 to 1948 the Canadian catch dropped from 34,000 tons to less than 500. The Washington and Oregon fisheries soon followed. After the 1948 to 1949 season the northern fishing fleets stopped operation, and the sardine canneries of the Northwest closed down. For a few more years the yield off California remained high. In 1951, however, the San Francisco fishing fleet returned with a disastrously low catch of 80 tons. With this, the main center of the industry closed down. Catches remained high in southern California waters for one more year, and then this fishery too collapsed.

Throughout all of this period the sardine industry remained unrestricted and refused to tolerate any limitation on its take. Whether or not such restrictions would have prevented the sardine disaster remains open to question, but it is most likely that the fishery could have been better maintained with intelligent regulation.

The final collapse of the sardine industry in United States waters was associated with failure in reproduction and survival of young fish. The expected addition to the population provided by the growth of young sardines to catchable size did not occur. Offshore waters in southern California, which were major spawning grounds in the past, are no longer producing young fish. A sardine fishery still exists in Mexican waters off the coast of Baja California, but it is not large enough to support a major fishing industry. Movement of sardines from Mexican to Californian waters, which occurred in the past, took place in 1955 to 1956 and allowed for an increase in catch in those years. However, this movement alone was not sufficient. There is evidence that changes in the condition of the ocean, resulting from shifts in currents or other causes, are involved in the depletion of the fishery. If this is true, little can be done except to hope that former conditions will return. However, since overfishing and the resulting depletion of breeding populations is a contributing factor, there is less excuse. Overfishing can be prevented. Fortunately, in 1955, the California legislature passed its first law limiting the catch of a marine, commercial fish. This law, intended to protect the anchovy fishery, on which the former sardine-fishing pressure has descended, has set a precedent for other laws that can provide needed protection for the sardine and other ocean fisheries.

A review of the situation in the 1970's, however, suggests that the former niche occupied by the sardine along the continental shelf of North America has been taken over by the anchovy.[10] Under these circumstances, even the absence of sardine fishing and the return of oceanographic conditions favorable to the sardine, would not necessarily lead to a recovery of sardine populations. Instead, the well-established anchovy might continue to thrive. Thus it can be seen that fishing pressure in the marine environment cannot be evaluated as a single factor. Although it may seem "common sense" that commercial fishing will not permanently reduce a fishery, when this fishing is balanced against all of the other factors operating for or against a marine species it may have consequences far beyond those that could readily have been predicted.

MARINE MAMMALS With the sardines one may still argue about the basic causes of the relatively permanent decline in population and the role played by human exploitation. It is a different situation with the marine mammals. Here the human factor is obviously predominant. Mammals, unlike fish, have no enormous powers of reproduction. The survival of the species depends on the survival of the one or two young produced each year.

The history of the whaling industry is one of the more colorful episodes in the saga of man. Initially, whaling consisted of the efforts of a few people who put out in small boats across the coastal waters to conquer and subdue the giant creatures who came from the far reaches of the ocean. In the Bay of Biscay off the Spanish coast during historical times, whaling was of this nature; the attempts to capture the right whales that came into these waters was little different from the more recent efforts of the Eskimos to capture and utilize the white whales, baluga, of the Arctic Ocean. But during the nineteenth century whaling became a much more intensive operation and the exploits of the Yankee whalers setting out from New Bedford, Mystic, and the other New England whaling villages have passed down in history and American literature. Hermann Melville's classic *Moby Dick* captures the spirit of the times. His fictional Captain Ahab of the whaling ship has been taken by some as exemplifying the entire spirit of our technological age: "All my means are sane, my motive and my object mad."[2]

There is little doubt that the efforts of these early whalers brought some species of whales to the verge of extinction. But the greatest effects were to come. The high value of whale oil, whale bone, whale meat, and all of the other products obtainable from these animals, provided an incentive to develop a more efficient technology for capturing them. In place of the hand-thrown harpoon came the harpoon gun, in place of the sail-powered whaling ship came the modern motor-driven factory ship with its satellites of hunter-killer vessels. In place of the laborious rendering of a captured whale into a compact booty of readily transportable valuables, came the capacity of reducing the entire animal, on the spot, into all of its commercially useful components. Whaling became big business, but the whales were not capable of producing in response to the new demands.[16]

The greatest impact was felt in Antarctic waters. Here the shrimplike krill, *Euphasia,* formed an important part of the zooplankton and was the food base for such giants as the blue or sulphur-bottomed whale, the largest of all mammals. We do not know how many blue whales there were in Antarctic waters, but their population has been estimated at about 200,000. To support this population it has been estimated that a total of 100 million tons of zooplankton, mainly krill, may have been required in each year. Motorized, efficient modern whaling was brought to bear on blue whale populations after the end of World War I. By 1930 to 1931 the annual catch of blue whales reached a peak of 29,400 animals. From then on the catch exceeded the sustainable yield from the blue whale population until it was finally apparent that if harvesting continued, even on an incidental basis, the whale would become extinct. In 1964 the blue whale was given complete protection by international agreement, and it has since shown some slight recovery.[10,16]

The whaling enterprise has shifted from the larger to the smaller whales. When blue whale stocks were depleted whaling shifted to the smaller fin whale. A peak catch of 28,000 animals was recorded in 1937 to 1938. From then on harvest exceeded the amount sustainable by what was an initial population of, at least, 200,000 animals. By the late 1960's the catch had declined to 3000 and the species was in danger. The humpback, also a moderately large whale, occurred in numbers that probably never exceeded 50,000 in Antarctic waters and could not support the pressure from the whaling industry. Catches of 2000 or more in a year in the Antarctic could not be sustained, since this species was also exploited in more northern waters. Pressure next descended on the sei whales which supported catches of up to 20,000 animals in the middle 1900's, but with their numbers also on the decline the catch was reduced to under 6000 in 1968 to 1969. Still smaller whales have been picked up in increasing numbers by the industry, and there has been talk of concentrating heavy exploitation on the small porpoises and dolphins, much to the dismay of those who regard these intelligent animals in the same category with domestic pets.[10,12,16]

In the 1970's considerable effort has been expended to offer complete protection to all whales to allow for recovery of their numbers. Although only a few species such as the right whale and blue whale have been considered as seriously endangered, there is little doubt that heavy exploitation could quickly reduce all species to this status. Unfortunately, the whaling industry has been little amenable to regulation.

Whales and their conservation exemplify a problem that besets the exploitation and conservation of most marine fisheries. The oceans are effectively no-man's-land. They belong traditionally to all nations and to no nations. Whoever gets there first has the right to capture and own their resources; their activities are not subject to any effective control. With the depletion of certain fisheries—the whale stocks, are an example—the need for international regulation and control became apparent. This need led to the formation of the International Whaling Commission, which supposedly was to regulate the activities of the whaling nations. In practice, however, the commission listened to the advice of its scientists, who were among the world's authorities on whale populations, but then decided, on political grounds, to ignore this advice. As a result, until recently, the take of whales has exceeded the limits that could be sustained. Conservation-minded people have, in the 1970's, finally taken the option of attempting to circumvent the International Whaling Commission. Thus, in 1971, all importations of whale products into the United States were stopped. However, the United States had long since lost its status as a major whaling nation. The Soviet Union and Japan, two of the principal whaling nations, showed no inclination to discontinue their decimation of whales.

Georg Borgstrom has pointed out some of the realities of marine ecology that have bearing on the conservation of whales. Around 500 pounds of phytoplankton must be used to produce 100 pounds of zooplankton.

MARINE FISHERIES

(a) At its peak the California sardine fishery produced 800,000 tons of fish per year. In the late 1940's and early 1950's it collapsed. **(b)** The Peruvian anchovy fishery. Most of the catch is reduced to fish meal in factories such as this. **(c)** Despite the efforts of international organizations to put an end to commercial whaling, Japanese and Russian whaling fleets continue, in the middle 1970's, to capture great numbers of marine mammals. **(d)** White whales provide the support for traditional Eskimo whaling in Canada. **(e)** The northern fur seal has been restored to abundance by means of an enforced treaty limiting the annual seal harvest.

d

e

This can, in turn, yield a maximum of 10 pounds of herring which then provide the basis for one pound of mackerel. Should tuna in turn feed on the mackerel, an ounce and a half of tuna might be produced. Thus a tuna weighing 100 pounds would represent a phytoplankton production of 500,000 pounds. The ratio of 5000 to 1 represents a high caloric loss. By contrast, the blue whale feeds on zooplankton directly and converts it into useful meat. If we have as a goal the production of protein useful to man from the oceans, we would go far to find a more handy and efficient plankton converter. We could be cultivating blue whales and their relatives as marine livestock equivalent to cattle on the land, and taking from them an annual sustainable crop. Instead we have treated them as we once did the American bison, and talk glibly about building plankton-harvesting devices that at their best would be less efficient than the whales.[2]

The inadequacies of human behavior have affected many kinds of marine mammals other than whales. Some, such as the Steller's sea cow of the Arctic, became extinct. Others, the manatees and dugongs, and the monk seals of the Mediterranean and Caribbean have been pushed to near extinction. Others, although once depleted, have been brought back to healthy levels. An outstanding example is the northern fur seal that hauls out to breed on the rocky Pribiloff Islands off the Alaskan coast. This species was once exploited by Russians, Americans, and Japanese and pushed to being in danger of extinction. One of the first international agreements affecting marine resources was signed by Russia, the United States, Japan, and Canada in 1911. Since then, the fur seal has been harvested annually on its breeding ground, but within a sustainable yield. It has increased from small numbers to a population that exceeds one million animals. It can continue forever to yield skins and other by-products for human use.

ANADRAMOUS FISHERIES[1,10,17] Particularly vulnerable to human pressures are the fish which migrate from fresh- to saltwater, spending a part of their life cycle in each environment. These species, known as *anadramous* fish, must face not only the hazards of ocean life but also the dangers to be found in streams and rivers. One example is the Atlantic salmon. Originally this was an abundant species which spawned and spent the early stages of its life cycle in the streams and rivers round the North Atlantic in Europe and America. As mature fish, they were found at sea and here they were commercially exploited. Within the freshwaters of Europe and America they received the attention of sport fishermen and were highly valued by anglers. A combination of dams and other obstacles constructed in their home streams and the ever-growing level of pollution in these waters led to major declines in fish populations. Those fish which successfully ran the gauntlet of hazards in freshwater were then subject to further decimation in the oceans. Concern for the future of the species resulted in increasing attention being given to its conservation during the late 1960's and early 1970's. As a result of the pressure by conservationists, the commercial fishing of this species by northern European nations was discontinued in 1971. However, the continuing pressure on its home streams gives rise to no optimism about its future recovery.

In Pacific waters, the Pacific salmon of several species compete with tuna for first place among commercial fish. Heavy exploitation by commercial fishermen combined with heavy sports fishing occurs, but it cannot be considered as the major cause of depletion. This is to be found in the freshwaters. The construction of Grand Coulee Dam on the Columbia blocked the upper reaches of the river to Chinook salmon spawning. Shasta Dam and other high dams on the Sacramento River and its tributaries have cut off most areas of spawning ground in California. To partially replace the reproduction lost by blocking off these spawning areas, fish hatcheries have been constructed on several river systems and these have helped to maintain the fishery. However, the continuing demand for water for power or irrigation, or for the control of floods will soon result in the damming of all of the main rivers of California, more dams in Oregon and Washington, and increasing dam construction in Canada and Alaska. These developments must force a dependence on the few remaining open streams and a much greater effort to develop and improve habitat conditions in these waters if salmon fishing is to be perpetuated.

A struggle has long been waged between those who wish to maintain open streams for fisheries and outdoor recreation, and those who wish to dam all waters for urban-industrial supplies, power, or irrigation. With few exceptions the representatives of the people in state legislatures and Congress have voted for dams. In consequence, there is less and less water for fisheries. Fisheries managers have worked minor miracles in their attempts to compensate for the increasing loss of fish habitat, but they are reaching their limits.

MARINE POLLUTION[17] Among the most common and persistent of human attitudes toward the ocean has been the view that it is the ultimate answer to the problem of waste disposal. This idea of the ocean as a dump has been encouraged by its apparent vast expanse and depth relative to the needs of man. Anything toxic or obnoxious, from atomic wastes and old war gases or ammunition, down to junked cars, sewage, and general urban debris has been placed in the oceans with a confidence that man had seen the last of it. Added to this, all of the outpourings of pollutants from streams and rivers reach the oceans, and much of the debris polluting the urban air eventually is deposited in ocean waters.

But the ocean is not a limitless dump, and in the 1960's and 1970's it became apparent that this attitude toward it was likely to create limitless problems. Perhaps more than anything else, the wreck of the *Torrey Canyon* off the coast of England in 1967 brought the situation into focus. The *Torrey Canyon* was one of a new generation of giant oil tankers used to transport oil from the fields of the Middle East or Latin America to refineries in Europe or the United States. In March, 1967, it ran aground off the coast of Cornwall in England and proceeded to spill its cargo of 36 million gallons of petroleum into the seas. The Cornish coast of England is a favored vacation spot and its beaches are highly valued. With the summer tourist season coming on, resort owners and all of those dependent on the tourist trade were faced with the prospect of an end to their prosperity. Oil-soaked beaches and oily waters guarantee that potential visitors will spend their holidays elsewhere. Furthermore, seabirds by the thousands became entrapped in the oil and died despite rescue efforts. In spite of a campaign on the part of the British government and local volunteers to clean up the oil, using detergents, napalm, and virtually everything else which could be thought of, damage was done. The oil spread along the coasts of England and reached the beaches of France, across the Channel. Investigations were launched to determine the extent of damage to fisheries, intertidal life, marine mammals and birds, and to recreation values generally.

Not long after the *Torrey Canyon* storm had died down, the world was given another example of the problems of ocean pollution. In the blue and placid Santa Barbara Channel off the coast of southern California, in another favorite tourist and recreation center, an oil well used to pump oil from the fields that lay deep beneath the channel waters began to leak. Oil poured upward to the surface of the water, formed an enormous slick, and began to move toward the beaches of Santa Barbara and adjoining communities. Again the *Torrey Canyon* pattern was repeated. Despite all efforts, great damage was done. In this case the federal Department of Interior, the agency most concerned with conservation, was held to blame for having issued leases to the oil companies which permitted them to drill in this vulnerable locality.

The news from around the world continues to record the wrecks of oil tankers, the flushing of oil bunkers by ships at sea, the leakage from undersea oil wells, and other continuing sources of oil pollution. In 1970 Thor Heyerdahl made one of his exploratory voyages in a papyrus ship from Africa to the West Indies—to prove that the Egyptians could have made the journey and thus influence the development of Amer-Indian civilizations. He reported encountering floating petroleum or tar almost throughout his Atlantic voyage. Other reports have added to the picture of a growing global problem that requires immediate international attention.

Yet oil is only one of many marine pollutants. The effects of pesticides on seabirds are discussed in more detail in Chapter 15. DDT residues are now being recorded from all parts of the oceans. A die-off of seabirds in the Irish Sea in 1969 is believed related to the heavy discharge of another industrial pollutant—polychlorinated biphenyls (PCBs)—produced and used in a variety of manufacturing processes. Mercury levels considered to be dangerous to man were found in tinned tuna and frozen swordfish in 1970 and 1971. Since these species feed across broad areas of the open ocean this led to the conclusion that mercury contamination had also become a global phenomena. The need for regulation and control of the discharge of pollutants into the oceans has become clearly apparent, but the means for accomplishing this remains unclear. The use of the oceans is still uncontrolled. Regulation is an international concern, but the difficulties of reaching agreements among sovereign nations are great, indeed, and the problems of enforcing such agreements are even greater. In 1972 a convention restricting ocean dumping was signed by many nations, but it remains to be seen if it will be effective.

ESTUARIES AND COASTAL WATERS[11,17,18] Compared to the pressures put on the resources and the environments of the open oceans, those affecting coastal and estuarine waters are much more severe. The history of the twentieth century, particularly its latter half, has been marked by man's movement to the sea. The coastal areas of America continue to attract a steady stream of immigrants from inland states. In Europe and in many other parts of the world a similar trend is evident. The coastline is an attractive place for living—recreation, in theory, at least, is available in one's front yard in the form of boating, fishing, swimming, and a variety of other shoreline or water sports. Coastal areas have naturally attracted industry and commerce through the appeal of cheap, waterborne transportation and the apparent availability of large quantities of water for industrial uses.

Use of the coastal zone, however, has seldom been planned to take into account the vulnerability of the environment. Instead, virtually every form of environmental affront has taken place. Thus, estuarine marshes and coastal swamps form a source of nutrients of great importance to marine aquatic life and also provide shelter and a nursery ground for a wide variety of otherwise oceanic species. They are not only highly productive themselves but are vital to the maintenance of productivity in a much wider oceanic area. To the developer, however, they represent areas to be dredged and filled in order to form platforms on which houses or other coastal accommodations can be built, or areas through which boat canals can be dredged to allow boat access to new residential areas.

Efforts to drain marshes along the coast have further resulted in the cutting of canals which move freshwater quickly to the sea. Where previously runoff moved slowly through a variety of winding channels, picking up nutrients and slowly mixing with saltwater, the new canals create massive outpourings of freshwater after each rain. This can disrupt the aquatic life in the bays or channels into which it is poured. Rapid drainage of freshwater has also caused a movement of saltwater inland through what were formerly freshwater aquifers. This has caused a salting up of water supplies needed by the new seashore communities.

Rivers and streams bring into the estuarine zone all of the pollutants and excess nutrients they have picked up in their flow across the lands. Added to this, new coastal communities often pour pollutants directly into the sea. Coastal and estuarine biotic communities suffer all the effects resulting from the concentrations of toxic substances and excessive fertilization. Undesirable planktonic blooms are balanced by the loss of more desirable species of aquatic life.

Dredging, draining, and the construction of coastal installations have changed offshore currents with the consequent erosion of existing beaches and deposition of sand in other areas where it is not wanted. Many efforts to correct this problem by the construction of groins and breakwaters have only accelerated the damage.

Many of the most valuable and interesting biotic communities occur on or near the coast. Pressure on the coastal zones often leads to their complete destruction. Coral reefs are blasted or plundered by those who seek fish, coral, or shells. Tidal pools and tidal marshes—where not polluted, dredged or filled—are often devastated by those who collect marine life for fun or profit.

In the United States many impressive steps were taken during the late 1960's and early 1970's to insure better protection and management of those coastal resources that were not already destroyed, but it is late in the game. Elsewhere in the world little is being done and devastation accelerates. Marine parks and reserves are badly needed. Effective protection for coastal lands, waters, and resources beyond the boundaries of any foreseeable system of parks and reserves is equally important. The health of the entire ocean can well hinge on the care we take of the waters near the coast and the lands in contact with them. It is incredible that we continue to be so careless.

INLAND WATER ENVIRONMENTS To a greater extent than marine environments, the aquatic environments of the continents and islands are highly diversified and marked by a wide range of physical and chemical conditions. Physical conditions vary from those of the boiling lakes of volcanic regions to permanently frozen bodies of water in polar or high mountain areas. Chemical extremes are represented by the clear lakes of certain high mountain and polar areas that contain few nutrients, and the lakes and inland seas of interior drainages that are so saline that only a few highly specialized forms of life can make use of them. A similar range is to be found among rivers and streams.

LAKES AND STREAMS[15,20] Lakes vary according to their age, their depth, their size, and with the conditions of their watersheds. Two broad categories are recognized, based on the relative levels of dissolved nutrients in their waters. One group of lakes is known as *oligotrophic* and includes the clear, cold lakes of high mountains, and of glaciated subpolar regions. These lakes commonly have rocky bottoms and rest in barren, infertile watersheds. Low water temperatures result in a high degree of oxygenation, but the lack of dissolved nutrients prevents an abundant growth of plankton. Rooted vegetation has difficulty becoming established on their rocky edges or bottoms. The level of life that can be supported is therefore low. There is a gradation from these nearly sterile lakes through to moderately fertile lakes. Such clear, cold lakes as Tahoe in the Sierra Nevada of California-Nevada, and Baikal in Siberia are considered as oligotrophic, but nevertheless they support a relatively abundant life. Tahoe, which connects through the Truckee River with Pyramid Lake in Nevada, supports a distinctive fauna. Baikal, long isolated from other water bodies, but of great size, supports a completely unique and highly varied fish fauna.

Associated with these lakes are the clear, cold streams of high mountain and subpolar regions, which are also of low-nutrient, oligotrophic character. Lakes and streams alike support many of the most highly valued sport fish—the cold-water fisheries of rainbow and brook trout, muskellunge, and northern pike. These often reach large size individually but, because of overall limitations in their food supply, seldom become abundant.

At the opposite extreme among freshwaters are the *eutrophic* lakes. These are usually warmer and characteristically have muddy or sandy bottoms, rounded contours, and gently sloping shorelines. Usually they are surrounded by watersheds in which soil has developed and matured and in consequence supplies the lakes with abundant nutrients through runoff or subterranean flow. Warm water causes an acceleration of life processes, and the abundance of nutrients encourages plant growth. Such lakes support abundant submerged, emergent, or floating aquatic vegetation. Throughout the lighted portion of their waters plankton blooms during the warm season of the year. Populations of invertebrates and fish, as well as aquatic amphibians and reptiles, are generally abundant and diversified. In temperate regions, where winter freezing normally occurs, these lakes develop seasonal problems. When ice and snow covers their surface, photosynthesis is inhibited or ceases. However, the decay of plant and animal life along with continued respiration by animals can cause oxygen exhaustion and die-offs of animal life. In subtropical and tropical regions where growth and photosynthesis can continue at a high rate throughout the year, lakes of this kind are among the most productive of ecosystems and yield a continuing abundance of fish and other aquatic life.

Over long periods of time most lakes will evolve from an oligotrophic to a eutrophic condition, as soils in their watersheds mature, as erosion occurs, and as nutrients become more abundant. But this is normally a slow, geologically timed process. *Accelerated eutrophication* of water bodies is a result of man-caused pollution and can bring serious damage to water bodies that have been valued either for their clear, cold water and the recreational and aesthetic values associated with this attribute, or for their sustained, high productivity, which can be swamped out by excessive supplies of nutrients, and excessive growth of certain plants, followed by high rates of decay and oxygen depletion.

The "ideal" eutrophic lake in the United States is one which supports an abundant population of black bass, lake perch, or the various sunfish. However, when such a lake becomes choked with plant growth, grows warmer, and develops a more variable oxygen supply, it becomes the home for catfish or carp. Still further eutrophication can lead to conditions unsuited to any fish and eventually to an environment suited only to blue-green algae or anaerobic bacteria.

The conditions described for lakes also apply to streams. Most large rivers that drain fertile watersheds are eutrophic, with a high-nutrient level and have many of the characteristics and problems of eutrophic lakes.

Zonation occurs in lakes as in the oceans, but to a lesser degree (Fig. 10–4). Large, deep lakes have a *littoral zone* around their margins within which rooted vegetation can grow—reeds and rushes, pondweeds and duckweeds. Beyond the littoral zone and lying over the deeper water in a *limnetic zone,* the lower limits of which are defined by the limits of light penetration, and within which active planktonic growth can occur. Below the limnetic zone is the dark, *profundal zone* where no photosynthesis occurs. This may still support abundant life, but it is dependent for its food on the lighted waters above or the littoral region of the shore. Particularly in temperate regions and in deeper lakes, zonation is further accentuated by *thermal stratification*. Surface waters are heated by the sun in summer and, as a result, become lighter and less dense than the deeper layers. The deeper layers may be maintained at a maximum density and constant temperature of 4° C. As one moves from surface to deeper waters, a sharp temperature gradient, or *thermocline* occurs. If the thermocline corresponds with or is below the level of the limnetic zone, then all photosynthesis occurs in the warmer waters and the profundal zone, as the summer progresses, may face oxygen depletion with

FIG. 10–4. Cross sections through oligotrophic and eutrophic lakes.

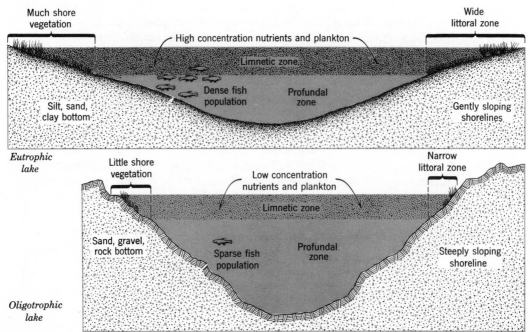

its consequences for life. In the autumn, however, as the weather cools, surface temperatures of the lake will decline and eventually reach the 4° level of the deeper waters. The thermocline disappears and the water from the two zones mixes freely, restoring oxygen to the deeper layers. As winter progresses the surface water cools, ice forms, and once again a stratification and thermocline is set up, although less severe than in summer. This again brings dangers of oxygen depletion if the winter remains cold. Spring warming of the surface, however, once again restores equal temperatures, a spring overturn occurs, and the waters are once again mixed. Both zonation and temperature stratification have consequences for the distribution of aquatic life and create separate ecologic niches within a water body, allowing for a greater variety of life. When lakes are managed for intensive fish production, these characteristics must be recognized and compensated for to maintain high levels of yield.

FISHERIES CONSERVATION AND MANAGEMENT IN THE UNITED STATES
The fisheries of the freshwater lakes and streams of North America attract annually an army of anglers numbering well over 20 million.[7] Dangling a hook and line into a quiet pond or flashing a trout fly over a splashing stream is a form of recreation with a traditional, and almost irresistible, appeal to a large segment of the American population. Because it is a form of sport open to participation by both sexes and all ages of people, it has a much larger group of followers than the more strenuous sport of hunting. The history of fish conservation, in America, resembles the conservation of game. In most instances responsibility for management of fisheries resources rests with a joint fish and wildlife agency.

BEGINNINGS
The history of freshwater fisheries in America can be traced through a period of early abundance, when streams ran clear and fish could be easily taken, to a time of serious depletion. The causes of depletion were basically the same as those which have affected other natural resources. Forests were cut, and streams that once supported abundant fish life deteriorated. Farmlands were mismanaged and erosion silted up lakes and streams. Debris, washed from overgrazed slopes, choked stream channels below. Pollution from mill or factory wiped out fisheries for miles below the source. Eventually, the situation became serious enough to cause alarm and action. In the 1870's the federal government entered the picture when a Bureau of Fisheries, forerunner of the present United States Fish and Wildlife Service, was created. State governments began to form fish-conservation commissions or agencies to look into the problem of restoring and improving fisheries.

Like game conservation, the conservation of fisheries went through a period of emphasis on protection through restrictive laws and of concern with the control of wild predators and then moved much more thoroughly into the field of artificial propagation and the introduction of exotic species. Most of the early state fish commissions were charged initially with the task of setting up fish hatcheries, where fish could be reared and then released to stock streams and lakes. They were also charged

FRESH WATER HABITATS

(a) Cold trout stream in Colorado.
(b) Oligotrophic lake in New Hampshire.
(c) Eutrophic lake in Connecticut.

a

b

c

with looking into ways of improving fisheries through the introduction of new species from other areas. Only much later did an ecological approach begin, with attention to providing suitable habitat for existing fish populations and research toward discovering actual causes of fisheries depletion.

The effect of the hatchery program on freshwater fisheries was far reaching. Whereas a good share of America's game birds and mammals are still truly wild animals reared in more or less natural habitats, America's freshwater fisheries are increasingly artificial. A wild fish in natural stream or lake is becoming more difficult to find, except in the still-existing wilderness of Canada and Alaska. The early history of fish conservation saw the mass movement of species from one side of the continent to the other, plus the introduction of many additional kinds from Europe and Asia. Even those streams that still support native species of fish are often stocked with hatchery-reared fish or their descendants.

FISHERIES MANAGEMENT In earlier days of fish conservation, the approach to the management of warm-water fisheries was much the same as for cold-water or trout fisheries, with increasing restrictions on angling which limited gear, seasons, numbers and size of fish that could be legally caught, combined with the development of a hatchery program. After a time, experience began to show that this approach did not make sense. Some lakes, heavily stocked with hatchery fish, began to produce less than other unstocked lakes. Fish populations, increased without reference to the food supply, were stunted in size and provided little incentive for angling. Some restrictions on take are obviously necessary—dynamite, poisons, and nets can finish off any population. However, once a general rule was established limiting sports-fishing gear to hook-and-line, further restrictions were often unnecessary. Studies in the reservoirs of the TVA and of various warm-water species in Midwestern lakes and ponds, where hatchery stocking and rigidly enforced seasons and creel limits had been the rule, showed that these measures were unnecessary. It was found that these lakes could be fished as heavily as anglers wanted to fish them and would still yield an abundance of fish from natural reproduction alone. The question was raised whether a warm-water lake could be overfished when recreation was the only incentive. With these studies came a shift in the emphasis of management, from artificial propagation and restrictions on take to the improvement of habitat and relatively unrestricted fishing.[13]

Since fish have a remarkably high rate of reproduction, given adequate spawning grounds, proper water conditions for hatching, adequate food, and enough weedy cover for protection, natural reproduction will produce increasing numbers of catchable-size fish. If the habitat is adequate, hatchery propagation of fish is unnecessary. If the habitat is protected and improved, nature will supply the fish.

With trout and other cold-water fish, it has also been realized that too much emphasis has been placed on hatchery production and not enough on habitat improvement. Nevertheless, trout fisheries often present a different problem, since the demand for fishing and the capacity of the habitat often do not coincide. With the best of management, natural propagation cannot meet the demands placed on some of the heavily fished cold-water lakes and streams. Although it is generally true that these waters are not "fished out" in the sense that the last fish have been caught, they can be "fished out" in the sense that all of the easily caught fish have been hooked. When this happens they no longer provide adequate recreation to fishermen. To meet popular demand, fish and game departments are forced to remain in the hatchery business, stocking streams and lakes with trout on a "put-and-take" basis. Trout are reared in hatcheries to legal or "catchable" size and then released in suitable places before the start of the fishing season. It is not necessary that these fish be able to survive permanently in the stocked waters but only that they survive long enough to be caught. Heavily fished areas may be restocked several times in a single season. Similarly, intermittent streams, sterile lakes, and reservoirs which could not support permanent fish populations can be stocked. These fishing grounds, if located near centers of population, will attract fishing pressure that would otherwise fall on the natural fish populations of productive lakes and streams. The more remote areas are thus preserved for the enthusiast who prefers more natural conditions.[1,10]

Deterioration of streams and lakes through failure to practice conservation on watershed lands remains a major problem. Logging in some areas, despite laws to the contrary, often results in the choking of streams with debris or the pollution of streams with organic wastes. Industries and cities still contribute to stream pollution. Poor farming practices, overgrazing, mining, and lumbering still cause increased erosion with consequent deterioration of watercourses. In addition, many practices advocated in the name of conservation, have caused much damage to fisheries. As discussed previously, the construction of high dams on rivers creates impassable barriers to migratory fish. Admittedly, the reservoirs formed behind the dams can provide a different type of fishing which may have equal or greater value, but this does not always occur. Low dams can be bypassed by fishways and ladders; high dams such as Shasta in California and Grand Coulee in Washington cannot. Although mature fish can be lifted over these dams by one device or another, young fish returning downstream experience high mortality during the trip over the dam. In addition to dams, irrigation canals prove a major hazard to fish life. Where possible these must be screened off to prevent fish from entering them and perishing. Unfortunately, the design, installation, and maintenance of adequate fish screens is expensive.

FARM PONDS AND FOOD FISH   One of the important developments which has come with the rise of the conservation movement has been an interest in farm fish ponds. Small ponds developed on farming lands not only serve in water conservation but, when stocked with fish, can be a permanent source of recreation, food, and sometimes income to the landowner. Many farm owners in the Middle West and South have developed their own home fishing grounds, stocked with bass or sunfish.[1]

In most other parts of the world, fish are important not so much for recreation as for food. Where populations are dense and space for livestock limited, much of the animal protein in the diet of the peoples comes from fish. The farm ponds of the United States have their counterpart elsewhere in the world. Where these contribute importantly to the local food supply, they are usually more intensively managed than in the United States and produce higher yields. German fish ponds, stocked with carp and fertilized, are reported to yield up to 1400 pounds per acre per year; whereas some of the fish ponds in Southeast Asia, where both fertilizer and fish food are added, give yields of as high as 13,500 pounds per acre.[15] Such high protein yields offer considerable promise for enriching the diet of the world's peoples. However, reservoirs, natural lakes and streams, canals, and swamps also contribute fish to the world food supply. It was estimated in 1967 that 15 percent of the world's commercial fish catch, or about 7 million tons of fish, was contributed by inland fisheries (FAO statistics).

WORLD OUTLOOK[2,9,10,13] Optimism that the ocean fisheries of the world could make increasing contributions to meeting growing demands for food was widespread during the 1950's and 1960's, and has been reflected in earlier editions of this book. Fisheries play a particular role in contributing protein, chronically deficient in the diet of a high percentage of the world population. Georg Borgstrom calculated that the world fisheries' yield in the middle 1960's represented protein equivalent to all of the cattle in the world. Between 1950 and 1970 the average increase in world fisheries catch was estimated by FAO at 7 percent per year, from a total of 21 million metric tons in 1950 to 70 million in 1970.[4] It was widely believed this increase could continue, up to a potentially sustainable yield of 100 million metric tons.[19]

In the past the northern oceans yielded most of the world's fish catch, and the technologically advanced nations took most of the harvest. More recently, many developing nations entered the marine fisheries business, and emphasis shifted to other waters. Between 1958 and 1968, for example, the fisheries yield of the Northeast Atlantic, traditional for European fishing, declined by half. In the same period the yield from the Southeast Pacific increased 42-fold. Increased fisheries yield resulted in part from the development of more efficient fishing technology, the entry of new fishing fleets into the business, and the harvesting of species lower in the food chains than those previously taken.[10]

What seemed to be ignored in the general optimism about oceanic fisheries was that much of the gain in the world harvest came from one fishery, the Peruvian anchovy. In 1970 it contributed over 12 million of the 70 million metric tons. In 1971 the anchovy fishery began to collapse, and from 1971 to 1974 world fisheries yields have gone down.[4,14]

The anchovies off the western coast of South America thrive in the nutrient-rich waters of the Humboldt Current. For centuries they yielded a minute part of their substance for the support of the Indians who occupied the nearby coasts. A far greater portion went to support the abundant sea birds which nested on rocky offshore islands.

In 1953 a small anchovy fishery was developed in Peru, which yielded a total of 37,000 pounds of fish. Thereafter, as the California sardine fishery collapsed, the Peruvian fishery was progressively developed. The fishing fleet increased, and processing factories that could reduce these small fishes to a dry fish meal were constructed on the mainland. By 1959 the annual yield had been increased to 1,909,000 tons, by 1962 to 6,275,000 tons, and finally by 1970 to 12 million tons. FAO has estimated that the sustainable yield of this fishery was 9.5 million tons, but in four of the years ending in 1970, the catch was in excess of this limit. By that time many of the symptoms of overfishing which characterized the last years of the California sardine fishery were in evidence—lower catch per unit of effort, increasing proportions of juvenile fish in the catch, and failures of the less efficient enterprises.

The collapse of the anchovy fishery, however, would have taken place in the absence of overfishing. It was caused primarily by a phenomenon known as *El Nino,* a change in the pattern of upwelling and in the flow of the cold Humboldt current, which has occurred before at unpredictable intervals.[14] The big question, however, is whether or not the anchovy will recover when the normal upwelling and current flow is resumed, or whether, as the California sardine, the combination of overfishing and current change will have brought a more lasting decline. In 1974 the answer was not apparent. It was obvious, however, that we know far less about oceanic fish populations than we should, and in far too many cases fisheries failures, apparently influenced by overfishing, were taking place. There was no cause for optimism about ever-increasing fisheries yields, or major contributions of fisheries to world food problems.[4]

What is particularly ironic about the Peruvian anchovy fishery is that, even at its peak yield, it made little contribution to feeding the protein-hungry people of the Third World. Georg Borgstrom has pointed out that the anchovy fishery could have provided all of the people in South America with an adequate protein diet. It could have met the minimum protein needs of 413 million undernourished people. Yet, with small exceptions it has not gone to hungry people at all. It has gone to the well-fed nations of the rich world, and has been used mostly to enrich the diet of domestic animals. Said Borgstrom:

The Peruvian-Chilean protein aid to the satisfied world overshadows, both in absolute and relative terms, anything done in the postwar period to alleviate the shortages of the Hungry World. . . . A similar tapping of invaluable protein resources but on a much more modest scale (approximately 100,000 tons) is taking place along the Atlantic Coast of South Africa. This protein also bypasses the protein-short continent of Africa in order to support largely European animal production. On the whole, close to one-half of the marine fish catch is channeled via fish meal and oil into the hopper of the satisfied world.[3]

If it were possible to increase world fisheries yields to 100 million tons or more, who would benefit? Would we then begin to solve the world's protein hunger? The Peruvian experience is not encouraging.

In the 1970's, furthermore, we must pay more careful attention to the energy drain, represented by the operation of the fisheries industry, compared to the energy yield in food calories. In the past, fishing used to yield a high return of food calories for a relatively small input of human energy. Today, however, the petroleum-powered fishing fleets and processing industries require a higher calorie input than they produce as calorie output. Like many forms of modern agriculture, high-technology fishing depends on a subsidy of cheap and abundant energy. But petroleum is no longer cheap, and the end of the supply is now in sight. Unless new cheap fuels can be found, ways to restore some form of low-energy input fishing must be found.

CHAPTER REFERENCES

Carson, Rachel, 1951. *The sea around us.* Oxford, New York.

Christy, Francis T., Jr., and Anthony Scott, 1966. *The commonwealth in ocean fisheries.* Johns Hopkins, Baltimore.

Cooley, R. A., 1963. *Politics and conservation. The decline of the Alaska salmon.* Harper & Row, New York.

Kinne, O., ed., 1970. *Marine ecology.* Vol. 1. Environmental factors. Wiley-Interscience, New York.

LeCren, E. D., and M. W. Holdgate, eds., 1962. *The exploitation of natural animal populations.* Wiley, New York.

Macan, T. T., 1963. *Freshwater ecology.* Longman, London.

Olson, T. A., and F. J. Burgess, eds., 1967. *Pollution and marine ecology.* Wiley, New York.

Sverdrup, H. V., M. W. Johnson, and R. H. Fleming, 1942. *The oceans.* Prentice-Hall, New York.

Walton Smith, F. G., and H. Chapin, 1954. *The sun, the sea, and tomorrow.* Scribners, New York.

Welch, P. S., 1935. *Limnology,* McGraw-Hill, New York.

LITERATURE CITED

1. Black, John D., 1954. *Biological conservation.* Blakiston, New York.

2. Borgstrom, Georg, 1965. *The hungry planet.* Macmillan, New York.

3. ———, 1971. Ecological aspects of protein feeding—the case of Peru. *The careless technology.* Natural History, New York.

4. Brown, Lester R., and Erik Eckholm, 1974. *By bread alone.* Praeger, New York.

5. California Department of Fish and Game, 1957. *Forty-fourth biennial report.* Sacramento.

6. Croker, Richard, 1954. *The sardine story—a tragedy.* Outdoor California, 15: 6–8.

7. Fish and Wildlife Service, 1956. *National survey of hunting and fishing.* Department of Interior, Washington, D.C.

8. Gordon, Seth, 1950. *California's fish and game program.* Senate of State of California, Sacramento.

9. Graham, Michael, 1956. Harvests of the seas. (See Thomas, 1956, in general references.)

10. Gulland, J. A., 1970. *The fish resources of the ocean.* FAO, Rome.

11. Hedgpeth, Joel, 1964. *Man and the sea.* Pacific Marine Station, Dillon Beach, California.

12. Holdgate, M. W., ed., 1970. *Antarctic ecology.* Academic Press, London, 2 vols.

13. Klingbiel, John, 1953. Are fishing restrictions necessary? *Wisconsin Cons. Bull.,* 18: 3–5.

14. Luftas, Tony, 1972. Where have all the anchoveta gone? *New Scientist,* 28 Sept., 583–586.

15. Odum, E. P., 1959. *Fundamentals of ecology,* Second edition, W. B. Saunders, Philadelphia.

16. Mackintosh, N. A., 1965. *The stocks of whales.* Fishing News (Books) Ltd., London.

17. Marx, Wesley, 1967. *The frail ocean.* Ballantine, New York.

18. Ricketts, E., and J. Calvin, 1962. *Between Pacific Tides.* Stanford, Palo Alto.

19. Schaefer, Milner B., 1965. The potential harvest of the sea. *Trans. American Fish. Soc.,* 94 (2): 123–128.

20. Welch, P. S., 1935. *Limnology,* McGraw-Hill, New York.

21. Wick, Gerald, 1974. Fishing off California. *New Scientist,* 61: 564–565.

11

increase
and
multiply—
the
problem of
population

In 1974 in Bucharest, Romania, representatives of most of the world's nations met for the United Nation's conference on world population. Perhaps the most worthwhile feature of the conference is that it happened at all, since this implied some recognition that there was a phenomenon known as the "world population problem." For the most part, however, the conference provided, not a forum for rational discussion of the problem, as had been intended, but a platform from which mutual recrimination and denunciation could be launched. There are few subjects, if any, more fraught with emotion than the subject of human population growth and its possible limitation. In some quarters, mere mention of it, brings out the worst in people. Nevertheless, the problem remains.

Throughout most of the world today there is an unprecedented growth in human numbers. This continuing increase not only intensifies all conservation problems, but nullifies many achievements of the past. Any type of rational management of the environment becomes more difficult as each new increment of population is added to the world's total — and in the middle 1970's each yearly increment amounts to nearly 80 million more people. With continued growth in population we face not only the loss of those values which contribute to the quality of living, but ultimately the collapse of civilization in any form that we have known it. Already it has meant the loss of many other forms of life, and this process will intensify. Any planning for conservation must take into account some method of limiting population growth, just as it must take into account means for prevention of war between nations.

One thing is certain. Population growth of the magnitude we have seen in recent years will *not* continue. Either people will begin to die in greater numbers than any of us would care to contemplate, or they will learn to limit birth rates. We are reaching the end of the line.

DISTRIBUTION OF PEOPLE In the middle 1970's the number of people in the world was nearing 4 billion. There is no possibility for giving exact figures, since for some parts of the world population estimates are not accurate. The available estimates are presented, however, in Table 12. From them it becomes obvious that Asia holds nearly two-thirds of the world's people. The rich countries of the world, confined with few exceptions to northern America, Europe, the Soviet Union, and Oceania, contain less than one-third of the world's people. The poor countries of Asia, Africa, and Latin America contains nearly half. In Table 13 the relation of people to in-

TABLE 12

People and Land

REGION	AREA OF LAND AND INLAND WATER IN SQUARE MILES	POPULATION 1970 ESTIMATES	PEOPLE PER SQUARE MILE
United States	3,676,000	205,000,000	56
Northern America	7,528,000	228,000,000	30
Latin America	8,767,000	283,000,000	32
Africa	11,635,000	344,000,000	30
Europe (excluding Soviet Union)	1,915,000	463,000,000	241
USSR	8,599,000	246,000,000	29
Asia (excluding Soviet Union)	10,300,000	2,056,000,000	199
Oceania	3,295,000	19,000,000	6
World (excluding Antarctica)	52,125,000	3,632,000,000	70

come, food, and land is presented. This shows the enormous unbalance between the rich and the poor world. Since figures can be misleading, one should recognize that the reality is even worse. The so-called poor world, developing world, less-developed nations, Third World, or whatever it's called, contains some comparatively rich nations and some extremely wealthy people. The really poor are poor indeed.

The United States' population in 1970 was approximately 204 million. Estimates in 1974 place it at 213 million, increasing at a rate of 0.7 percent a year. The 1970 population represented an increase of 30 million in the ten years since the last official census of 1960. These people were distributed over approximately 3.5 million square miles of land surface for an average in 1970 of 57 people per square mile of land, or 11 land acres per individual. An estimated 80 million people in 1970 lived in 30 large metropolitan areas, whereas 70 percent of the people, or 140 million, lived in urban areas: towns, cities, and suburbs (see Fig. 11–1).

In the United States population pressure is felt in terms of pollution, physical disorganization of cities and countryside, crowding in cities and recreation areas, and in other, at least tolerable, ways. In most of the

TABLE 13

People and Resources, 1970 Estimates

	NATIONS OF WORLD WHERE DIETS ARE ADEQUATE	NATIONS OF WORLD WHERE DIETS ARE DEFICIENT
Population	1,200,000,000	2,400,000,000
Annual population growth in percent	1.3	2.1
Density per 100 acres of agricultural land	17	53
Income in dollars per capita	1,302	115
Food consumption in daily calories per capita	3,023	2,203
Food consumption in grams protein per day	86.4	57.4

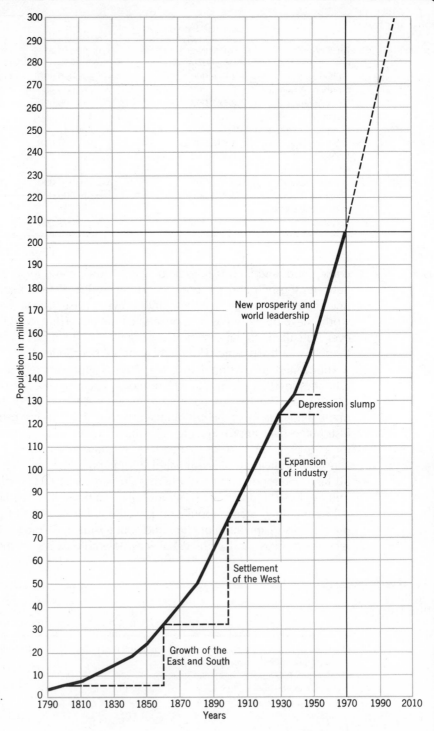

FIG. 11–1. Population growth in the United States (*source: U.S. Bureau of the Census*).

New prosperity and world leadership

Depression slump

Expansion of industry

Settlement of the West

Growth of the East and South

Population in million

Years

world population pressure is felt in terms of hunger and acute human misery. We expect, therefore, that the great demand for the means for halting population growth would come from the desperately poor, whereas the United States would be indifferent. But at the World Population Conference and other intergovernmental forums, the United States was one of the principal advocates for the limitation of population growth. The poor nations, for the most part, were against it. Why?

World population problems do not exist in isolation from other world problems. They are colored by the hangover from the days of political colonialism and imperialism, and affected by what many Third World politicians term the economic imperialism of today. The representatives of the poor countries point out that the United States and other rich countries not only have the economic wealth, but through this are capturing most of the resources of the earth. "Stop exploiting us, give us our fair share of resources, and then we will see how many people we can support," say many Third World leaders. China, with perhaps 800 million people, the most populous nation on earth, is now using highly effective means for halting population growth. Yet Chinese leaders say economic development must come first. India, however, with over 600 million people, the second most highly populated nation, takes a contrary view. Population growth, their leaders point out, wipes out all gains made through economic development. It will be necessary to explore in this and succeeding chapters the pros and cons of these arguments.

THE INCREASE IN PEOPLE It may not be realized that the population problem facing us today is essentially new, one arisen in the past century and without precedent in previous human experience. Our historical training, which emphasizes the events that took place in past centers of population, does not prepare us for this realization. To grasp the significance of what has occurred, we would need a history that cannot be written, for no one was there to record it. It would be a history of the vast open spaces of a little while ago, told by generations of buffalo and antelope and prairie wolf. It would be a story of a world that suddenly disappeared, of a changeless land suddenly completely transformed.

If we do not know for sure how many people we have on earth today, much less can we know the past numbers of man. However, by careful detective work in the files of history, by piecing together the scraps of information left by tax collectors, military commanders, and others concerned with the number of heads in their domains, demographers have reached some estimates of the growth of populations. All of these estimates point to a past time when the world was big, people were few, and the growth of populations was negligible. In Table 14 are some widely accepted estimates showing changes since 1650. It should be recognized that it took at least a million years for the human population of the earth to increase to the level of 1650. It took only 200 years for it to double again. Now the world's population is doubling in 35 years.

REGION	1650	1750	1800	1850	1900	1950	1970[a]	2000[a]
Anglo-America	1	1.3	5.7	26	81	166	228	354
Latin America	12	11.1	18.9	33	63	162	283	638
Europe	100	140	187	266	401	559	705	880
Asia	330	479	602	749	937	1,302	2,056	3,458
Africa	100	95	90	95	120	198	344	768
Oceania	2	2	2	2	6	13	19	32
World	545	728	906	1,171	1,608	2,400	3,632	6,130

[a] United Nations medium estimates (USSR included in Europe).

If population increase were to follow recent trends, there would be 22 billion people on earth in the year 2040, according to the United Nations estimates and, before a century had passed, we would long since have passed a point of world catastrophe.

To account for the great growth in population in relatively recent times, it is only necessary to look at the record of the most glowing accomplishments of modern times, told in our histories and recounted by our orators: the voyages of discovery, the settlement of the new worlds, the industrial revolution, the development of agricultural techniques, the "miracle of modern medicine." In a short time, in historical terms, vast new continents were suddenly opened to exploitation by a new kind of man, armed with the tools provided by the new technology and science. Populations, held in check for generations by their limited lands, found new lands with vast productivity. Acres that had once yielded a bare livelihood, provided a surplus when handled with new techniques. Diseases that once took their toll from all crowded populations fell back as food, medicine, and sanitation became available. Humanity, freed from the environmental resistance of the past, began to express more nearly its biotic potential.

The behavior of human populations today, in relation to their means of subsistence, has been such that there has been a widespread revival of the Malthusian outlook on populations. Thomas Malthus of England was one of the first to become concerned with the world population problem. In 1798 he published a book entitled *An essay on the principle of population as it affects the future improvement of society*.[2] The book stirred a controversy in its day, and today it can do the same. Some basic propositions of Malthus were:

1. Population is necessarily limited by the means of subsistence.

2. Population increases where the means of subsistence increase, unless prevented by very powerful checks. Furthermore, populations tend to increase at a geometric rate (1, 2, 4, 8, 16, etc.), whereas food supplies can usually only be increased at an arithmetic rate (1, 2, 3, 4, 5, etc.). Therefore populations tend to outstrip their means of subsistence.

3. The powerful and obvious checks to population increase, the checks that repress the superior power of population and keep its effect on a level with the means of subsistence are all resolvable into vice, misery, and potentially, perhaps, moral restraint.

When Malthus lived, the population of western Europe was pressing on the limits of the then existing food supply. The overseas colonial empires were yet to be fully exploited. Vice and misery were widespread, and moral restraint was at a minimum. Fortunately for mankind, but unfortunately for the reputation of Malthus, this situation soon changed, as the full impact of the industrial revolution on the new lands of the world was felt. For a time the means of subsistence increased much faster than population. Malthus was forgotten until populations too suddenly began to catch up.

The problem of overpopulation is not new; many lands have known it in the thousands of years that man has been on earth. The problem of world overpopulation is new. Once, population problems were local problems, and states whose peoples outran their means of subsistence suffered alone or affected but a few neighbors. The rise and fall of the Mayan empire of Central America created no concern in the courts of Europe. Only after it was gone, did European man find out it had existed. Today, however, our means of transportation and communication have changed the relative size of the world. Populations no longer starve in silence. Empires no longer die quietly.

Never before in human history was there a time when all of the world was on the map. All pieces of land are staked out and claimed, even the barren polar ice caps are the subject of international dispute, and nations are casting a speculative glance toward the resources of the moon. The grave fact that must be faced today is that there are no more land frontiers.

DYNAMICS OF POPULATION GROWTH

To understand the principles of human population growth, we need at first only review the principles governing the growth of animal populations in general. Population growth results when natality exceeds mortality, when there is an excess of births over deaths. The rate of population growth is dependent on two things: the biotic potential of the population and the amount of environmental resistance. The biotic potential for the human species is relatively low, by comparison with other species, but still high enough to cause serious concern where resources are limited. Fortunately, this maximum potential rate of increase is seldom realized. The environmental resistance, the sum of those factors that tend to prevent a population from achieving its biotic potential, includes all of the various mortality factors and all of the factors which inhibit the birth rate. In the latter group of factors, perhaps the most important is human social behavior—the blocks that we put in the way to prevent a maximum rate of population growth from being achieved.

a

b

CROWDING

(a) Hong Kong. How crowded can a city become before all systems break down? (b) A *favela* grows near downtown Rio de Janeiro. How do you prevent the continued influx of people into already overcrowded urban areas? (c) Urban confusion in New York. In the 1970's the financial problems of big city governments appear insurmountable. (d) There is still a choice. Not every place is crowded, yet. (e) But what about tomorrow?

c

d

e

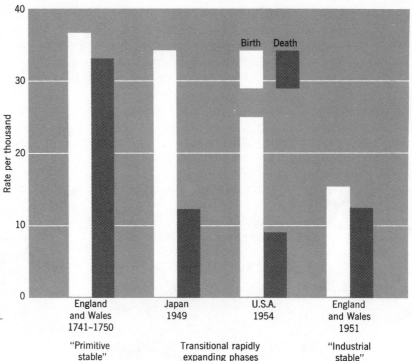

FIG. 11–2. Demographic patterns. Showing differences in birth and death rates in agricultural, industrial, and transitional societies (*data from Political and Economic Planning [1955] and U.S. Public Health Service*).

Demographers have postulated various patterns of population growth characteristic of different types of human societies. In the first type (Fig. 11–2) is the primitive agricultural society. In such a society large numbers of children are considered a blessing, partly because they represent extra hands to do the labor of the farm. Hence birth rates tend to be high. However, control of mortality factors is at a minimum. Medical knowledge and the application of sanitary techniques have not yet appeared. Diseases take an annual toll. With little individual care for children possible, accidents can be an important factor. If the population is in close balance with its food supply, as is usually true, starvation is a threat in years of crop failure. Such a society has limited ability to store food for use in emergency periods. Transportation is inadequate to ship food from areas of plenty to areas of scarcity. Consequently death rates are high. Birth and death rates achieve a rough balance, and the overall growth of population is slow.

At the other extreme, theoretically, is the industrialized society. In this society, large numbers of children are not considered a blessing because of the difficulty of providing them with the goods and services considered necessary in such a culture. Marriages tend to be delayed because of educational or employment needs. Family size is limited in a variety of ways; the overall birth rate is low. At the same time the death rate has been lowered. Medical facilities, adequate sanitation, and a relatively high material standard of living keeps mortality at a minimum. Again a rough balance is achieved between births and deaths, and the rate of population growth is kept low.

Obviously neither of these basic types of societies are the ones contributing to past and present rapid rates of population growth. Societies in which population growth is rapid can be described as those which have not yet reached either of these two stable states or which are in the process of change from one to another (Fig. 11–3). Examples from other animal species are illustrative.

Rapid population growth in wild animals is characteristic of a species

FIG. 11–3. Age pyramids for rapidly expanding, slowly expanding, and static populations, showing relative proportions of the different age groups (*data from Political and Economic Planning* [1955], *U.S. Bureau of the Census, and F. F. Darling* [1951], *American Scientist*, 39: 250).

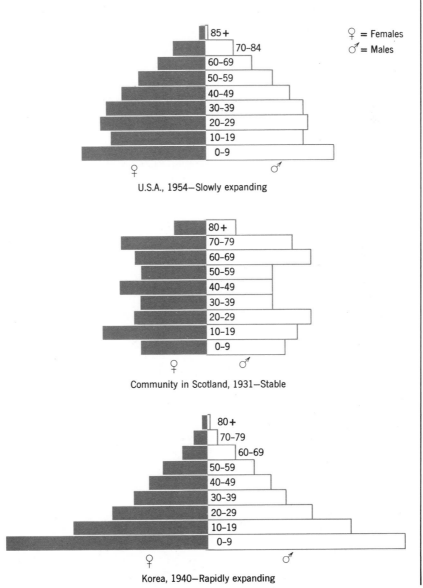

introduced into a new, favorable, and relatively unlimited environment. Thus, the starling or the English sparrow, when introduced into the United States, exhibited a remarkable rate of population increase. In such a new environment food supplies are plentiful. Disease and parasites are at a minimum because of the initial low population density. Predation losses, or accidental deaths, may be considerable at times, but the overall effect is slight. At the same time, because of the available space and the plentiful resources, birth rates are high. A similar pattern is exhibited by humanity when a new and productive land is colonized. Birth rates are high because large families not only can be provided for but help to bring in greater returns from the large amount of available land. Death rates, although not as low as in technologically advanced societies are nevertheless well below the birth rates, for epidemic disease and starvation losses are minimized. The balance is in favor of natality, and population growth is rapid. Such was the situation in the United States in the frontier days.

Rapid population growth in animals is also exhibited when some previously limiting factor has been removed from a stable population. Such a population increase is of the irruptive type exemplified by the Kaibab deer. As previously described, the removal of the limiting factor of predation permitted a spectacular increase in the deer population. This resulted in the carrying capacity of the habitat being surpassed, the food supply being destroyed, and finally in a die-off of the deer to a new low level. A similar pattern of population growth is exhibited when the introduction of medical supplies or sanitary techniques takes place in a society of the primitive agricultural variety. Thus the population of India is believed to have been relatively stable over a period of centuries. The British, however, introduced Western technology, medicine, and transportation. The result was a marked lowering in the mortality rate, not accompanied by a decrease in natality. The population began to grow rapidly. If India should proceed to become an industrialized society, an eventual lowering of the birthrate can be expected, and a new balance between births and deaths can be achieved. How large the population would grow before that time, however, is disturbing to contemplate. It has been sufficiently disturbing to the Indian leaders so they are now attempting to encourage a reduction in birthrate well before the process of industrialization can have much effect.

The concept that rapid growth of human populations is largely restricted to those nations in a state of demographic transition, from agricultural to industrial society, is a useful one. Events since World War II, however, have revealed that industrialization does not necessarily bring population stability. Table 15 reveals that some highly industrialized nations have high population growth rates. This has been true of the United States, particularly in the 1950's, and is true of many other industrialized countries. There is no good reason to assume full industrialization of nations such as Colombia or Kenya will necessarily bring marked decreases in the growth rates.

TABLE 15

Comparison of
Population Growth in
Various Nations, 1973

COUNTRY	POPULATION	ANNUAL RATE OF GROWTH	NUMBER OF YEARS TO DOUBLE POPULATION	BIRTH RATE PER 1000	DEATH RATE PER 1000
Germany, Federal Republic	59,400,000	0.0	—	11.5	11.7
Sweden	8,200,000	0.3	231	13.8	10.4
United Kingdom	57,000,000	0.3	231	14.9	11.9
United States	210,300,000	0.8	87	15.6	9.4
USSR	250,000,000	1.0	70	17.8	8.2
China	799,300,000	1.7	41	30.0	13.0
India	600,400,000	2.5	28	42.0	17.0
Indonesia	132,500,000	2.9	24	47.0	19.0
Brazil	101,300,000	2.8	25	38.0	10.0
Colombia	23,700,000	3.4	21	45.0	11.0
Kenya	12,000,000	3.0	23	48.0	18.0
Angola	6,100,000	2.1	33	50.0	30.0
World	3,860,000,000	2.0	35	33.0	13.0

Data from Population Reference Bureau, Washington, D.C.

Growth rates can also be misleading in the extent to which they conceal the size of the annual increment to the population. Costa Rica, with one of the highest growth rates of any nation, is still adding only around 65,000 people per year to the world population. The United States, with a much lower rate of growth, is adding nearly 2 million people each year. A growth rate of only 1 percent on the island of Barbados, where over 1500 people are found on each square mile, can be an intolerably high rate of increase. A rate of 2 percent in Canada, by contrast, may represent no immediate problem.

The disturbing fact about today's world is that areas which are already overpopulated have benefited from those factors that control mortality, but have yet to gain the incentive or knowledge needed to control birthrates. Consequently, population increase defeats efforts to raise living standards or to improve the quality of the environment.

CONTROL OF POPULATION SIZE The question of how to control population size is a familiar one to all who work with animal populations. The answers are simply stated but often are incredibly difficult to put into practice. For either animal or human populations, control of population growth must involve either a decrease in natality, an increase in mortality, or movement to a new area.

In the far north of America or Europe, populations of lemmings follow a pattern of cyclic increase and decline, with population peaks being reached every 3 to 4 years. At the peaks the numbers of lemmings are far greater than the area can support. At such times a mass emigration sometimes takes place. Vast numbers of lemmings drift out of the overpopulated area into new, and usually unfavorable, terrain. The end result of this movement is usually death for the emigrants. Such an emigration temporarily alleviates the problem of overpopulation. The alleviation, however, is never final. In another 2 or 3 years the remnant population has built up to another peak, and another overpopulation problem exists.

People are not lemmings, and their problems are more complex. Nevertheless, with human populations also, emigration alone provides no permanent solution to a population problem. Over the past three centuries, for example, many millions of people have left Europe and moved to new lands. This movement has not solved the problem of the homeland. Some countries which have contributed most to the emigrant stream are those that today have the most unfavorable balance between people and resources. The emigrants, in turn, have built the populations of the new lands to which they have moved until in some of these lands, too, the balance with resources is under threat. Emigration, with people or mice, can temporarily alleviate but not permanently solve a population problem.

With animal populations control of numbers is usually exercised by the device of increasing mortality. This may involve encouraging a greater amount of hunting, a higher level of predation, or with pest species even wholesale poisoning. Increasing mortality is also an answer, although an unpleasant one, to human population problems. Various peoples and cultures have tried many ways of doing this. Some eliminate the older members of the population. Thus, with some Eskimo tribes, a threat of food shortage and starvation for the tribe, may result in the older people removing themselves and going out alone into the tundra, thus in effect to their death. This is an emergency measure taken when the other consequences would be death for all. Other cultures attack the problem by eliminating the very young. Infanticide has been a common practice in primitive cultures, when the means for providing for another child are out of reach of a family. Some of the South Sea islanders, recognizing that the limited resources of the islands would support only a limited number of people, have solved the problem through a general acceptance of infanticide. The alternative was starvation. Still other cultures, including the more technologically advanced ones, have met the same problem by legalizing abortion. Although justifiable from many viewpoints other than population limitation, legalized abortion is no reasonable alternative to contraception.

The third way to control population size is not practical with wild-animal populations but is commonly used with domestic forms. This involves decreasing natality. This is perhaps the only acceptable way of limiting population size for those peoples with high respect for the individual and a "reverence for life." Decreasing the birth rate can be approached in a number of ways that vary both in effectiveness and in acceptability to various groups in the population. One approach is celibacy, encouraged by many religious groups but rarely effective on a mass basis. This means delaying either temporarily or permanently the sexual relationship. In a modified form, and a more common one, it means delaying those relationships that would be likely to lead to the production of offspring, or more frequently, delaying marrage. This is undoubtedly part of the reason for the relative stability of the population of Ireland in recent years. For economic and other reasons there has been a trend in this country toward delaying or permanently postponing marriage. In other technologically advanced countries this practice has had a depressing effect on birth rates during times of economic stress or of war. How long the practice would remain effective in the face of long-continued, or permanent, economic stress is certainly questionable.

In general, the sociological consequences and the effects on the individual of avoiding sexual relationships and postponing more permanent liaisons are undesirable. The reasons, in terms of personal well-being, are obvious. The practicality of this method for slowing down population growth over the world is most dubious.

Undoubtedly the means of controlling population growth most likely to be effective are those generally described as birth control. These involve little restriction on the sexual activities of the individual and are thus useful to the majority of the population. Two general types of birth control methods can be recognized: one involving so-called natural methods, the other involves mechanical or chemical methods. Of these, the first, or rhythm method, is the least effective, but is still the only acceptable form for members of some religious groups. In this method, coitus is restricted to the relatively infertile period of the menstrual cycle between menstruation and ovulation. For the individual this method is not highly reliable. If everyone in the population practiced it, it would lead to a reduction in birth rates. This technique has been used in India where for most of the population the materials needed for chemical or mechanical contraception are not available, but it has not had great success.

Mechanical and chemical methods of birth control are now widely used and are, at least in part, responsible for the reduced birth rates in the industrialized nations. The most acceptable and effective methods are birth control pills and intrauterine devices, both of which have only become widely available since the 1960's. They have been credited with the decline of birth rates during the past decade. Male contraceptives, such as condoms, are also effective, but only if men can be relied on to use them. Since women are the ones who experience the problems of pregnancy, parturition, and still take the brunt of most child care, they are more likely to exercise control than their male counterparts. More effective methods of birth control are still needed if population growth is to be slowed down without unnecessary and undesirable side effects on human relationships. The existing techniques, however, are adequate to accomplish the limitation of population growth that is required. First they must be made generally available, and perhaps more importantly the rights of women to control their own reproduction must be recognized at both political and social levels.

There has been much talk, at the World Population Conference and elsewhere, about the demographic lag, the time necessarily involved in turning off a high rate of population growth. A rapidly growing population necessarily has a high percentage of children and young people (Fig. 11–3). This means that if the birthrate of the existing adult population is brought down to a zero-growth, or replacement, level, there will still be additional population growth as the greater numbers of young people reach reproductive age. On this basis the inevitable growth of world population to a level of seven billion or more has been predicted, even assuming the need for population stability were everywhere recognized and the means for achieving it made available. In today's world, however, the most serious question is whether the existing world population level can be sustained, or whether mass mortality leading to population reduction is not inevitable. It is misleading to forecast continued growth when the means for supporting it are not in sight. Furthermore, any group of people can decide, right now, to put a stop to population growth; and if they put the decision into practice, there will be no further growth in their group. All that is required, in the long run, is to balance births against deaths, and growth will cease (ruling out immigration in this consideration). This need cause no hardship, nor does it mean those who wish to be parents will have to forego that privilege. It does mean, however, more planning ahead and social responsibility than most people care to exercise.

In the United States the philosophy that growth is good and that change, of whatever nature, is progress went for too long without challenge. We have a dynamic and expanding nature and people have been encouraged to look forward to a richer and better future, rather than concentrate on the inequities of the present. This attitude was perhaps acceptable when we were a pioneer nation, but the frontiers have long since gone. The belief that more people means more production and more customers to buy, and that business and industry can continue to expand in a limited space with limited resources, is today deadly. Unfortunately many technologists who work for business or government, and the economists who are selected as government advisers, still believe in scientific miracles, breakthroughs or, if necessary, even military takeovers of resource-rich areas. They thus encourage government leaders that we can continue to have business as usual, with ever-increasing production and profits.

For reasons to be further explored in the following chapters the only responsible attitude in the United States today is one which recognizes the need for controlling growth, not only of populations but for all resource-consuming sectors of the economy. We cannot solve the world population problem in America. We can, however, solve the American population problem and begin to slow down the drain on world resources, so that other people in other countries would no longer suffer from our excesses. If that were done we would at least have a moral foundation from which to advise other nations.

CHAPTER
REFERENCES

Brown, Harrison, 1954. *The challenge of man's future.* Viking, New York.

Brown, Lester R., 1974. *In the human interest.* W. W. Norton, Washington.

Brown, Lester R., and Erik Eckholm, 1974. *By breed alone.* Praeger, New York.

Carr-Saunders, A. M., 1936. *World population; past growth and present trends.* Clarendon, Oxford.

Cook, Robert C., 1951. *Human fertility; the modern dilemma.* Wm. Sloane, New York.

Day, Lincoln H., and A. T. Lincoln, 1965. *Too many Americans.* Delta Books, New York.

Osborn, Fairfield, ed., 1962. *Our crowded planet.* Doubleday, New York.

Vogt, William, 1948. *Road to survival.* Wm. Sloane, New York.

LITERATURE
CITED

1. Fraser Darling, F., 1951. The ecological approach to the social sciences. *American Scientist,* 39: 244–254.

2. Malthus, Thomas, 1926. *An essay on the principle of populations as it affects the future improvement of society, with remarks on the speculations of Mr. Godwin, M. Condorcet, and other writers.* Macmillan, London. (Originally published, 1798, St. Paul's, London.)

3. Political and Economic Planning, 1955. *World population and resources.* George Allen and Unwin, London.

4. Population Reference Bureau, 1973. *World Population Data Sheet.* Pop. Ref. Bur., Washington, D.C.

12

the devil's bargain— energy

In the middle 1970's the industrialized nations of the world still appear determined to continue on a collision course with environmental reality. Faced with a sudden increase in the price of petroleum set by the principal oil-producing countries, and with the inevitable exhaustion of this resource in the not-distant future, little effort has been made to restrict petroleum consumption. Instead all-out efforts are being pursued to find and develop new petroleum reserves, with little concern for environmental safeguards. New impetus has been given to gouging the face of the earth with strip mining for coal, oil shale, or the development of tar sands. Great new fleets of monster supertankers, built with little concern for safety or control are being launched to haul oil around the world's oceans. Concern for the safety of humanity and the biosphere is being set aside in a new rush to develop nuclear power as a substitute for petroleum and coal—and the problems created by nuclear wastes and the needs for safeguards are of serious magnitude. Alternative, safe sources of energy are receiving little attention, nor are people facing up to the need for revising what are basically unviable ways of life in favor of some more satisfying and enduring alternatives.

HISTORICAL BACKGROUND[7] For most of history humans have been minor consumers of the earth's stores of energy. The rate at which energy was being captured and stored from sunlight in the earth's vegetation far exceeded the rate of human consumption of plant and animal materials. People drew scarcely, if at all, on the reserves of materials captured by the biospheres of the past and stored in the rocks of the earth. Now, the situation has changed completely. The human species is boring ever deeper into the earth's crust and scraping its surface for its energy supplies, depleting the stores built up during the hundreds of millions of years of life's existence, and looking always for new sources of supply. Meanwhile there is no general agreement either about the availability of known fuels nor the likelihood of making available new sources of energy.

What are our energy needs, and the sources of supply? Initially each person needed to consume some 2500 to 3000 calories (kilocalories) of energy each day in the form of palatable, digestible, and nutritionally valuable foods. These provided the fuel to keep bodily processes in operation and to enable them to do work, which consisted for the most part of searching for more food. The energy was supplied by edible plants and animals. People played a variable role in the food chains of the ecosystems they occupied—part primary consumers, part secondary, usually the end carnivores, but occasionally providing food in turn for lion or leopard. Humanity was living on the earth's energy income and not drawing to any extent on its capital.

With the discovery of fire, energy consumption increased, and people began to draw on the short-term energy stores which had been accumulated over scores of years or even centuries by woody plants. With the Paleolithic age giving way to the Neolithic, domestic animals entered the picture and their energy was put to work for human purposes, to produce more food, to assist in the building of shelters, or to move people to new locations. Average consumption of energy, counting that burned and consumed by domestic animals may have reached 10 to 15 thousand calories per person per day. This level of consumption can be considered a definition of man's energy *needs*—food, fuel, and the manpower, horsepower, or cattlepower needed to produce and gather the food and fuel. All of these needs could be supplied by the earth's biota on a sustaining basis. All of the energy consumed above this basic level is consumed by choice, because we *want* to do certain things and to live in certain ways in certain places. However, with the increase in human populations to present levels, which has been a matter of human choice, and with the spread of civilization, also a matter of choice, our demands for energy have necessarily increased. These do not reflect basic needs, and when these demands come in conflict with other demands, such as the desire for a humane existence in an environment of high quality, then compromises must be made. We may well decide to consume less energy in order to maintain a better quality of existence. We may have to.

As human cultures became more diversified and particularly with the coming of civilization, people learned to draw on new sources of energy —notably wind and water. Wind was used to move sailing boats and thus to transport heavy materials or people over long distances. It was used also to turn windmills which produced the power to work machines or to process foods. Wind power is inexhaustible. During the past century, however, its use has declined with the decreasing availability of other energy sources. Waterpower was also developed at an early stage of human history, both as a means for transporting materials, for turning mills, and for activating machinery. During most of the history of civilization and, indeed, until the nineteenth century, the available sources of energy were primarily of a renewable nature—wind and water, wood and other vegetation, and animal life. Demands on wood for fuel were frequently excessive and led to widespread deforestation but, with human numbers limited, the effect on the biosphere as a whole was not damaging.

Somewhere in the distant past it was discovered the fossil fuels could be put to work. These, coal and its relatives (including, marginally, peat), petroleum, and natural gas, represented energy stored by animals and plants millions of years before. In the Middle East, oil and natural gas seeped from the ground and was burned for various purposes in the early days of civilization. The Chinese, in the pre-Christian era, learned to mine coal and to tap underground reservoirs of gas.[1] However, heavy use of these sources of fuel awaited the period of forest depletion and fuel scarcity in Europe, and most particularly the invention of the steam engine in the eighteenth century, and of electricity in the nineteenth. The extensive use of petroleum awaited the discovery of the internal combustion engine in the late nineteenth century. Since the beginning of the twentieth century the use of coal, petroleum, and natural gas has steadily accelerated and the fossil fuels have, in industrialized countries, largely displaced all other sources of energy. Their use is for the heating of spaces, for the powering of engines directly, or for the production of electricity, which can be transmitted over long distances to provide light, heat, or sources of mechanical power.

Since the advent of fossil fuels, the uses of other sources of energy declined *relatively* up until the advent of nuclear energy with the discovery of the atomic bomb. Nuclear power represents an entirely new power source for mankind. Its potentials, in theory, are virtually unlimited. In practice, with existing technologies and scientific knowledge, they are limited. After a slow start, the use of nuclear reactors to produce electricity is now underway, and it is widely believed that nuclear power will represent an increasing source of energy for the world. This will present humanity with a new set of problems including some not encountered before.

ENERGY USE IN THE UNITED STATES It must be recognized that the development and use of energy has been extremely uneven throughout the world. Some areas remain almost at Neolithic levels of energy production and consumption. Others have moved rapidly ahead, consuming ever-increasing amounts of energy. Of these, the United States is the outstanding example. In 1968 the average per capita consumption of energy from all sources was approximately 215,000 kilocalories per day.[5] In terms of the sum of fossil fuels, hydropower, and nuclear power, the United States consumed 35 percent of the world's supply to meet the needs of approximately 6 percent of the world's people. Energy consumption by the United States was nearly ten times greater than all of Latin America and approximately four times greater than all of Asia (excluding the USSR). The USSR, the second greatest national consumer of energy, used less than one-half the amount used by the United States.[48]

For what purposes did the United States use all of this fuel? Landsberg and Schurr have produced figures for 1960 which are still close enough for today's purposes. Thirty-five percent went for industrial purposes with general manufacturing the largest consumer. Twenty-five percent went for commercial and miscellaneous purposes, including agriculture and defense. Twenty percent was used for transportation, of which more than one-half went to operate private automobiles. Another 20 percent went into residential household operations, with heating the major source of consumption.[28] In other terms the people of the United States use twice as much fuel for heating their houses and for running their cars as all of the people of Latin America use for all purposes.

Where did the energy consumed in the United States come from? The following table is illustrative:[48]

TYPE OF ENERGY SOURCE	PERCENTAGE OF TOTAL UNITED STATES CONSUMPTION OF ENERGY (1967)	UNITED STATES CONSUMPTION AS A PERCENTAGE OF TOTAL WORLD CONSUMPTION OF THAT FUEL (1967)
Coal and lignite	23	20
Petroleum	42	36
Natural gas	33	64
Hydropower	1	22
Nuclear power	≤ 1	25
	100	

Although the United States is the greatest single consumer of energy, in total and on a per capita basis, it has been in the fortunate position of possessing most of the energy resources it needs. By contrast, other industrialized nations in Western Europe and Japan, as well as Australia and South Africa, have been dependent on imports of petroleum, almost completely, to keep their civilizations functioning. Japan has no oil, whereas Western Europe has no producing oil fields (as of 1974). The discoveries of oil under the North Sea have provided considerable oil reserves for Great Britain and Norway, but the difficulties of bringing these into production have been considerable. Most of the industrialized world has been dependent on the oil fields of the Middle East and North Africa (Table 16). The decision of the oil-exporting countries in 1973 to raise the price of oil from two dollars to more than ten dollars a barrel has had, therefore, a shattering effect on the economies of the entire world.

TABLE 16
Oil Reserves and Production—1974

AREA	PROVEN RESERVES IN BILLIONS OF BARRELS	DAILY PRODUCTION IN MILLIONS OF BARRELS
Middle East—North Africa	357	24
USSR	75	9
North America	50	12
Europe	26	0.05
South America	22	4
China	20	1
Black Africa	17	3
Southeast Asia—Australia	14	2
Total	581	55

Data from *Time*, January 6, 1975.

a

FOSSIL FUELS AND FISSION

(a) Strip mining for coal in Pennsylvania. Coal reserves are adequate to supply reasonable demands for energy for several centuries. However, many of the coal deposits cannot be mined without severe environmental disruption unless improved technologies are put into operation. (b) Oil refinery at Long Beach, California. During the past half century industrial civilization has grown almost totally dependent on petroleum. Now, oil reserves are inadequate to meet projected future demands. (c) Unnecessary generation of electricity results in waste of energy reserves. Distribution of electricity from centralized power plants has a disruptive effect on all environments through which power lines pass. (d) Nuclear fission power plant in Pennsylvania. Attempts to meet energy demands by increasing the numbers and size of nuclear plants will confront humanity with an unnecessary degree of risk and restriction.

b

c

d

What has been particularly disturbing about the world energy picture in the 1970's has been the almost complete dependence of civilization on fossil fuels, and particularly on petroleum, the annual increase in the consumption of these fuels (around 5 percent per year or more), and the knowledge that the supplies—particularly of petroleum and natural gas—are running out.

PROSPECTS FOR THE FUTURE What are the chances of maintaining the growing rate of energy consumption to meet the demands of increasing world populations and their hopes for higher standards of living? There is no general agreement, partly because we do not know for certain the extent of fossil fuel reserves, nor the ways in which use of fossil fuels will be affected by economic changes. In part the confusion lies in the ability to assess technological change, and in the disagreement about the extent of risk accompanying certain forms of energy development.

An optimistic view of the future is presented by Cambel (1970), who sees the supply of fossil fuels as adequate to carry us into the nuclear age; thereafter, with nuclear fission and nuclear fusion power available in virtually unlimited quantities, energy resources would no longer represent a problem for society.[5] By contrast, Brown (1954), while recognizing the potential of nuclear power, is concerned with the effects on society of following this high energy route and states:

With the consumption of each additional barrel of oil and ton of coal, with the addition of each new mouth to be fed, with the loss of each additional inch of topsoil, the situation becomes more inflexible and difficult to resolve. Man is rapidly creating a situation from which he will have increasing difficulty extricating himself.[7]

In *The Limits to Growth* (1972), Meadows et al., present the results of a study carried out at the Massachusetts Institute of Technology under the sponsorship of the Club of Rome.[34] Looking at fossil fuels, they assume initially the available petroleum reserves are 455 billion barrels of oil (see Table 16). Assuming no increase in present rates of consumption this supply would be exhausted in 31 years (2001 A.D.). However, rates of consumption have been increasing and are expected to continue to do so. Therefore, the available supply would be exhausted by 1990 A.D. Recognizing that reserves may be much greater, they make a further forecast on the assumption that there are 2275 billion barrels of oil to be found. This supply would be exhausted by 2020 A.D. Coal is much more abundant than petroleum, and their estimate of how long coal supplies would last, taking into account the exhaustion of petroleum, varies between 111 and 150 years, depending on whether high or low estimates of reserves are employed. Natural gas reserves are less abundant, relative to the rate of consumption, than petroleum, and this supply will be exhausted well before the end of this century.

The Limits to Growth allows very little room to squirm out of the popu-lation-resources dilemma. Obviously we must shift our economy away from petroleum in the near future, and away from a growing dependence on fossil fuels soon after that. Furthermore, Meadows et al., see no pros-pects of continuing growth based on nuclear power or any other form of energy, and they call for a stabilization of population, economy, and resource use.

Other evaluations of the situation by Ayres (1956),[1] Landsberg (1964),[27] Schaeffer (1970),[47] Cloud and Hubbert (1969),[9] and more recent writers confirm the view that the world economy must shift away from petro-leum in the near future and, regardless of how vast the world's coal re-serves may appear to be, they cannot supply the continued increase in energy demand for any comfortably long period of time.[45] Preston Cloud does not see any prospects for the "developing" world doing the hoped-

TABLE 17
Estimated Potential Energy Resources of the Earth[a]

ENERGY SOURCES	CONTINUOUSLY RENEWED YEARLY ENERGY INPUT	NONRENEWABLE ENERGY STORES
SOLAR ENERGY		
Solar radiation	350,000	
Solar energy stored for brief periods		
Wood, waste	50	
Waterpower, total potential	30	
developed	3	
Wind power	200	
Sea thermal power	100	
TIDAL POWER	1	
GEOTHERMAL ENERGY, minimum (readily available)	10	
FOSSIL FUELS		
Coal, known and accessible		6,000
Petroleum, known and accessible		1,000
Natural gas, known and accessible		400
Tars sands, known but not neces-sarily available (Canada)		200
Oil shale, known but not neces-sarily available (U.S.A.)		1,500
NUCLEAR FUELS		
Uranium-235 for 1973 reactors		1,500
Uranium-thorium for breeder reactors		100,000,000
Tritium-deuterium fuels for theoretical fusion reactors		300,000,000,000

[a] Adapted from Lars Kristoferson (*Ambio*, 2:181) and A. Lovins (1973).

NOTE. Total world energy consumption in 1970 was 50,000 terawatt hours, equal to the amount continuously supplied by wood wastes, or to 0.014 of 1 percent of the total solar energy input each year. *All figures are expressed in thousand terawatt hours. A terawatt equals 10^{12} watts, and is a measure of the total thermal energy content.*

for developing unless populations are stabilized at relatively low levels.[9]

We must realize that we are now living on the energy *capital* of the earth, whereas in earlier times we were living on the *interest,* and that, with this state of affairs, we are forced to expend increasing amounts of energy in order to gain an energy surplus. Thus the nuclear power industry has been subsidized by fossil fuel. Until recently more energy was expended in the mining, transportation, concentration, production, and disposal processes involving nuclear fuels than was gained in the output of nuclear plants. Also, it now takes a much greater energy investment to get oil or coal out of the ground, to process it, and to move it to the place where it is to be used than was true in the past. In the future, a still-greater investment of energy will be required. We can easily fool ourselves into thinking new energy resources can become available when, in fact, we would invest more fuel in their development than we would receive in return.[44]

It is possible to be both optimistic and pessimistic about the future of energy without being contradictory. The available energy from continuously renewable resources is enormous—if we learn how to use it and shape our societies to accommodate it. However, our present reliance on fossil fuels is leading us into serious difficulties, and pursuit of a new Age of Nuclear Power to replace the Age of Fossil Fuels could lead us into much worse straits. The availability of energy on earth is shown in Table 17. Each of these categories of energy will now be discussed.

ENERGY RESOURCES

SOLAR ENERGY

The yearly input of energy from the sun which reaches the surface of the earth is estimated to be 7000 times greater than the total human energy demand in 1970.[25] This is an inexhaustible supply of energy, and its use in any form does not contribute additional heat to the biosphere, unlike fossil fuel or nuclear energy. There are no problems of pollution associated with its use, except those related to the devices that may be used to capture or transport this energy. Obviously we already use solar energy either directly as the principal means of keeping warm, or indirectly, in food or other materials produced by plant and animal life. Solar energy also provides the energy available in wind power, waterpower, fuels made from wood or other vegetation, and in thermal gradients in the oceans or other water bodies. In the past solar energy was captured and stored in the form of coal and petroleum.

Solar energy can be used directly for space heating and cooling in all areas which have a high percentage of sunny days in each year. The dry tropics, of course, have an advantage, and it is here that the greatest potential for future use lies. Many homes are now heated by solar panels, which capture sunlight, and use it to heat water, which provides heat for homes. Solar stills have been manufactured and are used in some places: the Soviet Union, India, and North Africa for examples. These can provide freshwater from saline or alkaline water. Solar cookers are also in use in various parts of the world and can eliminate the need for wood or other fuels. Solar furnaces can generate the high temperatures required in many industrial processes.[6]

Solar power can be used to generate electricity making use of photovoltaic cells. This is still relatively expensive compared to other means of electricity generation, but comparatively little research and development has gone into this field, and it seems likely that in the future it will be both practical and economical.[20] In Australia it has been calculated that at 10 percent efficiency of conversion, from solar energy to electricity, 0.03 percent of the land surface could generate all of that country's energy needs.[19a] In the United States, to generate electric power requirements, it is estimated that 5000 square miles of desert surface, an area slightly more than 70 miles square, could produce all of the electric power needs of the nation.[19b]

The power companies in the United States, having jumped on the nuclear power bandwagon, have been sufficiently frightened by the potential competition of solar energy to devote considerable time and money to television advertising against it. One of their phrases was, "Ah, but what happens when the sun goes down?" Obviously what happens is one uses solar power during the daytime, when it is present in excess, to store energy in some other form. Batteries can be used on a small scale, but are expensive. For large-scale operations solar power can be used to pump water, during the daytime. This water can then be used to generate power hydroelectrically when the sun is not shining. Another approach is to use solar power to produce hydrogen from electrolytic dissociation of water. Hydrogen can be used as a fuel to run automobiles or other engines in much the same way as petroleum, but without the polluting effects of petroleum.

Any plan for centralized generation of electricity for the entire nation should be viewed with some suspicion, however. Such electricity has to be transported and this involves an energy-wasting national grid—power lines running in all directions, for example, or the need to transport the hydrogen to all parts of the country.[31] One of the advantages of solar energy is that it is available everywhere, and its use can be most efficient if decentralized. Home space heating and cooling, for example, presently consumes 20 percent of the energy used in the United States. If that alone were done through solar power, a great reduction in the demand for other fuels would occur.[28]

The use of solar distilling plants on a reasonably large scale, to provide freshwater from sea water, is one endeavor toward which sea-coast communities should be giving serious attention. The use of solar heat to process municipal waste for the production of methane gas, as a fuel, and fertilizers, or other useful end products, is another possibility that needs research and development.[3]

There is, however, no need to put all of our eggs in the solar-energy basket, or in any energy basket. A diversification of energy resources holds much greater promise. Development of solar energy as a power source has been held back because the industrialized world has decided to concentrate on petroleum as the principal source of power. Now that the end is in sight for that resource, governments have become committed to nuclear power—and once committed it is difficult for them to turn back.

WIND POWER Solar energy provides differential heating of the atmosphere, and this, in combination with the earth's rotation, generates the moving air masses or winds of the world. Enough energy is available each year in wind power to equal four times the total 1970 energy consumption of humanity.[25] In earlier years wind energy was used extensively for pumping, milling, and electricity generation. Home wind generators were frequent on middlewestern farms in America, until the Rural Electrification program launched by the government, at the urging of power companies, led to their displacement.

Certain massive schemes have been proposed for meeting all or most of the world's energy needs by using wind generators. Thus the Swedish State Power Board has calculated that a system of wind generators could supply most of that country's electrical needs,[24] and schemes have been advanced for generating most of the United States needs by a network of wind generators in the Great Plains, or on floating platforms off the coasts.[49] However, it seems most likely that a small-scale decentralized approach holds greater promise. Some farms now generate all of their electrical needs, including all household appliances, power machinery, and so forth, from relatively small and easily managed wind generators. Power is stored in batteries for use during those periods when the wind is not blowing. On a larger scale windpower, like solar power, can be used to pump water uphill, which can then be used to generate hydropower when the wind is not blowing.[4]

Along with solar power, wind power has the potential to reduce, or eliminate in some areas, the need for other fuels. Like solar energy, however, research into the potential of wind power has lagged behind because of the availability of cheap petroleum.

GEOTHERMAL, OCEAN THERMAL, AND TIDAL POWER Geothermal power is derived from heating which takes place within the earth's crust. It is manifested in volcanoes, geysers, and hot springs and in some parts of the world it has already been tapped and used for space heating or electricity generation. New Zealand, Iceland, Italy, and California are already making some use of geothermal power, and there is enough readily available to meet the energy needs of many areas in which volcanic activity takes place.[38] The greatest potential, however, may lie in making use of temperature differentials in nonvolcanic areas, where the rocks below the surface are warmer than the surface layer. This temperature differential can, in theory, be used to produce an electric current but the technology for this has yet to be developed.

In the tropical oceans, particularly, but also in other seas, a considerable temperature differential exists between cold water in the deeps and warm surface water. If the technology were developed this could be used to generate electricity in offshore, floating plants. Similarly, floating plants, in theory, could be used to generate electricity in the same way existing hydropower plants do, making use of such fast-flowing ocean currents as the Gulf Stream.[50]

Tidal power has been developed in some local areas, but never on a large scale. Its greatest potential lies in estuaries in which there is a great tidal range. By constructing barriers across such estuaries, one could use the high tide to push a flow of water through turbines and thus generate considerable amounts of electricity. The environmental implications of such constructions, however, would require considerable study to avoid interferences with other estuarine functions.[50]

FRESHWATER HYDROPOWER The hydroelectric potential of rivers and streams has already been extensively exploited in Europe and North America, making use of high dams and reservoirs from which water falls through turbines. As noted earlier, hydropower contributes only a small portion of U.S. power requirements, although locally it is often the principal source of electricity. Worldwide the full potential has not been developed but, at best, would not contribute any massive amounts of electricity to supply world demands unless all environmental considerations were to be set aside. Nevertheless, water power is a nonpolluting, ever-renewable source of energy. Small-scale developments have tended to be neglected in favor of giant dams, but many local communities could supply all of their electrical needs by use of hydropower in such a way that neither stream flow nor aquatic life were greatly disturbed. Hydropower will remain one of the many alternative energy sources which, under sensible management, could remove any need for massive development of fossil fuels or nuclear power.[32]

VEGETATION POWER Most of the world's people still meet their fuel requirements by burning wood, other vegetation, or animal dung which is secondarily derived from vegetation. This has had many disadvantages in some parts of the world, leading to deforestation and soil erosion, and to the waste of valuable fertilizer. Elsewhere, however, wood for fuel is one of many forest products which can be harvested on a sustainable basis without detracting from the production of other forest products. Wood fires, furthermore, have an attraction for people that exceeds their practical utility—perhaps because the human race has spent most of its existence sitting around campfires in the evening hours.

The potential contribution of wood for meeting total energy needs is small, although locally it can be of greatest significance. Other kinds of vegetation, either directly or in the form of plant or animal wastes, can make still more significant contributions to fuel requirements.

It has been proposed that corn be used to produce fuel without greatly reducing its value for other purposes. Fermented corn will yield ethanol from its starch, and this can be used directly as a fuel for motor vehicles or other engines, or in a mixture with gasoline. The other corn products, the proteins and oils can be used directly for animal fodder. Heat for the distilling units can come from corn stalks. Animal manures can be returned to fertilize the next crop of corn, and this particular system will produce milk, meat, or other animal products in addition to ethanol.[37]

Already in operation are many systems that produce methane from animal and plant wastes. Large-scale plants are in operation which produce methane from city sewage. Thus two-thirds of the 5000 sewage treatment plants in Great Britain produce their own methane, which is used to process sewage sludge and to meet other power needs in the plant. The Southend and Mogden plants in the London metropolitan area generate excess methane which is sold as heating gas. Methane production could, no doubt, be improved were this to be considered a principal objective of the sewage treatment plant. All such plants produce dried sludge which could be used as fertilizer in a reasonably organized economic system.[31] Smaller-scale methane-producing units can be used to generate fuel for farm use or for the use of small communities. Many of these are in operation in India and, since they produce fertilizer as well as fuel, are particularly valuable in those areas where animal dung would otherwise be used directly as fuel, with loss of its value as fertilizer. In addition to providing a substitute for natural gas, which is in short supply, methane can be used directly to fuel motor vehicles. During World War II a high percentage of the civilian motor vehicles in Europe operated on methane.[3]

Methane, methanol, ethanol and other gases, and alcohols derived from organic materials, as well as these materials in themselves, are all energy sources available to meet part of the needs of industrial civilization. None of them is a panacea, but we should cease to look for panaceas. Simple answers to complex problems always create new problems.

Energy can also be produced from the great variety of waste products that otherwise must be disposed of, at an energy cost, by large and small communities. The city of St. Louis, for example, now uses solid wastes in place of other fuels in some of its electrical power plants. Other cities are also pursuing this type of answer to the solid-waste pollution problem.[22] One suspects, however, that much of the material burned—waste paper, for example—could have better uses if we could devise the proper means of sorting, reclaiming, and recycling.

FOSSIL FUELS We have already noted that industrial civilization has become almost totally dependent on fossil fuels, starting this process of dependence in the eighteenth century and achieving nearly total dependence before the twentieth century was far advanced. It is also obvious that this dependence must cease and in the next few decades—well before the young people of today are far into middle age. We have already considered the supply of petroleum, coal, and natural gas. There are other fossil fuels to which the technological optimists are now looking with hope for the future.

Oil shales cover some 16,500 square miles of Colorado, Utah, and

Wyoming. It is estimated that these shales contain the equivalent of 600 to 3000 billion barrels of oil in the form of kerogen, which is converted into shale oil when heated to high temperatures. There is good reason to believe, however, that it would take a greater energy input to make shale oil available from most deposits than the energy output represented by the oil—that is, the shale oil system could be an energy sink rather than an energy resource. To make shale oil available, great amounts of water would have to be provided to operate the processing plants, and oil shale occurs where water is scarce. Road systems, towns, and processing plants would all have to be built at an energy cost. The mining machinery would require great amounts of fuel, the processing machinery still more. Furthermore, the end product would be a totally ruined countryside covered with great piles of rock debris and with vegetation and animal life destroyed. With the shortage of water in this region it is doubtful reclamation would be possible. Since we have already ruined some 4 million acres of land in this country through strip mining for coal or other minerals, one is appalled at the prospect of vastly increasing the amount of total wasteland in this new endeavor. It is extremely doubtful that any mining company would consider oil shale an economically profitable enterprise, if they had to bear the full cost of the operation. However, if the government, meaning all of the taxpayers, can be lured into paying most of the cost of development, the mining companies can make a tidy profit, and the fact that there is an energy drain instead of gain can be concealed.[30,44]

Tar sands occur in great quantities in the province of Alberta, Canada, and undoubtedly are found in other parts of the world. They represent a low-grade source of petroleum, which may equal one-fifth of the known petroleum reserves. It is likely that only a small proportion of the tar sands would yield a net gain of energy, since the energy costs of mining, hauling, and processing will be considerable, although presumably less than for oil shales. They are no long-term answer to fossil fuel needs.[30,44]

Peat occurs in great areas throughout the sub-Arctic regions of the world. Although not quite a fossil fuel, it is vegetation becoming a fossil fuel. Energy yield per kilogram of peat is necessarily much lower than for coal or petroleum since it is a less concentrated fuel. People have used peat for fuel during many centuries, and some countries with abundant peat supplies, such as Ireland, can supply a significant part of their energy demands from this source.[42] The environmental consequences of widespread peat removal, however, need considerable study, since peat bogs and other deposits are important regulators of water flow and infiltration in northern regions.

. There is no long-term answer for human energy needs in the field of fossil fuels. Furthermore, coal, petroleum, and natural gas are more than just fuels. They are important raw materials for the production of fertilizers, plastics, synthetic fibers, and a great variety of medicinal and other chemical products. If we make sparing use of these resources, they can be kept available for a long time. If we continue to accelerate our consumption of them, using them as our principal fuels, they will soon be gone. Ideally they should be specialized fuel sources, for use in processes where other energy sources are less satisfactory. Civilization should be weaned from fossil fuel and established on permanent, renewable energy supplies. Unfortunately, although most countries are now thinking in this direction, they can only see as far as nuclear power. This, however, presents us with what Alvin Weinberg has termed a "Faustian bargain." We can have all of the power we demand but, like Faust, must sell our soul to the devil to gain it by these means.

NUCLEAR ENERGY The world first became aware of the energy potential from atomic fission when in 1945 an atom bomb was dropped on Hiroshima, obliterating a good part of the city and its people. Soon after, to relieve any doubts, a second bomb was used to destroy Nagasaki. The horror of these events and the developments that followed have dogged the footsteps of all who work with nuclear power and seek to harness the atom to do constructive work. The development of atomic energy was shrouded from the beginning in secrecy. While the United States and Russia, and later Great Britain, France, and China continued to test atomic and then hydrogen bombs, apparently with little regard for world opinion or environmental consequences, an atmosphere of distrust and suspicion greeted any government pronouncements about the dangers, or their absence, from fallout, and later about the potential hazards surrounding the development of nuclear power. This situation was not improved when the chronicle of blunders, misleading information, and apparent attempts to deceive the public became known through books such as *Science and Survival* by the biologist Barry Commoner.[11]

Radioactive elements are those elements, such as radium, which undergo spontaneous disintegration. In this process they give off ionizing radiation and change ultimately into other stable elements. The ionizing radiation of interest to ecology is of two basic kinds: that consisting of particles of atomic or subatomic size, and that consisting of electromagnetic radiation. In the former category are *alpha* particles, relatively large in size and with little ability to penetrate far through air or more solid media, and *beta* particles, which are high-speed electrons with greater penetrating power. Both of these particles are capable of doing biological damage near their point of origin through causing ionization of the molecules that make up living protoplasm—breaking up or disrupting these components of cells. In the second category are *gamma* rays, which are related to x rays—radiation similar to visible light, but with extremely short wavelengths. These readily pass through organic material and can do damage throughout the body, although this damage is more diffuse. Shields of lead or other heavy metals are used to screen against them.[43]

The measurement of radioactivity is based generally on the amount of radiation energy given off by the emitting materials, the rate at which atomic disintegrations take place, or on the dose of radiation energy received by an organism. Thus the *curie* is the quantity of a radioactive substance in which 3.7×10^{10} atoms will disintegrate per second and, consequently, will give off that number of alpha or beta, plus gamma radiation. It is the equivalent of one gram of radium. Since 37 billion particles per second is a high, quickly lethal, rate of radiation, the more common measurements related to environmental conditions are *millicuries* (one-thousandth of a curie) or *microcuries* (one-millionth of a curie).[43]

The *roentgen* or *rad* is a measure of the dosage of radioactivity absorbed by living tissue, and amounts of 100 ergs of energy per gram of tissue. One thousandth of a rad, the millirad, is a convenient measure for dosages commonly encountered in the human environment.[13] A further term in common use is *rem,* meaning "roentgen equivalent man," and is a measure of radiation absorbed by the entire body.[12]

Radioisotopes are radioactive forms of otherwise stable elements and are formed when stable atoms are hit by ionizing radiation. Thus carbon-14 is a radioisotope of normal carbon, carbon-12, and is formed when atmospheric nitrogen is bombarded by cosmic rays. It is a naturally occurring radioactive isotope. The naturally occurring radioactive elements, uranium and thorium, are those employed in the atom-splitting process that gives rise to massive releases of energy, used destructively in bombs, or when controlled and regulated, used to generate heat that can, in turn, generate electricity. Uranium and thorium are spontaneously radioactive and break down slowly to form, eventually, stable elements.

In the nuclear fission process an atom of uranium-235 is bombarded with a neutron—one of the many kinds of atomic particles. This splits the nucleus of the atom into two pieces with the release of a large amount of energy. The nucleus, in this process, gives off additional neutrons, which strike other U-235 atoms in a chain reaction. One pound of uranium-235, subject to fission, can give off as much energy as 1500 tons of coal.[7]

Uranium-235 is an isotope of uranium that is not abundant. Uranium-238, which is more common, can also be used as nuclear fuel. It must, however, first be transformed by bombardment with neutrons into plutonium-239, which is fissionable. Similarly, thorium must be transformed into fissionable uranium-233 before it can be used as fuel.[7]

In the fission process, when an atomic bomb is exploded in the atmosphere, great amounts of energy are released along with great amounts of radiation. This radiation bombards atoms that are present in the environment and converts many of them into radioactive isotopes. Furthermore, the breakdown products of the explosion include a variety of radioisotopes. The length of time these persist in the environment varies. Each isotope is said to have a *half-life,* which is the time required for half of the atoms in any given quantity of radioactive material to disintegrate. Carbon-14, which occurs naturally throughout the atmosphere and in all living tissue, has a half-life of 5568 years, meaning that for any quantity present in the environment now, one-half will still be present in 5568 years. Strontium-90 and cesium-137, two of the isotopes more dangerous to living organisms, have half-lives, respectively, of 28 and 33 years. This means they decay more rapidly than carbon 14 and thus, for a given amount, are more radioactive. Worse, strontium-90 is chemically similar to calcium and is deposited in its place in bone tissue. Here it emits beta particles that can do important damage to metabolic processes occurring in or near the bone. Furthermore, these elements can accumulate in the environment in considerable quantity and thus can become concentrated in their passage through food chains. By contrast, iodine-131 has a half-life of only 8 days and does not persist in the environment. However, if it is ingested it may become strongly concentrated in the thyroid gland and do serious damage during its active period.[13,51]

The biological danger from radioisotopes depends in part on their concentration in the external environment; in part on the degree to which living creatures concentrate the elements in their organs or tissues; and in part on the half-life of the isotopes involved. However, this biological danger must be weighed in the balance with the "normal" condition of the biosphere. Radioactive elements and isotopes are natural components of the environment. The elements uranium, radium, and thorium, along with radioisotopes of carbon, rubidium, hydrogen, and potassium all contribute natural radiation. The total amount of naturally occurring radiation, known as *background radiation,* amounts to an estimated one-tenth of a roentgen or rad per year, or an exposure for an average person in a lifetime to the total of seven roentgens. The Council of Environmental Quality has presented data to indicate that the average annual dosage of radiation a person receives is as follows:[12]

SOURCE	DOSE IN MILLIREMS
Natural background	125.0
Medical sources (use of x rays and isotopes)	55.2
Fallout—from all previous atomic explosions	1.5
Miscellaneous (occupational, TV sets, luminous wrist watches, etc.)	2.2

Viewed in this way, the danger from fallout seems trivial. The United Nations has estimated that the average person living in the United States from the period of heavy nuclear testing in the 1950's and early 1960's until the year 2000 will have received a total dosage of radiation from fallout amounting to 110 millirems, less than the amount received annually from normal background radiation.[12] Should we therefore relax about the dangers and hazards from the use of nuclear energy for power production? Many think we should not. In part the reason is this—no radiation is good for you. Any increase in the level of radiation to which people are exposed is potentially harmful. Radiation does cause cancer. Radiation does cause mutations. Radiation can produce a variety of other harmful effects. We still have inadequate knowledge of the effects of continued exposure to low levels of radiation. Organisms can concentrate radioactive isotopes to a dangerous degree within their bodies even when the general level of radiation in the environment is low.

Despite the present tendency to discount the importance of fallout, the reasons listed above were sufficient to cause the United States and the Soviet Union in 1963 to sign a treaty banning atmospheric testing of atomic or hydrogen bombs. Treaties of this nature do not occur frequently. This one has not been broken thus far in 13 years. This suggests that governments do not like the risks.

However, the major sources of environmental concern today are not the effects of bomb explosions but the more pedestrian uses of atomic energy for the generation of electricity. The establishment of nuclear power stations has, from the first, been fraught with controversy. This was partly because of the tendency of the power companies to plan their locations in some of the most scenic and attractive places in the countryside, and partly because of an opposition to the plants themselves. The "battle of Bodega Head" in California pitched the forces of the Pacific Gas and Electric Company against the environmentalists of that time over the issue of constructing a nuclear plant in the middle of an important center for marine and intertidal research, and on a scenic peninsula of high aesthetic value. The power company lost.

The nuclear power plant of today uses heat generated by controlled nuclear fission to heat water into steam which then turns a turbine that generates electricity. The principal is not greatly different from an oil-or-coal-fired plant, but the fuel is uranium, and the amount of heat generated is enormous. Such plants require great quantities of water as a coolant and necessarily give off heated water.[14] They release, in the water, a small amount of radioisotopes, and release also a small amount through smokestack discharge into the atmosphere. They are not atomic bombs, and it is said that they cannot produce an atomic explosion.[11] They are, however, subject to various kinds of accidents that could inadvertently release large amounts of radioactive material into the environment.[29]

The principal isotopes given off are tritium (a hydrogen isotope), krypton-85, manganese-56, and xenon-133 (based on the proposed Calvert Cliffs plant in Maryland), but smaller quantities of a great number of other isotopes are also produced.[46] Atomic Energy Commission experts, who set the safety standards, say the amounts produced are trivial. Other experts, however, are seriously concerned, particularly in view of possible biological concentration. That this can be significant is illustrated by the fact that adult swallows, exposed to stack effluents, may concentrate radioactive materials to levels 75,000 times higher than those found in the air; radioactive phosphorus may be concentrated 150,000 times higher in phytoplankton than in the water in which these live, and 850,000 times higher in filamentous green algae than in the surrounding water.[48] There are numerous, and disturbing, figures measuring all kinds of biological concentration.

It is not only radioactivity, however, but heat that is a source of concern among conservationists. Nuclear power plants, because they must be kept cooler than fossil-fuel plants, use far more water than any other type of industrial installation. In passing through the reactor the water becomes heated. On discharge back into a river, or the ocean, it may raise the overall temperature of the water body significantly. This can have major biological effects. Thus for the proposed Calvert Cliffs power plant in Maryland (two units each generating 800,000 kilowatts of electricity):

For each unit, cooling water from the Bay will be required at about 2500 cubic feet per second, equivalent to a lake one foot deep and 7.7 miles square each day. This water cools and condenses the steam leaving the plant's turbine-generator, and it is estimated that there will be at 10° F. rise of temperature when the cooling water flow is 1,200,000 gallons per minute.

This statement by a group of Johns Hopkins University professors who opposed the construction of this plant is further expanded with the comment that: "the Calvert Cliffs plant is of special consequence because of its size—the volume of its heated effluent water will place it after the Susquehanna, Potomac, and James as Maryland's fourth largest 'river'. . . ." This group believed, and showed evidence to support the belief, that such an output will have major and probably deleterious effects on the biotic communities of Chesapeake Bay.[46]

The construction of a nuclear power plant in tropical regions presents a different kind of problem. Thus the proposal of the Florida Power and Light Corporation to construct a nuclear plant on Turkey Point in Biscayne Bay, Florida, was opposed almost universally by environmental scientists because of the damaging effect the heated effluent water would have on the biota of Biscayne Bay. In this case the temperature of the bay in summer was already high. Addition of heated water in great quantities would raise it above the level of tolerance for many kinds of life. If cooling of effluent water were provided by holding it in cooling ponds, running it through cooling towers, or in other ways, the problem of heating the Bay would be resolved, but there would still be that of adding heat to the total environment.

There has been considerable concern that a growing reliance on nuclear power, and in particular on nuclear fusion, if this can be developed, would cause serious heat problems for the biosphere as a whole. Too much warming of the earth's atmosphere, above the level provided by solar energy and its direct derivatives, could bring about serious climatic changes. If the average world temperature were to increase by 3° C., it has been predicted that the polar ice caps would melt and flood all of the low-lying coastal areas of the earth. Such an increase in temperature could be brought about not only through increasing consumption of fossil fuels and nuclear power, but by any great increase in the atmospheric levels of carbon dioxide which would retard the heat from being radiated into outer space. Several studies of this problem have been carried out—for example, by Lamont Cole, or Cornell,[10] by the Council on Environmental Quality,[12] and by the Study of Critical Environmental Problems (SCEP) group at Williams College in 1970.[48] All emphasize the need for careful monitoring, while not seeing any immediate global problem. The SCEP study foresaw local effects around cities and other areas of heavy power consumption, and these could have important environmental consequences.

At a time when there is a continuing shortage of energy, the idea of wasting heat should be unacceptable and all future heat-producing plants, whether nuclear or fueled by other means, should be planned so that maximum use of the excess heat will be provided for. In most electrical power plants the efficiency of conversion from energy contained in the fuel to power contained in electric current is not high. For the United Kingdom, MacKillop has calculated that the efficiency of electrical generation is no more than 27 percent in most power plants. The balance of the energy in the original fuel is lost as heat. In coal-fired plants there is an output of waste heat of 1300 megawatts for every 1000 megawatts of electricity generated; for nuclear plants 2100 megawatts of heat are lost for every 1000 megawatts of electricity produced. One approach to this problem has been tried at Vasteras, Sweden, where the heat produced from the power plant is used for local district heating (or cooling). For every 1650 megawatts of fuel input, 500 megawatts of electricity and 900 of useful heat are produced. Only 200 megawatts is lost as waste heat.[31]

In the middle 1970's it would appear that the government of the United States has committed the country to a full pursuit of nuclear power as an answer to the nations energy needs. The score sheet of nuclear plants and their generating capacity in 1974 was as follows:[23]

STATUS	NUMBER OF PLANTS	MEGAWATTS, ELECTRICAL CAPACITY
Licensed by Atomic Energy Commission to operate	45	28,183
Owned by AEC	2	940
Under construction	60	57,970
Planned and ordered	105	115,948
Announced	21	24,270
Total	233	227,948

Most of these plants are of the conventional type, usually they are light-water reactors, which use water as a coolant and heat-transfer system. They, for the most part, will burn uranium-235 as fuel.[33] Some of them—and most likely a high percentage in the future—will be liquid-metal-fast-breeder reactors (LMFBR). These use liquid sodium as a heat-transfer medium. As fuel they can use the common form of uranium, U-238, mixed with plutonium. In operation they convert U-238 into plutonium, and thus breed more fuel as they operate. None are in operation in the United States (in 1975), although both France and the Soviet Union have put fast-breeder reactors into operation. The Soviet plant was subject to an accident shortly after it started to operate.[35] How serious this was, and what caused it has not been revealed. The French plant is producing electricity. Opposition to fast-breeder reactors in the United States, based on both the economics and safety of the plants, has delayed construction and forced a review of the entire system.[39,41]

The safety of the nuclear plant system, and particularly of the breeder reactors which produce great amounts of plutonium as end products, is based on a number of considerations. First is the danger of an accident to the reactor core itself with the possible massive release of radioactivity into the surrounding environment; but more pervading is the fact that we still have no sensible system for handling radioactive wastes. Plutonium is an exceedingly toxic metal in addition to being the basic material for nuclear bombs.[2] Since its half-life is over 24,000 years any plan for its disposal has to look as far into the future as the lifetime of *Homo sapiens* on earth. Where do you put great quantities of this metal, and who will look after them so they do not endanger life on earth? How do you prevent this substance from getting into the hands of people who will use it for nuclear blackmail of humanity?[33,40] Is there any reason to trust the private power companies who already control large quantities of this material? Is there any good reason to take such risks? This writer cannot see any.

NUCLEAR FUSION The ultimate energy panacea which is being held forth by some as the answer to all energy problems is nuclear fusion. Whereas all nuclear plants in operation (and those proposed) are fission plants which essentially harness the fission process of the atom bomb, nuclear fusion harnesses the nuclear fusion processes of the hydrogen bomb. It makes use of the same sort of reaction which takes place within the sun and, in theory, would produce far greater amounts of energy than any fission process. The fuels involved are isotopes of hydrogen contained in heavy water, deuterium (H_3O), and are sufficiently abundant in ordinary sea water so that fuel supply represents no foreseeable problem. The waste products are also hydrogen isotopes which could be recycled for fuel. There is, consequently, no problem of radioactive pollution or waste storage, but heat will be a serious problem.

Nuclear fusion technology will certainly be one of the most advanced and complicated on earth if it is ever developed past the pilot stage. It seems doubtful it could ever be made available for any but the most technologically advanced countries. Furthermore, the economics of the entire enterprise require serious investigation. Amory Lovins has evaluated fusion power in this way:

Some would say that no nuclear source can be clean and safe; and that though nuclear power is admirable when properly sited, the source and user should be rather widely separated—say, about 150 million km.

We happen to have one nuclear fusion plant in operation which meets these requirements: the sun. Do we need another?[30]

ENERGY CONSERVATION Perhaps one of the most disturbing features concerning the high consumption of energy in the United States and other industrialized nations is the amount of energy lost as sheer waste. The loss of energy as waste heat from power plants has already been referred to, but this is only one of many examples.

The private motor car, fueled by petroleum which is burned in an internal combustion engine is highly inefficient, both in its design and in the way in which it is employed. American automobiles, which are larger and have engines which consume more fuel per mile than most of their foreign counterparts, add to the unnecessary waste of energy. Gerald Leach has noted that road transport in America, buses, trucks, and automobiles, uses 43.5 percent of all oil consumed. The comparable figures in Western Europe are 17.6 percent. Air transport, particularly that employing jet planes, is more energy inefficient than road transport, whereas rail transport is relatively efficient. The following table illustrates:[16]

	BTU CONSUMPTION PER PASSENGER MILE	BTU CONSUMPTION PER TON/MILE OF FREIGHT
Jet plane	7150	63,000
Private automobile	5400	
Railroad train	2620	750
Passenger bus	1700	
Highway trucking		2400
Ship		500
Bicycle at 8 mph	310	

Despite the relative inefficiency of road transport, the U.S. government has spent $40 billion in development of the interstate highway system, compared to only $900 million in assistance to railroads during the same period.

a

ENERGY ALTERNATIVES

(a) Taal Volcano, Philippines. Areas of volcanic activity are likely to be suitable to geothermal energy generation. (b) Geothermal power plant at Wairakei, New Zealand. It produces 10 percent of New Zealand's electricity. (c) Solar furnace at Odeillo, France. On a smaller, decentralized scale solar energy could now be used to greatly reduce the demand for other energy resources. (d) Windmills have supplied energy for useful purposes for many centuries. More recently wind generators have been developed for the production of electricity.

b

c

d

TABLE 18

Comparison of Production of Energy by Fast-Breeder Reactor Program as Compared to Other Means[a]

ENERGY SOURCE	PROJECTIONS TO 2000 A.D.	
	GENERATING CAPACITY (OR SAVINGS) MILLIONS OF KILOWATTS	PERCENTAGE OF TOTAL U.S. ENERGY DEMAND
Solar energy		
Photovoltaic	140	7
Solar thermal	40	2
Heating and cooling buildings	35	2
Wind generators	170	9
Bioconversion	25	1
Total solar	410	21
Geothermal energy	80	4
Conservation of electricity	236	12
Grand total	765	37
AEC estimate of production from LMFBR program	435	23

[a] From Scientist's Institute for Public Information, 1974.[18]

Space heating—residential, commercial, and industrial—also represents a great waste of energy. This is partly because of the means employed, but equally important is the lack of proper building design and insulation. Great savings of energy—in winter for heating, in summer for cooling—could be accomplished by proper insulation alone. Still greater savings could be had if energy saving was given proper consideration in the planning and design of structures.

It will be noted in the next chapter that present methods of high-energy input agriculture represents a serious waste of energy as well as having other undesirable features.

These are only some examples of ways in which energy is wasted and could be conserved. Lovins has pointed out that if per capita energy use in the United States were reduced to the same level as in France, the amount saved would be enough to give everyone else on earth one-fourth more energy than they now have. He states:

In the USA, for example, a politically acceptable strategy could be devised and implemented within two years of an orderly reduction of the energy growth rate by perhaps 0.3–0.5 percentage points a year, reaching zero within about a decade despite continuing population growth. The author believes that without prohibitive cost or disruption, the level of US energy consumption could then be smoothly reduced, at a rate of perhaps 1–2%/yr, by a factor of at least two over the ensuing two or three decades—again despite continuing population growth.

In other words, through energy conservation and some redeployment of economic activity, we could maintain a high standard of living without any need for massive nuclear development, or of scraping the earth for the last of the fossil fuels.[30]

In Table 18 are shown calculations by the Scientist's Institute for Public Information which demonstrate how the goals, proposed by the Atomic Energy Commission for the liquid-metal-fast-breeder-reactor (LMFBR) program, could be reached by other means—with energy conservation one of the most important.[18]

In 1974 the Ford Foundation released the results of the most thorough study of American energy policy which has yet been carried out. They examine three scenarios: the historical growth scenario in which we plow ahead as we have in the past, but faster, encouraging growth and

FIG. 12–1.

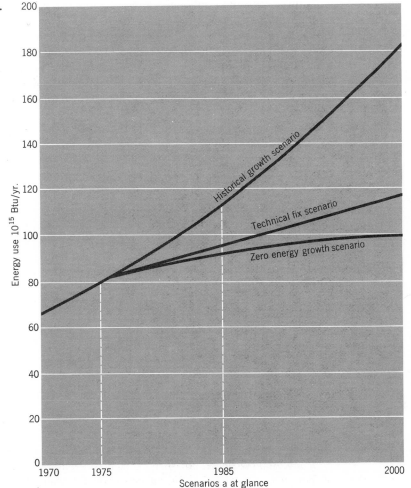

Scenarios a at glance

grasping everywhere for the fossil fuel and nuclear power to support it; the technical fix scenario, in which we seek to avoid waste and increase technical efficiency without slowing growth or changing our patterns of economic activity greatly; and finally, the zero-energy-growth scenario, in which the aim is to level off the rate of energy consumption in the United States. We can achieve and maintain zero energy growth without anybody being the worse off materially or economically. Figure 12–1 shows the rates of energy consumption that would be involved in each of these scenarios.[17]

The world is at a crossroads where the choice of energy policy may determine whether or not civilization will survive and whether or not life in that civilization would be endurable for those who care about individual freedom or the quality of the environment in which they live. Among the most distressing features of recent trends in energy ownership, distribution, and consumption has been the great concentration of real power, including political power, in a few hands. Anyone who lived through the so-called energy crisis of 1973–1974 knows the extent to which those who control the flow of oil and electricity can bring all others to their knees. The development of a diversity of energy resources, with emphasis on local energy autonomy would be strong insurance against the loss of social and political freedom in the future. A final word from Ivan Illich seems appropriate to end this chapter:[21]

A low energy policy allows for a wide choice of life styles and cultures. If, on the other hand, a society opts for high energy consumption, its social relations must be dictated by technocracy and will be equally distasteful whether labelled capitalist or socialist.

CHAPTER REFERENCES

Ford Foundation Energy Policy Project, 1974. *A time to choose. America's energy future.* Ballinger, Cambridge, Mass.

Illich, Ivan D., 1974. *Energy and equity.* Calder and Boyars, London.

Lovins, Amory B., 1973. *World energy strategies: facts, issues, and options.* Earth Resources Research Ltd., London.

Meadows, Donella H. et al., 1972. *The limits to growth.* Signet, New American Library, New York.

National Academy of Science, 1969. *Resources and man.* W. H. Freeman, San Francisco.

LITERATURE CITED

1. Ayres, Eugene, 1956. The age of fossil fuels. *Man's role in changing the face of the earth.* University of Chicago Press, Chicago.
2. Bair, W. J., and R. C. Thompson, 1974. Plutonium: biomedical research. *Science,* 183: 715–722.
3. Bell, C., S. Boulter, D. Dunlop, and P. Keiller, 1973. *Methane, fuel of the future.* Andrew Singer, Bottisham, United Kingdom.
4. Bruckner, Arthur, 1974. Taking power off the wind. *New Scientist,* 61: 812–814.

5. Cambel, Ali B., 1970. Energy for a restless world. *Science and technology in the world of the future.* Wiley-Interscience, New York.

6. *Catalyst,* 1974. World News. *Catalyst,* 4: 2.

7. Brown, Harrison, 1954. *The challenge of man's future.* Viking Press, New York.

8. Cade, C. Maxwell, 1968. Wavelengths of life and death. *New Scientist,* 39: 588–591.

9. Cloud, Preston, 1969. *Resources, population, and quality of life.* Proceedings, AAAS, Boston, Mimeo.

10. Cole, Lamont C., 1971. Thermal pollution. *Man's impact on environment.* McGraw-Hill, New York.

11. Commoner, Barry, 1963. *Science and survival.* Viking Press, New York.

12. Council on Environmental Quality, 1970. *Environmental quality.* C.E.Q., Washington, D.C.

13. Comar, Cyril L., 1966. Biological aspects of nuclear weapons. *Human ecology.* Addison-Wesley, Reading, Mass.

14. Curtis, R., and E. Hogan, 1970. The myth of the peaceful atom. *Eco-crisis,* Wiley, New York.

15. Dahlberg, Kenneth A., 1973. Toward a policy of zero energy growth. *Ecologist,* 3: 338–341.

16. Entwistle, Robert, 1973. The crisis we won't face squarely. *Sierra Club Bull.,* 58: 9–12, 32.

17. Ford Foundation Energy Policy Project, 1974. *A time to choose. America's energy future.* Ballinger, Cambridge, Mass.

18. Gillette, Robert, 1974. Breeder reactor debate: the sun also rises. *Science,* 184: 650–651.

19a. Hall, John, 1974. Bright ideas. *Nature,* 247: 331.

19b. Hall, David G., 1974. Tapping the sun's energy. *National wildlife,* 12: 18–20.

20. Hammond, Allen, 1974. Solar power; promising new developments. *Science,* 184: 1359–1360.

21. Illich, Ivan, 1974. Energy and social disruption. *Ecologist,* 4: 45–52.

22. Kasper, William C., 1974. Power from trash. *Environment,* 16: 34–38.

23. Kenward, Michael, 1974. Energy file. *New Scientist,* 63: 469.

24. ———, 1974. Energy file. *New Scientist,* 63: 332–333.

25. Kristoferson, Lars, 1973. Energy in society. *Ambio,* 2: 178–185.

26. Kubo, A. S., and D. J. Rose, 1973. Disposal of nuclear wastes. *Science,* 182: 1205–1211.

27. Landsberg, H. H., 1964. *Natural resources for U.S. growth.* Johns Hopkins, Baltimore.

28. Landsberg, H. H., and S. Schurr, 1968. *Energy in the United States.* Random House, New York.

29. Lewis, Richard, 1973. Shippingport—the killer reactor? *New Scientist,* 59: 552–553.

30. Lovins, Amory B., 1973. *World energy strategies: facts, issues and options.* Earth Resources Research Ltd., London.

31. MacKillop, Andrew, 1973. Unravel the grid. *Ecologist,* 3: 412–418.

32. ———, 1973. *Hydropower.* Wadebridge Ecological Centre, Wadebridge, Cornwall.

33. McPhee, John, 1973. The curve of binding energy. *New Yorker,* Dec. 3: 54–145; Dec. 10: 50–108; Dec. 17: 60–97.

34. Meadows, Donella H., et al. *The limits to growth*. Signet, New American Library, New York.
35. *Nature*, 1974. Soviet reactor accident: official. *Nature*, 248: 468.
36. *New Scientist*, 1974. Plutonium cancer warning spells trouble for breeders. *New Scientist*, 61: 542.
37. ———, 1974. Feedback. *New Scientist*, 62: 415.
38. Norman, Colin, 1974. Geothermal energy in California. *Nature*, 247: 81.
39. ———, 1974. Concerted criticism of breeder reactors. *Nature*, 248: 202–203.
40. ———, 1974. The Strangelove scenario. *Nature, 248: 725*.
41. Novick, Sheldon, 1974. Nuclear breeders. *Environment*, 6: 15.
42. O'Donnell, Sean, 1974. Ireland turns to peat. *New Scientist*, 63: 18–21.
43. Odum, Eugene P., 1959. *Fundamentals of ecology*. W. B. Saunders, Philadelphia.
44. Odum, Howard T., 1973. Energy, ecology, and economics. *Ambio*, 2: 220–223.
45. Osburn, Elburt F., 1974. Coal and the present energy situation. *Science*, 183: 477–481.
46. Ray, Carleton, et al., 1969. Statement of concern. *Environment*, 11: 20–27.
47. Schaeffer, M. B., 1970. *The resources base and prospective rates of development in relation to planning requirements*. Center for Study of Democratic Institutions, Santa Barbara.
48. SCEP, 1970. *Man's impact on the global environment*. M.I.T. Press, Cambridge.
49. Wade, Nicholas, 1974. Windmills: the resurrection of an ancient energy technology. *Science*, 184: 1055–1058.
50. Walton Smith, F. G., 1974. Power from the ocean. *Sea Frontiers*, 20: 87–89.
51. Woodwell, George M., 1967. Radiation and the pattern of nature. *Science*, 156: 461–470.

13

feeding the people

○
In 1974 most of the nations of the world were represented at the World Food Conference in Rome—to explore ways to meet the immediate food crisis in which tens of millions of people were facing the prospect of famine. The results were negligible. Some emergency food relief was provided, but for the most part, the conference was simply another opportunity for the poor nations to denounce the rich nations, and for the socialist world to vilify the capitalist world. Since it was a food conference, it could not, by the rules, spend much time talking about population or environment. Since all three are totally interrelated, attention to one topic alone would have, at best, produced a further imbalance for planet Earth. Nevertheless, producing enough food for four billion people to eat remains a desperate problem in the middle 1970's, and one which can only grow more severe.

During World War II it became apparent to all who were looking ahead to postwar years that a concerted effort would be needed to restore order to the chaos created by the destruction and dislocation resulting from the war. A famine in Bengal in 1943, during which millions died, was a portent of problems to face many areas unless great improvements were made in the food and agricultural status of most nations. Consequently, in Quebec in October, 1945, the states of the new United Nations joined together to form the Food and Agriculture Organization of the United Nations (FAO). The purpose of FAO was stated at its first conference by Lester B. Pearson of Canada:

FAO will bring the findings of science to the workers in food and agriculture, forestry and fisheries everywhere . . . . It will assemble, digest, and interpret information to serve as a basis for the formulation of policy, national and international. It can suggest action, but only through the activities of governments themselves can the objectives be finally won.[29]

FAO, among its other objectives, sought to increase world food supplies at a rate exceeding the growth of population, with a view to restoring the balance between food and population, initially to what existed in 1939, before World War II, but hopefully to move from there to end shortages of food everywhere.

In 1955, after 10 years of effort, FAO could announce some success and some failure.[7] In 1939, 49 percent of the world received less than 2200 Calories (kilocalories) of food energy daily, an amount believed to be the minimum for a person doing active work. By 1955, according to figures published by the Political and Economic Planning Group in Great Britain, 66 percent of the world population received less than 2200 calories per day. The situation had deteriorated. Still, in some areas there was success and FAO in 1955 was hopeful:

What is almost within human grasp is nothing less than the abolition of primary poverty in the last strongholds of poverty, and bringing of the low-income peoples, not to equality of income with the wealthiest peoples, but to within hailing distance, so that there is no longer a wide social and material gap between them.[29]

In 1965, after 20 years of effort, a pattern had clearly emerged. In the technologically advanced countries, which were initially well off in food supply, it proved to be possible to increase food supplies more rapidly than populations grew. In most of the world, where the food situation was critical, it proved to be difficult, if not impossible to increase food supplies at a rate equal to population growth. Despite great efforts, the amount of food produced lagged behind, so there was less food per head than before. All of Africa, all of Asia outside the USSR, and most of Latin America had an average consumption of less than 2000 calories per person per day. The director-general of FAO stated:[8]

The outlook is alarming. In some of the most heavily populated areas the outbreak of serious famine within the next five to ten years cannot be excluded. And, if food output everywhere just kept pace with population growth at the present level of consumption, by the end of this century the number of people who would be subject to hunger and malnutrition would be double what it is today.

By 1973 the situation had grown more desperate. Great numbers of people were starving in the drought-stricken region of the Sahel, on the borders of the Sahara, and it is likely we will never know how many died. Still greater numbers in India and Bangladesh seemed likely to die from hunger. Again the director-general of FAO stated to the press:

But in the name of reason, can this world of the 1970's, with all of its scientific prowess and its slowly growing sense of common purpose, go on enduring a situation in which the chances of enough decent food for millions of human beings may simply depend on the whims of one year's weather? Is this a tolerable human condition? Emphatically not.

Thus, we have progressed toward our goal of freedom from hunger, and reached the World Food Conference of 1974. Meanwhile the famine which would kill tens of millions, or hundreds of millions has not yet hit. It remains to be seen if 1975 will be the year of the big famine, predicted by some experts.[23] By one device or another those who are hungry seem to have managed to scrape together enough food to keep alive, if just barely alive.

Throughout this period when the world food situation has grown worse, we have witnessed some of the most remarkable gains in agricultural production, exceeding all expectations, in certain areas of the world. This too has been the period of the Green Revolution, which was to put an end to hunger, and seemed for a few brief years as though it would do just that.

AMERICAN AGRICULTURE

In Chapter 5, some of the history of American agriculture was traced, and it was noted it was a success story in terms of productivity. Corn yields, during the period from 1900 to 1950 averaged less than 2 metric tons per hectare. From 1950 to 1970 they were tripled, up to 6 metric tons per hectare. In 1972 the United States produced more than 141 million tons of corn—far more than any other country.

The success of American farm production was sufficiently obvious during the 1950's that it became government policy to encourage the retirement of land from agriculture into soil banks, conservation reserves, and the like. This good feature takes out of production those lands that were marginal, or in need of restoration. It led to an increased area available for forestry, wildlife, and recreation. Nevertheless, food production on the remaining areas continued to soar, and by 1961 the United States had an embarrassingly high food surplus. Along with Canada, Australia, and Argentina it was a principal contributor to the world's grain reserves. In 1961 reserve stocks of grain reached a level of 154 million metric tons. In addition, the idle U.S. cropland had a grain potential of 68 million metric tons. This was enough grain to meet all the world's grain needs for 95 days.[4] Why then was anybody hungry? Partly because farmers and all of the middlemen who profit from transporting, storing, or speculating on farm products are in business to make a profit and do not give food away free. The government, meaning all of us, can buy this food with tax dollars, and then give it away free. This was done on a fairly massive scale as part of the Food for Peace program, when 7.9 billion dollars worth of food aid was provided during the period 1960 to 1970. In order that this not look like a giveaway the recipient countries, in theory, paid for it. In fact they paid in money which could not be taken out of their country, and in the case of India, which received 3.2 billion dollars worth of food, the debt was finally canceled.[12] However, it is still not feasible to transport and distribute grain on a sufficiently massive scale to provide everybody with enough food—not when the grain is grown in the American Midwest, and the hungry people are in southeast Asia. The food provided helped prevent outright famine, but did not solve the food problem.

In 1974, however, the total grain reserves of the world had dwindled to 90 million metric tons. All of the once-idle U.S. farmland was back in production. This reserve was only adequate to meet world grain needs for 26 days.[4] In other words, the means for staving off famine, or buffering against the failure of food crops in any one year, were no longer there.

The success of American agriculture in boosting food production resulted from the interaction of a number of factors. Before World War II most American farms were diversified to some degree. Because horses were commonly used to pull farm machinery, cows were kept to produce milk and butter, and poultry for meat and eggs, at least some of the land was employed in growing feed for animals or as pasture. This resulted in at least a minimum amount of crop rotation. However, starting in the 1920's and becoming almost universal after World War II, farm livestock was replaced by farm machinery. Labor that used to be done by man or horse was done by machines burning petroleum. This led to a much greater output per man, although not necessarily a greater output per acre. Increased yields per acre resulted partly from the development of new varieties of crop plants—various hybrid corns and wheats which could produce much higher yields than the old breeds. These new hybrids, however, required massive fertilization if they were to reach their production potential. Consequently the use of chemical fertilizers, which were easily applied by machines, expanded greatly. Three elements in particular—phosphorus, nitrogen, and potassium— were required in large quantities, and in some farms lime was also needed to prevent soil acidity from building up. Many of the new crops also required irrigation, even in relatively high rainfall areas, since even a short period of less-than-optimum water supply could greatly reduce yields. With high value, high-yielding crops, diversification began to disappear on farms, and practices of crop rotation were abandoned. Farmers became specialists in producing a particular crop, and often were as dependent on the grocery store for their own food needs as any city person.

The spread of single-crop monocultures over wide areas brought a situation in which the danger of crop loss to insects or diseases was increased. This was overcome partly by a massive use of insecticides and fungicides and partly by the development of new pest-resistant strains of crop plants. The latter, however, do not retain their resistance for long since new strains of disease or new varieties of insect pests develop to take advantage of them. The plant breeder, therefore, is in a continual race to develop still newer strains of plants before the diseases catch up with the older ones. Even so, in 1970, 15 percent of the field corn in the United States was lost to the Southern corn leaf blight.[11]

The disappearance of most hand labor, and the use of machinery resulted in new problems also with farm weeds. This encouraged a growing use of herbicides such as 2-4D, 2-4-5T, and others.

Production of meat from poultry, hogs, beef cattle, or sheep also became a highly mechanized operation and one in which the specialist replaced the generalized farmer. New breeds of animals capable of fast growth, high milk production, or high egg yield were maintained under highly artificial conditions. Per capita consumption of beef increased from 70 pounds in 1910 to nearly 120 pounds in 1970, and a similar increase took place in the consumption of poultry.[4] All of this livestock, however, was fed by acreage which might otherwise have been used in producing food for direct human consumption. At best, about 20 percent of the food energy in grain becomes available as food energy in meat.

Between 1940 and 1970 the number of operating farms in the United States decreased from 6.3 million to 2.8 million, and the average farm size increased from 167 acres to 400 acres. In other words, small farmers tended to be forced out of business, whereas large company-owned farms—agrobusinesses—increased. The reason for this was partly because the massive investment in farm machinery is not economically feasible for the small holder. Between 1950 and 1970 the value of farm machinery in use in agriculture tripled, whereas the cost of operations, repairs, and depreciation on this machinery doubled. The actual number of people living on farms and engaged in agriculture decreased remarkably between 1940 and 1970. In 1940, 23 percent of the U.S. population lived on the farm—a total of 32 million people. By 1970 the numbers of farm people had declined to 9 million, or 4.8 percent of the total population.[24] These figures suggest that great efficiency has been achieved, where far fewer people can produce much more food. However, the figures are misleading. No figures are available to show how many people are employed in the industries that store, transport, process, and distribute farm crops, or in the industries that produce the farm machinery, fertilizers, pesticides, electric power, and fuel used on the farm. In earlier days most of the activities connected with the production, processing, and use of food were carried out on the farm, using only those energy sources available on the farm—man power and horse power. Now the activities are carried out elsewhere, and the actual farm population does only a small part of the labor involved in the whole process of providing food for people.

Far from being a total success story, it may well be that American agricultural practices in the 1970's will stand as an example for the rest of the world of how *not* to grow food. The reasons for this become apparent when we examine the energy side of agricultural production.

The massive increase in the cost of petroleum which took place in 1973, caused everybody to look more seriously at the ratios between energy input and energy output in a variety of processes, including agriculture. For American agriculture a number of analyses became available. David Pimentel et al. examined the energy picture for American corn production and discovered that we were using the equivalent of 80 gallons of gasoline per acre per year to produce corn, and that the ratio of energy input to energy output had become steadily less favorable from 1940 to 1970. They pointed out that if American techniques were used to feed all of the world's four billion people, the petroleum required in farm production alone would exhaust the world's reserves in less than 30 years—without any other uses of petroleum.[26] Yet, corn is not one of the high-energy-demanding crops, and Pimentel et al. only examined the energy actually used on the farm, or used in the processes which directly supply the farm. The energy requirements of the entire food production process are much greater.

M. J. Perelman calculated that the agricultural production process in the United States involved the employment of the equivalent of 150 gallons of gasoline per capita, to yield the equivalent in food energy of 30 gallons of gasoline per capita. In other words, 5 Calories were required to produce 1 Calorie.[24]

Hirst, in 1974, wrote that food production uses 12 percent of the total energy consumed in the United States. His calculations showed that energy use on the farms, food processing, food transportation, food distribution, and food preparation involves the input of 8 fossil-fuel-energy calories for every one Calorie of food consumed.[13,14] Yet agriculture is supposed to be a process in which free solar energy is converted into useful food energy, and to produce an energy surplus. Over most of the world, most of the time, it has. For example, so-called "primitive" agriculturalists, the Tsembaga people of New Guinea are said to manage an output of 20 food Calories for every Calorie of energy put into its production.[27] In Chinese wet rice agriculture a yield of 50 Calories for every 1 Calorie input is obtained.[17] These, however, are labor intensive, and not machine intensive ways of growing food.

In the analysis of energy use in corn production, Pimentel showed that farm machinery and fertilizers were principal consumers of fossil-fuel energy.[26] Nitrogen fertilizer is usually produced from natural gas, but can be produced from petroleum. Fossil fuel is used in large quantities to power the fertilizer plant as well as serving as the raw material for nitrogen production. With the increased cost of fuel, nitrogen fertilizer prices have also gone up—and in the poorer countries have become difficult to obtain. Phosphates are mined, rather than being produced in a factory, and are less energy demanding. Nevertheless, Morocco has virtually controlled phosphate exports, and has raised prices so that phosphates also are no longer readily available to poor farmers. Thus, problems of world food supply, already difficult enough, have been complicated because the agricultural system developed in the United States and Western Europe has been sold to the developing countries of the world. With high costs of fuel and fertilizer this system is breaking down.

THE GREEN REVOLUTION During the 1950's the Rockefeller Foundation sponsored a program in Mexico to adapt United States high-yield agriculture to Mexican conditions. Much of the effort went into developing a new hybrid dwarf wheat which would respond adequately to massive applications of fertilizer and would mature early. Through the efforts of Norman Borlaug and his associates this new variety of wheat was produced, widely planted, and as a result, Mexican grain yields began to soar. In 1941 Mexico produced only 50 percent of the wheat its people consumed. By 1960, despite an increase in population of 60 percent, Mexico was self-sufficient in wheat production. This was the beginning of what was to be known as the Green Revolution.[4]

In the 1960's, the International Rice Research Institute in the Philippines was successful in the development of new hybrid rices which showed similar characteristics of quick response to massive fertilizer applications. In the late 1960's and early 1970's high-yield wheats and rices were planted in many countries—the Philippines, Kenya, Pakistan, and India among them. Grain yields were tripled wherever an abundance of irrigation water, fertilizer, agricultural machinery, pesticides, and related inputs could be provided. Some agriculturalists believed the world food crisis had been forever ended. But then the problems began.[4]

Drought conditions were prevalent in the early 1970's, and without abundant water the new "miracle" grains produced less than the old native varieties. Extensive monocultures devoted to single varieties of wheat or rice proved far too susceptible to insect and disease attack— despite, or because of, the massive use of pesticides.[22] Furthermore, the new agricultural systems required heavy capital investment in machines, fertilizers, and the like and essentially were not available to any except the wealthier landowners. Small farmers were forced off their land. Unable to even afford the new high cost grains, many of them were pushed out to the marginal lands where they attempted once more to scratch out a subsistence living. Others were forced to join the hungry crowds in the slums of the big cities.[9,10] On top of all this came the increased price of oil and fertilizer in 1973, and all agricultural development schemes in Third World countries were hard hit. By 1974 there was no longer much talk about the Green Revolution, nor much optimism about supplying world food needs. Meanwhile, everywhere, marginal lands were again being farmed, often at great environmental cost. The loss of farmlands to soil erosion, salinization, and all the other ills which result from poor management, was tending to cancel any gains that resulted from bringing new land into production. In some areas, at least, the experts were beginning to turn at long last to an examination of traditional peasant agricultural methods to see if high yields might yet be produced without high inputs of energy and money. It was realized some of the older methods had been very good indeed.[1,21,25]

ALTERNATIVES There is nothing essentially wrong with an agricultural system which involves higher inputs of energy than are received in food output—providing the energy put in is cheap and inexhaustible. We use fuel in much more wasteful ways than in food production, and often for no worthwhile gain of any kind. However, an agricultural system based on a massive input of petroleum energy cannot endure since petroleum is no longer cheap and, certainly by the end of the century, will be scarcely available for this use. What then are the alternatives? Some hope that the combination of nuclear power and accelerated development of coal and oil shale can keep this agricultural system working. Others point out it is time to develop a new system, perhaps still a high-energy-input system, but one which makes use of locally available, renewable or inexhaustible resources, such as solar, wind, water, or vegetation power in place of fossil fuel or nuclear power.[2,21] Furthermore, since human labor is the one resource that is in abundant supply, many would urge that getting people back on the land is a first requirement. Thus Gould has pointed out that when English farm lands, producing under the machinery-fossil fuel-chemical fertilizer system, are occupied by housing developments food output actually goes up. The reason is the intensive hand care people give to their backyard vegetable gardens.[10]

There are many examples of people around the world who have practiced highly sophisticated and productive agriculture without benefit of machinery or inputs from the petroleum or chemical industries. China, for example, has apparently carried out an agricultural "miracle" in providing adequate food for its 800 million people. In the 1940's famine was a way of life, and death, for the Chinese people, of which there were then only 400 million. Now with the population doubled there is apparently no threat of starvation, and China is exporting grain. Intensive land care, high labor input, and most particularly the recycling of organic "wastes" play a large part in this success story.

In discussions and papers presented at the Cambridge symposium on the "Future of Traditional 'Primitive' Societies" in 1974, the generally successful agricultural practices of many people who live entirely outside the urban-industrial technocracy were reviewed. Notably successful are the Ifugao people of Luzon in the Philippines, who are noted for their elaborate terraces built on the lower slopes of the mountains they occupy. In addition to permanent, terrace agriculture they make use of a shifting "swidden" agriculture on the higher or steeper slopes, and take advantage of a great variety of forest crops and products from the uncultivated areas. An agriculturally supported density of 237 people per square kilometer lives in a reasonably affluent style of life. Crop diversification, intensive care of every square meter of land, and great attention of recycling of organic materials are involved in this successful land use.[6] Many tropical root crops, of course, have much higher yields than grain crops. Thus 30 tons per hectare of cassava can be harvested in Nigeria, using improved breeds of plants, but building on traditional methods.[25] By contrast 6 tons per hectare of American "high-fossil-fuel" corn are produced,[4] or 11 tons of "miracle-rice" (IR 24 variety) on experimental plots.[1] According to Vass, in Malaya on combination hog-fish-vegetable farms as much as 15,000 pounds of pork, 1500 pounds of fish, and an unestimated quantity of vegetables per hectare are produced. Admittedly there is some input of energy and chemicals into this system, but the yields are high by any standards.[28]

There is no option to suddenly shift from current methods of agriculture employed in North America, Western Europe, Japan, or those Third World countries that have followed these patterns—not unless we are

a

b

FOOD AND HUNGER

(a) There could be enough food for everyone, but only if the numbers of people can be stabilized and present levels of food production greatly increased. **(b)** In the 1970's drought hit the Sahelian region at the edge of the Sahara. Millions of domestic animals died and most people were left with little or no food. Here a nomad family forages for leaves from the few trees that remain alive. **(c)** In the 1970's the likelihood of severe famine confronts the people of Bangladesh. **(d)** Emergency grain shipments have thus far helped to reduce the number of deaths from starvation. But world grain reserves are no longer abundant. **(e)** Should America continue to try to feed the world?

really prepared to see mass starvation. There is, however, an absolute necessity to move forward now, while fossil fuels and materials are still available, to develop agricultural systems that are highly productive and *can be permanently sustained.* We cannot afford to continue practices that lead to soil erosion or to continue depletion of soil fertility. We cannot continue world systems which involve the sacrifice of the productivity and resources of one area in order to support people in another. World food banks, such as the ones proposed at the World Food Conference, are no substitute for a reasonable degree of local self-sufficiency.[12] Each people, each region, each nation should look to their own means for self-support. If they can produce surpluses of one commodity or another without sacrifice of their own long-term future, it will be to their advantage to do so. But surpluses gained at the sacrifice of long-term productivity are always a poor bargain—except perhaps for the exploiter who gains a quick profit. Agricultural systems based on the continued depletion of scarce, nonrenewable resources represent a sacrifice of future well-being to present affluence. If the human race is to have a long-term future they must be replaced.

CHAPTER REFERENCES

Brown, Lester R., and E. P. Eckholm, 1974. *By bread alone.* Praeger, New York.
Borgstrom, Georg, 1965. *The hungry planet.* Macmillan, New York.
President's Science Advisory Committee, 1967. *The world food problem.*
UNESCO, 1970. *Use and conservation of the biosphere.* Natural Resources Research 10, UNESCO, Paris.
Vogt, William, 1948. *Road to survival.* Wm. Sloane, New York.

LITERATURE CITED

1. Allen, Robert, 1974. New strategy for the Green Revolution. *New Scientist,* 63: 320–321.
2. Blaxter, Kenneth, 1974. Power and agricultural revolution. *New Scientist,* 61: 400–403.
3. Borgstrom, Georg, 1974. The food-population dilemma. *Ambio,* 3: 109–113.
4. Brown, Lester R., and E. P. Eckholm, 1974. *By bread alone.* Praeger, New York.
5. Chapman, Duane, 1973. An end to chemical farming. *Environment,* 15: 12–17.
6. Conklin, Harold C., 1974. Ifugao ethnography. *Aerial photography in anthropological field research.* Harvard University Press, Cambridge, Mass.
7. FAO, 1956. *The agricultural division of FAO, a summary of its organization, development and accomplishments.* FAO, Rome.
8. ———, 1965. *The state of food and agriculture.* FAO, Rome.
9. Franke, Richard W., 1974. Miracle seeds and shattered dreams in Java. *Natural History,* 83: 10–18, 84–88.
10. Gould, Nicholas, 1974. England's green revolution. *Ecologist,* 4: 58–60.
11. Gruchow, Nancy, 1970. Corn blight threatens crop. *Science,* 169: 3949.
12. Hardin, Garrett, 1974. Living on a lifeboat. *Bioscience,* 24: 561–568.
13. Hirst, Eric, 1974. Food-related energy requirements. *Science,* 184: 134–138.
14. ———, 1973. Living off the fuels of the land. *Natural History,* 82: 20–22.

15. Janzen, Daniel H., 1973. Tropical agroecosystems. *Science,* 182: 1212–1219.

16. Laurie, Peter, 1974. Pig ignorant. About self-sufficiency. *New Scientist,* 63: 472.

17. Lovins, Amory B., 1973. *World energy strategies: facts, issues, and options.* Earth Resources Research Ltd., London.

18. Mende, Tiber, 1973. *From aid to re-colonization. Lessons of a failure.* Harrap, London.

19. *New Scientist,* 1974. Methane—the most natural gas. *New Scientist* 61: 407.

20. Odum, Howard T., 1973. Energy, ecology, and economics. *Ambio,* 2: 221–227.

21. Omo-Fadaka, Jimoh, 1974. Industrialisation and poverty in the Third World. *Ecologist,* 4: 61--63.

22. Paddock, William C., 1970. How green is the Green Revolution? *Bioscience,* 20: 897–902.

23. Paddock, W., and E. Paddock, 1967. *Famine-1975!* Little, Brown, Boston.

24. Perelman, M. J., 1972. Farming with petroleum. *Environment,* 14: 8–13.

25. Pickstock, Michael, 1974. Filling Nigeria's larder. *New Scientist,* 63: 452–456.

26. Pimentel, David et al., 1973. Food production and the energy crisis. *Science,* 182: 443–449.

27. Rappaport, R., 1971. The flow of energy in an agricultural society. *Scientific American,* 224: 116–134.

28. Vass, K. F., 1963. Fish culture in freshwater and brackish ponds. *The better use of the world's fauna for food.* Symposium of the Institute of Biology, no. 11.

29. Yates, P. L., 1955. *So bold an aim.* FAO, Rome.

14.

putting things together— minerals

The exploiters of mineral resources have held a special, privileged role in human society since the beginnings of the industrial revolution—and most likely for long before that. Minerals were considered so precious and essential for the development of technology and civilization that those who sought them, those who arranged to have them brought out of the earth, and those who processed them have been given concessions rarely granted to other groups in society. This does not mean the miners themselves were well treated—far from it. Mining was work for slaves—hard, dirty, and dangerous. Later, miners were to be exploited for the lowest of wages under conditions of maximum hazard. Even today, with trade unionism firmly established, mining is rated as one of the most dangerous and unpleasant occupations. But those who own the mines are in a different category.

In the settlement of the United States during the nineteenth century, every effort was made to encourage exploitation of natural resources and settlement of the lands. However, national policy was not well defined. Opinions varied as to whether federal lands containing valuable minerals should be sold for a profit to the government, held in public ownership but leased to mining interests who would pay rents or royalties, or simply disposed of free of charge to those who extract their mineral resources. Quite naturally, those who wished to mine favored the latter alternative.

The issue was brought to a critical point by the California Gold Rush of 1849–1850. Most of the gold was found on public land. This had become the property of the United States when California entered the Union. However, prospectors and miners staked claims to mineral-bearing land and proceeded to exploit gold without any legal right to do so. As time passed, those who held substantial mineral resources attempted to establish their right to this ownership. Their friends in Congress in 1866 managed to sneak through an amendment to an unrelated bill which provided that anyone could obtain title to a mining tract and all of its minerals by filing a claim with the General Land Office, and by paying a nominal fee of 5 dollars an acre. Upon an expenditure of 1000 dollars in "improvements" to the claim, complete ownership of the land and its minerals was obtained.[10,13]

The 1866 Act applied only to "hard rock" mines and limited an individual's holding to 200 feet along the ore's vein. In 1870 an act was passed providing for the sale of placer mines based on alluvial deposits, at the cost of 2.50 dollars per acre for those who had registered an appropriate claim. Finally, the Mining Act of 1872 replaced the two preceding acts and gave the mining interests virtually unlimited rights on public lands. These included the right of entry for the purpose of prospecting, and the right to claim and develop mineral resources, and included all public lands except those specifically withdrawn from such uses. Thus even the National Wilderness System, established in 1964, and otherwise protected against disturbance, is available to mining interests. Obviously great fortunes could be and were made from the public wealth thus given away to private interests.[10,13]

In the presidency of Theodore Roosevelt, and through the influence of Gifford Pinchot, the idea that the public should benefit directly from public resources became established. Thus, in 1908 when one individual sought to take over the rim of the Grand Canyon through staking a series of mining claims on the overlooks, Roosevelt withdrew the area from the public domain and proclaimed it the Grand Canyon National Monument. In this category it was, like the National Park, exempt from mining claims. Furthermore, Roosevelt attempted to establish a leasing system for minerals and other resources of value including choice sites for hydro-electric installations. Unable to accomplish this during his administration, he still managed to reserve 75 million acres of public land bearing coal and phosphate resources, thus preventing private claims. The concept of mineral leasing of public resources finally became a reality with the passage by Congress in 1920 of the Mineral Leasing Act.[13] However, the question of special rights for mining companies remained an active one, and was one of the issues studied by the Public Land Law Review Commission in its report issued in 1970.[8]

The PLLRC recommended the principal of "maximum economic efficiency" apply to lands classified as being of principle value for their mineral resources. This was, of course, a far cry from the principle of multiple use of public lands for which conservationists had fought so long. The "dominant-use zoning" principle further recommended by the PLLRC would essentially turn over mineral lands to the exploiters with no other rights of use being recognized. Essentially, the recommendations of the Commission were pleasing to the miners, who retained all of their rights and privileges, but scarcely pleasing to anyone else who might have some other interest in lands containing mineral resources, or in the environment to be affected by the development of those lands.[8] In 1975 the recommendations of the PLLRC have not been approved by Congress.

The destructive impact of mineral extraction on the environment has in certain places been serious. An example of how bad things can get is again provided by the California Gold Rush. In pioneer California the mining interests and grazing interests virtually controlled the government. The early miners of Gold Rush days did little harm with their placer mining, but such small-scale activity was soon replaced. Streams were dammed and diverted to allow the gravels and sands of their beds to be worked over. In the process, aquatic resources were destroyed, whereas erosion and siltation were accelerated. However, in 1853 an even more destructive practice started: hydraulic mining. In this a jet of water was directed against a hill or mountain to wash away the gold-bearing deposits. These were then passed through sluices in which the gold was extracted. All of the rocks and debris were then washed on down the stream, or piled up in great drifts. An enormous amount of siltation and erosion resulted. Stream channels and major rivers were choked with silt. Winter and spring floods carried this debris over farmlands, destroying their productivity. Farmers attempted suits against the mining companies, with no success. Finally, after the town of Marysville was destroyed by a flood in 1875, which covered it with mining debris, the courts responded. After a long battle, in 1884, a permanent injunction against hydraulic mining was granted. By then, of course, millions of dollars worth of damage had been done, but the miners were not held responsible. Much of the land damaged during this period has yet to recover. Damage was done also by the practice of dredging rivers to extract gold from their gravels and, as might be expected, the mining companies were again not held responsible for the environmental damage that resulted from this activity.[10,13]

More than 4 million acres in the United States have been seriously damaged by surface mining. Although mining for fuels is responsible for the largest part of this damage, nonfuel minerals have also contributed. In some other countries the situation is even more severe. Surface mining for tin has damaged great areas of Malaysia. In Australia, mining for titanium ore along the beaches has had serious consequences for the biotic communities of the coastal zone as well as recreational beaches. In New Caledonia the entire top surface is being removed from much of the island in order to obtain nickel. In Nauru, Ocean, and other Pacific phosphate islands, entire islands are being destroyed to obtain this mineral. Always the mining companies are spared the consequences of their activities, both because of their political power and the realization that industrial civilization may grind to a halt, if the metals and other minerals it consumes at an ever-growing rate are not made available.

Occasionally, conservation interests win a struggle, at least for the interim. Through an all-out political campaign, British conservationists prevented the Rio Tinto Zinc Corporation from mining the Snowdonia National Park in Wales. In Papua-New Guinea, the new government has put a stop to some of the more destructive copper-mining activities. But, more often the results favor the mining interests. A look at the world resource picture helps explain why.

MINERAL WANTS AND NEEDS
It was noted in a previous chapter that the actual *needs* of humanity for energy are not the same as the *wants* or *demands* of people who live in a technological civilization. The same statement can be made about our needs for the raw materials from which the artifacts of technological civilization are formed. The human race existed for tens of thousands of years without making any use of the metallic resources of the earth. It

was not, in fact, until the coming of civilization that use of metals, and the demand for things made from mineral resources became of any consequence. In early civilization building stone, clay suitable for bricks or pottery, copper, tin, and a few other metals were sought and traded widely. Fraser Darling has told me that the devastation of forests, in northern China in areas where clay suitable for the making of fine pottery and porcelain is found, is responsible for the highly eroded landscapes which may still be seen there, thousands of years later. The wood was required in great quantities for the firing of these materials. Undoubtedly the smelting of copper had serious environmental effects in local areas of the ancient world, and took its toll in human health.

With the further development of civilization the demand for other metals increased—weapons of steel held the secret of success in warfare. By the time of the Roman Empire, the civilized states were placing heavy demands on the metals and nonmetallic minerals of their regions. Yet the demands were to grow enormously with the coming of industrial civilization. The age of fossil fuels has also been the age of iron and steel, an age of constant searching of the earth's crust, the ocean's waters, and the sea bottoms for additional supplies of minerals. Today's sophisticated and intricate technology requires elements which were scarcely known a few decades ago—the use of beryllium in rocketry is an example, or that of zirconium in nuclear power plants.

Much of the demand is for materials to be transformed into more or less worthless junk—all of the playthings and throwaways of civilization. Still more goes into the production of things which could be made to last, but instead are made to be replaced after a few years of use. The automobile is a prime example. Robert Entwistle has pointed out that the automobile industry alone uses 55 percent of the lead, 37 percent of the zinc, 21 percent of the steel, 14 percent of the nickel, and 10 percent of the aluminum consumed in the United States.[4] At long last cars are being recycled, but the practice is late in coming and hardly universal.

MINERAL SUPPLIES Supplies of metals and nonmetallic minerals are not evenly distributed around the world. One can find iron, nickel, gold, or sulfur almost anywhere on earth, but the quantities are so low and the dispersal so great that the energy expended in gathering, processing, and concentrating these supplies is too great to be considered. We are largely dependent on those areas where, through the action of various geological processes, the metals or other minerals are concentrated in quantities sufficient to justify the energy costs involved in their extraction and processing.

Some idea of what is available, in the broadest sense, is provided by a consideration of the elements which make up the earth's crust, the atmosphere, and the oceans. This is shown in Table 19. It will be obvious many of the materials used in considerable quantities by civilization are not present in abundance on earth. Only because high concentrations exist in certain areas is it possible to make use of them.

a

b

INDUSTRIAL POLLUTION

(a) A man-made rival for the Grand Canyon—the Bingham copper mine in Utah. (b) Total devastation in Tennessee caused by fumes from copper smelting. (c) Copper mining and smelting in Arizona. Will the Tennessee experience be repeated? (d) Steel mills in Wales and workers' housing. Is there a need for "progress" at any cost? (e) Junked cars—a rich potential ore?

c

d

e

TABLE 19[9,12]
Composition of the
Earth's Crust and
Biosphere

ELEMENT	PERCENTAGE BY WEIGHT IN EARTH'S CRUST	PERCENTAGE COMPOSITION OF	
		ATMOSPHERE	OCEANS
Oxygen	46.60	20.99	85.79
Silicon	27.72	trace	trace
Aluminum	8.12	trace	trace
Iron	5.00	trace	trace
Calcium	3.63	trace	0.05
Sodium	2.83	trace	1.14
Potassium	2.59	trace	trace
Magnesium	2.09	trace	0.14
Titanium	0.44	trace	trace
Hydrogen	0.14	0.01	10.67
Nitrogen	trace	78.03	less than 0.002
Argon	trace	0.94	trace
Carbon	trace	0.03	0.002
Chlorine	trace	trace	2.07

A deposit of any mineral is known as an *ore,* if the mineral is present in such concentration and quantity that it can be extracted profitably under the technological or economic conditions which exist, or can be foreseen for the short-term future. It follows that certain mineral deposits which are not *ores* today will be *ores* tomorrow if prices go up, technology changes, or important demands arise. *Reserves* of minerals constitute those ores that are known to exist (measured or indicated reserves), or can be inferred to exist, at a high probability (inferred reserves). *Potential reserves or ores* are those known to exist and would become ores if technological or economic conditions changed.[7]

It is impossible, therefore, to speak with accuracy about the supplies, demands, or future prospects for any of the nonliving materials used in technological civilization. We do not know, in the first place, the location of all available supplies. Each year brings some new discoveries, and often these are of great quantities. Second, we do not know what demands will be. If we shift from automobiles as they now exist—and obviously we must—to other vehicles or means of transportation, then demands for some metals (e.g., for batteries for electric cars) may go up, whereas demands for the heat-resistant metals used in high-temperature internal-combustion engines will go down. Finally, new discoveries and improvements in technology may affect both demand and supply.

The present demands for metals in the United States are presented in Table 20. The number of metals consumed on a large scale in the United States (expenditure of more than one dollar per person for them) has increased from two in 1900 (copper and iron) to eleven in 1970 (chromium, lead, zinc, aluminum, silver, gold, nickel, tin, uranium). By the year 2000 it is believed by some forecasters that more metals will be added to this group, notably titanium, magnesium, sodium, molybdenum, niobium, and tantalum.[14] This is, of course, being optimistic about the future of technological civilization.

To attempt to forecast the future is to run into the conflicts between technological optimists and the others. Some believe that new discoveries, the development of new synthetics and composites, more efficiency in production, and substitution of plentiful for scarce materials will keep supplies of essential materials available into the indefinite future.[14] However, a great number of more pessimistic viewpoints deserve some attention. These take into account not only present demand, but also the steady increase in demand that has now gone on for several decades. They take into account not only the needs of the industrialized nations of today, but also the change in the demand picture if all nations are brought to a high standard of living, and have requirements equivalent to the now industrialized world. From these viewpoints there is no doubt that all known supplies of many minerals that are now required by civilization will be exhausted before the end of the century. Even if great new ores are discovered, if demand continues to increase, the time when civilization will run out of these materials will not be greatly postponed. The following list is illustrative of the minerals that are in short supply:[2,3,6,7]

Silver	Tin	Platinum
Mercury	Copper	Uranium-235
Lead	Tungsten	Molybdenum
Zinc	Gold	Nickel

Not everyone will agree on this list. However, if we extend the horizon past the year 2000 then still other metals and minerals would have to be added to it. Furthermore, the industrialized nations do not neces-

TABLE 20		
Estimated Per Capita Consumption of Metals in the United States,[1] 1975		POUNDS PER PERSON PER YEAR
	Steel	1550
	Copper	26
	Lead	20
	Zinc	17
	Aluminum	47
	Chromium	20
	Manganese	11
	Nickel	2.1
	Tin	1.2
	Antimony	0.1
	Magnesium	1 to 10
	Molybdenum	0.4
	Cadmium	0.1
	Cobalt	0.2
	Tungsten	0.1
	Beryllium	0.1

sarily control the reserves of the minerals they require in great quantity, and we can expect continuing pressure from the Third World nations to receive better prices for those minerals they do control. Copper and cobalt from Zaire, tin from Malaysia, tungsten from China, and chromium and manganese from Southern Africa are all likely to cost more in the future than the industrialized world would like to pay.

The mineral resources of the ocean floor are going to receive increasing attention in the future, as the technology for mining them at an economical profit becomes available. There are undoubtedly great concentrations of manganese, cobalt, nickel, copper, zinc, and phosphates at the bottom of the sea.[11] The environmental costs of mining them, however, could be staggering.

It must be recognized that civilization first made use of the most accessible, highest grade, and easily workable deposits of minerals. When these were exhausted, or became too difficult to obtain, attention shifted to other deposits or to substitute materials. Technological civilizations came into existence because certain ores could be worked readily with relatively primitive technology. But these ores were the first to be depleted. Now we are drawing, for the most part, on ores which can only be extracted by an advanced technology and with high expenditures of energy. If technological civilization were to break down to any serious extent—such as would result from a major war—we would have difficulty obtaining the tools and machines required to extract the minerals needed to build new tools and machines. Technological civilization is built, not only on the accumulation of knowledge passed down from the past, but also on the accumulation of tools, implements, and machines—the processed and manufactured products of past technology. Any serious shattering of this framework could bring conditions under which we might not be able to recover. The old, easily accessible sources of materials no longer exist—they were "worked out" long in the past.[1]

The exploitation and use of mineral resources is likely to be determined in the future by the energy cost. Recognizing that petroleum will be exhausted (unless a serious conservation program begins), and that coal cannot last indefinitely in the face of increasing demand, the idea that we can forever make use of lower and lower grades of ores will have to be abandoned. Instead, it is likely we will learn, when energy costs are counted, that there are many things we can just as well do without— and perhaps be happier for their absence.[5]

On the brighter side, we do not really consume most of the mineral resources we use. The copper and bronze implements of ancient Egypt and Babylonia are still around today. Materials become dispersed, oxidation occurs, but the rate of loss is not necessarily high—especially for metals. A skyscraper or a junkyard can be regarded as a rich potential ore. We can reclaim or recycle many of the minerals we now discard, and fortunately the energy cost of doing so is not necessarily high.[5] Reclamation and recycling can be forced, not only by the scarcity or energy cost of new materials, but by the cost of pollution and disposal brought about by our current ways of doing things. In the future there will probably be less talk about renewable, or nonrenewable resources, and more emphasis on *recyclable* resources. However, the total amount of minerals in use at any one time will always be limited. We cannot recycle a building and continue to live in it.

CHAPTER REFERENCES

National Academy of Sciences, 1969. *Resources and man.* W. H. Freeman, San Francisco.

United Nations, Statistical yearbooks. United Nations, New York.

U. S. Bureau of Mines, Minerals yearbooks. Government Printing Office, Washington, D.C.

LITERATURE CITED

1. Brown, Harrison, 1954. The challenge of man's future. Viking Press, New York.
2. Cloud, Preston, 1969. Resources, population and quality of life. Proceedings, AAAS, Boston, mimeo.
3. Dunham, Sir Kingsley, 1974. How long will our minerals last? *New Scientist,* 61: 129–130.
4. Entwistle, Robert, 1973. The crisis we won't face squarely. *Sierra Club Bull.,* 58: 9–12, 32.
5. Lovins, Amory B., 1973. *World energy strategies: facts, issues and options.* Earth Resources Research Ltd, London.
6. Meadows, Donella et al., 1972. *The limits to growth.* Signet, New American Library, New York.
7. Netschert, Bruce C., and H. H. Landsberg, 1961. *The future supply of the major metals.* Resources for the Future, Washington.
8. Pyle, Hamilton K., ed., 1970. *What's ahead for our public lands?* Natural Resources Council of America, Washington.
9. Riley, Charles M., 1959. *Our mineral resources.* Wiley, New York.
10. Roske, Ralph J., 1968. *Everyman's Eden. A history of California.* Macmillan, New York.
11. Schaefer, Milner, 1970. *The resources base and prospective rates of development in relation to planning requirements.* Center for Study of Democratic Institutions, Santa Barbara.
12. Smith, Guy-Harold, ed., 1965. Conservation of mineral resources. *Conservation of natural resources.* Wiley, New York, pp. 327–349.
13. Udall, Stewart, 1963. *The quiet crisis.* Holt, Rinehart and Winston, New York.
14. Westbrook, J. H., 1970. Materials for tomorrow. *Science and technology in the world of the future.* Wiley-Interscience, New York, pp. 329–365.

13

the final limits— pollution

One of the characteristics of the human animal is a wide range of environmental tolerance, the ability to continue to exist under conditions from which most species would flee. This has enabled human societies to spread over the face of the earth, to increase and multiply despite what would appear to be a great number of physical handicaps. People can't fly without machines, they can't run very fast, they are not very strong—but they have an incredible ability to "take it," to endure. A few other species—rats, mice, starlings, pigeons—seem able to tolerate the conditions under which people live, and they accompany mankind around the world. Fleas, lice, and house flies also qualify. This human trait, however, seems to be one which would actually permit people to destroy the biosphere. The ability to accept thoroughly unwholesome conditions, can permit these conditions to finally build up to the danger point. There is no doubt, if nothing else works, pollution can set the final limits to human growth and expansion. There are limits to the amounts and kind of poisons the living systems of the biosphere can tolerate, before they begin to unravel and fall apart so that life on earth begins to disappear. We do not know precisely where those limits are, and this is what encourages people to gamble. We take a risk whenever we add to the earth's burden of pollution, but if the stakes seem reasonably high, if a profit can be made, there are always people willing to take the risk. So we go on playing Russian roulette with the environment, hoping that nobody has put extra loaded cartridges into the cylinder.

Pollution has been a theme running throughout this book, and some aspects of it have already been discussed at length. This chapter looks at other aspects of the problem, and perhaps we can find ways in which it can be all tied together. There is little doubt that pollution usually results from a failure to realize and act on the knowledge that in the biosphere the rules of physics apply—all actions have equal and opposite reactions.

THE PESTICIDE PROBLEM In the desperate race to produce food faster than populations would grow, humanity has resorted to some desperate measures. In Chapter 13 we noted that a characteristic of American agriculture since World War II, and of most agriculture in the developed world has been the employment of pesticides. This has been forced by the spread of monocultures which leave great areas planted to a single variety of a single crop species, and the extent to which mechanical and chemical devices have replaced human labor on the farm. Starting during World War II a whole new variety of pesticides were produced by the chemical industries, and the use of these has gone hand and hand with the new agriculture, spreading with the Green Revolution into the countries of the Third World.

The first of the new pesticides was DDT, developed on a large scale during the war when it proved effective in controlling populations of lice, fleas, and other disease-bearing insects. The initial impact of this chemical on both public health and agriculture was so encouraging that it was adopted and widely used with little investigation of its side effects. The use of DDT virtually eliminated malaria in some parts of the world. The use of this and other related insecticides knocked back populations of crop-destroying insects, and contributed to the gains in agricultural yield. But, unfortunately, biotic communities are complex and not amenable to such simple solutions to human problems.

Insect pests initially can be controlled by an application of a pesticide such as DDT at a level not harmful to birds and mammals. Control, however, is not eradication, and some insects always survive. Frequently these will be individuals most resistant to the pesticide. If this resistance is inheritable, a DDT-resistant population of cinch bugs, bag worms, scale insects, or other pests will breed following several applications of this chemical.[29] It then becomes necessary to increase the dosage or find a more lethal chemical. Eventually, control efforts may lead to applications of poisons at levels toxic to birds, mammals, or to man himself. Insects breed rapidly and produce large numbers of offspring. It takes relatively little time to develop pesticide-resistant populations. The slower breeding vertebrates are not so fortunate. But this is only part of the problem.[29]

In 1962, Rachel Carson attracted national attention to pesticides with the publication of her book, *Silent Spring*. In her words the consequences of our continued careless use of pesticides might result one year in the arrival of a springtime in which "There was a strange stillness. The birds, for example—where had they gone? Many people spoke of them, puzzled and disturbed. . . . On the mornings that had once throbbed with the dawn chorus of robins, catbirds, doves, jays, wrens, and scores of other bird voices there was no sound; only silence lay over the fields and woods and marsh." *Silent Spring* has been accused of scientific inaccuracy, but Miss Carson's emotional approach accomplished what a thousand scientific papers could not do—awakened the people to an awareness of the hidden dangers of pesticides. Later, more sober accounts, but equally valid indictments, were to appear. These were well presented in Robert Rudd's book, *Pesticides and the Living Landscape*.[29]

The pesticides which have been effectively and widely used in recent decades are organic in nature. One group, the chlorinated hydrocarbons, includes DDT, DDD, dieldrin, chlordane, and endrin among others. The other group, the organophosphates, includes malathion, parathion, and TEPP. Of the two, the first group has presented the most problems. DDT, for example, persists on soil and vegetation long after it has been applied. Repeated dosages may therefore be consumed by animals. It is also a broad-spectrum pesticide, meaning it effects many kinds of animals other than the particular insect for which it was intended. It is a cumulative poison; animals store it in their fatty tissues and may build up high concentrations in their internal organs even though the initial field concentration was at a level not toxic to most species. The organophosphates, although highly poisonous, are generally not cumulative nor do they as a rule persist on the ground.[29] (Table 21).

As a method for control of pests, the most widely employed pesticides have this disadvantage: since they affect the entire community and not just the pest species, they kill off the predators and parasites which normally feed on the insect as well as the pest itself. They thus simplify the biotic community and generate instability. Lacking effective enemies, the pest species can increase more rapidly and to higher levels, before the populations of its former predators and parasites can recover sufficiently to again exercise some control. The control chemicals thus tend to create a continuing demand for more or better control chemicals. The agriculturalist who seeks to protect his crops is likely to make this de-

TABLE 21
Relative Toxicity of Pesticides

PESTICIDE	LD^{50} IN MILLIGRAMS PER KILOGRAM BASED ON WHITE RATS[a]	LC^{50} AT 11°C. MILLIGRAMS PER LITER OF WATER BASED ON FISH[b]
CHLORINATED HYDROCARBONS		
Aldrin	40.0	0.0082
Dieldrin	46.0	0.0055
DDT	250.0	0.005
Endrin	12.0	0.0044
Heptachlor	90.0	
Lindane	125.0	n.e. at 0.03[c]
Toxaphene	69.0	0.0022
Endosulfan	110.0	
Telodrin	4.8	
ORGANOPHOSPHATES		
Malathion	1500.0	0.55
Parathion	8.0	0.065
Methyl parathion	15.0	
Azinphosmethyl	15–25	0.055
TEPP	1.6	
Mevinphos	6.0	0.83
Ethion	208.0	0.42
Temik	1,0	
Trichlorphon	450.0	n.e. at 1.0
CARBAMATES		
Carbaryl	540.0	
Zectran	15–36	n.e. at 1.0

Source. Kevin P. Shea, 1969, "Name Your Poison," *Environment,* 11 (7): 30.[32]
[a] Dose required to kill 50 percent of population.
[b] Concentration in water required to kill 50 percent of population.
[c] No effect.

mand. If other methods were available, he might turn to them, but chemical control seems simple, cheap and, initially at least, effective.

An example of the kind of problem which has developed has been presented by Rudd.[29] In the 1930's a reddish fire ant was accidentally introduced into Alabama and, thereafter, spread widely throughout the southern states. These ants built earth mounds that interfered with crop cultivation, they were capable of delivering a stinging bite, and they reportedly did some damage to crops and livestock. In 1957 the United States Department of Agriculture took action against them in cooperation with the states involved. A major program of control started using the chlorinated hydrocarbons, dieldrin and heptachlor. During 1957 to 1958 over two and a half million acres were aerially sprayed with these chemicals. As a result, "Fish, wildlife, livestock, and poultry suffered losses; the destruction of wildlife bordering on catastrophic." Outbreaks of other insect pests, presumably stimulated by the destruction of their natural enemies, took place. Fifteen million dollars were spent on the control program. The fire ant remained in the South.[29]

At Clear Lake, California, the use of DDD to control a gnat population caused a reduction to near elimination in the population of the western grebe, a diving bird for which the lake was famous. Subsequent studies revealed that the grebes concentrated the chemicals in their tissues to a level 80,000 times as great as the amount originally applied to the lake.[29] Elsewhere, control programs against spruce budworms and gypsy moths, insects which do serious damage to forests, caused significant wildlife losses from DDT poisoning. Dieldrin and aldrin, used against Japanese beetles, caused wildlife mortality. Elsewhere in the world, in Japan for example, losses of wildlife to a point of near extinction for some species have been reported.[38] In Ecuador, massive fish kills followed the spraying of banana plantations with a fungicide. In Malaya, the use of insecticides in oil palm plantations stimulated much more serious outbreaks of the bagworm pest than those which occurred before the pesticide was used.[7] In the tropics generally, where biological controls are normally more operative, the potential hazards from continued use of pesticides are known to be high, but have yet to be fully assessed.[10]

Yet all this was only a beginning and it was not until the late 1960's and early 1970's that the results began to accumulate. Perhaps the basis for the trouble is illustrated in this small table based on studies in Lake Michigan:[17]

	DDT CONCENTRATION (PARTS PER MILLION)
General environment	
Lake bottom sediments	0.0085
Small invertebrates	
(zooplankton)	0.41
Fish	3.00 to
	8.00
Herring gulls	3,177.00

Since DDT is not broken down appreciably by biological action (it is not strongly biodegradable), it accumulates as it passes up the food chain from one organism to another. Initially low concentrations in the environment become very high, indeed, when they reach the terminal organisms in the food chain, the meat-eating or fish-eating organisms.

In England, birds of prey began to decline in numbers starting in the early 1950's. The cause was not known. A little later a similar decline was observed in the United States. Slowly the story began to unravel.[31] The first evidence of the trouble, although it was not recognized as such at the time it was published, was in an article entitled "Stimulatory effects of chlordane on hepatic microsomal drug metabolism in the rat" by L. G. Hart and his co-workers, which appeared in the *Journal of Toxicology and Applied Pharmacology*.[16] Essentially, these researchers had found chlordane, a relative of DDT, reduced the ability of the liver to produce the enzymes needed to render harmless the activity of drugs (barbiturates). This article appeared in 1963. In 1964 it was found that the use of DDT to control mosquitoes, blackflies, and gypsy moths in the Lake George area of New York caused a complete loss of lake trout fry.[3] Similarly, in 1966, Joseph Hickey and his associates at the University of Wisconsin presented the data on pesticides in Lake Michigan shown above.[17]

It was not until 1967 that investigations began to focus on the cause of loss of the birds of prey. In that year Derek Ratcliffe in England found that eggshell weight and thickness had decreased from 8 to 24 percent in birds of prey in England between pre-1947 (when DDT came into wide use) and the post-1947 period.[27] The next year, Joseph Hickey and his associates reported similar findings in raptorial and fish-eating birds in North America.[18] This was then related to findings by D. B. Peakall in New York showing that DDT or dieldrin caused a rapid metabolism and breakdown of sex hormones in birds.[26] Data then began to accumulate from many directions. By 1970 there was no longer the slightest doubt that DDT and its relatives, through interfering with the sex hormonal regulation of metabolism in birds, was leading to the production of thin-shelled eggs, or eggs without shells, and was further interfering with the survival of any young which escaped the breakage of eggs during the process of nesting. In 1970 disturbing reports came in from the Channel Islands of California: a virtually complete failure of the brown pelican to bring any nests through to a successful hatch as a result of DDT accumulation. Pelican eggs contained 2600 parts per million of DDE (a product of the metabolism of DDT).[14] Similarly the double-crested cormorants, pelagic cormorants, common murres, and common egrets along the California coast showed similar effects. Plankton in the coastal waters was contaminated with DDT, which thus entered the food chain. Catches of mackerel off the California coast were seized and condemned when it was shown they contained 20 times more DDT than the allowable "safe" level for human consumption.

It had become increasingly apparent in 1970 that we were in danger of losing all of the birds that are high on food chains—hawks, eagles, falcons, owls, herons, egrets, and seabirds—and that there was no reason to expect the effects of pesticides to stop there. Fish and aquatic invertebrates of many species proved to be particularly vulnerable, and great damage has been reported to food fish production in some areas. Deaths and reproductive losses of marine mammals have also been attributed to accumulations of organochlorine pesticides, of which DDT is the most widespread. George Woodwell has estimated that as much as one billion pounds of DDT alone might now be circulating in the biosphere.[36] It has been found from the Antarctic to Greenland—in areas where it has never been employed but has drifted on air or water currents.[33] Charles Wurster found that, at a level of 100 parts per billion in seawater, DDT could drastically reduce photosynthesis in plant plankton, the base of all oceanic food chains.[37]

Studies carried out by the University of Miami revealed that oil slicks in the ocean appeared to concentrate oil—soluble pesticides such as DDT and dieldrin. One oil slick investigated off Miami revealed 10,000 times more dieldrin in the thin surface film of oil than in the water immediately below. This could, of course, bring great danger to surface-feeding marine life, including the animal plankton. Studies carried out by the National Science Foundation and the National Ocean and Atmospheric Agency revealed the widespread distribution of petroleum in the form of tar balls throughout the oceans. Again these were found to contain dissolved organochlorine pesticides as well as the equally dangerous PCBs (polychlorinated biphenyls) in high concentrations. Since these tar balls attract marine organisms, probably for shelter, the likelihood of their poisoning is increased.[6,32]

We have once again put ourselves into a dilemma. The World Health Organization, faced with controlling malaria and other insect-borne diseases does not want to abandon DDT which is relatively cheap, and still effective enough against some disease vectors. Agricultural and forestry departments, seeking to increase yields, do not want to give up these tools. But the end results of these humanitarian activities could be disastrous.

Action has been taken in many nations to ban the use of DDT and its relatives—Sweden and Switzerland are examples. In others such as Great Britain, the use of organochlorines is carefully controlled. In the United States such uses are under some measure of control. But in the developing nations of the world the use of these pesticides is still expanding. If they would stay in place, this would not be so bad, but stream flow, ocean currents, and air movements take them everywhere. At what point does the system break down?

Ironically enough the answer to the pesticides problem, insofar as agricultural production is concerned, is the same answer to the problem of how to wean agriculture from its fatal dependence on fossil-fuel energy—encouraging diversity and natural ecological processes. Studies in the Soviet Union have shown that where DDT is used, the soil fauna is also knocked out and takes four years to recover.[12] Yet the same soil fauna, and flora as well, is needed to maintain the soil fertility which would reduce the need for chemical fertilizers. Encouraging the nitrogen-fixing organisms in the soil can remove the need for massive applications of the energy-wasting artificial nitrogen fertilizer. Experience in many parts of the world has shown that with a high crop diversity, the need for pest control is greatly reduced if not eliminated. Biological controls, using predatory insects, or the disease organisms which attack pest insects has been highly effective against scale insects, Japanese beetles, and other crop pests—but this activity receives far less support than goes into the development of new chemical poisons.[29]

Thus with pesticides, as with most pollutants, the answer is not simple, since the problem lies with the entire agricultural system. A highly mechanized, low manpower, high energy farming system creates the demand for pesticides. A diversified, organically balanced system that receives a lot of human care does not require the poisons and may, over the long run, produce more food.

AIR POLLUTION There are many experts who give air pollution first rank among conservation problems because of its potential for threatening the life and health of millions of people, and ultimately perhaps, all life on earth. It is not a new problem, except for its present global dimensions. People have been affected seriously and have been killed by polluted air ever since the Industrial Revolution.

Particulate matter in the air, in the form of dust or smoke, has caused problems to human health and comfort in some places at some times throughout history. To this was added, starting with the Middle Ages and increasing ever since, the by-products of the combustion of coal and later of petroleum. In this century the internal combustion engine has become a major source of air pollutants. Since World War II, radioactive elements from nuclear explosions and power plants, and the wide range of new chemical pesticides have joined the list of poisons in the air. To these can be added a whole range of other materials produced by industry or transportation: dust from cement factories, fumes from pulp mills, exhausts from jet planes, aerosols from spray cans, PCBs and heavy metals from other industrial processes, and so on. We are adding new and potentially dangerous chemical pollutants to the air faster than we can analyze the effects or dangers from the existing ones. In many places we have reached a crisis stage. A new word, *smog,* has been added to the language to describe the poisonous mixture which has taken the place of what was once harmless fog and haze.

The recent history of air pollution disasters starts with the Meuse Valley in Belgium. In December, 1930, a heavy concentration of smog in this area killed 60 people. In October, 1948, Donora, Pennsylvania experienced a high concentration of air pollutants which caused widespread respiratory illness resulting in 17 deaths. In London, a long period during which there were many minor disasters caused by the cities infamous "black fogs" culminated in December, 1952, when 4000 people were believed to have died from breathing polluted air. In all of these disasters, the primary blame was placed on high concentrations of sulfur dioxide, a by-product of coal combustion or of the burning of fuel oil with a high sulfur content. The polluters were both the ordinary citizens, burning coal or fuel oil to heat their houses, and the factories and other industrial plants which burned large quantities of these fuels.[8,13]

There has been more than a little success in cleaning up the visible, particulate pollution resulting from coal and fuel oil combustion. In Pittsburgh which was once known for its dirty air, the factories no longer pour out visible smoke and ash, and the buildings are no longer coated with soot. In London the black fogs are a thing of the past. Sulfur dioxide, however, is more difficult to remove. It is invisible, and people are less likely to complain about it. Nevertheless, it combines with the moisture in the air to form sulfuric acid droplets. Starting in the 1960's, and becoming steadily worse, sulfur dioxide, without the particulates which used to partially neutralize it, is falling out as "acid rain" in Scandinavia, the eastern United States, and elsewhere. What effects this will have on vegetation, animal life, man-made structures, and people themselves has yet to be fully analyzed, but we know the effects will not be good. Attention to one component of a polluting system, therefore, may simply make the action of the other components more severe.

Air pollution crises usually result from weather conditions. Normally in daytime air temperatures will decrease from the ground upward. Warmed air, near the ground, will rise, and as it does so will cool. This upward movement of air will carry pollutants away from the zone where people live. Wind will carry them away from their area of origin, disperse them, and mix them. Under certain conditions, however, the normal air temperature gradient changes. For example, a mass of warm air may move in with a weather front, and overlay the cooler air below. A *temperature inversion* will result. Inversions also occur as a result of the cooling of the air near the ground during winter. This creates a stagnant layer of cold air, and the familiar winter mists of the countryside. On seacoasts, also, there may be a movement in summer of cooler air from over the ocean, which will force the warm air inland upward, and may then be held for long periods near the ground until it becomes warmer than the air above. With such inversions, the upward movement of air is prevented and pollutants are trapped within the zone where human activities are concentrated.

Inversions frequently persist for several or more days during times when there is little horizontal air movement to carry pollutants away from their source. The frequency at which inversions occur varies from one place to another. New York, which produces enormous quantities of air pollutants, escapes disaster because inversions are relatively infrequent and seldom persist for long. Los Angeles, with a lower total output of pollutants, has frequent inversions and long periods of heavy smog.[8,24,25]

A region, such as the Los Angeles basin, within which air masses rest and develop uniform characteristics differing from those in an adjoining area, is known as an *airshed*. Sources of pollution anywhere within an airshed can affect the entire region within it.

Air pollution is regarded primarily as a threat to human health. It has been estimated by Lave and Seskin that if air pollution were reduced 50 percent there would be a saving to the United States of over 2 billion dollars just from the time lost in work and the medical expenses from bronchitis, pneumonia, lung cancer, cardiovascular diseases, and other related sicknesses.[19] However air pollution also directly damages buildings and other structures. The cost of repair and prevention runs into additional hundreds of millions of dollars, and becomes critical when architectural masterpieces or historical monuments of great value are involved. Air pollution affects all plant and animal life. Pine trees are particularly susceptible and have been damaged greatly in the mountains around Los Angeles, as well as elsewhere. Lichens, which dominate the arctic tundras are highly vulnerable to sulfur dioxide pollution.[30] The cut-flower industry and many kinds of agricultural crops have been pushed out of the area of heavy air pollution in southern California.[24,25]

There are two major types of air pollution in the United States: that resulting primarily from the burning of coal and high-sulfur fuel oils, which characterizes the eastern and midwestern part of the country and that resulting primarily from other causes, particularly automobile engines. The two intergrade in many places, and locally a different kind of pollution—for example, that emanating from pulp mills—is more important. Throughout the United States the automobile has risen to first place as a cause of air pollution, and in California it has long held this position. It has been estimated that 42 percent of air polluting emissions in the United States are produced by transportation.[9]

Los Angeles, one of the first cities faced with a major air pollution problem, has done many things to try to solve it. In 1947 the California legislature passed an enabling act assigning the authority to California counties to control stationary sources of air pollution. Los Angeles County moved to control the emissions from industrial plants and to stop the burning of refuse in municipal dumps. Next, a more difficult step was taken through forbidding the burning of trash in home incinerators. Space heating of buildings was the next target, and the use of high-sulfur fuels was forbidden. Despite all of these controls, smog problems grew worse. In 1955 the California legislature passed an act creating multiple-county Air Pollution Control Districts, thus providing for uniform regulations in counties sharing a common airshed. However, in southern California it had become apparent that the major offender, the source of 80 percent of pollution, was the automobiles, and this could not be controlled by a local district. In 1960 a state Motor Vehicle Pollution Control Board was established. Through the action of this board, it is now mandatory that all new motor vehicles registered in the state be equipped with devices which reduce the quantity of pollutants in automobile exhausts. These devices, however, are still inefficient, and the pollution problem remains, and grows worse.[24,25]

Automobile-caused air pollution is a symptom of a sick transportation system. It will probably not be solved by tacking more and more expensive devices on automobile exhaust systems. It could be solved by providing a healthier form of transportation. Yet the federal government can provide 40 billion dollars to build an interstate highway system for automobiles and trucks, while doing very little to promote relatively nonpolluting and energy-efficient rail or other rapid public transportation systems. It has been known for years how to develop relatively nonpolluting engines which burn renewable fuels. Yet billions of dollars go into devising new varieties of gasoline engines which waste energy, pollute the air and end up in the category known as "solid waste." It is argued that the American people do not wish to give up their motor vehicles. It is undoubtedly true that Americans and others like to have private, high-speed vehicles for personal transportation. But they have not been given much choice.

NOISE POLLUTION   Most primates are noisy animals and man is no exception. Anyone who has listened to a pack of baboons getting settled for the night in Africa develops a better perspective on the racket frequently heard in human gatherings. It is no news that cities are noisy places. The fact has been commented on since the Towers of Babel were first constructed. But in the technologically advanced sections of the world, noise pollution has reached new dimensions. Some ideas of the magnitude of the problem are shown in Table 22, prepared by the Council on Environmental Quality.[5] The decibel scale shown is a measure of the energy level of sound. The scale is logarithmic, meaning a level of 130 decibels is 10 times as great as one of 120 and 100 times as great as one of 110. In a quiet environment the sound level will be about 50 decibels or less, at 80 decibels the sound level becomes annoying. Nevertheless in the cities, people are commonly exposed to levels of 110 decibels or more—that of nearby riveting machines, jet takeoffs at the airport, or those mind-deadening institutions known as discotheques.

Steady exposure to sound at levels of 90 decibels or more is believed to cause loss of hearing. Other effects of noise on man are only now being pinpointed, but they include direct physiological as well as psychological effects. There appear to be individual differences in tolerance to noise and wide differences in tolerance to different kinds of noise—high frequency whines are more difficult to withstand than dull roars, sudden and unexpected sounds cause more reaction than those which are regular or anticipated.

Although much more research on the effects of noise must be conducted before we can speak with any certainty, there seems no good reason for putting up with as much noise as is now forced on urban dwellers. Many cities and some states are now attempting to enforce

POLLUTION: HOW MUCH IS TOO MUCH?

(a) Smog. Do we really want fresh air? **(b)** Where do the children play when fish can't live in the water? **(c)** Spraying pesticides on corn—the wrong way to go. **(d)** Pesticide consequences. **(e)** Oil slick surrounds the Statue of Liberty in New York Harbor. **(f)** What happens when the newer, bigger oil tankers spill their petroleum in some bay or enclosed sea?

d

e

f

TABLE 22
Weighted Sound
Levels and Human
Response

DECIBEL LEVEL[a]	REPRESENTATIVE SOURCES OF SOUND	HUMAN RESPONSE TO SOUND LEVEL
150		
140	Aircraft carrier deck jet flights	Painfully loud
130	Limit of amplified speech	
120	Jet takeoff at 200 feet	
	Discotheque	
	Auto horn at 3 feet	
110	Riveting machine	
	Jet takeoff at 2000 feet	
100	Shout at 0.5 feet	Very annoying
	New York subway station	
90	Heavy truck at 50 feet	Hearing damage (8 hours)
	Pneumatic drill at 50 feet	
80		Annoying
	Freight train at 50 feet	
70	Freeway traffic at 50 feet	Telephone use difficult
60	Air conditioning unit at 20 feet	Intrusive
	Light auto traffic at 50 feet	
50		Quiet
	Living room	
40	Bedroom	
	Library	
30	Soft whisper	Very quiet
20	Broadcasting studio	
10		Just audible
0		Threshold of hearing

Source. Council on Environmental Quality (1970) from Department of Transportation.[5]
[a] Weighted sound levels based on frequency response of human ear.

anti-noise regulations and to force manufacturers to build machinery and equipment with lower noise ratings. The federal government is now moving into this area with the setting of standards and with research on acoustical problems.

Probably the greatest national attention to the subject of noise was directed toward the plan to develop the supersonic transport. The SST, like all planes which fly faster than the speed of sound, creates a sonic boom all along its flight corridor. This noise level would be intolerable to those who would have to live with it and, in addition, is capable of creating structural damage. Furthermore, the SST would create a much higher level of airport noise, even flying at subsonic, than any existing jet plane. Although the federal administration had guaranteed the SST would not be permitted to fly over inhabited areas, the opponents to the project were skeptical about such promises. Opposition to noise, as much as any other factor, helped contribute to the defeat in Congress of the proposal to develop an American SST.

THE URBAN SYSTEM There are two factors which contribute particularly to the noise pollution levels in human communities. One is the nature of those communities themselves, often developed without planning or with limited, one-sided planning which did not take into account the necessity for flow of goods, people, and energy in and out. This results in an unnecessary degree of destruction and construction of buildings, the constant tearing up of streets, the movement of unnecessary traffic through residential and commercial areas, and all of the other factors contributing to urban confusion. Second, there is the nature of the entire technological process in which tools, vehicles, and equipment are designed only with the view of the job to be done. No consideration is given to how the tool will be used, by whom, and where. A jackhammer may be quite efficient for breaking up concrete—but the employment of jackhammers under crowded city conditions means intolerable noise levels. A chain saw is an efficient tool for cutting trees, but is an absolute insult to the ears of people who are seeking peace and solitude.

SEWAGE AND AGRICULTURE The problems related to the disposal of human and animal organic wastes have been partly discussed in preceding chapters. We have cities which must find some way of getting rid of sewage and other wastes produced by millions of people. We also have agricultural soils being depleted of organic material by monocultural practices, which forces the employment of excessive amounts of energy-demanding nitrate fertilizers, as well as other chemicals. The fertilizers, washing from farmlands and into streams, lakes, or estuaries create an additional pollution problem. The system is obviously disrupted, and what could be a healthy recycling does not take place.

The magnitude of the urban sewage problem cannot be dismissed lightly. New York City must do something with 5 million cubic yards of sewage sludge—the end product of its sewage treatment plants, each year. It has tackled the problem by hauling it in barges, 11 miles off shore and dumping it. The sewage dumping ground has long been an unhealthy part of the ocean, since about 15 square miles of ocean bottom are now covered with a concentrated mass of sludge, and can support only anaerobic forms of life. In theory this sludge is supposed to work its way down a submarine canyon into the ocean deeps. However, it has not obliged, and recently has been working its way back toward the beaches. Properly processed and returned to the land, this could be valuable fertilizer. Left alone it is a menace to marine life and a health threat to people.[28]

Chicago, by contrast, has attempted to solve its problem in a more rational way, using it to restore the soils of about 36,000 acres of marginal farm lands and strip-mined areas. Although the digested and chemically treated sludge represents no menace to health, citizens in the recipient areas have filed suit against the city of Chicago to prevent further dumping, since they fear some unknown disease hazard may creep upon them.[21] The belief that anything organic is filthy is widespread among Americans—an unfortunate by-product of mishandled health education, and a direct product of advertising campaigns by those who sell disinfectants and deodorants to the gullible. The principal health hazard in sewage sludge from urban areas results from concentration of heavy metals. This is a result of the failure to separate chemical and industrial wastes from household sewage and can represent a formidable problem where sludge is used in food plant production. However, all of the cities' sewage could be used on soils which were not being used in food production, until such time as the separation of organic and nonorganic wastes can be effected. The nation's strip-mined areas alone could absorb all of the urban sludge and would be at least partially restored as a result.[21]

One of the most absurd sewage disposal problems has been that resulting from new methods of livestock production. The concentration of great numbers of animals in small areas of feed lots, poultry batteries, and the like results in the production of large quantities of manure which must then be removed. For some time this has been dumped into streams, thus adding to the burden of stream and lake pollution. It obviously belongs back on the farm where it would enrich and improve the soil. However, with farms mechanized and chemicalized, the bother of collecting and spreading manure has been too great for the landowners. Now, with the high cost of chemical fertilizer, one can expect a greater interest in obtaining manure, and some reports indicate that this particular pollution problem may be a thing of the past.

A POTPOURRI OF POLLUTION Many books have been filled just by listing some of the various kinds of pollution and the problems resulting from them. No attempt is made here to be comprehensive, but some additional points deserve mention. During studies of the possible effects of the SST on the atmosphere, it was discovered that the nitrogen oxides in the exhaust of these big planes, released in the stratosphere at the altitudes used for supersonic flight, had the potential for destroying the ozone layer of the stratosphere. This is the chief atmospheric barrier to ultraviolet radiation. A great increase in ultraviolet radiation reaching the earth's surface would do more than just cause sunburn. It could create a serious hazard for many forms of animal life and vegetation. More recently it was discovered that the explosion of hydrogen bombs in the atmosphere would produce similar results if many of them were to be set off.[22] Still more recently it was shown that the fluorocarbon gas used in pressurized spray cans, refrigeration, and various other processes could also produce similar effects. None of these things—SSTs, hydrogen bombs, or pressurized spray cans—can be considered essential to a high standard of living or even important to the "American way of life." Why do we prefer to gamble for such dubious winnings?

The poisoning of many people in Japan with methylmercury, in the Minamata case described in Chapter 6, was followed by the realization that fish and people in Sweden and other Baltic Sea countries were being exposed to excessive amounts of organic mercury. You might have expected that the use of mercury salts as a fungicide for the protection of agricultural seeds might have been abandoned as a result of this. But it was not. In Iraq, in 1973, 6000 people were poisoned by eating seed grain treated with methyl mercury.[1] In 1974 it was necessary to kill 50,000 calves in Italy, 30,000 in Holland, and additional numbers in other European countries because phenyl mercury acetate became mixed up in their feed.[34] Heavy metals of other kinds continue to pile up in the human environment despite their known hazards. Heavy cadmium concentrations have been found in sea otters off the California coast,[35] and high concentrations of arsenic in crabs along the Canadian Pacific coast.[20] Tetraethyl lead is spewed from automobile tail pipes around the world although even relatively low concentrations of lead have been associated with nervous and behavioral disorders, whereas high concentrations are fatal.[2] The simple concept that people should not be allowed to poison other people, even though it is very profitable and convenient to do so, has apparently not been accepted by all the people. Those who are not made noticeably ill, or who have not had their friends and relatives poisoned, prefer not to get involved.

Donella and Dennis Meadows et al. have summed the situation up well in *The Limits to Growth:*[23]

virtually every pollutant that has been measured as a function of time appears to be increasing exponentially. . . . It is not known how much CO_2 or thermal pollution can be released without causing irreversible changes in the earth's climate, or how much radioactivity, lead, mercury or pesticide can be absorbed by plants, fish, or human beings before the vital processes are severely interrupted.

So, meanwhile shall we play another round of Russian roulette? You bet your life. Or would you rather think twice about economic growth and progress?

CHAPTER REFERENCES

Carson, Rachel, 1962. *Silent spring.* Houghton Mifflin, Boston.

Farvar, M. T., and J. P. Milton, 1972. *The careless technology.* Natural History, Doubleday, New York.

Meadows, Donella et al., 1972. *The limits to growth.* Signet. New American Library, New York.

Rudd, Robert L., 1964. *Pesticides and the living landscape.* Univ. Wisconsin Press, Madison.

SCEP, 1970. *Man's impact on the global environment.* MIT Press, Cambridge.

LITERATURE CITED

1. Bakir, F. et al., 1973. Methyl mercury poisoning in Iraq. *Science,* 181: 230–241.

2. Bryce-Smith, D., and H. A. Waldron, 1974. Lead, behaviour and criminality. *Ecologist,* 4: 367–377.

3. Burdick, G. E. et al., 1964. Accumulation of DDT in lake trout. *Trans. Amer. Fisheries Soc.,* 93: 127–136.

4. Carson, Rachel, 1962. *Silent spring.* Houghton Mifflin, Boston.

5. Council on Environmental Quality, 1970. *Environmental quality.* Government Printing Office, Washington.

6. _____, 1973. *Environmental quality.* Government Printing Office, Washington.

7. Conway, R. C., 1965. Crop pest control and resource conservation in tropical Southeast Asia. *Proc. Conf. on Nature and Natural Resources in tropical Southeast Asia,* IUCN, Morges, Switzerland.

8. Cousins, Norman et al., 1966. *Freedom to breathe.* Mayor's Task Force on air pollution in the City of New York., New York.

9. Entwistle, Robert, 1973. The crisis we won't face squarely. *Sierra Club Bull.,* 58: 9–12, 32.

10. Farvar, M. T., and J. P. Milton, 1972. *The careless technology.* Natural History, Doubleday, New York.

11. Franke, Richard W., 1974. Miracle seeds and shattered dreams in Java. *Natural History,* 83: 10–18, 84–88.

12. Gilyarov, M., 1968. Soil fertility and zoology. *Nature and Resources,* UNESCO, Paris, 4: 13–15.

13. Gordon, Mitchell, 1965. *Sick cities.* Penguin, Baltimore.

14. Gress, Franklin, 1970. *Sea bird egg contamination.* Center for Short-lived phenonema, Smithsonian Inst., Cambridge, Mass.

15. Gress, Franklin, R. W. Risebrough, and F. C. Sibley, 1971. Shell thinning in eggs of the common murre, *Uria aalge,* from Farall on Islands, California. *Condor,* 73: 368–369.

16. Hart, L., R. Shultice, and J. Fouts, 1963. Stimulatory effects of chlordane on hepatic microsomal drug metabolism in the rat. *Toxicology and Applied Pharmacology,* 5: 371–386.

17. Hickey, Joseph, J. Keith, and F. Coon, 1966. An exploration of pesticides in a Lake Michigan ecosystem. *Jour. Applied Ecology,* 3: 141–154.

18. Hickey, Joseph, and D. W. Anderson, 1968. Chlorinated hydrocarbons and eggshell changes in raptorial and fish-eating birds. *Science,* 162: 271–272.

19. Lave, Lester B., and E. P. Seskin, 1970. Air pollution and human health. *Science,* 169: 723–733.

20. LeBlanc, P. J., and A. L. Jackson, 1973. Arsenic in marine fish and invertebrates. *Marine Pollution Bull.* 4: 88–90.

21. Lewis, Richard, 1974. The "prairie plan" for waste disposal. *New Scientist,* 63: 544–545.

22. Lewis, Richard, 1974. Bombs. *New Scientist,* 64: 132–133.

23. Meadows, Donella et al., 1972. *The limits to growth.* Signet. New American Library, New York.

24. Middleton, J. T., and D. C. Middleton, 1962. Air pollution and California's state control program. *Bull. Div. of Refining,* Sacramento, 42: 636–641.

25. Middleton, J. T., 1965. Man and his habitat: problems of pollution. *Bull. Atomic Scientists,* 21: 5.

26. Peakall, D. B., 1967. Pesticide-induced enzyme breakdown of steroids in birds. *Nature:* 216: 505–506.

27. Ratcliffe, Derek, 1967. Decrease in eggshell weight in certain birds of prey. *Nature:,* 215: 208–210.

28. Rogers, Michael, 1974. It'll knock 'em dead on Broadway. *Rolling stone,* 14 Mar.

29. Rudd, Robert L, 1964. *Pesticides and the living landscape.* Univ. Wisconsin Press, Madison.

30. Schofield, Edmund, and W. L. Hamilton, 1970. Probable damage to tundra biota through sulfur dioxide destruction of lichens. *Biological Conservation,* 2: 278–279.

31. Shea, Kevin P., 1969. Unwanted harvest. *Environment,* 11: 12–16, 28–31.

32. Shea, Kevin P., 1973. PCB. *Environment:* 15: 25–28.

33. Tatton, J. O., and J. H. Ruzicka, 1967. Organochlorine pesticides in Antarctica. *Nature,* 215: 346–348.

34. Tinker, Jon, 1974. Mercury, calves and wallpaper. *New Scientist,* 63: 227.

35. Vandevere, Judson E., and J. A. Mattison, Jr., 1970. Sea otters. *Sierra Club Bull.,* 55: 12–15.

36. Woodwell, George M., 1967. Toxic substances and ecological cycles. *Scientific American,* 216: 24–31.

37. Wurster, C. F., Jr., 1968. DDT reduces photosynthesis in marine phytoplankton. *Science,* 159: 1474–1475.

38. Yamashima, Y., 1966. Recent progress of nature conservation and preservation of natural resources in Japan. Proc. 11th Pacific Science Congress, Tokyo, Mimeo.

16

the urban-industrial-technological trap

$\overset{\circ}{\text{I}}$n the 1970's people belonging to the biosphere cultures (Chapter 4) control the world. People who are still basically ecosystem oriented still exist but are scarcely able to control their own small areas of land. The biosphere cultures are centered in the metropolitan areas of the world. Each metropolis depends—not on any local ecosystem—but on the resources of the biosphere. Food and drink come in from everywhere: coffee from Colombia, tea from Sri Lanka, bananas from Panama, olive oil from Italy, oranges from South Africa, pineapples from Hawaii, and so on. Fuel may come from Saudi Arabia or Venezuela. Minerals come from Zambia, Jamaica, Rhodesia, Chile, and Peru. Manufactured goods flow out from the metropolis to change and influence all parts of the world. Money and technology also flow out to dominate and control. In the United States in the middle 1970's, more than three quarters of the people are urban—not city people, necessarily, but more likely suburban, or living in the satellite towns that surround the big cities. It is in the cities where the greatest achievements of humanity are to be found, and also the worst failures. It is in the cities where the greatest conservation battles are being fought, and it is city people who decide the fate of other areas.

One of the most disturbing features of life in a modern city is the feeling of helplessness and dependence. The larger and more complex the metropolis, the less able is each individual to help himself. One is totally dependent on the continued functioning of the urban society for everything—food, clothing, water, transportation, light, heat—all of the necessities for survival. Self-sufficiency and independence are only words. Instead one must rely on some unknown or impersonal "them" who are responsible for providing everything. When things go wrong, when the garbage is not hauled, or the sewage lines break, when water doesn't flow and telephones don't work, it is always "they" who are to blame, but nobody knows who "they" are. They may be identified with city government or the big corporations, but both are equally impersonal, and both seem totally interrelated. This helplessness and dependence may account for the great flight to the suburbs and then to the exurbs, which has characterized the years since World War II. There, at least, one can have a plot of ground, a home workshop, and less of a feeling of being hemmed in. But as the suburbs expand outward, those in the inner rings begin to develop the same trapped feeling.

To say most American people are urban means they live in towns with a population of 2500 or more. The term "urban" to the Census Bureau means just that. A little more than a third of the people in the United States are actually city people, meaning that they live in cities of 100,000 or more. However, more than two thirds of the population are related to a large town or city, and live either within it, in its suburbs, or in smaller associated communities. The great majority of Americans therefore relate to the country's metropolitan areas, the cities, and their satellites. During the census period 1960–1970 many of the country's central cities actually lost population. The 25 largest cities gained only 710,000 people in that period. However the 25 largest metropolitan areas gained 8.9 million people. The older central cities tend to be left increasingly to the elderly, the poor, and the people of the ethnic minority groups.

During the half century from 1910 to 1960 the population of the United States doubled. The urban population, however, tripled. In 1910, 46 percent of the population was urban. In 1960, 70 percent was urban. The growth of some cities was enormous. Populations in Los Angeles increased eightfold, in Albuquerque, twentyfold; in Phoenix, fortyfold. The rapid growth and sheer mass of people in some metropolitan areas not only complicated old problems, but added a whole new dimension of problems.

In the 1970's, in many large American cities, the city heart has deteriorated, with slum conditions widespread. The metropolitan edge has deteriorated with the unplanned spread of suburbs, most of which offer a minimum of environmental amenities. The spread of unplanned highway "strip towns," and the development of an urban fringe area—neither farm nor city but of neglected land in transition—has made the situation worse. Traffic congestion in and around cities has become extreme. In an effort to solve this problem freeways, parking lots, and other automobile-oriented enterprises have cut into and often shattered the earlier city framework, sometimes destroying scenic and historical areas as well as urban open space in the process. Pollution of air and water has become chronic. In many areas water shortages exist, or are threatened.

Yet the greatest problem may be presented not by the existing situation but by the prospect of future growth. If some forecasters prove correct we would have to build accommodations for double the present urban population within 35 years. If they are correct we must build the equivalent of metropolitan Washington each year. However, there is nothing inevitable about this process. We could decide to live in a different way.

THE WORLD
SITUATION If the American situation is depressing, the world situation often appears hopeless. According to the United Nations, the rate of urbanization is most rapid in developing countries. Where, in 1920, the urban population was 100 million it is predicted that by 2000, the urban population will be 2 billion. The Secretary-General of the United Nations has pointed out:[22]

However, in most areas, governments have neither prepared for, nor have they been able to cope with, the mass migration into urban areas. In the large cities, slums of the most wretched nature often become the environment of people who once lived in greater dignity and better health on rural lands. Pollution of air, water, and land, concentrated in urban areas, have become universal problems, threatening man's health. Diseases associated with urban living in developing nations has increased greatly despite advances in medicine. Noise and congestion in urban areas add to physical and mental distress.

It is paradoxical that the greatest creations of humanity—the cities—have become the places least suited to human occupancy. But the paradox is caused by the history of cities and the sudden shattering of their frameworks by too rapid growth. A city adequate for the needs of pedestrians cannot be adjusted quickly to accommodate hordes of motorists. A city built to house 50,000 people with a circumscribed space cannot be stretched to accommodate five times as many without serious disruption of its former framework. For many years, American city planners made pilgrimages to Europe and came back shaking their heads in amazement at the ways in which European cities had resisted the disruptive forces which plagued those of America. They do so no longer.

The supposedly greater environmental wisdom of the older civilizations of Europe vanished as soon as population pressure, and particularly, economic affluence, reached critical levels. It was then realized that the European did not necessarily love his quaint old dwelling; nor did he ride a bicycle instead of an auto by personal choice. Today historic and picturesque quarters of London and Paris are mushrooming with high-rise buildings all too reminiscent of Omaha or Kansas City. New towns in France exemplify the worst in "plastic modern" architecture. The traffic congestion in Rome must be experienced to be believed, even by a visitor from New York. Air pollution from Milan blots out the landscapes of Lake Como. The Swiss mountains are invaded by ugly developments to accommodate tourists, and many of the once-distinct towns and villages are merging together in a continuous urban sprawl. But, despite the now obvious problems, the situation in Europe, where population growth is slow, seems idyllic compared with that in developing countries. The Secretary-General of the United Nations reported:[22]

In most developing nations it has rarely been possible to provide in advance the urban planning and design. . . . Migration into cities is often associated with the importation of disease such as trachoma, tuberculosis, parasitosis, and skin diseases. The influx of people tends to bring enormous pressure on water supplies and arrangements for waste disposal, with the consequent appearance of diarrhoeal diseases. Overcrowding of premises and sites is typical. Inadequate housing accommodation is accompanied by shanty-type construction and further

THE URBAN-INDUSTRIAL-TECHNOLOGICAL TRAP

388

unsatisfiable demands are made upon water supply and waste disposal facilities. Food supplies may be inadequate, badly distributed or prepared, and sold under unhygienic conditions . . .

In rapid urbanization every form of publicly provided service, including transport and education, tends to be overloaded. Schools are heavily overcrowded, and as a result attendance tends to fall, and juvenile delinquency becomes more common. Social change often leads to disintegration of the family and other primary institutions of society. . . . The stress that often accompanies accelerated change results in emotional tension and a feeling of insecurity. These may find their expression in mental breakdowns, psychosomatic manifestations, suicide attempts, increased frequency of crime, drug dependence and anti-social behavior. . . . The magnitude of the problem in some developing nations appears to defy solution by anything less than a massive national and international effort.

These words, written in 1969, called for a United Nations Conference on the Human Environment. The conference was held in 1972, but there has been no massive national and international effort to date. The U.N. will try again in Vancouver in 1976 with the United Nations Conference on Human Settlements. There is no reason to expect any greater results than those which have followed the Environment Conference, the Population Conference, and the World Food Conference. In other words, we can expect things to get worse.

The test for the ability of a modern technologically advanced nation to cope with its urban problems may well come in Tokyo—which suffers acutely from uncontrolled growth, pollution, and urban confusion. It seems to function only because of the ability of the Japanese citizen to endure the intolerable. The test for the Third World may well be Calcutta, which has degenerated into a state of misery and chaos from which there seems no way out.

URBAN PATTERNS AND PROBLEMS It is impossible here to do more than give an outline of some of the problems facing metropolitan areas. Most of our towns and cities grew originally with little overall planning or control. They reflect thousands of individual decisions and hundreds of partial plans. These have contributed in some areas to a rich texture of interesting urban diversity, in others to ugliness and confusion. Past efforts to achieve some order in the cities have to a large extent taken the line of separating urban functions through zoning. Zoning laws have separated the industrial areas where people work in producing goods; the commercial areas where people shop or work at office jobs; and the residential areas where people sleep and carry out much of their social life. The latter are further divided into areas of single-family detached homes and areas of multiple-family housing represented by high-rise apartments or other high-density housing.[10] Such a separation of urban functions was inhibited originally by transportation facilities. In the nineteenth century and earlier, it was necessary to be within walking distance of work and shopping areas. With the development of individual transportation by private automobile, however, it became possible to separate these urban functions widely. Thus the development of residential suburbs, extending often in uniform patterns for many miles beyond the former city boundaries, occurred.

Cities, by their very nature, present problems of transportation. They are areas in which agricultural produce is processed or consumed and areas in which the various products of industry are manufactured. There must be a constant flow of goods into and out of the city. The modern industrial city often grew up around the railroad junction. The central railway station was in many American cities the focus around which hotels, entertainment centers, stores, and offices were grouped. The railway line was later the axis along which the city expanded into the countryside, the means by which city people travelled to seek recreation, the basis for the existence of satellite towns, resorts, and other urban-oriented developments. Within the city, public transportation systems, horsecars or, later, electric trolleys served to move people from the industrial or commercial centers to the residential districts. With the rise of the private automobile and the gasoline- or diesel-powered truck, however, this old framework of the city was disrupted. New urban centers, more readily accessible by automobile, arose, and the area around the railway station disintegrated into a "skid row" or slum district. Highways, rather than rails, provided the new avenues for urban expansion into the countryside. Public transportation facilities disintegrated.

With ever-growing numbers of automobiles the traffic jam became a permanent part of the urban scene. The difficulties of reaching the city center and of parking when there, along with other factors, led to a breakdown of the central city. Business and industry followed the people to the surburbs. New centers of work and commerce, dispersed widely around the periphery of the urbanized area, began to replace the old centralized urban core. The central city became a place where the poor concentrated, where ethnic minority groups were forced to live, and where housing, schools, and all other urban facilities deteriorated. Cities, in the old sense of vital, thriving centers of human activity and interest, appeared to be dying.[7,8,10]

The suburbs have been the subject of many sociological studies since the end of World War II and have been blamed for many of the ills of modern society. Yet there is little doubt most people who have moved there from the central city have gained a marked improvement in living conditions. The suburbs have become the established center of the American middle-class family, since they offer security and space for the raising of children in congenial surroundings. They have been consistently rejected by the adolescent and young adult who find them restrictive and dull. They have little appeal to the intellectual. In one form or another, however, they are likely to remain as part of urbanized America.[1,3]

There have been many different approaches to urban renewal. Some center on the belief the automobile is here to stay and seek, through the construction of freeways and adequate parking facilities, to develop new patterns of automobile-oriented urban centers and residential areas. Others believe that the automobile is by its nature inimical to healthy cities and seek the development of clean, attractive, high-speed public transportation systems which will replace the private car, combined with pedestrian-oriented centers of shopping, business, and entertainment. Some seek to retain and rejuvenate the old urban residential areas, now frequently deteriorated into slums.[10] This approach has been followed with marked success in Georgetown in the nation's capital, in the North Beach area of San Francisco, Greenwich Village in New York, the French quarter in New Orleans, and elsewhere.

A more common approach to urban renewal is demolition and re-development. The old congested centers of Philadelphia, Pittsburgh, southwest Washington, D.C., and other cities have been replaced by gleaming new towers of office buildings and high-rise apartments. Such an approach is frequently disastrous for those people who lived in the old areas, but cannot afford to live in the new.[10]

The garden city concept, for which Ebenezer Howard was the best known early advocate, has many followers today.[9] The new towns of Reston, Virginia and Columbia, Maryland essentially follow this pattern, with a major emphasis on the clustered development of housing around recreation lakes and surrounded by green areas of open space. In both of these towns and in many other developments, emphasis has been placed on the formation of what is essentially an urban village within an urban town in a city. It is hoped such small, unified communities will give the individual greater opportunity and scope for activity in the affairs of his society, and a greater feeling of personal identity.[24]

No one approach to urban development or renewal provides the answer for the cities of the future. Indeed, it is to be hoped no single urban pattern will be allowed to prevail to the same extent in the future as, for example, the uniform, detached-house suburban pattern was allowed to prevail after World War II. Our understanding of cities, and of people, is far from complete, and we would do well to be skeptical of those who would offer us packaged solutions for all of our urban problems. Indeed, the preservation or creation of urban diversity, to provide different ways of living, old and new, in different kinds of cities, for people of differing tastes, and thus to allow a maximum degree of individual choice, is the most human approach to the future development of urban environments.

URBAN OPEN SPACE Few would question that one of the greatest needs in our society is for open space in or near the cities suited to and available for various forms of outdoor recreation. With 70 percent of our population living in urbanized areas, and with the amount of leisure time growing in each decade, the demand for recreation space close to urban areas is both large and increasing.

In addition to its value for recreation, open space, in the form of areas growing trees or other plants and supporting various forms of wild animal life, adds beauty and variety to cities, gives them a definition, shape, and identity they might otherwise lack, and generally adds to the pleasure of living in them.[12]

One of the first big steps toward the reservation of urban open space in the form of city parks came in New York in the 1850's. At this early date, the pressure of urban populations on land in or near the cities was already great. Few people could afford a long train or boat journey to a distant recreation area. Most were forced to spend all of their time within the city and to seek whatever recreation it had to offer. William Cullen Bryant could foresee a future when the need for public parks in the city would be intense. Consequently, through his efforts in what was to become the middle of Manhattan, a major area of 700 acres was purchased for very little and was developed by Frederick Law Olmsted into New York's Central Park. The value of the land in Central Park would today be beyond the reach of government purchase if it had been at any time opened for development. But Central Park has stood through the years, and New Yorkers would not tolerate its development as real estate. It is impossible to measure the ways in which it has contributed to the welfare and enjoyment of New Yorkers.[18]

Not to be left far behind, San Francisco in the 1870's set aside and later developed a still larger Golden Gate Park in an area now surrounded by urban housing and high-value real estate. In the 1890's in Boston, Charles Eliot and others went a step farther and developed not just a park but a park system, providing a variety of kinds of urban open space and room for many types of recreational activity. In the second decade of this century, Chicago also developed a park system including the outstanding Cook County Forest Preserve.[18]

It was once relatively easy to purchase and set aside open space in or near cities and to develop it for parks and recreation. Now with increasing populations and skyrocketing land values, it is extremely difficult. As the need for open space grows, the possibility of a city or county government being able to afford to buy it appears to decrease. Most cities today have open-space plans showing the areas they would like to open up, keep open, or develop for recreation. Few have great success in putting the plans into operation, since the pressure for real-estate development can usually persuade the landowner to sell to the developer and convince the city government it is in their best interest to allow development to take place.[2,23,25]

One of the greatest problems has come, not from the acquisition of open space but the preservation of that already required. Parks and other open areas seem an easy answer to the location of public facilities. The land can be used at no charge and requires no clearing away of existing structures. Consequently, there has been a regrettable tendency to locate freeways in parks, sometimes disguised as parkways or scenic highways, as well as to locate other urban facilities which are incompatible with the use for which the park was intended. There is also an unfortunate tendency to locate highways in areas which might otherwise be acquired with relative ease for future parks or other urban recreation space. Each such proposal must be vigorously opposed by those who favor parks or, simply, would rather have a beautiful city than one which is easy to get to and easy to leave. Battles against freeway development have been fought in nearly every major city from San Francisco to Washington.[8,25]

It has been suggested by some planners that one approach to the urban open-space problem would be for planning authorities to give it highest priority in planning, to regard it as a fixed quality, and all other urban elements as relatively more movable. Such a procedure is needed, but its implementation will depend on the resolve of the citizenry of each town and city and their desire to maintain their communities as environments suitable in all respects for their inhabitants.[25]

TRANSPORTATION

For most of man's history, travel within a city was on foot, and transportation of goods was conducted by human porters or domestic animals drawing carts of various kinds. Travel between centers of population was, for people "of importance," by carriage of one sort or another, or by boat. The famous Roman roads which are still in use today were laid out to facilitate travel by chariot between the capital and regional centers of the Italian peninsula, but travel to the far reaches of the empire was usually by water transport. Proximity to navigable waters determined the location of many of the world's great cities and favors their continuance today. Transportation is not exclusively an urban concern, but it is in and around our urban centers that transportation problems have become hopelessly snarled.

Methods for improving water-based transport showed their greatest enhancement during the period from 1870 to approximately 1940, with the replacement of a dependence on sails or oars by steam- and then diesel-powered engines. Speed of transportation was increased somewhat, although the sailing clippers at times made the transatlantic run nearly as quickly as did the diesel-powered liner; but, more important, reliability was markedly improved. In more recent decades there have been some radical advances—hovercraft moving on a cushion of air now regularly cross the Channel between France and England, nuclear powered submarines can stay at sea and remain submerged for much longer periods of time and move faster than their petroleum-driven predecessors, giant supertankers have capacities not believed possible in the recent past—nevertheless, the average level of ocean transport has shown little improvement. Travel by ship across the ocean has now become a luxury for those who feel they can afford to spend extra time in their travels or simply wish to spend a completely restful vacation.

a

CITIES—PROBLEMS AND ANSWERS?

(a) The endless city—Los Angeles. Is bigger better? **(b)** Paris destroying itself—the new office tower in Montparnasse. **(c)** The freeway and the city—no answer to urban transportation needs. **(d)** Total confusion in New York. **(e)** and **(f)** New towns in England. Is this the way to go?

b

c

d

e

f

Others, who once were forced to take this time, now crowd their schedules with other activities.

The environmental impact of waterborne transport has been considered to some degree in relation to pollution problems. Other problems resolve around the dredging of waterways, which can have disastrous effect on aquatic resources, and the construction of new waterways. Pressure for the latter is determined by the fact that water transport is still the cheapest form of transportation for goods which are bulky and need not be delivered quickly. This has led to considerable dispute in some recent instances. Thus in 1971 President Nixon called a halt, one hopes permanently, to efforts to construct a barge canal across north-central Florida. The effort to prevent this construction dates back to the 1930's when the Army Corps of Engineers was first authorized to construct a Florida ship canal. Dangers of pollution to the underground aquifers that carry much of Florida's useful freshwater and the destruction of a semitropical river wilderness, the Oklawaha, were major factors in the halting of this canal, in which 50 million dollars had already been expended.[5] However, in 1971, plans were still being advanced to construct a sea-level canal across Panama, despite the warnings by marine scientists of the potential dangers which would follow from the mixing of aquatic life from the Pacific and the Caribbean.[21]

As noted earlier, the greatest problems of land-based transportation have resulted from the shift from railways for intercity transport, and the shift from surface trolleys and underground subways for inner-city transport, to a one-sided dependence on the private automobile and motor truck. Highway construction, favored by taxes on petroleum that were earmarked for this specific purpose, has been carried out in ways completely disproportionate to human needs. All other systems of transport have suffered from neglect with the exception of the air transport, which has also undergone one-sided development.[15]

The comfort and convenience attached to the private motor car, as well as the sheer pleasure derived from its ownership and operation cannot be ignored. Nevertheless, the automobile, as it is presently constructed and used, is completely impractical for movement within high-density urban areas. The needs of the cities for rapid, convenient, and comfortable mass transit systems have long been obvious; not that these systems are the single answer to urban transportation problems, but they are an obviously important part of any answer. Despite this, in Washington, D.C., Congress blocked construction of a much-needed subway system, which had been in a planning stage for many years in an effort to force on the city an unwanted addition to its freeway system—an addition which would not only displace city residents but would pour more vehicles into an already badly congested downtown area. The subway was held up for so long it now seems likely it will be out of date and inadequate by the time it has been constructed.

Opposition to the construction of airports near the city reached a high level during the late 1960's and early 1970's. In Tokyo, farmers and students fought pitched battles with the police to prevent construction of new airport facilities. In London's outskirts similar battles are threatened by those who oppose the destruction of residential areas, urban areas, or valued nature reserves to make room for an additional airport. In Florida the plans to construct a giant jet port in the Big Cypress Swamp, north of Everglades National Park, intended to serve the cities of Miami and Tampa, were brought to a halt after 13 million dollars had been expended. The opposition of conservationists, based on the damage the jetport would cause to the Everglades and Big Cypress environments, was sufficient to halt construction.

The opposition to the construction of new airports, however, does not solve the problem. Existing airports, saturated with plane traffic, are both dangerous and inefficient. The inefficiency is related particularly to the failure to integrate air terminals with any effective form of surface transportation. It has long been a complaint that one can spend more time getting from the city to the metropolitan airport than it takes to fly across the country. Inattention to the comfort and safety of passengers has been accompanied by greater attention to larger and faster planes—in other words to what has been the most efficient part of the system. This led to investment by airlines in jumbo jets and, most peculiarly of all, to a drive to develop an unneeded and generally unwanted supersonic transport. Fortunately in 1971 Congress decided to veto any further federal support for the SST. In France and the USSR, however, where governments seem strangely entranced by technology, SSTs have been built and attempts are being made to get them into regular service. The fact that the first Russian SST crashed at the Paris Air Show did not help their cause greatly, and England has apparently lost interest in the Anglo-French Concorde SST.

Urban centers require efficient and flexible transportation systems. Precisely what form these systems should take is difficult to predict in advance—but their use of nonrenewable fuels must be eliminated before many years have passed. There is not the slightest doubt the present reliance on petroleum-driven motor cars and airplanes as an answer to transportation needs must be abandoned. Cities shaped around the motor car must be reshaped to fit systems of mass transportation.

THE URBAN SYSTEM It is generally accepted, in theory, that urban communities represent systems within which the various parts necessarily interact. They have many features in common with natural ecosystems, but also marked differences. The modern metropolis is a supraecosystem—a system which affects and is affected by a wide range of natural ecosystems, and cannot be circumscribed within anything less than the entire biosphere. All modern cities are tied together by networks of transportation and communication, so that Paris and New York are more closely interrelated and interacting today than Philadelphia and New York were in colonial times.

Urban systems are necessarily built up from a network of subsystems—transportation being an example. These are tied together in various ways. The subsystems through which food, water, and materials move into a city, and the one through which wastes move out or are, hopefully, recycled, are obviously related to subsystems of transportation and communication. Unlike natural systems, however, where increasing complexity leads (or seems to lead) to greater stability, urban systems appear to have had the opposite tendency. Increasing size and complexity lead to greater fragility, that is, to greater dangers of disruption from disturbance. Thus a breakdown somewhere in the electrical power grid covering the northeastern United States brought the city of New York to a total halt in 1965, since there were no adequate buffering or compensating devices. A strike by sanitation workers disrupted many years of progress in the system for sewage disposal in England, and led to unacceptably high levels of water pollution. The work of a few Arab hijackers has affected and slowed the world's air transport system. Part of this vulnerability and much of the confusion in urban existence results from the failure to treat urban communities for the systems they are and to plan accordingly. Part of it, however—perhaps the most important part—is the result of excessive centralization of control and of power.

In the first of these causes, it is too common for those concerned with one subsystem—and transportation is the notorious example—to work in isolation from all other subsystems. The one-sided development of highways leads to the neglect of transportation as a whole, and of the effects of highways on everything else. Similarly, builders of suburban tracts commonly work without consideration of the effect of their community on transportation, sewage disposal, water supply, schools, and all of the other parts of the broader urban community to which the new tract will belong. It is the job of the metropolitan planners to be aware of these things, but many planners are not environmentally trained, and all are ruled by politicians, who often reflect special interest pressures.

Perhaps the greatest failure in urban planning and development is the tendency to get carried away by the technological game of building and developing, and to forget that the city is intended to be the home for a particular type of animal, the human being. This is a species noted for individuality and diversity, for aggressive and territorial tendencies in behavior, and is frequently characterized by bad temper and destructiveness. Thus the new and shiny housing developments intended to improve the lot of slum dwellers are commonly hated by those who are forced to live in them. They seldom function in the way the designers had intended. Studies of what the people concerned really want seldom precede the development of mass housing that people are then forced to accept. Studies of how people react to new towns and communities are rarely financed, since it is embarrassing to the developers and government officials to consider past failures. It is easier to go on building tomorrow's failures.[31]

The energy crisis will force a restructuring of urban areas. There is no doubt that a high degree of self-sufficiency could be developed within small, urban-suburban neighborhoods. Attention to local development of renewable energy supplies: solar, wind, or whatever is most available would unhook these communities from complex and centrally directed power webs. Community systems for handling organic wastes with the generation of methane and the production of fertilizers are feasible.[13] Community gardens for food production within the cities already characterize some European cities, and could do much to remove dependency on outside food sources. There are many things which could be done—all involve opening up the urban network, decentralizing its functions, developing local sufficiency and reliance and, perhaps most importantly, developing a *sense of community*.

There is no good reason for supinely accepting continued urban growth. Much of this takes place because nothing is done to encourage people to remain on the land, and because villages and small towns suffer from public neglect. A move toward strengthening the rural settlement pattern and for providing in village and town the means of livelihood, and centers for intellectual and cultural advancement could be accomplished by government action. It could also be accomplished by individuals, if they have the will to do so, whether or not government shows much interest. Someone has suggested Los Angeles be set aside as a "national degradation preserve" in which all efforts to protect or improve the environment would be forbidden, and only uncontrolled economic growth would be allowed. The same thing could be recommended for New York. People of the future may value these "living museums" (providing anything can still be kept alive within them) as examples of how not to develop a human community.

THE TECHNOCRATIC SOCIETY Critics of the present organization of the biosphere cultures have spent considerable time in analyzing and defining its faults and problems. It is difficult to find anyone who is not a critic of society, although some confine their criticism to a few aspects of modern life, whereas others spend time looking for scapegoats to whom the blame can be attached. It is difficult, however, to affix blame in modern industrial society. In earlier kingdoms and empires, one could always blame the monarch since he presumably had complete power and control. In the America of the 1970's, however, one can force out of office a president, vice-president, and most of the other higher officials of administration—and yet, everything remains about the same. The more closely one examines the total system, the more it becomes apparent nobody is really in charge.

Lewis Mumford has examined the development of technics and technology in a two-volume work which reviews the history of mankind from this perspective.[14] He defines the present technological organization as a megamachine. In his view this originated with the first civilizations

—the builders of pyramids and towers of Babel. In these earlier empires the megamachine was powered by human components rather than by mechanical engines. Civilization thus was the first form of human organization that reduced the individual to being a cog or component of a machine rather than an equal partner in a human enterprise. George Leonard, who sees in Civilization (with a capital C) itself the cause of today's human problems, has commented on this concept: "We of Civilization are the direct heirs of the first man who was moved to think of another human being as a component. We are the heirs of that component himself."[11]

Characteristic of the megamachine was the institution of slavery, of armies, of separate priesthoods removed from the people who alone could talk to the gods, of organized warfare and mass murder, and of the organization of working masses to build structures for the glory of those who held power.

In its original form, the megamachine broke down with the fall of the ancient empires. In Europe, at least during the long period following the fall of Rome, society came to be organized on a more human scale. However the tradition of the megamachine lived on and was to be re-born with the industrial revolution and the rise of the modern nation-state.

The industrial revolution grew from a highly organized and efficient medieval technology. This operated on a small, human scale with emphasis on individual skill and excellence. The machines that were organized in the factories of the industrial revolution were themselves turned out by individual craftsmen who were drawing from a long tradition. Mumford believes that if this original craftmanship and small technology

had not been condemned to death by starvation wages and meager profits, if it had, in fact, been protected and subsidized as so many of the new mechanical industries were in fact extravagantly subsidized, right down to jet planes and rockets today, our technology as a whole, even that of "fine technics" would have been immensely richer— and more efficient.

The industrial revolution, with its creation of a new megamachine and its reduction of people to components and parts of an industrial process, depended on the rise of a new form of nation-state and its professional armies. In the old empires, the emperor might be deified, but the state was not. The new nation-states, however, were endowed with godlike qualities. One was supposed to live and die for a strange spiritual entity known as "la belle France," "Mother Russia," or "Uncle Sam." Loyalty to this spirit was supposed to take precedence over one's love of family, friends, community, or the hills of home. Such idolatry could only occur in a world from which God had been effectively banished—through the increasing dualism of institutional Christianity, or the abandonment of any meaningful spiritual beliefs. "My country right or wrong" is not a statement compatible with the teachings of Christ, but is one expected of followers of the goddess Columbia.

Mumford defined modern technology as follows:

The last century, we all realize, has witnessed a radical transformation of the entire human environment, largely as a result of the impact of the mathematical and physical sciences upon technology. This shift from an empirical, tradition-bound technics to an experimental mode has opened up such realms as those of nuclear energy, supersonic transportation, cybernetic intelligence and instantaneous distant communication.

The growth of this technology, based on the application of science and mathematics to industrial processes, has resulted in its encompassing the world. With its massive size and rate of growth it is the dominant force in the biosphere, compared to which nation-states and international organizations appear as mere adjuncts. It exists in the Communist and capitalist world and dominates all who are caught up in its network.

Jacques Ellul has called the existing state of affairs the "Technological Society," and points out one of its characteristics is that technology must prevail over the human being—everyone must play his role to keep the system turning over.[4]

Theodore Roszak has used the term "technocracy" and defines it as

that society in which those who govern justify themselves by appeal to technical experts, who, in turn, justify themselves by appeal to scientific forms of knowledge. And beyond the authority of science there is no appeal. . . . Technocracy easily eludes all traditional political categories. Indeed it is characteristic of the technocracy to render itself ideologically invisible.[20]

George Leonard sees the problem this way: Civilization, he says, is "that mode of social organization marked in general by political states, markets, legal sanctions and social hierarchies, wherever in the world it occurs." He further describes how the end of this Civilization is now taking shape—and most people today begin to notice it is indeed unravelling at all of its seams.[11]

No matter what it is called or how it is defined, it is now obvious to anyone who thinks about it, that we in America no longer live—if, indeed, we ever lived at all—in a society where "private enterprise" produces goods for the benefit of the people and is watched over by a benign government which has always the long-term interest of the people at heart. Yet, not very long ago many Americans believed just that. Maybe some still do.

In the technocratic society, built along capitalist lines, the separation of government and private industry scarcely exists in practice. Private industry performs public work—the building of highways, dams, war machinery, and schools. Much of the action at the government level is directed toward subsidization, regulation, or development of the private sector. The Atomic Energy Commission existed to promote the development of nuclear power by private industry. The fact that it was also supposed to regulate itself and industry created a contradiction which led to its split in 1974 into two agencies. The whole complex, however, is geared toward continuing economic growth along directions which are difficult to modify. Decisions are made collectively and cannot easily be reversed by the person who may be the current general manager, chairman of the board, or even president of the United States. Planning for growth in a particular direction involves consultations among representatives of many industries and branches of government. Once a decision is made, contracts and subcontracts are let. People are employed and go to work. New government agencies may come into existence. If it should be discovered after a few years that the original decisions were mistaken and the direction is wrong the discoverer will hesitate to announce this, even if he occupies a high position. Once turned on, the technocracy rolls on, and he who would stop it will throw people out of work, disrupt the economy, and will probably be fired himself.[19]

A principal activity of the world technocracy, through most of its national branches, has always been preparation for war. War is the biggest growth industry, but it is not to be called by its own name. Instead it is referred to as national defense. In 1975 the Department of Defense has requested Congress to give it 95 billion dollars to use in war preparations. This guarantees that a high percentage of the American population will be employed in research, development, or construction related to the various components of the war machine. During the peak years of the American involvement in Indochina, we were spending 20 billion dollars a year for the destruction of that region and its peoples. For many years it was recognized by some that the war was morally wrong and by others that it was not being won—but it was easier to go on accelerating the destruction than to turn off or reverse the megamachine.

Productivity in the mechanical rather than the biological sense is a principal activity of a technocracy. It is measured in terms of gross national product or GNP. Anything produced, whether useful or not, enhances the GNP. Anything destroyed, if its destruction involves payrolls and machines, enhances the GNP. War always boosts the GNP. Production for waste particularly characterizes American technocracy. Quality and durability of products would lead to decreased consumption and therefore to decreased production and thus a decline in the GNP. Production for profit need not be an incentive in a technocracy. In the socialist model represented by the USSR, the same processes take place as in the United States. There, however, prestige, position in the hierarchy, and other rewards take the place of the profit motive.

All of the activities of the technocratic society are oriented toward the goal of "progress," which is defined in terms of continuing economic growth. Yet the system is wasteful, destructive of the environment, and unresponsive to human needs except for those which can be satisfied with material goods. Furthermore, it is almost beyond human control. The technocratic society could continue to operate so long as energy supplies and raw materials were abundant. Now that they are no longer cheap or abundant, changes must be made. The technocracy must be modified or it will grind to a halt.

The technocratic society, depending as it does on resources from throughout the biosphere, must endeavor to extend its influence globally. Thus assistance to Third World countries, during the period since the old colonial empires broke down, has consisted for the most part of investment in major developments: industries, big dams, massive irrigation schemes, or developments for tourism. All of these tend to strengthen the local technocracy and to tie it into the global technocracy. Considering that billions of dollars are spent on such "aid," it is remarkable how little of it seems to trickle through and actually improve the lot of the average person in the recipient countries. Instead the contrast between rich and poor becomes greater. Often, however, there is a comforting growth in the GNP which disguises the fact that the poor people remain as poor as before.

Jimoh Omo-Fadaka has described how industrialization and a high rate of growth in the GNP have disguised the realities of life in Jamaica.[17] Between 1950 and 1965, the GNP grew at an annual rate of 7.2 percent. However, the per capita income of the Jamaican people declined. Unemployment climbed to 19 percent in urban areas and 10 percent in rural areas. Although 140 factories were built, that created 9000 new jobs, some 10,000 jobs were lost in the sugar industry alone through mechanization. Thus economic development, poured in from the top, brought increased poverty and misery. After examining the situation in other developing countries Omo-Fadaka recommends building from the bottom, starting with small-scale decentralized communities. These communities must relate to agricultural lands farmed by methods that are labor intensive and require small inputs of imported energy. Low-cost local energy production, on a small scale, using wind, water, and solar power needs be encouraged. Aid should be concentrated in providing and developing low-cost building materials and in establishing village industries and workshops which encourage local crafts.[13]

There is more than a little danger that people will vote for a greater concentration of power in the name of greater efficiency and in protest against the chaos which is growing throughout technocratic society. This is the route taken in Italy, Germany, and Japan before World War II. It is being taken in many erstwhile democracies in the Third World, where military dictatorships have replaced the former governments. Although it is not inconceivable that a greater centralization of power could lead to more effective environmental protection and even to greater economic

a

b

c

THE TECHNOLOGICAL SOCIETY

(a) Conflict in ways of life. Must the technological society always prevail?
(b) Destruction in Vietnam — where the "megamachine" broke down.
(c) A "technocratic" solution to the world's problems.

well-being for the people, it is impossible that any society geared to continued economic growth and expansion along the lines that have been followed to date can protect the human environment. Without such environmental protection, the society must eventually collapse. The other direction is toward decentralization of power, both in the political sense and in terms of energy production and distribution. This is the one which appears to hold greater hope for the future of the human environment, and for individual freedom. It needs careful exploration.

Howard Odum has warned of the dangers, and states the terrible possibility that economic advisers who do not understand ecological processes will insist on continued growth with our last energies. There would then be "no reserves with which to make a change, to hold order, and to cushion a period when populations must drop". The end result could be that "At some point the great gaunt towers of nuclear installations, oil drilling, and urban cluster will stand empty in the wind for lack of enough fuel technology to keep them running."[16]

I cannot provide the answers for the problems of today's societies. If this book can point out directions that are wrong, that are environmentally insupportable, it may help you choose. If it can further explore some avenues which may lead in the right direction, from a conservation viewpoint, then that choice may be easier to make.

CHAPTER REFERENCES

Duhl, Leonard J., ed., 1963. *The urban condition.* Basic Books, New York.

Geddes, Patrick, 1915. *Cities in evolution.* Williams & Norgate, London.

Hall, Peter, 1966. *The world cities.* World University Library, McGraw-Hill, New York.

Mumford, Lewis, 1961. *The city in history.* Harcourt, Brace & World, New York.

————, 1967. *The myth of the machine. Technics and human development.* Harcourt, Brace & World, New York.

————, 1970. *The myth of the machine. The pentagon of power.* Harcourt Brace Jovanovich, New York.

Roszak, Theodore, 1970. *The making of a counter culture.* Faber and Faber, London.

LITERATURE CITED

1. Alonso, William, 1964. The historic and structural theories of urban form: their implications for urban renewal. *Land Economics,* 40: 227–231.
2. Burrough, Roy J., 1966. Should urban land be publicly owned? *Land Economics,* 42: 11–20.
3. Dasmann, R. F., 1968. *A different kind of country.* Macmillan, New York.
4. Ellul, Jacques, 1964. *The technological society.* Alfred Knopf, New York.
5. Florida Defenders of the Environment, 1970. *Environmental Impact of the Cross-Florida barge canal with special emphasis on the Oklawaha Regional Ecosystem.* FDE, Gainesville, Florida. .
6. Fraser Darling, Frank, and R. F. Dasmann, 1969. The ecosystem view of human society. *Impact of Science on Society,* 19: 109–121. UNESCO, Paris.
7. Gordon, Mitchell, 1965. *Sick Cities.* Penguin, Baltimore.
8. Gruen, Victor, 1964. *The heart of our cities.* Simon and Schuster, New York.

9. Howard, Ebenezer, 1902. *Garden cities of tomorrow.* Faber and Faber, London (1946 ed.).

10. Jacobs, Jane, 1965. *The death and life of great American cities.* Random House, New York.

11. Leonard, George B., 1972. *The transformation.* Delacorte Press, New York.

12. Lynch, Kevin, 1960. *The image of the city.* MIT Press, Cambridge.

13. MacKillop, Andrew, 1972. Low energy housing. *Ecologist,* 2: 4–10.

14. Mumford, Lewis, 1967, 1970. *The myth of the machine.* 2 vol. Harcourt Brace Jovanovich, New York.

15. Nelson, Robert A., and P. W. Shuldiner, 1970. Transportation, lever of progress—20-year prospects. *Science and Technology in the World of the Future,* Wiley, New York.

16. Odum, Howard T., 1973. Energy, ecology and economics. *Ambio,* 11: 220–227.

17. Omo-Fadaka, Jimoh, 1974. Industrialisation and poverty in the Third World. *Ecologist,* 4: 61–63.

18. Outdoor Recreation Resources Review Commission, 1962. *Outdoor Recreation for America.* Government Printing Office, Washington.

19. Reich, Charles A., 1970. *The greening of America.* Bantam Books, New York (1971 ed.).

20. Roszak, Theodore, 1970. *The making of a counter culture.* Faber and Faber, London.

21. Rubinoff, Ira, 1971. Central America sea-level canal: possible biological effects. *Man's impact on environment.* McGraw Hill, New York.

22. United Nations, 1969. *Problems of the human environment.* Report of the Secretary General, New York.

23. Weismantel, W., 1966. How the landscape affects neighborhood status. *Landscape Architecture,* 56: 190–194.

24. Whyte, W. H., 1964. *Cluster development.* American Conservation Association, New York.

25. Zisman, S. B., 1966. Urban open space. *Transactions North American Wildlife Conference.* Wildlife Management Institute, Washington.

17

different
ways,
different
places

THE ATTACK ⌐here have been many invasions of the territories of others by groups
AGAINST HUMAN └who had developed greater skills in warfare. The sweep of the Mongols
VARIETY across Asia and into Europe during the days of Genghis Khan and his
successors was one of the most far reaching and devastating. However,
nothing in previous history was to equal the onslaught of the Europeans
against the rest of the world that began in the fifteenth century. Combined in it were the personal quests for gain and fame of its leaders, the
peculiar intolerance of medieval Christianity, and the general distrust
of all things foreign that most people share.

When Columbus reached the West Indies in 1492 it was a tragic day
for all of the peoples and the cultures of America. Where the Spanish
and Portuguese colonizers were to set foot, death soon followed. It
was not just that the invaders of America put down armed opposition
and took the Indians into slavery, but the diseases they introduced that
did the worst damage. Developed as they were in long isolation from
Eurasia, the American peoples had no immunity or resistance to even the
milder ailments which the invaders brought. Hundreds of thousands
of Indians died from the new diseases, which wiped out whole peoples
and shattered cultures even where people survived. The Arawak peoples
of the West Indies were to totally disappear, as did the original Indians
of Florida.[15]

With Cortez and Pizarro, the unique Indian civilizations of Mexico
and Peru were totally destroyed. In these instances sheer butchery played
a major role, but disease was to finish the job. Humanity lost an important cultural heritage in the process, but the jobs of looting and destroying were so thorough that we are not yet fully aware of how much was
lost.

The invasion of the British and French into North America started another long process of destruction of tribes and cultures. Much of the
damage occurred here too as a "side effect" of the actual invasion—
through the agency of disease, or the incompatibility of contrasting cultures. However much of the killing and disruption was deliberate.
Smallpox was spread with infected blankets. Entire tribes were massacred
with no better excuse than the one advanced by General Sheridan: "the
only good Indians I ever saw were dead." There were massacres on the
other side as well, but most seem to have been provoked by those who
could not realize that they were stealing other people's land and destroying their livelihood, or would not care if they did realize. Treaties signed
in the most solemn manner between the Indian nations and the government of the United States were broken or set aside whenever the con-

venience of the invaders demanded it. Tribes were rounded up and placed on reservations in unfamiliar territory where the means of self-support were not available. For the Plains Indians, the buffalo which had been their source of food, shelter, clothing, and their entire way of life, were destroyed—so that they became wards of the government and charity cases.[1,9]

Yet some Indians survived. Much was lost in the destruction which took place, but many traditions were maintained. Today the Indian nations are beginning to reconstitute themselves and to reaffirm what was best in the old traditions. Fortunately, unlike many peoples who were similarly attacked in other parts of the world, the North American Indians had some eloquent spokesmen. Thus Chief Standing Bear of the Oglala Sioux had this to say about the coming of the invaders:[11]

We did not think of the great open plains, the beautiful rolling hills, and winding streams with tangled growth as "wild." Only to the white man was nature a "wilderness" and only to him was the land "infested" with "wild" animals and "savage" people. To us it was tame. Earth was bountiful and we were surrounded with the blessings of the Great Mystery. Not until the hairy man from the east came and with brutal frenzy heaped injustices upon us and the families we loved was it "wild" for us. When the very animals of the forest began fleeing from his approach, then it was that for us the "Wild West" began.

It is difficult to generalize about Indians. There were many peoples and all differed in varying degrees from one another. Some were hunter-gatherers, others were skilled farmers. Some lived in civilized communities, others scarcely bothered to put up shelters at their camping grounds. However, there was a relationship to nature closely interwoven with religious belief which seemed to characterize most, if not all, of these peoples. Again, Chief Standing Bear is an adequate spokesman:[11]

Kinship with all creatures of the earth, sky and water was a real and active principle. For the animal and bird world there existed a brotherly feeling that kept the Lakota safe among them and so close did some of the Lakotas come to their feathered and furred friends that in true brotherhood they spoke a common tongue. . . . The old Lakota was wise. He knew that man's heart away from nature becomes hard; he knew that lack of respect for growing, living things soon led to lack of respect for humans too. So he kept his youth close to its softening influence.

Much was lost for humanity and for any understanding of conservation when the Indian peoples and cultures were shattered. One can hope that today, when more people are conscious of such things, some of the values lost can be regained.

Ethnic diversity developed over hundreds of thousands of years of human cultural evolution because people lived in geographically separate areas with differing environments. A different way of seeing the environment was necessary, and different behavior was enforced, if one was an Eskimo in the Arctic compared to a Pygmy in the Congo forest. With growing populations and the spread of people over the earth, it was inevitable that isolation of human groups would break down. This process also modified cultural differences as one group learned new techniques, art forms, or ways of living from the other. Much of the breakdown, however, came from the impact of civilization on people who lacked the power and organization of the civilized states, and was not a voluntary change or relinquishment of the old ways. Thus the black people of Africa were uprooted and hauled away by the armies of civilization and transported to other lands. As slaves they could scarcely maintain their old ways of living—their societal patterns were broken and pushed away. However, the culture which appears superior under one set of circumstances will not always continue to be superior when circumstances change. Many civilizations have vanished, whereas those who seemed backward and inferior to the city dwellers have persisted in their cultural ways. In times some of these gave rise to new technologically advanced cultures. Protection of cultural variety on earth is one way of insuring that the human race will continue to survive, as well as a way for providing a more interesting world for all who live today. It has the further advantage of offering freedom to those who may not care to follow the ways of life available in their particular society.

During the nineteenth century, when the worst impact of European societies against other peoples was being felt, the Europeans had reached a high level of chauvinism and self-conceit. It was almost inconceivable to a nineteenth-century American or European that anyone could prefer ways of living different from his own. The so-called blessings of industrial civilization were forced on other people. The "saving grace" of Christianity also was forced on them whether they liked it or not. Still, today the advocates of the technocratic society cannot believe that other people might have insights regarding living with the earth, or their relationship with the universe, that the technocratic world has lost. Today it is said that all people must be "developed." Earlier the word was "Christianized" or civilized."

There would be no point in reviewing what has happened in the past, nor any reason to condemn people of past generations for their acts, if the same process did not still continue. All over the world, where different cultures exist apart from the biosphere cultural network, they are being attacked and destroyed. It is not that this destruction necessarily represents a firm policy on the part of the government concerned, although it sometimes does. More often there is a lack of any rational policy, and a belief that given time the problem will solve itself. Regrettably the problem does solve itself. The peoples concerned die, or their cultures are destroyed.

In my opinion one reason for the extreme prejudice against so-called primitives is based on the way they lived—a relaxed and easy way, with much time for dance and song and ceremony.[12] They behaved as though they were still in the Garden of Eden, whereas the Judeo-Christian tradition told the Europeans that mankind had been driven from the Garden and must now earn its bread with the sweat of its brow. If the "savages" were not working and suffering then they must be made to work and suffer for the good of their souls. Furthermore, in warmer climates, many of the people had the habit of running around happily without clothes, and some were quite relaxed in their sexual behavior. This particularly upset the missionaries and the more "uptight" leaders of the Europeans who felt it a God-given duty to put clothes on these "pagans"—teach them that their bodies were ugly and sex was bad. One has seen the same prejudice and hatred boil up in present American society in reaction to the hippie movement of the 1960's. That the hippie could be relaxed and happy and sexually free could not be tolerated.

ECOSYSTEM PEOPLE TODAY Throughout the world in various remote areas people who are sometimes called primitive continue to hold out. Of course, they are not primitive, but have simply taken different directions in their social and cultural evolution. They are ecosystem people in that they are totally dependent on a local ecosystem or a few adjoining ecosystems, and cannot call on a biosphere network to help them through their difficulties. The ecosystems they occupy have nothing in common except they represent the extremes—they are too hot, too dry, too wet or cold or mountainous to be of interest to the biosphere cultures—or they were until recently.[3] One pervasive quality these people have in common is that they lack political influence. They belong to the *Fourth World,* and are not represented by the governments of the other three worlds. Were the world arranged in a more rational manner they would be autonomous. They were autonomous in the past, and many behave today as though they still are. After all what have the Amazonian Indian tribes to do with Brazil? Brazil, like most countries, is an international legal fiction. It exists within its present boundaries because a pope in the fifteenth century drew a line on the map to divide the New World between Spain and Portugal. The Indians happened to live in what was to be called the Portuguese area—but they had never heard of Portugal and many today have not heard of Brazil. They do know that invaders with guns are trying to kill or capture them, and since they were always warriors, they fight back.[8,12]

A second quality these ecosystem people have in common is that most of them have learned to live in a sustainable balance with their environment. Without overexploitation of its resources, and without need of outside sources of energy and materials, they live quite well and have done so for centuries.

The Indian anthropologist, L. P. Vidyarthi, has pointed out that the ecosystem people in India, where there are some 38 million people who live outside of the dominant biosphere cultures, have developed a style of life which he characterizes as a nature-man-spirit complex.[17] Figure 17–1 diagrams this idea as a triangle of which the two sides—human society and the natural world—are held in balance by the third side, the spiritual world. It is the relationship of people through their spiritual beliefs with the natural world which permits them to maintain the necessary rhythms of planting and harvesting, hunting, fishing, and gathering. The religions are the old nature religions and have nothing to do with formal churches, but much to do with personal transcendence. Destroy the religion, as the missionaries from the biosphere cultures seek to do, and the balance between humans and nature falls apart. Destroy their environment and people and their beliefs will collapse—and this is happening in many areas.

There is little doubt that the hunter-gatherers of the world are in the most desperate straits. This is because they require a relatively large area for their subsistence—they cannot survive when crowded from the outside. Not much better off are those who practice a shifting agriculture, but depend basically on hunting and gathering to maintain a nutritionally adequate diet. The Indians of the American tropics are mostly in that category. They have been and are more and more being subjected to brutal treatment which is in the process of destroying them.[8]

The gradient of cultures moves from pure hunting and gathering to various combinations with shifting agriculture, then on to a less shifting, but more rotational agriculture, and finally to a more or less permanent, peasant agriculture such as is represented by the Ifugao of the Philippines. Along another track it moves from pure nomadic herding to varying degrees of combination of herding with agriculture or with other forms of sedentary culture. All of these groups are under pressure and many have been totally shattered by the biosphere cultures. Few people around the world are much worried about them, since most who are caught up in the biosphere network have difficulty enough keeping themselves alive. Yet these peoples have lessons to teach the world

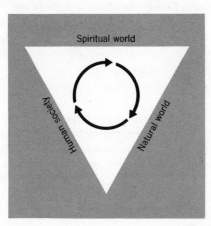

FIG. 17–1. The balance in those ''primitive'' cultures where ''God is alive. Magic is afoot.''

that we have yet to consider seriously. They offer a hope for the future, if for no other reasons than they have learned to live happily and in balance with their environment without drawing heavily on any of the earth's resources.

CONSERVATION OF CULTURES
It is today considered morally reprehensible that one dominant group of humans should exterminate another group who differ from them racially, genetically, or culturally. Nevertheless, the practice continues in one way or another. To halt it, the first step would be to recognize what is ethically or morally a law, even if it has not been enacted in any binding legal form: that these people have the right to the lands or resources on which they have always lived or on which they have always depended. This means suspending the "right of conquest" once and for all. It means forbidding those who have more power or greater numbers from invading, stealing, destroying, or bargaining away the lands and resources which have traditionally and rightfully belonged to these people. It means, at most, recognizing them as the autonomous nations they always have been, *in fact*, and giving that recognition status *in law*. At least, it means recognizing their property rights within a particular nation, again by law, and agreeing not to interfere with these rights. In the United States, insofar as the Indians are concerned, it means recognizing and adhering to the treaties which were once signed, and then providing adequate compensation for the damages the people have suffered since the treaties were broken. For those tribes who were crushed and set aside without treaties, it means negotiation to restore their fair share of land and property.

For those more fragile people, who have not been much exposed to biosphere culture and would be damaged by such exposure (the Amazonian Indians are mostly in this category), a further policy of "hands off" must be enforced in respect to their lands and resources. This means that within their territories these people would have a right to exclude all visitors. It means that the prevailing dominant culture on the outside would forbid its agents from entering these territories. This would apply to those agents of spiritual destruction, the missionaries, and the agents of nature destruction from industry and business. This does not mean that the ecosystem people would be in any way prevented from leaving their territory, from joining the dominant culture or from changing their ways as they see fit. It does mean that they would have a breathing space, and would be granted once and for all the right to determine their own future.

There are other steps which should be taken, in view of the past abuse many of these people have suffered, but these need to be determined on an individual basis. If these two requirements can be accepted by governments, a beginning at least will have been made. During 1974, the government of Australia has, at long last, recognized fully the rights of its aboriginal peoples to the lands which had much earlier been set up

a

c

b

THE FOURTH WORLD

(a) Nomads in the Sudan. Pressured from all sides, it is unlikely that traditional pastoral nomads can continue with their old ways of life. (b) Eskimos. The impact of "biosphere people" has already largely destroyed the old "ecosystem cultures" of the Arctic. (c) Survivors. Despite a century of attack and neglect, the Indians of the United States retain their tribal identities. (d) Hitting back. Indians take over the Federal Bureau of Indian Affairs office, as they pursue their "trail of broken treaties." (e) Still isolated. American Indians in Amazonia are being attacked today by those who favor "progress." (f) Independent. Papua, New Guinea seeks new ways to develop that will protect its diversified cultural heritage.

d

e

f

as aboriginal reserves. These rights include mineral rights, with the result that great wealth is now available to the aborigines to use as they see fit. The aborigines, with some isolated exceptions, have been so knocked around and battered by their contact with the technocratic world, that they can no longer be considered ecosystem people, but their rights remain, and the step taken by Australia is an enlightened one. One hopes that other countries would follow the example. For some countries, however, it seems that only the unrelenting pressure of international public opinion can result in a change.

DEVELOPING HUMAN DIVERSITY Since there is more than a little reason to doubt the continuing viability of technocratic societies as they are now functioning, it would appear that any groups who have alternative ways of living should be encouraged, whether they are traditional ecosystem people or simply disaffected members of the biosphere cultures.

There has always been a tendency among some people to reject the ways of technocracy and to seek simpler and more satisfying ways of life. During the eighteenth century, when the global technocracy was still taking shape, the Romantic poets, artists, and philosphers were repelled by it and developed a "counterculture" in opposition. Jean-Jacques Rousseau and William Blake were noted for their unrelenting opposition to the new industrializing world with its "dark, satanic mills."[14] For every rebel whose name is remembered there were a thousand others who simply dropped out, who left the cities and sought satisfaction on the periphery—as cowboys or trappers on the American frontier and as shepherds, sailors, fishermen. Some joined tribes and became essentially Indians, or "honorary" blacks in Africa. Some disappeared into the exotic and nonindustrialized countries of Asia to become a part of their people. Fletcher Christian and his companions joined Polynesia when they mutinied and took H.M.S. *Bounty* to Pitcairn Island.

The dropout rate has accelerated since the nineteenth century and has, in the past decade, become impressive. In the United States, starting in the 1960's great numbers of young people attempted to develop alternative life-styles. Some have remained in the cities. For a time they were successful with creating "countercultural villages" within the city, in the Haight-Ashbury district of San Francisco and in Greenwich Village, Berkeley, and elsewhere. Most of these urban communities folded under the attention of the popular news media, and the onslaught of organized crime, organized law enforcers, and mass tourism. However, in a less flamboyant way, many urban pockets remain where people reject the values of the mass society and attempt to develop at least a minimum dependence on the technocracy. Those who have fled to the land, however, have had more success. The establishment of rural communes or other forms of intentional communities based on agriculture or the use of other natural resources has passed beyond the experimental stages. In its early years it was inevitable that mistakes would be made, and many of the new communities collapsed. Many of the people involved had no experience outside the city and were unprepared for the complexities of human behavior and of natural ecosystems.[7] However, many learned from their mistakes and have continued their efforts. Some have been successful in developing unconventional energy resources, and some have produced bountiful crops from areas where the soils and climate have been considered unsuitable for agriculture. A great reservoir of inventiveness and determination has been tapped and there is little doubt that greater successes will be achieved. One needs only to keep up with such journals as *Mother Earth News, Resurgence, Alternative Sources of Energy* or the *Journal of the New Alchemists* to learn that there is much happening.

It would be most appropriate if governments were to reserve certain areas of the planet—both land and water—for the practice of nontechnocratic ways of life. Waters could be set aside for fishing; land areas for hunting, trapping, and food gathering; grazing lands for nomadic herding; and other lands of better than average productivity for low-energy-input and organic agriculture. Special attention should also be given to the protection of primitive and more recent nonindustrial arts, crafts, and other skills. It would help guarantee the future survival of humanity, as well as make life endurable now, if such steps and encouragement could be given nationally and internationally. However, one need not wait for governments to act—at least not in those countries which are still reasonably democratic and still have adequate space for their people. There are always spaces in the interstices of the technological society where people can survive by other means—and people have displayed considerable ingenuity in locating these "ecological niches" which have been ignored by the prevailing culture.

ACTION FOR SURVIVAL If all of the more intelligent, more sensitive, more humane people were to drop out of the technocratic world, the people with dead souls who were left behind, as well as those who simply have not understood the realities of their world, might well succeed in destroying all life on earth. Everyone has a dual duty: to work on their own, if necessary, to establish a way of life which can be sustained—or has some hope for the future, and to work within the dominant culture to try and set it on a saner course. There is no single way out of the environmental and social dilemmas in which humanity is caught. We must seek the way we are able to pursue and seems to offer the greatest scope for our own talents, but we must do our best to influence the total society, by whatever means seem most likely to turn it from its self-destructive course. We must use every possible means to avoid another war—and the means will have to include "thinking the unthinkable": unilateral disarmament. If the United States were to announce to the world that it would henceforward cut back 10 percent each year on military expenditures and devote the money (10 billion dollars the first year) to assistance for the poor people of the world—the precedent set might be contagious. At least no great risk would be taken for the first few years when we already have enough armament to blow up the world more than once.

There is no doubt in my mind that the best hope for environmental conservation lies in the gradual (but not too gradual) dismantling of the "megamachine" or technocratic society. Some 500 years before the birth of Christ it was written in the *Tao Te Ching*, attributed to the philospher Lao Tzū:[5]

If the government is sluggish and inert, the people will be honest and free from guile. If the government is prying and meddling, the people will be discontented. Is it realized that the ultimate ideal is the absence of government? Otherwise, the straight will become the crooked, and the good will revert to evil. Verily, mankind have been under delusion for many a day.

Considerably more recently the economist E. F. Schumacher wrote:[16]

An entirely new system of thought is needed, a system based on attention to people, and not primarily attention to goods. . . . Therefore we must learn to think in terms of an articulated structure that can cope with a multiplicity of small-scale units. If economic thinking cannot grasp this it is useless.

We cannot follow the *Tao Te Ching* all at once, even though we have had many examples of the straight becoming crooked, and good reverting to evil at the highest level of government. Neither can we suddenly break up the country into small-scale units, unless we are prepared to endure a period of chaos. But we can begin. The *Blueprint for Survival*, prepared by the staff of the *Ecologist* in Great Britain proposes steps for the dismantling of the British megamachine, aiming at the development of small, relatively self-sufficient communities, using ecologically sound, labor-intensive agriculture, and local and renewable energy resources. These would be held together nationally by communications and public transportation, but at the national level would be done only those things that cannot be better handled at the local level.[4] If one examines the Swiss system of government, where the power and authority resides for the most part in the small cantons, it will be noted that relatively little has to be done at the national level.

It would be far easier for the United States to move toward ecologically sound, sustainable systems of agriculture, resource utilization, business and industry, and trade and commerce. Not only does it have sufficient resources—including energy—to sustain itself during the transition period, it has, at the present time, the most environmentally educated citizenry, and an enormous reservoir of potential enthusiasm among its young people.

OLD ANSWERS AND NEW?

(a) Terrace agriculture. The Ifugao people of the Philippines support a high-density population from diversified agriculture without benefit of machines, pesticides, or imported energy. (b) Alternative community in the United States. Some people are seeking new answers to the tired, old problems of the technological world.

We should not, however, plan for a nation of agricultural communes any more than we should plan for a total technocratic centralized dictatorship. Schumacher points out the duality of economic requirements which do not lend themselves to a single answer:[16]

For his different purposes man needs many different structures, both small ones and large ones, some exclusive and some comprehensive. Yet people find it most difficult to keep two seemingly opposite necessities of truth in their minds at the same time. They always tend to clamour for a final solution, as if in actual life there could ever be a final solution other than death.

Even Switzerland recognizes the need for a national railroad network, whereas Australia has encountered the problems which result from each state choosing narrow or wide gauge rail lines to suit itself.

There is no way in which humanity will endure on this planet unless each of us, in some degree, is willing to undergo the kind of "transformation" George Leonard has called for—a realization of the full significance of our own potential as human beings, of our relationship to the world of nature, and to the universe.[10] We cannot return to the view of the universe and the way of living of primitive peoples, but we must become once more, at the basic level, ecosystem peoples capable of supporting ourselves from the resources of our own lands and waters. This does not mean cutting ourselves off from the rest of the world—it does mean ending a slavish dependence on systems of technological organization over which we no longer have control. It does not mean abandoning trade and commerce, from which we could gain many worthwhile benefits—it does mean freeing ourselves from a total reliance on the coming and going of giant jets, tankers, cargo trucks, and railroad freight.

Writing in *Planet Drum*, Jerry Gorsline and Linn House have described the change that is needed:[6]

We have been awakened to the richness and complexity of the primitive mind which merges sanctity, food, life and death—where culture is integrated with nature at the level of the particular ecosystem and employs for its cognition a body of metaphor from and structured in relation to that ecosystem. We have found therein a mode of thinking parallel to modern science but operating at the entirely different level of sensible intuition, a tradition that prepared the ground for the neolithic revolution; a science of the concrete, where nature is the model for culture because the mind has been nourished and weaned on nature; a logic that recognizes soil fertility, the magic of animals, the continuum of mind between species. Successful culture is a semipermeable membrane between man and nature. We are witnessing North America's postindustrial phase right now, during which human society strives to remain predominant over nature. No mere extrapolation from present to future seems possible. We are in transition from one condition of symbiotic balance—the primitive—to another which we will call the future primitive . . . condition having the attributes of a mature ecosystem: stable, diverse, in symbiotic balance again. . . . If we wish to integrate our cultures with nature we do so at the level of the ecosystem which everywhere has a common structure and progression but everywhere varies specifically in composition and function according to time and place.

There is no single answer to the question of how we become ecosystem people again. No one answer will ever be the right one for any two groups in two different places. Each of us must build with what we have and what we can learn in the place we choose to live. Each must bear in mind the responsibility for the human environment and the human race. The ways out we find will be difficult but strangely rewarding if we learn once more to hear the song of birds and the message of the wind, if we can see the stars and once more learn to appreciate the earth beneath our feet.

The American Indians said it very well in the past, and in the 1970's one of them, Don Juan, the Yaqui sorcerer, has said just enough:[2]

This earth, this world. For a warrior there can be no greater love.

CHAPTER REFERENCES   *Ecologist,* 1972. Blueprint for survival. *Ecologist,* 2: 1–43.

Lee, R. B., and I. DeVore, 1968. *Man the hunter,* Aldine Press, Chicago.

Meggers, Betty J., 1971. *Amazonia. Man and culture in a counterfeit paradise.* Aldine Press, Chicago.

Schumacher, E. F., 1973. *Small is beautiful.* Harper Torchbooks, New York.

LITERATURE CITED

1. Brown, Dee, 1970. *Bury my heart at Wounded Knee.* Bantam Books, New York (1972 ed.).
2. Castaneda, Carlos, 1974. *Tales of power.* Simon and Schuster, New York.
3. Dasmann, R. F., 1974. Difficult marginal environments and the traditional societies which exploit them: Ecosystems. Symposium on the Future of Traditional "Primitive" Societies. Cambridge, U. K., Mimeo.
4. Ecologist, 1972. *Blueprint for survival. Ecologist,* 2: 1–43.
5. Giles, Lionel, 1905. *The sayings of Lao Tzū.* John Murray, London.
6. Gorsline, Jerry, and Linn House, 1974. Future primitive. *Planet Drum,* San Francisco, Issue 3.
7. Houriet, Robert, 1971. *Getting back together.* Abacus, London (1973 ed.).
8. Indigena et al., 1974. *Supysaua. A documentary report on the conditions of the Indian peoples in Brazil.* Indigena and American Friends of Brazil, Berkeley, Calif.
9. Keith, Shirley, 1972. The AmerIndian tragedy. *Ecologist,* 2: 13–22.
10. Leonard, George, 1972. *The transformation.* Delacorte Press, New York.
11. McLuhan, T. C., 1971. *Touch the earth. A self-portrait of Indian existence.* Pocket Books, New York.
12. Meggers, Betty J., 1971. *Amazonia. Man and culture in a counterfeit paradise.* Aldine Press, Chicago.

13. Neel, James V., 1970. Lessons from a 'primitive' people. *Science* 170: 815–822.

14. Roszak, Theodore, 1972. *Where the wasteland ends*. Doubleday, New York.

15. Sauer, Carl O. 1964. *The early Spanish Main*. Univ. California Press, Berkeley.

16. Schumacher, E. F., 1973. *Small is beautiful*. Harper Torchbooks, New York.

17. Vidyarthi, L. P., 1974. The future of traditional "primitive" societies: a case study of an Indian shifting cultivation society. Symposium on the Future of Traditional "Primitive" Societies, Cambridge, U. K., mimeo.

18. Waller, Robert, 1971. Out of the garden of Eden. *New Scientist*, 2 Sept., 528–530.

204 and 205: **(a)** U.S. Forest Service; **(b)** USDA; **(c)** Grant Heilman; **(d)** U.S. Forest Service. *Pages 208 and 209:* **(a)** H.W. Silvester/Rapho-Photo Researchers; **(b)** Marc Riboud/Magnum; **(c)** George Holton/Photo Researchers.

CHAPTER NINE **Opener:** Grant Heilman. *Pages 222 and 223:* **(a)** Jim Yoakum; **(b)** Charles J. Ott/National Audubon Society; **(c)** U.S. Forest Service; **(d)** Jen & Des Bartlett/Bruce Coleman; **(e)** Andy Bernhaut/Photo Researchers. *Pages 232 and 233:* **(a)** Tom Willock/National Audubon Society; **(b)** Harry Engels/National Audubon Society; **(c)** Leonard Lee Rue III/National Audubon Society; **(d)** John H. Gerard/National Audubon Society. *Pages 244 and 245:* **(a)** Camerapix/Rapho-Photo Researchers; **(b)** Tom Hollyman/Photo Researchers; **(c)** Grant Heilman; **(d)** Katherine Young; **(e)** Grant Heilman. *Pages 248 and 249:* **(a)** Phoenix Zoo Photo; **(b)** John Borneman/National Audubon Society; **(c)** George Holton/Photo Researchers; **(d)** George Rodger/Magnum; **(e)** Marc & Evelyne Bernheim/Woodfin Camp; **(f)** Russ Kinne/Photo Researchers. *Pages 252 and 253:* **(a)** Paolo Koch/Rapho-Photo Researchers; **(b)** George Holton/Photo Researchers; **(c)** Georg Gerster/Rapho-Photo Researchers; **(d)** Harvey Barad/Photo Researchers.

CHAPTER TEN **Opener:** Russ Kinne/Photo Researchers. *Page 262 and 263:* **(a)** Alan Pitcairn/Grant Heilman; **(b)** Grant Heilman; **(c)** Russ Kinne/Photo Researchers. *Pages 272 and 273:* **(a)** Wide World Photos; **(b)** Georg Gerster/Rapho-Photo Researchers; **(c)** Transworld Feature Syndicate; **(d)** Morris Huberland/National Audubon Society; **(e)** Karl W. Kenyon/National Audubon Society. *Pages 282 and 283:* **(a)** Grant Heilman; **(b)** and **(c)** Robert Perron.

CHAPTER ELEVEN **Opener:** Jason Laure/Woodfin Camp. *Pages 298 and 299:* **(a)** Inger McCabe/Rapho-Photo Researchers; **(b)** Georg Gerster/Rapho-Photo Researchers; **(c)** Jan Lukas/Rapho-Photo Researchers; **(d)** George Whiteley/Photo-Researchers; **(e)** J.W. Cella/Photo Researchers.

CHAPTER TWELVE **Opener:** Paolo Koch/Rapho-Photo Researchers. *Pages 314 and 315:* **(a)** Grant Heilman; **(b)** Georg Gerster/Rapho-Photo Researchers; **(c)** Jack & Betty Cheetham/Magnum; **(d)** Grant Heilman. *Pages 332 and 333:* **(a)** Josephus Daniels/Rapho-Photo Researchers; **(b)** and **(c)** Almasy; **(d)** John Bryson/Rapho-Photo Researchers.

CHAPTER THIRTEEN **Opener:** Thomas Hopker/Woodfin Camp. *Pages 348 and 349:* **(a)** Marc & Evelyne Bernheim/Woodfin Camp; **(b)** FAO. Photo by F. Botts; **(c)** Donald McCullin/Magnum; **(d)** FAO; **(e)** Grant Heilman.

CHAPTER FOURTEEN **Opener:** Almasy. *Pages 358 and 359:* **(a)** J. Allan Cash/Rapho-Photo Researchers; **(b)** State of Tennessee Department of Conservation; **(c)** EPA-Documerica. Photo by Cornelius Keyes; **(d)** Gerry Cranham/Rapho-Photo Researchers; **(e)** Grant Heilman.

CHAPTER FIFTEEN **Opener:** Ray Ellis/Rapho-Photo Researchers. *Pages 376 and 377:* **(a)** Paul E. Sequeira/Rapho-Photo Researchers; **(b)** Max & Kit Hunn/National Audubon Society; **(c)** Grant Heilman; **(d)** Bob Harrington, Michigan Department of Natural Resources; **(e)** EPA-Documerica. Photo by Chester Higgins, Jr; **(f)** Georg Gerster/Rapho-Photo Researchers.

CHAPTER SIXTEEN **Opener:** Georg Gerster/Rapho-Photo Researchers. *Pages 394 and 395:* **(a)** Georg Gerster/Rapho-Photo Researchers; **(b)** Bill Raftery/Monkmeyer; **(c)** Elliott Erwitt/Magnum; **(d)** Bruce Davidson/Magnum; **(e)** George Rodger/Magnum; **(f)** Pete Loud DeWys. *Pages 404 and 405:* **(a)** Henri Cartier-Bresson/Magnum; **(b)** Philip Jones Griffiths/Magnum; **(c)** U.S. Air Force.

CHAPTER SEVENTEEN **Opener:** Marc & Evelyne Bernheim/Woodfin Camp. *Pages 416 and 417:* **(a)** Almasy; **(b)** Karl W. Kenyon/National Audubon Society; **(c)** Hiroji Kubota/Magnum; **(d)** Wide World Photos; **(e)** Dr. Robert Carneiro and Cornell Capa/Magnum; **(f)** Elliott Erwitt/Magnum. *Page 421:* *(a)* Almasy; **(b)** David Campbell/Photo Researchers.

index

Pages in *italics* refer to illustrations.